A FIELD GUIDE TO THE
BIRDS
OF EASTERN AND CENTRAL
NORTH AMERICA

Hudson Bay

MANITOBA

QUEBEC

LAB.

NFLD.

ONTARIO

N.B.

ME.

N.S.

N.D.

MINN.

WISC.

MICH.

VT.

N.Y.

N.H.

MASS.

CONN.

R.I.

S.D.

IOWA

PENN.

NEB.

ILL.

IND.

OHIO

N.J.

DEL.

KANS.

MO.

W.VA.

VA.

MD.

KY.

Atlantic Ocean

OKLA.

ARK.

TENN.

N.C.

S.C.

MISS.

ALA.

GA.

AREA COVERED BY THIS BOOK

TEXAS

LA.

FLA.

MEXICO

Gulf of Mexico

Roadside Silhouettes

1 MOURNING DOVE
2 HOUSE SPARROW
3 GRACKLE
4 STARLING
5 COWBIRD
6 RED-WINGED BLACKBIRD
7 KINGFISHER
8 BLUE JAY
9 MOCKINGBIRD
10 SONG SPARROW
11 SHRIKE
12 FLICKER
13 BLUEBIRD
14 NIGHTHAWK
15 ROBIN
16 KILLDEER
17 PHEASANT
18 PURPLE MARTIN
19 BARN SWALLOW
20 CLIFF SWALLOW
21 KESTREL
22 CARDINAL
23 MEADOWLARK
24 KINGBIRD
25 HORNED LARK
26 PHOEBE
27 BOBWHITE
28 CROW

THE PETERSON FIELD GUIDE SERIES®

A FIELD GUIDE TO THE

BIRDS

OF EASTERN AND CENTRAL

NORTH AMERICA

Fifth Edition

ROGER TORY PETERSON

AND

VIRGINIA MARIE PETERSON

SPONSORED BY THE NATIONAL AUDUBON SOCIETY,
THE NATIONAL WILDLIFE FEDERATION, AND
THE ROGER TORY PETERSON INSTITUTE

HOUGHTON MIFFLIN COMPANY
BOSTON   NEW YORK

Chapter opener photographs © Roger Tory Peterson

Library of Congress Cataloging in Publication Data

Peterson, Roger Tory, date.
    A field guide to the birds of eastern and central North America /
Roger Tory Peterson and Virginia Marie Peterson. — 5th ed.
    p. cm. — (The Peterson field guide series)
Rev. ed. of: A field guide to the birds. 4th ed. 1980.
ISBN 0-395-74047-9
ISBN is 0-395-74046-0 (flexi-bind)
1. Birds — North America. I. Peterson, Virginia Marie, 1925–
II. Title. III. Series.

QL681 .P45 2002
598'.097—dc21   2001051879

Book design by Anne Chalmers
Typeface: Linotype-Hell Fairfield; Futura Condensed (Adobe)

Printed in Singapore

TWP 13 12 11 10 9 8 7 6

TO THE BIRD WATCHERS OF THE WORLD

WHO

TRUSTED, REVERED, AND LOVED

MY HUSBAND,

ROGER TORY PETERSON

— *Virginia Marie Peterson*

Contents

FOREWORD

Long before I saw him, I knew him. Everyone did, at least everyone important in my life. It was a crowded setting, the grand opening of one of the most historic exhibitions of its kind, "Animals in Art," at the Royal Ontario Museum.

The year was 1975, and many distinguished people were there, but the one I was most anxious to meet was Roger Tory Peterson. I had hoped for an introduction, but I didn't expect it. I couldn't believe it when he looked me in the eye and told me he had seen a wildebeest painting of mine in Bristol Foster's house in Nairobi. He then took me aside, led me through the show, and proceeded to comment on and critique my paintings and others. As I was to learn through the years, this was classic Peterson. Never an idle chit-chatter, he was an absorbed and interested observer.

He changed my life in immeasurable and positive ways. My own life and career received an almost immediate impact through the connection Roger made for me to Bob Lewin and Mill Pond Press, as well as Lars-Eric Lindblad and Lindblad Tours. But that is not important when compared to the enormous influence Roger's life's work had on the planet. My first *Peterson Field Guide to the Birds* came as my twelfth-birthday present from my mother. It has been joined by many others since, but that first one is still a treasured possession. This little book was the doorway into the wonderland of natural history. It has, in fact, been the doorway for countless millions of other people worldwide. *A Field Guide to the Birds,* first published in 1934, created the trail for countless field guides to follow. They are still following year by year.

Two things were crucial in the evolution of the field guide. First was the recognition of the importance of naming things. The second was the fact that Peterson chose birds to start with.

For most of human history, our species has lived close to nature and therefore has been familiar with the names of their neighbors of other species. Even today, the few remaining tribes of hunter-gatherers can name thousands of kinds of plants and animals and what they do through the seasons. In our modern society, it has been said that the average person knows only 10 wild plants but can recognize 1,000 corporate logos. It should be the other way around. How can we hope to preserve and protect biodiversity if we don't even know the inhabitants of the ecosystem? The key to repairing this damaging information gap is the field guide. If I had my way, field guides would be standard texts in every classroom, and learning to know other species would be an important part of school curricula.

It is difficult to say whether young Roger chose birds or whether the subject of bird study chose him. There is something universal and compelling about birds. Peterson's close friend, Victor Emanuel, has said, "Birds have attracted the interest of more people than any other living things because of the variety and vividness of their colors, the beauty of their voices, and their complex behavior." Peterson often observed that "they are the most intensely alive of all creatures — often moving, darting, hopping, flying, or at times migrating thousands of miles." By observing them and appreciating them, birders seem to absorb some of this tremendous life force and therefore stay very much alive themselves.

I have been a birder since the age of 12 when I started my first Peterson-based bird list. I have evolved strong opinions through the years about what makes the most useful field guide. Peterson has it just right, to my taste. I became exasperated by "artsy" attempts at awkward poses and foreshortened positions. Vegetation and bits of habitat are superfluous, in my view. For comparison's sake, similar species should be in standardized similar poses. Attempts at shading should be minimized, used only to inform the shape of the bird. Anything else is distracting and confusing. It is not easy. I tried it once. I did one plate of curlews for a proposed, but never published, book on shorebirds of the world by John Williams. It was agony. Admittedly, curlews, with their subtle mottling, are no picnic to portray. I vowed never to attempt it again, and my admiration for Roger Tory Peterson increased by leaps and bounds. He regularly spoke to me and others of the "ball and chain" effect that working on a field guide produces. The discipline is staggering: You cannot get loose and sloppy even once. You must always pay attention, not only to the detail, but to the general shape and form. A Red-tailed Hawk is not just a Red-shouldered Hawk wearing a different coat. The birds have a different "feel."

Roger Tory Peterson was born in Jamestown, New York, on August 28, 1908. The bird artist in him began in 1919 in the seventh grade. He relates the story: "Miss Hornbeck gave each of us a small watercolor box and a Louis Agassiz Fuertes color plate from the portfolio *Birds of New York*. I was given the blue jay to copy. When our efforts were finished they were put on the blackboard . . . but my blue jay was credited to Edith Soule, the girl who sat across the aisle. I was upset and made it plain that it was mine." That same spring he saw a Yellow-shafted Flicker, exhausted from its migration, like a lump of brown feathers. He poked it. "I saw the red patch on the head and those wild eyes in the moment before it flew away. The contrast between what I thought was dead and what was very much alive made an enormous impression on me. It was like a resurrection that touched one so deeply that ever since then birds seem to me to be the most vivid expression of life." The eloquence of that last sentence sums up the artist, the naturalist, the thinker, and the communicator. All of these qualities seemed to be part of him all of the time.

In 1922, he bought his first camera (a Primo No. 9 4 × 5" plate camera) and his first binocular (four-power opera glasses). The following year he began his first bird list, which grew to almost 5,000 during his lifetime. At the age of 17, he went to work at the Union Furniture Factory in Jamestown, to decorate Chinese lacquer cabinets. From 1927 to 1928, he studied drawing at the Art Students League in New York City. His drawing and painting studies continued at the National Academy of Design from 1929 to 1931.

He began participating in a number of naturalist organizations such as the Linnaean Society and the Bronx County Bird Club. His career as an educator began as counselor of nature study at a YMCA camp in Michigan (one summer) and then Camp Chewonki in Maine (five summers). From 1931 to 1934, he taught arts and natural history at the Rivers School, a private boys' school in Massachusetts. His pupils included Elliot Richardson, later attorney-general of the United States, who in 1974 declared Peterson the teacher who had influenced him most.

It was during his time teaching in Maine that he began work on his first field guide to the birds. In 1929, Bill Vogt, the editor of *Bird-Lore* magazine (later *Audubon* magazine) suggested, "Roger, you know these things — the field marks — and you're also an artist. Why don't you pass on your knowledge in a book?" The historic moment arrived in 1934. After rejection by three New York publishers, Houghton Mifflin, a small Boston publisher, had the courage to take on this "risky" venture but only on condition that Peterson take no royalties on the first 1,000 books. The whole edition was only 2,000 copies. They were sold out in less than three weeks, and the book was immediately reprinted. Thus began an enterprise that changed the world. There have been four revised and expanded editions of the *Field Guide to the Birds of Eastern and Central North America* since then. More than 7 million copies of the two North American Field Guides to the birds (east and west) have been sold. In 1947, the Peterson Identification System was extended by Houghton Mifflin to cover other nature subjects. The series now embraces more than 50 titles.

During World War II, Peterson used his system to prepare a plane-spotting training manual for the Air Corps. He later worked for the Air Corps in pioneering research on the effects of DDT on wildlife. His friend and fellow naturalist Rachel Carson built on these efforts and eventually produced the landmark environmental book *Silent Spring*. Peterson was an activist in the banning of DDT in Connecticut, resulting in the rebounding of Osprey and other bird populations. Roger Tory Peterson worked with Peter Scott in helping to found the World Wildlife Fund, and his efforts resulted in the creation of a national park at Lake Nakuru in Kenya.

His awards are numerous: 23 honorary doctorate degrees, the Conservation Medal of the National Audubon Society, the Gold Medal of the World

Wildlife Fund, the Linnaeus Gold Medal of the Royal Swedish Academy, and Master Bird Artist at the Leigh Yawkey Woodson Art Museum in Wisconsin. Most prestigious was the Presidential Medal of Freedom, the highest honor awarded to an American civilian and presented by Jimmy Carter in 1980. But the greatest honor of all will always be his place in the hearts, minds, and eyes of birders the world over. The idea that you could put in your pocket information that would open the door to understanding and enjoying the wonders of life on our planet is a very powerful notion indeed. That little 1934 book has gone from strength to strength through its various editions. Every species has been sweated over, brush stroke by brush stroke.

In 1976, Roger's wife, Virginia Marie Peterson, began an exhaustive study of bird distribution in North America for maps in the revised eastern field guide (390 maps done in three years) and the revised western field guide (440 maps done in six years). This couple worked and traveled as a team for the last decades of Roger's life. My wife, Birgit, and I were privileged to travel with them in various parts of the world. I recall an incident that illustrates Roger's acute ability to pay attention to nature. We were standing with a group of Lindblad travelers in a Tokyo park, waiting to tour a nobleman's house. We were all chatting, and Roger was half-listening to us and totally listening to nature. At a lull in the conversation, he said, "I am not sure, there are either four or five different species of cicada singing at this moment." He didn't know their names, but he distinguished between their songs.

A major culmination of the couple's teamwork resulted in the Roger Tory Peterson Institute of Natural History in his hometown of Jamestown, New York. It was dedicated in 1993 as an educational beacon for teachers and for the study of nature. Peterson said, "We must reach all mentors of children, their teachers and those who teach teachers. We must give them the tools and instill in them a responsibility for creating in their young charges a knowledge and love of nature." As Baba Dioum, an African environmentalist, says, "In the end we will conserve only what we love, we will love only what we understand and we will understand only what we are taught."

It is a great honor to be asked to do the introduction for this fifth and final edition of Roger Tory Peterson's "birder's bible," the *Field Guide to the Birds of Eastern and Central North America*. Virginia Peterson wrote to me, "Today I was looking at Roger's fifth edition bird plates which he finished some time ago. They are gorgeous." She enclosed a picture of the final plate of flycatchers that he was working on the day he died.

As I look at these final and unfinished images, I am very moved. Many years ago, I visited, deep underground, an ancient tomb in the Valley of the Kings at Karnak in Egypt. One wall had beautifully delineated figures, birds, mammals, and inscriptions. They were finished in color. But as we proceeded through the tomb, some drawings were uncolored and were only outlines, then vague sketches, and finally emptiness. The royal personage had died, and work had stopped. It was all so fresh you could imagine that the artists would come in tomorrow and continue their work. I have the same vivid immediacy as I gaze at this plate of flycatchers. I can see the studio and follow the strokes of the hand of the master. This work in progress implies that Roger's life's work will never finish. Indeed it does go on in the lives and efforts of millions of people. It will never end but will continue to expand like ripples in a pond. That is the criterion for a person's importance. How big and lasting is the circle of ripples that his life has made? Roger Tory Peterson's life has been one of the most important lives of the last 100 years.

Mimi Westervelt, Virginia's daughter, leaves us with a word portrait of her stepfather:

"At age 87, he's crouched down, camera to his eye, in some brush along a wetland focusing on a butterfly. He's just walked through some thorny mass of greenbrier, or thistle, or multiflora rose, and his legs and arms are all scraped up, but he never mentions it. Because he doesn't feel it. His head and neck are thick with insects, but he never flinches. Because he doesn't feel them. He doesn't see them. He doesn't hear them. All he sees is that butterfly. As long as he hadn't just run out of film, Roger knew how to focus."

That one word is the key to the man. Through his life and his work, he has shown us how to focus on nature. And that is just what this world needs.

Robert Bateman

Dr. Peterson was working on this flycatcher plate on the day
he died. This exemplifies the dedication he had to completing this revision.
The plate was finished by H. Douglas Pratt and appears on page 229.

PREFACE

Roger Tory Peterson's consuming passion in his later years was to complete the fifth edition of his *Field Guide to the Birds of Eastern and Central North America*. After the publication of his *Western Birds* in 1990, he immediately set about this formidable task — and he almost made it. The morning of July 28, 1996, Roger was painting his final bird plate. He died peacefully in his sleep later that day. He had completed 85 percent of his book.

Some months before his death, while we were working in the studio on the fifth edition, Roger came into my map room and asked, "Dear, what if I don't finish it?" Believing that he would live to be 100 years old, I said, "Roger, don't worry — it will get done." Always aware of how much Roger wanted to offer his new field guide to the legion of bird watchers who were waiting for it, and feeling the weight of my promise to him, I began planning. After his estate was settled, I gathered the most knowledgeable consultants possible to help me. Only with their expert help was the fifth edition of this field guide completed. I owe a great debt of heartfelt gratitude to the following people.

- Noble Proctor, professor of biology at Southern Connecticut State University, author, and world birder, who worked closely with Roger for more than 30 years, was the natural choice to complete the text. He also helped check the art and final maps.

- Paul Lehman, former editor of the American Birding Association magazine *Birding* and university instructor, updated and added maps to my final map roughs. Paul is widely recognized as the authority on the distribution of North American birds.

- H. Douglas Pratt, staff research associate of Louisiana State University Museum of Natural Science, is an acclaimed bird artist and specialist on the birds of Hawaii and the tropical Pacific. Doug painted the four rare flycatchers on Roger's final plate. Beautifully painted are the Cuban Pewee, La Sagra's Flycatcher, Variegated Flycatcher, and Loggerhead Kingbird. The additional flycatchers in the finished plate are Roger's paintings from his *Field Guide to Mexican Birds*.

- Pete Dunne, director of Cape May Bird Observatory in New Jersey and vice president of natural history information for New Jersey Audubon Society, introduced several innovations to the content and design and provided editorial counsel for this fifth edition. He is considered one of birding's most capable spokespersons.

- Robert Bateman wrote the foreword. He is acclaimed as one of the world's foremost wildlife artists.

In the years before his death, Dr. Peterson and I researched the original map material. My research background involved infrared spectroscopy for the U.S. Coast Guard Research and Development Center, where I developed methods for identifying oil spills. I wrote the original U.S. Coast Guard Infrared Field Manual for Oil Spill Identification. My research on the fifth-edition maps was curtailed in 1997 because of the pressures of settling my husband's estate. Knowing the maps would need current updating, and after conferring with Paul Lehman, I handed over to him my rough maps and all the map data I had collected from experts in every state east of the 100th meridian, plus the eastern Canadian Provinces. Paul's expert map update has given to this fifth edition the most accurate and current information on bird ranges.

This field guide is the culmination of more than 60 years of watchful, careful revisions of the Peterson classic, A Field Guide to the Birds, which was included in The New York Public Library's Books of the Century in 1996. This book and the Peterson Field Guide Series have been credited with being a powerful catalyst for the modern environmental movement. Paul Ehrlich, professor of biology at Stanford University, naturalist, and author of more than 20 books, wrote, "In this century no one has done more to promote an interest in living creatures than Roger Tory Peterson, the inventor of the modern field guide. His greatest contribution to the preservation of biological diversity has been in getting tens of millions of people outdoors with Peterson Field Guides in their pockets."

In the original 1934 edition of A Field Guide to the Birds, there were only four plates in color, with 26 in black and white. In the 1947 edition, all the old plates were retired and replaced by 60 new ones, with 36 in color. The 1980 edition progressed to 136 color plates. In this fifth edition, the progression continues, with Peterson offering 151 color plates with more than 1,800 bird paintings. Eighty-five plates have had birds added or modified, fifty-nine plates are from the fourth edition, and seven plates are totally new.

Roger delayed finishing his final plate of accidental flycatchers for months, trying to get more information on La Sagra's Flycatcher. On the day he died, he was working on the flycatchers. This last bird plate is unfinished and is included in the front matter of the book. Roger's struggle to paint his final birds is evident.

Virginia Marie Peterson

ACKNOWLEDGMENTS

We shall not list again the many correspondents and others who contributed notes or helped in other ways with the previous editions. We would, however, like to thank those who offered suggestions for this new edition with maps, general identification materials, and other tangible ways that helped to make this edition as complete as possible.

MAP ACKNOWLEDGMENTS: ALABAMA: T. Imhof, G. Jackson, S. McConnell; **ARKANSAS:** D. Catanzaro, M. Parker, B. Shepherd, K. Smith, M. White; **COLORADO:** T. Leukering, C. Wood; **CONNECTICUT:** M. Ardwin, T. Baptist, L. Bevier, H. Golet, H. Hunter, N. Proctor, M. Szantyr, J. Zeranski; **DELAWARE:** M. Barnhill, L. Fleming, G. Hess, R. West; **FLORIDA:** B. Anderson, B. Pranty, W. Robertson, H. Stevenson, G. Woolfenden; **GEORGIA:** A. Ashley, W. Baker, G. Beaton, B. Bergstrom, K. Blackshaw, B. Blakeslee, M. Chapman, L. Davenport Jr., H. DiGioia, J. Greenberg, D. Guynn Jr., M. Harris, J. Hitt, M. Hodges, M. Hopkins Jr., W. Hunter, M. Oberle, J. Ozier, J. Paget, J. Parrish, S. Pate, T. Patterson, T. Schneider, P. Sykes, S. Willis, B. Winn; **ILLINOIS:** H. D. Bohlen, R. Chapel, V. Kleen, W. Serafin, E. Walters, W. Zimmerman; **INDIANA:** K. Brock, J. Castrale et al., E. Hopkins, C. Keller; **IOWA:** J. Dinsmore, J. Giglerano, B. Hoyer, L. Jackson, K. Kane, T. Kent, P. Lohmann, C. Thompson; **KANSAS:** C. Ely, C. Hobbs, M. Robbins, S. Seltman, M. Thompson, J. Zimmerman; **KENTUCKY:** D. Roemer, B. Palmer-Ball Jr.; **LOUISIANA:** J. V. Remsen, M. Swan, D. Wiedenfeld; **MAINE:** P. Adamus, L. Brinker, E. Pierson et al; **MARYLAND:** C. Robbins; **MASSACHUSETTS:** P. Alden, R. Lockwood, W. Petersen, R. Veit; **MICHIGAN:** R. Adams Jr., C. Black, R. Brewer, A. Byrne, G. McPeek, C. Smith; **MINNESOTA:** K. Eckert, R. Janssen; **MISSISSIPPI:** J. Jackson, S. Peterson, T. Scheifer, J. Wilson; **MISSOURI:** D. Easterla, C. Hobbs, B. Jacobs, P. McKenzie, M. Robbins, J. Wilson; **MONTANA:** T. McEneaney; **NEBRASKA:** P. Johnsgard, W. Mollhoff, L. Padelford, R. Silcock; **NEW JERSEY:** P. Dunne, V. Elia, D. Hughs, P. Lehman, J. Walsh; **NEW HAMPSHIRE:** D. Abbott, C. Foss; **NEW MEXICO:** J. Oldenettel; **NEW YORK:** R. Andrle, P. A. Buckley, T. Burke, J. Carroll, W. D'Anna, A. Farnsworth, E. Levine; **NORTH CAROLINA:** C. Brimley, H. Brimley, H. Davis, J. Fussell, J. Gerwin, D. Lee, H. LeGrand, T. Pearson, N. Siebenheller, W. Siebenheller, D. Wray; **NORTH DAKOTA:** G. Berkley, R. Martin, R. Stewart; **OHIO:** B. Peterjohn, D. Rice, L. Rosche, W. Zimmerman; **OKLAHOMA:** J. Arterburn, W.. Carter, J. Grzybowski, J. McMahon, G. Schnell, G. Sutton, D. Wood; **PENNSYLVANIA:** D. Brauning,

N. Pulcinella; **RHODE ISLAND:** R. Enser; **SOUTH CAROLINA:** J. Cely, D. Crawford, P. Crawford, M. Dodd, A. Farnsworth, S. Gauthreaux, J. Gerwin, T. Murphy, W. Post, P. Wilkinson; **SOUTH DAKOTA:** C. Lippincott, R. Martin, R. Peterson, The South Dakota Ornithologists' Union; **TENNESSEE:** B. Linsey, C. Nicholson, J. Robinson, B. Stedman, S. Stedman, J. Wilson; **TEXAS:** K. Arnold, R. Baker, K. Benson, G. Blackloack, E. Kincaid, G. Lasley, M. Lockwood, H. Oberholser, J. Rappole, M. White; **VERMONT:** D. Kibbe, S. Laughlin; **VIRGINIA:** N. Brinkley, T. Dalmas, R. Peake, Virginia Society of Ornithology; **WEST VIRGINIA:** W. Argabrite, A. R. Buckelew Jr., G. Felton, G. A. Hall; **WISCONSIN:** D. Flaspohler, B. Harriman, S. Matteson, S. Robbins Jr., D. Tessen; **BRITISH COLUMBIA:** R. Cambell et al; **LABRADOR AND NEWFOUND-LAND:** C. Brown, K. Knowles, P. Linegar, B. Mactavish, W. Montevecchi, J. Pratt, P. Ryan, J. Selno, J. Wells; **MANITOBA:** B. Carey, C. Curtis, G. Holland, B. Knudsen, R. Koes, W. Neeley, P. Taylor; **NORTHWEST TERRITORIES:** W. E. Godfrey; **NEW BRUNSWICK:** B. Dalzell; **NOVA SCOTIA:** B. Dalzell, A. Erskine, B. Maybank, I. McLaren, R. Tufts; **ONTARIO:** M. Cadman, B. Curry, P. Eagles, F. Helleiner; **QUEBEC:** Y. Aubry, P. Bannon, C. Cormier, A. Cyr, N. David, J. Gauthier, J. Larivee, G. Savard, R. Yank; **ST. PIERRE AND MIQUELON:** R. Etcheberry; **SASKATCHEWAN:** A. R. Smith; **MEXICO:** S. N. G. Howell, S. Webb.

ADDITIONAL HELP: P. Alden, P. Bacinski, W. Boyle, W. Burt, V. Emanuel, K. Garrett, F. Gill, K. Kaufman, K. Parkes, A. Poole, J. V. Remsen, J. Rowlett, B. Russer, P. Stettenheim, W. Sladen, R. Sundell, P. Vickery.

The professionalism and support of Elaine Lillis and Elizabeth Gentile were invaluable. At Houghton Mifflin, Lisa White's editorial expertise, creative insight, and dedication to the project were indispensable. Anne Chalmers and Terry McAweeney provided editorial and technical support and guidance. Paul Jones photographed the plates, and Sandy Sherman copyedited the text. Larry Rosche created the electronic map files from Paul Lehman's data.

A FIELD GUIDE TO THE
BIRDS
OF EASTERN AND CENTRAL
NORTH AMERICA

CONSERVATION NOTE

Birds undeniably contribute to our pleasure and quality of life. But they also are sensitive indicators of the environment, a sort of "ecological litmus paper," and hence more meaningful than just chickadees and cardinals that brighten the suburban garden, grouse and ducks that fill the sportsman's bag, or rare warblers and shorebirds that excite the field birder. The observations and recording of bird populations over time leads inevitably to environmental awareness and is a signal of possible change.

To this end, please support the cause of wildlife conservation and education by contributing to or taking an active part in the work of the following organizations: the Nature Conservancy (4245 North Fairfax Drive, Suite 100, Arlington, VA 22203; www.nature.org), National Audubon Society (700 Broadway, New York, NY 10003; www.audubon.org), the Defenders of Wildlife (1101 14th Street, N.W., # 1400, Washington, D.C. 20005; www.defenders.org), the Roger Tory Peterson Institute of Natural History (311 Curtis Street, Jamestown, NY 14701; www.rtpi.org), the National Wildlife Federation (1400 16th Street, N.W., Washington, D.C. 20036; www.nwf.org), the World Wildlife Fund (1250 24th Street, N.W., Washington, D.C. 20037; www.wwf.org), Cornell Laboratory of Ornithology (159 Sapsucker Woods, Ithaca, NY 14850; www.birds.cornell.edu), Ducks Unlimited (One Waterfowl Way, Memphis, TN 38120; www.ducks.org), BirdLife International (Wellbrook Court, Girton Road, Cambridge CB3 0NA, UK; www.birdlife.org.uk) as well as your local Landtrust and Natural Heritage Programs and your local Audubon societies and bird clubs. These and so many other groups that have come into the forefront of bird conservation in the last 20 years merit your support.

INTRODUCTION

BIRD SONGS AND CALLS

Not everything useful for identifying birds can be crammed into a pocket-sized field guide. In the species accounts, I have included a brief entry on voice, and I have tried to interpret these songs and calls in my own way, trying to give birders some handle on the songs they hear. Authors of bird books have attempted with varying success to fit songs into syllables, words, and phrases. Musical notations, comparative descriptions, and even ingenious systems of symbols have also been employed. To supplement this verbal interpretation, there are tapes available for nearly every region of the world, CDs for some countries, such as our *Eastern/Central* and *Western Bird Songs*, and specific CDs covering individual groups to include nightjars and frogmouths, owls and wrens. The *Birding by Ear* CDs provide a step-by-step method for learning how to develop your listening and identification skills. Preparation in advance for particular species or groups greatly enhances your ability to identify them. Some birders do 95 percent of their birding by ear, and there is no substitute for actual sounds — for going afield and tracking down the songster and committing the song to memory. However, an audio library is a wonderful resource to return home to when attempting to identify a bird heard afield. Caution: when using tapes to attract hard-to-see species, limit the number of playbacks, and do not use them on rare and threatened species.

BIRD NESTS

The more time you spend afield becoming familiar with bird behavior, the more skilled you'll become at finding bird nests. It is as exciting to keep a bird nest list as it is to keep a life list. Remember, if you happen to find a nest during the breeding season, leave the site as undisturbed as possible. Back away, and do not touch the nest, eggs, or young birds. Often squirrels and several other mammals, grackles, and cowbirds are more than happy to have you "point out" a nest and will raid it if you disrupt the site or call attention to it. Many people find young birds that have just left the nest and may appear to be alone. Usually they are not lost but are under the watchful eye of a parent bird and are best left in place rather than scooped up and taken to a foreign environment. In the winter, nest hunting can be great fun and has little impact as most nests will never be used again. They are easy to see once the foliage is gone, and it can be a challenge to attempt to identify the maker. Books such as *A Field Guide to Birds' Nests* and *A Field Guide to Western Birds' Nests,* both in this series, will expand your ornithological expertise.

WATCHING BIRDS

A valuable tool for learning bird identification is my video, *Watching Birds,* which shows more than 200 species in their native habitats, is narrated, and has the species' songs or calls.

THE MAPS AND RANGES OF BIRDS

A number of species have been added to the avifauna of eastern North America since the previous edition of this field guide was published in 1980. Taxonomic splits have resulted in such "new" species as Saltmarsh and Nelson's Sharp-tailed Sparrows and Eastern and Spotted Towhees. Successful introductions of some species have resulted in self-sustaining, growing populations of Trumpeter Swans, Yellow-chevroned and White-winged Parakeets, and Eurasian Collared-Doves (the latter was introduced to the Bahamas, then arrived in the U.S. on its own). And a good number of additional vagrant species — out-of-range visitors from faraway lands — continue to be found. Some species that were formerly thought to occur only exceptionally have, over the past several decades, become much more regular visitors and sometimes even local breeders. It is not always certain if such changes in status are the result of actual population increases or if they merely reflect better observer coverage and advances in field identification skills.

The ranges of many species have changed markedly over the past 50 or more years. Some are expanding because of protection given them, changing habitats, bird feeding, or other factors. Some "increases" may simply be the result of more field guide–educated birders being in the field, helping to more thoroughly document bird populations and distributions. Other avian species have diminished alarmingly and may have been extirpated from major parts of their range. The primary culprit here has been habitat loss, although other factors such as increased competition or predation from other species may sometimes be involved. Species that are in serious decline in eastern North America run the gamut, from the American Bittern to the Loggerhead Shrike and Bewick's Wren.

Range maps need to be of sufficient size to denote adequate detail and to include written information on such topics as population trends and extralimital occurrences. Thus, the informative range maps in this Field Guide have been purposely placed near the back of the book where they can be reproduced in a large size not possible near the main body of the text. The maps are organized taxonomically, following the order published by the American Ornithologists' Union; their page numbers are given in the appropriate species accounts. In addition, thumbnail maps are placed in the main text next to the species accounts to give the reader a quick overview of a species' range without needing to turn the page. Because of the small size of these thumbnail maps, the ranges have been exaggerated so that they are visible. Turn to the full-size maps at the back of the book for accurate range information.

HABITATS

Although I have seen thousands of meadowlarks, I have never seen one in oak woodland. Likewise, I have never seen a Wood Thrush in a meadow. Just as a fisherman lives near the sea, a lumberjack near the forest, and a cab driver in the city, so each bird has its niche — its place to "make a living." Birders know this, and if they want to go out to run up a large day list, they do not remain in one habitat but shift from site to site based on time and species diversity for a given type of habitat. On listing days such as this, the more birds they find the more fun it is.

Gaining a familiarity with a wide range of habitats will greatly enhance your overall knowledge of the birds in a specific region, increase your skills, and add to your enjoyment of birding.

A few birds do invade habitats other than their own at times, especially in migration. A warbler that spends the summer in Maine might be seen, on its journey through Florida, in a palm. In cities, migrating birds often have to make the best of it, like the woodcock found one morning on the window ledge of a New York City office. Strong weather patterns can also alter where a bird happens to appear. Hurricanes, for example, can be a disaster for many species. As these violent storms sweep over the ocean, the calm eye can often "vacuum" up oceanic species that seek shelter in its calmness. Upon reaching land, these normally offshore species are faced with an entirely strange habitat and account for sightings such as a Yellow-nosed Albatross heading up the Hudson River or a White-tailed Tropicbird in downtown Boston.

Most species, however, are quite predictable for the major portion of their lives, and for the birder who has learned where to look, the rewards are great.

To start, familiarize yourself with individual habitat types. Become familiar with the dominant plant types that are indicators — for example, oak-beech woods, grass-shrub meadows, salt or fresh wetlands — and keep accurate records of what species you find in each. In a short period of time you will have a working knowledge of the predominant species in each habitat, and this will help you with your identification by allowing you to anticipate what might be found there.

The seasonal movements of birds at your sites will provide an overview of migrant species that come through at a given time and will be a reference point for future visits during these migration periods. An oak forest dotted with migrant warblers in spring may revert to relative quiet accented by the repetitive calls of a Red-eyed Vireo or drawn-out call of an Eastern Wood-Pewee in midsummer.

Be sure not to overlook cities and towns, where well-adapted species can be found. Common Nighthawks rest and nest on flat rooftops and can often be heard at night over the busiest of streets. Peregrine Falcons have shown remarkable adaptability, nesting on strategic ledges in the walled canyons of many cities. The fertile grounds for hunting Rock Doves and starlings seem to suit this raptor quite well.

Ecotones are edges where two habitat types interface—a forest and a shrub meadow, for example. As this is not a gradual change, ecotones offer habitat for species in both of the adjoining areas and are therefore rich in bird life. One can be recording forest species such as Red-eyed Vireo singing in the woodlands on one side and White-eyed Vireos in the thickets on the other.

The changes in habitat over the years will also affect your favorite birding areas. Fields turn to shrubby lots and then woodlands. Bobwhite and meadowlarks may move on, but Indigo Buntings and Field Sparrows establish themselves. This dynamic is normal in the natural world. However, man's alterations to this process have had great impact. Forest fragmentation is an example. As land development continues, it is having an effect on numerous species. A sudden disruption has a more drastic effect than a slow change, which allows for adaptation. As we divide up habitat with roadways, we have created a greater edge effect, and this allows Brown-headed Cowbirds to penetrate into forest areas where they would not have ventured in the past. They now parasitize many more species than before, and such parasitization is leading to marked declines in total numbers of many species. This forest fragmentation is also impacting the success rate of nestling fledging by altering prime habitat requirements for obtaining food to raise the young. If young birds are not fledged, then the input of replacement young into fall migration is nonexistent.

Some species are obligates to a specific habitat type, and searching these areas greatly improves your chance of finding them. These include Golden-crowned Kinglets in coniferous woodlands and the Kirtland's Warbler of Michigan that frequents only Jack Pine woodlands of a specific height. Even in migration, many species remain faithful to selected habitats, such as waterthrushes along watercourses. Running or dripping water has proven to be an important attractant for migrating warblers, and in areas such as the Dry Tortugas off Florida, where fresh water is at a minimum, a water drip can be a goldmine for migrant warblers.

All habitat types should produce at least a few species, and the more diverse the habitat, the greater the number of birds. You can increase your skills and enjoyment of birding by moving from habitat to habitat.

SUBSPECIES AND GEOGRAPHIC VARIATION

Many species of birds inhabit wide geographic areas. The Song Sparrow (*Melospiza melodia*), for example, breeds throughout North America, from Mexico north into Alaska. In such a wide-ranging species, there are clearly geographic subsets within the population that show distinct local plumage pattern and song variants. When the distinct geographic forms of a species reach a point when the population is dominated by individuals that are recognizably different from typical individuals of the "parent" species, the local group is formally designated a subspecies of the parent species. The subspecies is named by attaching a third, subspecific name to the Latin name of the species. Thus, the pale Song Sparrows of the southwestern deserts of North America are called *Melospiza melodia saltonis*, to distinguish that form from another subspecies. With at least 31 recognizable subspecies, the Song Sparrow ranks among the highest of North American birds in the number of its geographic varieties.

Often a subspecific group is so distinct from the parent species that several members can be easily recognized by birdwatchers. A good example of this is the Dark-eyed Junco (*Junco hyemalis*). With 12 subspecies, at least 5 are easily discerned: the Oregon (*J. h. oreganus*), Pink-sided (*J. h. mearnsi*), White-winged (*J. h. aikeni*), Slate-colored (*J. h. hyemalis*), and Gray-headed (*J. h. caniceps*). For the birder, identification of subspecies can add greater challenges to birding and, when documented, valuable information, especially when subspecies are reclassified to full species status. Such has been the case in the West, with the recent splitting of the Western Flycatcher (*Empidonax difficilis*) into the Pacific-slope Flycatcher (*E. difficilis*) and the Cordillerian Flycatcher (*E. occidentalis*). Field studies of the Sage Grouse (*Centrocercus urophasianus*) leading to the separation of the Greater Sage-Grouse (*C. urophasianus*) and the Gunnison Sage-Grouse (*C. minimus*) prove how valuable these studies of subspecific populations can be. The differences between the Bicknell's Thrush (*Catharus bicknelli*) and the Gray-cheeked Thrush (*C. minimus*) illustrate how subtle the field marks can be between species and why they had been relegated to subspecific status. The shifting of this line between subspecies and species is an ongoing one. Recording data on location and numbers can prove helpful in completing a picture of a species' distribution or even a new species that has been overlooked.

In this edition, species that have distinct subspecies easily recognized afield, such as the Yellow-rumped Warbler (*Dendroica coronata*) and the Dark-eyed Junco (*Junco hyemalis*), have been represented. When afield, challenge yourself to discern the subspecies. It will increase your visual and listening skills and add a new level of understanding and enjoyment of birds.

Veteran birders will know how to use this book. Beginners, however, should spend some time becoming familiar in a general way with the illustrations. The plates, for the most part, have been grouped in a taxonomic sequence. However, in cases where there is a great similarity of shape and action, I have grouped similar-appearing birds to help in identification. For example, vireos have been shown to be close relatives of shrikes. However, I have placed some of them in the older, conventional way nearer the warblers, which are similar in shape and action, and, indeed, the two groups often move together. I hope this will aid the beginner in making a field identification and not frustrate the true taxonomist to any great degree.

The beginning birder will also find that familiarization with visual categories is a great help in pinpointing the plates that most likely hold the identification:

1. Ducks and ducklike birds

2. Gulls and terns

3. Long-legged waders such as herons

4. Shorebirds and smaller waders

5. Fowl-like birds such as grouse

6. Birds of prey

7. Flycatchers

8. Warblers

Within these groupings it will be seen that ducks do not resemble loons; gulls are readily distinguishable from terns. The thin bills of warblers immediately differentiate them from the seed-cracking bills of sparrows. Birds that could be confused are grouped together when possible and are arranged in identical profile for direct comparison. The arrows point to outstanding "field marks" which are explained opposite. The text also gives aids such as voice, actions, habitat, etc., not visually portrayable, and under a separate heading discusses species that might be confused. The brief notes on general range are keyed by number to detailed three-color range maps in the rear of the book (pp. 333–410). Thumbnail versions of the maps also appear next to the species accounts for quick reference.

In addition to the 152 plates of birds normally found in the area of this field guide, there are 8 color plates depicting accidentals from Eurasia, the sea, and the tropics, as well as some of the exotic escapes that are sometimes seen.

WHAT IS THE BIRD'S SIZE?

Acquire the habit of comparing a new bird with some familiar "yardstick" —a House Sparrow, a robin, a pigeon, etc., so that you can say to yourself, "smaller than a robin; a little larger than a House Sparrow." The measurements in this book represent lengths in inches (with centimeters in parentheses) from bill tip to tail tip of specimens on their backs as in museum trays. However, specimen measurements vary widely depending on the preparator, who may have stretched the neck a bit. In most cases the species accounts give minimum and maximum lengths, but in life, not lying in a tray, most birds are closer to the minimum lengths given.

WHAT IS ITS SHAPE?

Is it plump like a starling (left) or slender like a cuckoo (right)?

WHAT SHAPE ARE ITS WINGS?

Are they rounded like a bobwhite's (left) or sharply pointed like a Barn Swallow's (right)?

WHAT SHAPE IS ITS BILL?

Is it small and fine like a warbler's (1); stout and short like a seed-cracking sparrow's (2); dagger-shaped like a tern's (3); or hook-tipped like that of a bird of prey (4)?

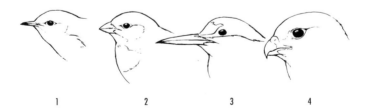

1   2   3   4

What Shape Is Its Tail?

Is it deeply forked like a Barn Swallow's (1); square-tipped like a Cliff Swallow's (2); notched like a Tree Swallow's (3); rounded like a Blue Jay's (4); or pointed like a Mourning Dove's (5)?

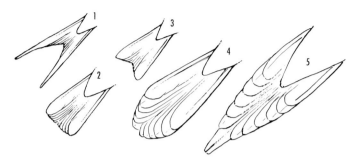

How Does It Behave?

Does it cock its tail like a wren or hold it down like a flycatcher? Does it wag its tail? Does it sit erect on an open perch, dart after an insect, and return as a flycatcher does?

Does It Climb Trees?

If so, does it climb in spirals like a Creeper (left), in jerks like a woodpecker (center) using its tail as a brace, or does it go down headfirst like a nuthatch (right)?

How Does It Fly?

Does it undulate (dip up and down) like a flicker (1)? Does it fly straight and fast like a dove (2)? Does it hover like a kingfisher (3)? Does it glide or soar?

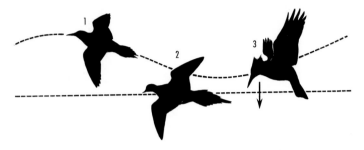

Does It Swim?

Does it sit low in the water like a loon (1) or high like a gallinule (2)? If a duck, does it dive like a scaup or a scoter (3) or does it dabble and upend like a Mallard (4)?

Does It Wade?

Is it large and long-legged like a heron or small like a sandpiper? If one of the latter, does it probe the mud or pick at things? Does it teeter or bob?

What Are Its Field Marks?

Some birds can be identified by color alone, but most birds are not that easy. The most important aids are what we call field marks, which are, in effect, the "trademarks of nature." Note whether the breast is spotted as in the Wood Thrush (1); streaked as in the thrasher (2); or plain as in a cuckoo (3).

Tail Patterns

Does the tail have a "flash pattern"—a white tip as in the kingbird (1); white patches in the outer corners as in the towhee (2); or white sides as in the junco (3)?

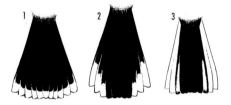

Rump Patches

Does it have a light rump like a Cliff Swallow (1) or flicker (2)? The Northern Harrier, Yellow-rumped Warbler, and a number of the shorebirds also have distinctive rump patches.

EYE-STRIPES AND EYE-RINGS

Does the bird have a stripe above, through, or below the eye, or a combination of these stripes? Does it have a striped crown? A ring around the eye or "spectacles"? A "mustache" stripe? These details are important in many small songbirds.

WING BARS

Do the wings have light wing bars or not? Their presence or absence is important in recognizing many warblers, vireos, and flycatchers. Wing bars may be single or double, bold or obscure.

WING PATTERNS

The basic wing patterns of ducks (shown below), shorebirds, and other water birds are very important. Notice whether the wings have patches (1) or stripes (2), are solidly colored (3), or have contrasting black tips (Snow Goose, etc.)

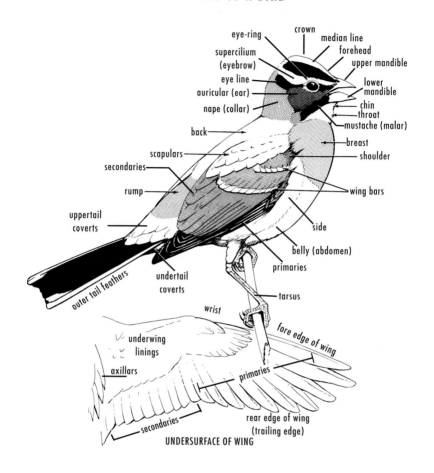

TOPOGRAPHY OF A BIRD

crown
eye-ring
median line
supercilium (eyebrow)
forehead
upper mandible
eye line
lower mandible
auricular (ear)
chin
nape (collar)
throat
back
mustache (malar)
scapulars
breast
secondaries
shoulder
rump
wing bars
uppertail coverts
side
belly (abdomen)
primaries
outer tail feathers
undertail coverts
tarsus
wrist
fore edge of wing
underwing linings
axillars
primaries
secondaries
rear edge of wing (trailing edge)

UNDERSURFACE OF WING

OTHER TERMS USED IN THIS BOOK

GENDER SYMBOLS: ♂ means male, ♀ means female. These symbols are used frequently on the plates, sparingly in the text.

RARE: Annual or probably annual in small numbers.

CASUAL: Not annual. These species are beyond their annual range but recur at regular intervals.

ACCIDENTAL: One record or a very few records that form no seasonal or regional pattern.

VAGRANT: Outside of its normal range limits.

LOCAL: Limited population within its range.

INTRODUCED: Not native; deliberately released.

EXOTIC: Not native; either released or escaped.

IN PART: A well-marked subspecies or morph—part of a species.

LIFE LIST

Keep a Life List. Check the birds you have seen.

This lists covers the eastern half of the continent west to the 100th meridian including the species of the Lower Rio Grande Valley in Texas. It includes only those species that are described and illustrated in the main body of this field guide. It excludes most of the extreme rarities and most introductions and escapes as depicted on pages 328–329.

For a checklist covering the entire North American region see the *ABA Checklist: Birds of the Continental United States and Canada,* compiled by the Checklist Committee of the American Birding Association, P.O. Box 6599, Colorado Springs, CO 80934. It lists every species that has occurred north of the Mexican border.

In the following list, birds are grouped first under orders (identified by the Latin ending *-formes*), followed by families (*-dae* ending), sometimes subfamilies (*-nae* ending), and then species. Sequencing of orders and families follows the American Ornithologists' Union's *Check-list of North American Birds* (1998 and 42nd supplement 2000) as do the scientific names for genus and species. They are not given below but will be found in the species accounts throughout the book. The vernacular names given here are the ones decided upon by the A.B.A. Checklist Committee. They are essentially the same as those adopted by the A.O.U. The list includes all of the birds shown on the plates, except for some of the accidentals that have not been verified.

ORDER GAVIIFORMES
LOONS: Gaviidae

__ Red-throated Loon
__ Arctic Loon
__ Pacific Loon
__ Common Loon
__ Yellow-billed Loon

ORDER PODICIPEDIFORMES
GREBES: Podicipedidae

__ Least Grebe
__ Pied-billed Grebe

__ Red-necked Grebe
__ Horned Grebe
__ Eared Grebe
__ Western Grebe
__ Clark's Grebe

ORDER PROCELLARIIFORMES
ALBATROSSES: Diomedeidae

__ Black-browed Albatross
__ Yellow-nosed Albatross

SHEARWATERS, PETRELS: Procellariidae

- __ Northern Fulmar
- __ Cape Petrel
- __ Black-capped Petrel
- __ Bermuda Petrel
- __ Mottled Petrel
- __ Herald Petrel
- __ Cory's Shearwater
- __ Greater Shearwater
- __ Sooty Shearwater
- __ Manx Shearwater
- __ Little Shearwater
- __ Audubon's Shearwater

STORM-PETRELS: Hydrobatidae
- __ Wilson's Storm-Petrel
- __ White-faced Storm-Petrel
- __ European Storm-Petrel
- __ Band-rumped Storm-Petrel
- __ Leach's Storm-Petrel

ORDER PELECANIFORMES
TROPICBIRDS: Phaethontidae
- __ Red-billed Tropicbird
- __ White-tailed Tropicbird

BOOBIES, GANNETS: Sulidae
- __ Northern Gannet
- __ Blue-footed Booby
- __ Masked Booby
- __ Red-footed Booby
- __ Brown Booby

PELICANS: Pelecanidae
- __ American White Pelican
- __ Brown Pelican

CORMORANTS: Phalacrocoracidae
- __ Double-crested Cormorant
- __ Neotropic Cormorant
- __ Great Cormorant

ANHINGAS: Anhingidae
- __ Anhinga

FRIGATEBIRDS: Fregatidae
- __ Magnificent Frigatebird
- __ Lesser Frigatebird

ORDER CICONIIFORMES
HERONS, EGRETS, BITTERNS: Ardeidae
- __ Great Blue Heron
  - __ "Wurdemann's" Heron
  - __ "Great White" Heron
- __ Great Egret
- __ Reddish Egret
- __ Tricolored Heron
- __ Little Blue Heron
- __ Snowy Egret
- __ Little Egret
- __ Western Reef-Heron (ssp of Little Egret)
- __ Cattle Egret
- __ Green Heron
- __ Black-crowned Night-Heron
- __ Yellow-crowned Night-Heron
- __ Least Bittern
- __ American Bittern

IBIS, SPOONBILLS: Threskiornithidae
- __ White Ibis
- __ Scarlet Ibis
- __ Glossy Ibis
- __ White-faced Ibis
- __ Roseate Spoonbill

STORKS: Ciconiidae
- __ Wood Stork
- __ Jabiru

NEW WORLD VULTURES: Cathartidae
- __ Black Vulture
- __ Turkey Vulture
- __ King Vulture

ORDER PHOENICOPTERIFORMES
FLAMINGOES: Phoenicopteridae
- __ Greater Flamingo

ORDER ANSERIFORMES
DUCKS, GEESE, SWANS: Anatidae

WHISTLING-DUCKS: Dendrocygninae
__ Fulvous Whistling-Duck
__ Black-bellied Whistling-Duck

SWANS, GEESE: Anserinae
__ Mute Swan
__ Trumpeter Swan
__ Tundra Swan
__ Pink-footed Goose
__ Greater White-fronted Goose
__ Snow Goose
    __ "Blue" Goose
__ Ross's Goose
__ Canada Goose
__ Barnacle Goose
__ Brant

TRUE DUCKS: Anatinae
Dabbling Ducks: Anatini
__ Muscovy Duck
__ Wood Duck
__ Eurasian Wigeon
__ American Wigeon
__ Gadwall
__ Green-winged Teal
    __ "Eurasian" Teal
__ Mallard
__ Mottled Duck
__ American Black Duck
__ Northern Pintail
__ White-cheeked Pintail
__ Garganey
__ Blue-winged Teal
__ Cinnamon Teal
__ Northern Shoveler

Bay Ducks: Aythyini
__ Canvasback
__ Redhead
__ Ring-necked Duck
__ Tufted Duck
__ Greater Scaup
__ Lesser Scaup
__ Common Eider

__ King Eider
__ Steller's Eider
__ Harlequin Duck
__ Long-tailed Duck
__ Black Scoter
__ Surf Scoter
__ White-winged Scoter
__ Common Goldeneye
__ Barrow's Goldeneye
__ Bufflehead

Sea Ducks/Mergansers: Mergini
__ Smew
__ Hooded Merganser
__ Red-breasted Merganser
__ Common Merganser

Stiff-tailed Ducks: Oxyurini
__ Masked Duck
__ Ruddy Duck

ORDER FALCONIFORMES
OSPREY: Pandionidae
__ Osprey

HAWKS, EAGLES, KITES: Accipitridae
KITES: Elaninae, Milvinae
__ Hook-billed Kite
__ Swallow-tailed Kite
__ White-tailed Kite
__ Snail Kite
__ Mississippi Kite

HARRIERS: Circinae
__ Northern Harrier

BIRD HAWKS: Accipitrinae
__ Sharp-shinned Hawk
__ Cooper's Hawk
__ Northern Goshawk

EAGLES, BUZZARD HAWKS: Buteoninae
__ Bald Eagle
__ Common Black-Hawk
__ Harris's Hawk

__ Gray Hawk
__ Roadside Hawk
__ Red-shouldered Hawk
__ Broad-winged Hawk
__ Short-tailed Hawk
__ Swainson's Hawk
__ White-tailed Hawk
__ Zone-tailed Hawk
__ Red-tailed Hawk
    __ "Krider's" Red-tailed Hawk
    __ "Harlan's" Red-tailed Hawk
__ Ferruginous Hawk
__ Rough-legged Hawk
__ Golden Eagle

CARACARA, FALCONS: Falconidae
__ Crested Caracara
__ Collared Forest Falcon
__ American Kestrel
__ Aplomado Falcon
__ Merlin
__ Gyrfalcon
__ Prairie Falcon
__ Peregrine Falcon

ORDER GALLIFORMES
GUANS, CHACHALACAS, CURASSOWS: Cracidae
__ Plain Chachalaca

PARTRIDGES, GROUSE, TURKEYS, OLD WORLD QUAIL: Phasianidae
PHEASANTS, PARTRIDGES: Phasianinae
__ Gray Partridge
__ Ring-necked Pheasant

GROUSE, PTARMIGAN, PRAIRIE-CHICKENS: Tetraoninae
__ Spruce Grouse
__ Willow Ptarmigan
__ Rock Ptarmigan
__ Ruffed Grouse
__ Sharp-tailed Grouse
__ Greater Prairie-Chicken

__ Lesser Prairie-Chicken

TURKEYS: Meleagridinae
__ Wild Turkey

NEW WORLD QUAIL: Odontophoridae
__ Scaled Quail
__ Northern Bobwhite

ORDER GRUIFORMES
RAILS, GALLINULES, COOTS: Rallidae
__ Yellow Rail
__ Black Rail
__ Clapper Rail
__ King Rail
__ Virginia Rail
__ Corn Crake
__ Sora
__ Purple Gallinule
__ Common Moorhen
__ American Coot
__ Caribbean Coot (ssp. of American Coot)

LIMPKIN: Aramidae
__ Limpkin

CRANES: Gruidae
__ Sandhill Crane
__ Common Crane
__ Whooping Crane

ORDER CHARADRIIFORMES
PLOVERS, LAPWINGS: Charadriidae
__ Northern Lapwing
__ American Golden-Plover
__ European Golden-Plover
__ Black-bellied Plover
__ Common Ringed Plover
__ Semipalmated Plover
__ Wilson's Plover
__ Killdeer
__ Piping Plover

__ Snowy Plover
__ Mongolian Plover
__ Mountain Plover

OYSTERCATCHERS: Haematopodidae
__ American Oystercatcher

STILTS, AVOCETS: Recurvirostridae
__ Black-necked Stilt
__ American Avocet

JACANAS: Jacanidae
__ Northern Jacana

SANDPIPERS: Scolopacidae
__ American Woodcock
__ Common Snipe
__ Short-billed Dowitcher
__ Long-billed Dowitcher
__ Black-tailed Godwit
__ Hudsonian Godwit
__ Bar-tailed Godwit
__ Marbled Godwit
__ Whimbrel
__ Eurasian Curlew
__ Long-billed Curlew
__ Upland Sandpiper
__ Spotted Redshank
__ Common Greenshank
__ Greater Yellowlegs
__ Lesser Yellowlegs
__ Solitary Sandpiper
__ Spotted Sandpiper
__ Willet
__ Ruddy Turnstone
__ Red Knot
__ Sanderling
__ Semipalmated Sandpiper
__ Western Sandpiper
__ Red-necked Stint
__ Least Sandpiper
__ White-rumped Sandpiper
__ Baird's Sandpiper

__ Pectoral Sandpiper
__ Sharp-tailed Sandpiper
__ Curlew Sandpiper
__ Dunlin
__ Purple Sandpiper
__ Stilt Sandpiper
__ Buff-breasted Sandpiper
__ Ruff
__ Wilson's Phalarope
__ Red-necked Phalarope
__ Red Phalarope

SKUAS, GULLS, TERNS, SKIMMERS: Laridae
SKUAS, JAEGERS: Stercorariinae
__ South Polar Skua
__ Great Skua
__ Pomarine Jaeger
__ Parasitic Jaeger
__ Long-tailed Jaeger

GULLS: Larinae
__ Band-tailed Gull
__ Black-tailed Gull
__ Mew Gull
__ Ring-billed Gull
__ California Gull
__ Great Black-backed Gull
__ Glaucous Gull
__ Iceland Gull
    __ "Kumlien's" Gull
__ Thayer's Gull
__ Herring Gull
__ Lesser Black-backed Gull
__ Black-headed Gull
__ Bonaparte's Gull
__ Laughing Gull
__ Franklin's Gull
__ Little Gull
__ Ivory Gull
__ Ross's Gull
__ Sabine's Gull
__ Black-legged Kittiwake

TERNS: Sterninae
__ Gull-billed Tern
__ Caspian Tern
__ Sandwich Tern
__ Royal Tern
__ Roseate Tern
__ Common Tern
__ Arctic Tern
__ Forster's Tern
__ Least Tern
__ Bridled Tern
__ Sooty Tern
__ White-winged Tern
__ Black Tern
__ Large-billed Tern
__ Black Noddy
__ Brown Noddy

SKIMMERS: Rynchopinae
__ Black Skimmer

AUKS, MURRES, PUFFINS: Alcidae
__ Dovekie
__ Common Murre
__ Thick-billed Murre
__ Razorbill
__ Black Guillemot
__ Atlantic Puffin

ORDER COLUMBIFORMES
PIGEONS, DOVES: Columbidae
__ Rock Dove
__ White-crowned Pigeon
__ Eurasian Collared-Dove
__ Ringed Turtle Dove (domestic variant)
__ Mourning Dove
__ White-winged Dove
__ Common Ground-Dove
__ Inca Dove

ORDER PSITTACIFORMES
PARROTS: Psittacidae
__ Budgerigar
__ Monk Parakeet
__ White-winged Parakeet
__ Yellow-chevroned Parakeet
__ Red-crowned Parrot

ORDER CUCULIFORMES
CUCKOOS: Cuculidae
__ Black-billed Cuckoo
__ Yellow-billed Cuckoo
__ Mangrove Cuckoo
__ Smooth-billed Ani
__ Groove-billed Ani
__ Greater Roadrunner

ORDER STRIGIFORMES
BARN OWLS: Tytonidae
__ Barn Owl

TYPICAL OWLS: Strigidae
__ Eastern Screech-Owl
__ Great Horned Owl
__ Snowy Owl
__ Barred Owl
__ Great Gray Owl
__ Northern Hawk Owl
__ Burrowing Owl
__ Boreal Owl
__ Northern Saw-whet Owl
__ Long-eared Owl
__ Short-eared Owl

ORDER CAPRIMULGIFORMES
NIGHTHAWKS, NIGHTJARS: Caprimulgidae
__ Lesser Nighthawk
__ Common Nighthawk
__ Antillean Nighthawk
__ Common Pauraque
__ Common Poorwill
__ Chuck-will's-widow
__ Whip-poor-will

ORDER APODIFORMES
SWIFTS: Apodidae
__ White-collared Swift
__ Chimney Swift
__ Vaux's Swift

HUMMINGBIRDS: Trochilidae
__ Green Violet-ear
__ Buff-bellied Hummingbird
__ Bahama Woodstar
__ Ruby-throated Hummingbird
__ Black-chinned Hummingbird
__ Anna's Hummingbird
__ Calliope Hummingbird
__ Broad-tailed Hummingbird
__ Rufous Hummingbird
__ Allen's Hummingbird

ORDER CORACIIFORMES
KINGFISHERS: Alcedinidae
__ Belted Kingfisher
__ Ringed Kingfisher
__ Green Kingfisher

ORDER PICIFORMES
WOODPECKERS: Picidae
__ Red-headed Woodpecker
__ Golden-fronted Woodpecker
__ Red-bellied Woodpecker
__ Yellow-bellied Sapsucker
__ Downy Woodpecker
__ Hairy Woodpecker
__ Red-cockaded Woodpecker
__ Three-toed Woodpecker
__ Black-backed Woodpecker
__ Northern Flicker
    __ "Yellow-shafted" Flicker
    __ "Red-shafted" Flicker
__ Pileated Woodpecker

ORDER PASSERIFORMES
TYRANT FLYCATCHERS: Tyrannidae
__ Northern Beardless-Tyrannulet
__ Greenish Elaenia
__ Caribbean Elaenia
__ Olive-sided Flycatcher
__ Eastern Wood-Pewee
__ Yellow-bellied Flycatcher
__ Acadian Flycatcher

__ Alder Flycatcher
__ Willow Flycatcher
__ Least Flycatcher
__ Eastern Phoebe
__ Say's Phoebe
__ Vermilion Flycatcher
__ Ash-throated Flycatcher
__ Great Crested Flycatcher
__ La Sagra's Flycatcher
__ Great Kiskadee
__ Social Flycatcher
__ Piratic Flycatcher
__ Variegated Flycatcher
__ Couch's Kingbird
__ Western Kingbird
__ Eastern Kingbird
__ Gray Kingbird
__ Loggerhead Kingbird
__ Scissor-tailed Flycatcher
__ Fork-tailed Flycatcher
__ Masked Tityra

SHRIKES: Laniidae
__ Loggerhead Shrike
__ Northern Shrike

VIREOS: Vireonidae
__ White-eyed Vireo
__ Bell's Vireo
__ Black-capped Vireo
__ Yellow-throated Vireo
__ Blue-headed Vireo
__ Warbling Vireo
__ Philadelphia Vireo
__ Red-eyed Vireo
__ Yellow-green Vireo
__ Black-whiskered Vireo

CROWS, JAYS, MAGPIES: Corvidae
__ Gray Jay
__ Blue Jay
__ Green Jay
__ Brown Jay

__ Florida Scrub-Jay
__ Black-billed Magpie
__ Eurasian Jackdaw
__ American Crow
__ Tamaulipas Crow
__ Fish Crow
__ Chihuahuan Raven
__ Common Raven

LARKS: Alaudidae
__ Horned Lark

SWALLOWS: Hirundinidae
__ Purple Martin
__ Tree Swallow
__ Northern Rough-winged
    Swallow
__ Bank Swallow
__ Cliff Swallow
__ Cave Swallow
__ Barn Swallow

CHICKADEES, TITS: Paridae
__ Carolina Chickadee
__ Black-capped Chickadee
__ Boreal Chickadee
__ Tufted Titmouse

PENDULINE TITS: Remizidae
__ Verdin

NUTHATCHES: Sittidae
__ Brown-headed Nuthatch
__ Red-breasted Nuthatch
__ White-breasted Nuthatch

CREEPERS: Certhiidae
__ Brown Creeper

WRENS: Troglodytidae
__ Cactus Wren
__ Rock Wren
__ Canyon Wren
__ Carolina Wren
__ Bewick's Wren
__ Winter Wren

__ House Wren
__ Sedge Wren
__ Marsh Wren

BULBULS: Pycnonotidae
__ Red-whiskered Bulbul

KINGLETS: Regulidae
__ Golden-crowned Kinglet
__ Ruby-crowned Kinglet

OLD WORLD WARBLERS: Sylviidae
GNATCATCHERS: Polioptilinae
__ Blue-gray Gnatcatcher

OLD WORLD FLYCATCHERS: Muscicapidae
__ Northern Wheatear

THRUSHES: Turdidae
__ Eastern Bluebird
__ Mountain Bluebird
__ Townsend's Solitaire
__ Veery
__ Gray-cheeked Thrush
__ Bicknell's Thrush
__ Swainson's Thrush
__ Hermit Thrush
__ Wood Thrush
__ Clay-colored Robin
__ Rufous-backed Robin
__ American Robin
__ Varied Thrush

MOCKINGBIRDS, THRASHERS: Mimidae
__ Gray Catbird
__ Northern Mockingbird
__ Sage Thrasher
__ Brown Thrasher
__ Long-billed Thrasher
__ Curve-billed Thrasher

STARLINGS: Sturnidae
__ European Starling
__ Hill Myna

PIPITS: Motacillidae
__ American Pipit
__ Sprague's Pipit

WAXWINGS: Bombycillidae
__ Bohemian Waxwing
__ Cedar Waxwing

NEW WORLD WARBLERS: Parulidae
__ Bachman's Warbler (extinct?)
__ Blue-winged Warbler
__ Golden-winged Warbler
    __ "Brewster's" Warbler
    __ "Lawrence's" Warbler
__ Tennessee Warbler
__ Orange-crowned Warbler
__ Nashville Warbler
__ Northern Parula
__ Tropical Parula
__ Yellow Warbler
__ Chestnut-sided Warbler
__ Magnolia Warbler
__ Cape May Warbler
__ Black-throated Blue Warbler
__ Yellow-rumped Warbler
    __ "Myrtle" Warbler
    __ "Audubon's" Warbler
__ Black-throated Gray Warbler
__ Golden-cheeked Warbler
__ Black-throated Green Warbler
__ Blackburnian Warbler
__ Yellow-throated Warbler
__ Pine Warbler
__ Kirtland's Warbler
__ Prairie Warbler
__ Palm Warbler
__ Bay-breasted Warbler
__ Blackpoll Warbler
__ Cerulean Warbler
__ Black-and-white Warbler
__ American Redstart
__ Prothonotary Warbler
__ Worm-eating Warbler

__ Swainson's Warbler
__ Ovenbird
__ Northern Waterthrush
__ Louisiana Waterthrush
__ Kentucky Warbler
__ Connecticut Warbler
__ Mourning Warbler
__ Common Yellowthroat
__ Gray-crowned Yellowthroat
__ Hooded Warbler
__ Wilson's Warbler
__ Canada Warbler
__ Golden-crowned Warbler
__ Yellow-breasted Chat

BANANAQUIT: Coerebidae
__ Bananaquit

TANAGERS: Thraupidae
__ Scarlet Tanager
__ Summer Tanager
__ Western Tanager

NEW WORLD SPARROWS: Emberizidae
__ White-collared Seedeater
__ Olive Sparrow
__ Green-tailed Towhee
__ Eastern Towhee
__ Spotted Towhee
__ Bachman's Sparrow
__ Botteri's Sparrow
__ Cassin's Sparrow
__ Rufous-crowned Sparrow
__ American Tree Sparrow
__ Chipping Sparrow
__ Clay-colored Sparrow
__ Field Sparrow
__ Vesper Sparrow
__ Lark Sparrow
__ Lark Bunting
__ Savannah Sparrow
    __ "Ipswich" Sparrow
__ Seaside Sparrow

__ "Cape Sable" Seaside
   Sparrow
__ Nelson's Sharp-tailed Sparrow
__ Saltmarsh Sharp-tailed Sparrow
__ Le Conte's Sparrow
__ Henslow's Sparrow
__ Baird's Sparrow
__ Grasshopper Sparrow
__ Fox Sparrow
__ Song Sparrow
__ Lincoln's Sparrow
__ Swamp Sparrow
__ White-crowned Sparrow
__ White-throated Sparrow
__ Golden-crowned Sparrow
__ Harris's Sparrow
__ Dark-eyed Junco
   __ "Slate-colored" Junco
   __ "Oregon" Junco
__ McCown's Longspur
__ Lapland Longspur
__ Smith's Longspur
__ Chestnut-collared Longspur
__ Snow Bunting

CARDINALS, ALLIES: Cardinalidae
__ Crimson-collared Grosbeak
__ Northern Cardinal
__ Pyrrhuloxia
__ Rose-breasted Grosbeak
__ Black-headed Grosbeak
__ Blue Bunting
__ Blue Grosbeak
__ Lazuli Bunting
__ Indigo Bunting
__ Varied Bunting
__ Painted Bunting
__ Dickcissel

BLACKBIRDS, ORIOLES, ALLIES: Icteridae
__ Bobolink
__ Red-winged Blackbird
__ Eastern Meadowlark

__ Western Meadowlark
__ Yellow-headed Blackbird
__ Rusty Blackbird
__ Brewer's Blackbird
__ Common Grackle
__ Boat-tailed Grackle
__ Great-tailed Grackle
__ Shiny Cowbird
__ Bronzed Cowbird
__ Brown-headed Cowbird
__ Orchard Oriole
__ Hooded Oriole
__ Bullock's Oriole
__ Spot-breasted Oriole
__ Altamira Oriole
__ Audubon's Oriole
__ Baltimore Oriole

FINCHES, ALLIES: Fringillidae
__ Common Chaffinch
__ Brambling
__ Pine Grosbeak
__ Purple Finch
__ House Finch
__ Red Crossbill
__ White-winged Crossbill
__ Common Redpoll
__ Hoary Redpoll
__ Pine Siskin
__ Lesser Goldfinch
__ American Goldfinch
__ Evening Grosbeak

OLD WORLD SPARROWS: Passeridae
__ House Sparrow
__ Eurasian Tree Sparrow

PLATES

LOONS. Family Gaviidae.

Large, long-bodied swimmers with daggerlike bills; may dive from the surface or slowly sink. Run along water to take off, nest on land at water's edge. Sexes alike. Immatures more scaly feathered above than winter adults. **FOOD:** Small fish, crustaceans, other aquatic life. **RANGE:** Northern parts of N. Hemisphere. **NO. OF SPECIES:** World, 5; East, 4.

RED-THROATED LOON *Gavia stellata* (in flight p. 44)   Common

M 1

25" (63 cm) Sharp thin bill, distinctly uptilted. *Summer:* Dark brownish gray back, uniform gray head with a dark *rufous throat patch,* striped nape. *Winter:* Similar to other loons but smaller, slimmer; carries head at upward angle; back, head, and neck paler, with less contrast or pattern. Back flecked with white. **SIMILAR SPECIES:** (1) Common Loon is larger, bill straight. (2) Pacific Loon, slender, straight bill. **VOICE:** When flying, a repeated *kwuk.* On arctic breeding area, bubbling yodeling sounds. **RANGE:** Arctic; circumpolar. **HABITAT:** Coastal waters, bays, estuaries; in summer, nests at margins of tundra lakes, coastal lagoons.

PACIFIC LOON *Gavia pacifica* (in flight p. 44)   Rare

M 2

25" (63 cm) Smaller than Common Loon, with a thinner, straight bill. *Summer:* Crown and nape rounded, *pale gray.* Back checkered, divided into four areas. *Winter:* Note sharp separation of black-and-white neck pattern. Bill more slender than Common Loon's but not upturned as in Red-throated Loon. Often has trace of a chin strap. **SIMILAR SPECIES:** See Arctic Loon. **VOICE:** A deep, barking *kwow.* Falsetto wails, rising in pitch. **RANGE:** E. Siberia, n. Canada. Winters mainly along Pacific Coast. **HABITAT:** Ocean, open water; in summer, tundra lakes.

ARCTIC LOON *Gavia arctica*   No Eastern record to date

27" (68 cm) Formerly regarded as conspecific with Pacific Loon. Slightly larger. In breeding plumage, lacks pale nape of Pacific and is slightly larger-headed and longer-billed. When sitting, shows a more distinct white patch at waterline than Pacific Loon.

COMMON LOON *Gavia immer* (in flight p. 44)   Common

M 3

28–36" (70–90 cm) Large, long-bodied, low-swimming; bill thick, daggerlike. *Breeding:* Black head and bill. *Checkered back, barred white necklace. Winter:* Dark above, whitish below. Note *stout, straight bill* and *strongly indented neck pattern.* **SIMILAR SPECIES:** See other loons, cormorants. **VOICE:** In summer, falsetto wails, weird yodeling, maniacal quavering laughter; at night, a tremulous *ha-oo-oo.* In flight, a barking *kwuk* or low yodel. **HABITAT:** Lakes, bays, ocean edge; in summer, woodland lakes and ponds. In winter, chiefly coastal or large unfrozen lakes.

YELLOW-BILLED LOON *Gavia adamsii*   Vagrant

33–38" (83–95 cm) Similar to Common Loon, but bill mostly *pale ivory or straw-colored,* distinctly uptilted; straight above, slightly angled below. In winter, *paler* head and neck than Common Loon; usually shows a *dark ear spot.* Bills of most winter Common Loons are pale but upper ridge is *dark to tip.* **HABITAT:** Tundra lakes in summer; coastal waters in winter. May appear on inland lakes.

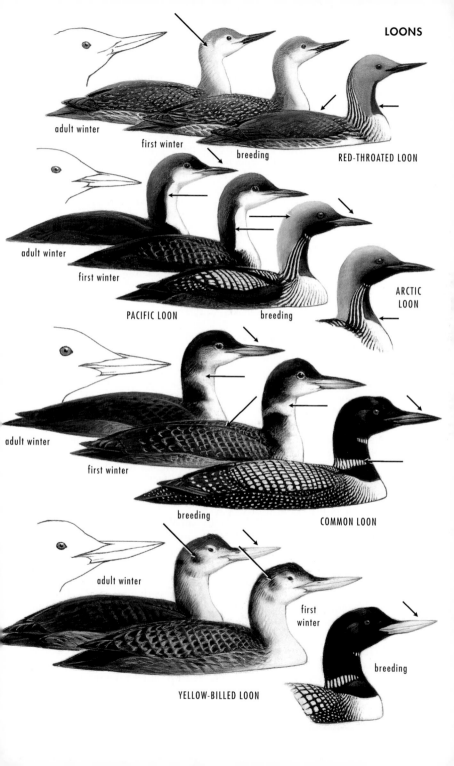

LOONS

adult winter

first winter

breeding

RED-THROATED LOON

adult winter

first winter

PACIFIC LOON

breeding

ARCTIC LOON

adult winter

first winter

breeding

COMMON LOON

adult winter

first winter

breeding

YELLOW-BILLED LOON

Ducklike divers with flat, lobed toes, thin neck, tail-less look. All but the Pied-billed have white wing patches, pointed bills. Sexes alike. Most young have striped heads. May dive from the surface or slowly sink. Flight labored (with a drooping neck). **FOOD:** Small fish, other aquatic life. **RANGE:** Cosmopolitan. **NO. OF SPECIES:** World, 19; East, 7.

PIED-BILLED GREBE *Podilymbus podiceps* Fairly common

M 4

13" (33 cm) A small brown diver of ponds, marshes. Note thick, un-grebelike "chicken bill" and puffy white undertail. No wing patch. *Breeding: Black throat patch* and *ring* around pale bill. *Winter:* Throat patch and bill ring *absent. Juvenile:* Striped on head. **VOICE:** (mainly on breeding grounds) *Kuk-kuk-cow-cow-cow-cow-cowp-cowp;* also whin-nying. **HABITAT:** Ponds, lakes, marshes; in winter, also salt bays. Migratory in North.

HORNED GREBE *Podiceps auritus* Common

M 5

12–15" (30–38 cm) *Breeding:* Note combination of *golden ear tufts* and *chestnut neck. Winter:* Dark above, white below, with its black *cap clean-cut to eye level;* white foreneck, thin straight bill. **VOICE:** Harsh *kerra*'s and squeaky trills on breeding grounds. Usually silent in winter. **HABITAT:** Lakes, ponds, coastal waters.

EARED GREBE *Podiceps nigricollis* Rare in East

M 7

12–14" (30–35 cm) *Breeding: Peaked* black head, golden ear tufts, thin *black* neck. *Winter:* Similar to Horned Grebe but overall slimmer; bill slightly upturned; cap ill defined, dusky neck. Gray cheek sets off white throat, *white ear patch.* Some cheeks can have smudged appearance. Rump is usually raised well above water. **VOICE:** On breeding grounds a froglike *poo-eep* or *krreep.* Usually silent in winter. **HABITAT:** Prairie lakes, ponds; in winter, open lakes, salt bays, coastal waters.

RED-NECKED GREBE *Podiceps grisegena* Uncommon

M 6

18" (45 cm) A large, almost loonlike grebe. *Breeding:* Long *rufous* neck, *light cheek,* black cap, long bill with *yellow base. Winter:* Grayish (including neck); *white crescent* on side of face. In flight, double *white* wing patch. **HABITAT:** Lakes, ponds; in winter, salt water.

LEAST GREBE *Tachybaptus dominicus* Uncommon and restricted

9½" (24 cm) A very small *slaty grebe,* smaller than Pied-bill, with *white wing patch* (often concealed), puffy undertail coverts, a slender *black* pointed bill, *golden or red eye.* In winter, *throat white.* **HABITAT:** Ponds and lake edges. **RANGE:** Extreme s. Tex.

WESTERN GREBE *Aechmophorus occidentalis* Very rare in East

M 8

25" (63 cm) A large slate-and-white grebe with a *long neck.* Black of cap extends *below eye.* Bill long, *greenish yellow* with a dark ridge on upper mandible. **VOICE:** Two-noted *crik-crik.* **HABITAT:** Rush-edged lakes, sloughs; in winter, large lakes, bays, coastal waters.

CLARK'S GREBE *Aechmophorus clarkii* Accidental

M 9

Very similar to Western Grebe. *White surrounds eye; bill orange-yellow.* Downy young are white, not gray. **VOICE:** A slurred one-note *creeet* or *criiik.* **HABITAT:** Same as Western Grebe. Range overlaps that of Western Grebe.

lobed foot of grebe

GREBES

juvenile

adult winter

breeding

downy young

PIED-BILLED GREBE

winter variant

winter

breeding

bill (Horned)

HORNED GREBE

winter variant

winter

breeding

bill (Eared)

EARED GREBE

immature

winter

breeding

RED-NECKED GREBE

winter

breeding

LEAST GREBE

display

WESTERN GREBE

CLARK'S GREBE

SHEARWATERS, ETC. Family Procellariidae.

Birds of the *open sea*, with stiff-winged gliding flight (several flaps followed by short glide) over the waves. Bills with tubelike external nostrils. Wings narrower than those of gulls, tail shorter. Sexes alike. On their nesting grounds, they are noisy at night; at sea, usually silent. **FOOD:** Fish, squid, crustaceans, ship refuse. **RANGE:** Oceans of world. **NO. OF SPECIES:** World, 72; East, 7 (+ 4 or 5 accidental).

CORY'S SHEARWATER *Calonectris diomedea* Fairly common

M 12

21" (53 cm) Large, pale seabird; *gray* head blends into white of throat; bill *dull yellow*. Belly all white; rump usually dark with indistinct or no white. **SIMILAR SPECIES:** Greater Shearwater has dark-capped look, black bill, white rump, smudge on belly. Cory's has more pronounced bend to wing than Greater, and wingbeat tends to be slightly slower. **RANGE:** Breeds in Azores, Canaries, and other islands in e. Atlantic; also in Mediterranean. Ranges to coastal U.S. in summer. **HABITAT:** Open ocean.

GREATER SHEARWATER *Puffinus gravis* Common

M 13

19" (48 cm) Dark above and white below, scaling above waves on stiff wings, is likely to be this shearwater or Cory's. This species has a *dark headcap* separated by a light band across nape. Note also *white rump patch* and *dark smudge on belly*. **SIMILAR SPECIES:** See Cory's Shearwater. **RANGE:** Breeds mainly on Tristan da Cunha Is. in s. Atlantic. Ranges at sea north to s. Greenland, Iceland, and back, May–October. **HABITAT:** Open ocean, usually well offshore.

SOOTY SHEARWATER *Puffinus griseus* Common

M 14

17" (43 cm) Size of Laughing Gull; looks all dark at a distance and scales over waves on narrow rigid wings. Note *whitish linings* on undersurface of the wings. **SIMILAR SPECIES:** See dark jaegers (white in primaries), p. 170, and dark-morph Northern Fulmar, p. 321. **RANGE:** Breeds in New Zealand, s. S. America; ranges in summer to N. Atlantic, N. Pacific. **HABITAT:** Open sea, but more likely to be seen from shore than most other shearwaters.

MANX SHEARWATER *Puffinus puffinus* Uncommon

M 15

13" (33 cm) A small *black-and-white* shearwater; half the bulk of Greater Shearwater; *no white* at base of tail. Dark cap extends below eye. Wingbeat quicker than Greater or Cory's. **RANGE:** Breeds on sea islands off Europe. **EAST:** Has bred in Nfld., Mass. Increasing. Regular at sea from Nfld. to N.C.; casual Fla.

AUDUBON'S SHEARWATER *Puffinus lherminieri* Fairly common

M 16

12" (30 cm) A very small dark-backed shearwater, similar to Manx but with slightly browner upperparts and dark under tail. Wings *shorter*, tail *longer*. **SIMILAR SPECIES:** See also Little Shearwater, p. 32. **RANGE:** Breeds Bermuda, W. Indies, Cape Verdes, Galapagos, etc. **EAST:** Visitor at sea off Atlantic and Gulf Coasts of se. U.S.

SHEARWATERS

GREATER
SHEARWATER

CORY'S
SHEARWATER

SOOTY
SHEARWATER

MANX
SHEARWATER

AUDUBON'S
SHEARWATER

tubed bill of
shearwater

NORTHERN FULMAR *Fulmarus glacialis*   Common

M 10

18" (45 cm) A stiff-winged oceanic glider, stockier than a shearwater; swims buoyantly. Note bull neck, rounded forehead, *stubby yellow bill* with tubed nostril, large dark eye, short tail. Primaries may show a *pale flash* at base. Leg color variable. *Dark morph* (less frequent in Atlantic): Smoky gray, yellowish bill. Intermediates are often seen. **VOICE:** A hoarse grunting *ag-ag-ag-arrr* or *ek-ek-ek-ek-ek.* **RANGE:** Northern oceans of N. Hemisphere. **HABITAT:** Open ocean; breeds colonially on open sea cliffs.

BLACK-CAPPED PETREL *Pterodroma hasitata*   Uncommon

M 11

16" (40 cm) Larger than Audubon's or Manx Shearwater and looks quite similar to Greater Shearwater. Note white forehead, *white collar,* and white rump patch extending to tail. **RANGE:** Caribbean. Regular in Gulf Stream well offshore north at least to Cape Hatteras. Accidental inland after storms.

BERMUDA PETREL (CAHOW) *Pterodroma cahow*   Rare

15" (38 cm) Breeds on Bermuda only. One of world's rarest seabirds. Differs from Black-capped Petrel by grayer rump, absence of white collar. **RANGE:** Known only from certain small islets off northeast end of Bermuda (a few pairs), where they come and go at night. Sightings becoming more regular off Cape Hatteras.

LITTLE SHEARWATER *Puffinus assimilis*   Vagrant

10½–12" (26–30 cm) Smaller than Audubon's Shearwater (p. 30), with a shorter tail. Very rapid, almost alcidlike wingbeats. Bluish legs contrast with white undertail coverts (Audubon's has pinkish legs, dark undertail coverts). Manx Shearwater (p. 30) is larger; wings longer; black on face extends below eye level. Reported S.C., N.C., Me., N.S.

HERALD PETREL *Pterodroma arminjoniana*   Rare

16" (40 cm) Dark, intermediate, and pale morphs. Most N. American records are dark, differing from Sooty Shearwater by absence of silvery wing linings. Light area at primary base suggest a jaeger. Feet and legs black. Reported annually off N.C. coast.

MOTTLED PETREL *Pterodroma inexpectata*   Vagrant

14" (35 cm) Identified by white chest, dark belly, and black stripe on fore edge of the white underwing.

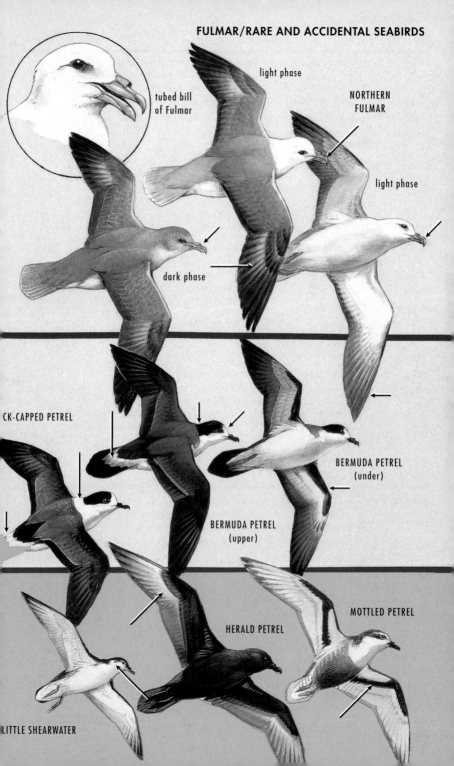

FULMAR/RARE AND ACCIDENTAL SEABIRDS

tubed bill
of Fulmar

light phase

NORTHERN
FULMAR

light phase

dark phase

CK-CAPPED PETREL

BERMUDA PETREL
(under)

BERMUDA PETREL
(upper)

HERALD PETREL

MOTTLED PETREL

LITTLE SHEARWATER

STORM-PETRELS. Family Hydrobatidae.

Small dark birds that flit over the ocean. Like shearwaters, large pe-
trels, etc., they nest on sea and coastal islands, returning to burrows at
night. Nostrils in tube on top ridge of bill. Sexes alike. **FOOD:** Plankton,
crustaceans, small fish. **RANGE:** Oceans of world (except Arctic). **NO. OF
SPECIES:** World, 20; East, 3 (+ 2 or 3 accidental).

WILSON'S STORM-PETREL *Oceanites oceanicus*   Common

M 17

7" (18 cm) Smaller than Purple Martin; sooty with a paler wing panel
and conspicuous *white rump patch; tail squared off.* Yellow-webbed
feet may show beyond tip of tail. Skims like a swallow, pausing to flut-
ter and patter over water. **RANGE:** Breeds in Antarctic; in summer, to N.
Hemisphere. **HABITAT:** Open ocean. Often follows ships. (Leach's
Storm-Petrel does not.) Can be "chummed in" by tossing out ground
fish, suet, puffed wheat in fish oil, etc. Occasionally seen from shore.

LEACH'S STORM-PETREL *Oceanodroma leucorhoa*   Scarce

M 18

8" (20 cm) Note *forked tail.* Otherwise similar to Wilson's Storm-Petrel but browner; wings longer, more angled, white rump patch slightly
divided. In flight, it bounds about erratically, suggesting a nighthawk's
flight. The breeding storm-petrel of the N. Atlantic (but less often seen
than Wilson's Storm-Petrel). Does not follow ships. **VOICE:** At night, in
flight on breeding grounds, rhythmic falsetto hooting notes. From burrows, long crooning trills. **RANGE:** N. Atlantic, N. Pacific. **HABITAT:** Open
ocean; nesting colonies in turf on offshore islands.

BAND-RUMPED STORM-PETREL *Oceanodroma castro*   Rare

M 19

7–8" (18–20 cm) Very similar to Leach's Storm-Petrel but with shorter
wings, more shearwater-like flight; tail square and larger pale wing
panel. White of rump is broad, forming a straight band (not divided as
in Leach's) and extending onto flanks and undertail coverts. (E. Atlantic, Pacific.)

CASUAL OR ACCIDENTAL SEABIRDS
AND COASTAL SPECIES

EUROPEAN STORM-PETREL *Hydrobates pelagicus*   Vagrant

6" (15 cm) Smaller than Wilson's Storm-Petrel; shorter legs, which do
not extend beyond the square tail. Yellow on feet not on webs. Shows a
whitish underwing patch. (e. N. Atlantic.) Reported Sable I., N.S.

WHITE-FACED STORM-PETREL *Pelagodroma marina*   Vagrant

8" (20 cm) A storm-petrel with a white head and white underparts,
dark crown, and eye patch. Very long legs. Bounds "kangaroo style"
over water when feeding. (Se. Atlantic, sw. Pacific, Indian Ocean.)
Usually seen far offshore.

STORM-PETRELS

tubed bill of
storm-petrel

WILSON'S

LEACH'S

BAND-RUMPED

lower

upper

WHITE-FACED

EUROPEAN

Leach's

Wilson's

Band-rumped

European

WHITE-RUMPED STORM-PETRELS

BLACK-BROWED ALBATROSS *Thalassarche melanophris* Vagrant
32–34" (80–85 cm) Wingspan 7½' Suggests a huge Great Black-backed Gull, but with a short *blackish tail* and a very large yellow bill (adult) with a hooked tip. Immature has dark bill. A *dark eye streak* gives it a frowning look. In stiff-winged gliding flight, shows white underwing broadly outlined with black. (Resident of cold oceans of S. Hemisphere.)

YELLOW-NOSED ALBATROSS *Thalassarche chlororhynchos* Vagrant
29–34" (73–85 cm) Wingspan 7–7½' Similar to Black-browed Albatross, but bill is *black*, with a *yellow ridge* on upper mandible. In flight, underwing is whiter, with narrower black edging. (Cold oceans of S. Hemisphere.)

RED-FOOTED BOOBY *Sula sula* Vagrant
26–30" (65–75 cm) Adults have *bright red feet*. Bill pale blue. *White morph:* Gannetlike; white, with black tip and trailing edge of wing (as in Masked Booby), but tail *white. Dark morph:* Brown back and wings, paler head; white tail and belly. Immature birds similar to Brown Boobies but are paler, buffy brown and have dark trailing edge to wing and orange feet. Resident of tropical oceans. Occasional sight records, especially of young birds at Dry Tortugas.

LESSER FRIGATEBIRD *Fregata ariel* Vagrant
31" (78 cm) Smaller than Magnificent Frigatebird; male distinctive, with a *round white patch on each flank* beneath wing. Female has chestnut (not gray) collar on hindneck. (Tropical oceans.)

RED-BILLED TROPICBIRD *Phaethon aethereus* Vagrant
24–40" (60–100 cm) Differs from White-tailed Tropicbird (p. 40) in being slightly larger, having a closely *barred back, bright red* to slight orange (not yellow) bill, and having more black on wing and out into primaries. (Tropical oceans.)

BAND-TAILED GULL *Larus belcheri* Vagrant
20" (50 cm) A black-backed gull with a clean-cut *black band* across tail. Bill broadly tipped with *red*; feet yellow. *Winter:* Head blackish. (S. America.) Several records on Gulf and East Coasts.

MEW GULL *Larus canus* Vagrant
16–18" (40–45 cm) (Called Common Gull in Europe.) Smaller and darker backed than Ring-billed Gull, with a small, short, *unmarked*, greenish yellow bill. (*Caution:* In winter, bill may show dark smudge.) Legs *greenish*. Immature looks like a "pint-sized" young Ring-billed Gull with a small bill (N. Eurasia, nw. N. America.)

ACCIDENTAL SEABIRDS

overhead

BLACK-BROWED
ALBATROSS

BLACK-BROWED
ALBATROSS

dark morph

YELLOW-NOSED
ALBATROSS

FOOTED
OBY

LESSER
FRIGATEBIRD ♂

RED-BILLED
TROPICBIRD

white morph

breeding

MEW GULL

winter

BAND-TAILED GULL

PELICANS. Family Pelecanidae.

Huge water birds with long flat bills and great throat pouches (flat when deflated). Necks long, bodies robust. Sexes alike. Flocks fly in lines, alternating several flaps with a glide. In flight, head is hunched back on shoulders, long bill resting on breast. Pelicans swim buoyantly. **FOOD:** Mainly fish, crustaceans. **RANGE:** N. and S. America, Africa, se. Europe, s. Asia, E. Indies, Australia. **NO. OF SPECIES:** World, 8; East, 2.

AMERICAN WHITE PELICAN
Pelecanus erythrorhynchos

Locally common, wanders

M 24

62" (155 cm) Huge (wingspread 8–9½'). White with black primaries and a great orange-yellow bill. When breeding, ridge of bill has a "centerboard." Immature has a dusky bill. Does not plunge from air like Brown Pelican but scoops up fish while swimming. Flocks fly in lines, often soaring high on thermals. **SIMILAR SPECIES:** (1) Swans have no black in wings. (2) Wood Stork and (3) Whooping Crane fly with necks extended, long legs aft. (4) Snow Goose is much smaller, with a small bill; noisy. **VOICE:** In colony, a low groan. Young utter whining grunts. **RANGE:** W. and cen. N. America, winters to se. U.S. **HABITAT:** Lakes, marshes, salt bays.

BROWN PELICAN *Pelecanus occidentalis*

Common

M 25

50" (125 cm) A ponderous *dark* water bird (spread 6½'); adult with much *white* about head and neck. Immature has a brown head and back, whitish underparts. Size, shape, and flight (a few flaps and a glide) indicate a pelican; dark color and habit of *plunging bill-first* identify it as this species. Lines of pelicans scale close to water, almost touching it with wingtips. **VOICE:** Adults silent (rarely a low croak). Nestlings squeal. **RANGE:** Coasts; U.S. to n. and w. S. America. **HABITAT:** Salt bays, beaches, ocean. Perches on posts, boats.

FRIGATEBIRDS. Family Fregatidae.

Dark tropical seabirds with extremely long wings (with a greater span in relation to weight than that of any other birds). Bills long, hooked; tails deeply forked. Not seen floating on water. **FOOD:** Fish, jellyfish, squid, young birds. Food snatched from water in flight, scavenged, or taken from other seabirds. **RANGE:** Pantropical oceans. **NO. OF SPECIES:** World, 5; East, 1 (+ 1 accidental).

MAGNIFICENT FRIGATEBIRD *Fregata magnificens*

Locally common

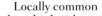

M 30

38–41" (95–103 cm); wingspread 7–8'. A large black seabird with extremely long, angled wings and a scissorlike tail (often folded in a point). Soars with extreme ease. Bill long, hooked. *Male:* All black with a red throat pouch (inflated in display). *Female:* White breast, dark head. *Immature:* Head, breast white. **VOICE:** Voiceless at sea. A gargling whinny during display. **RANGE:** Gulf of Mexico, tropical Atlantic, e. Pacific. **HABITAT:** Oceanic coasts, islands.

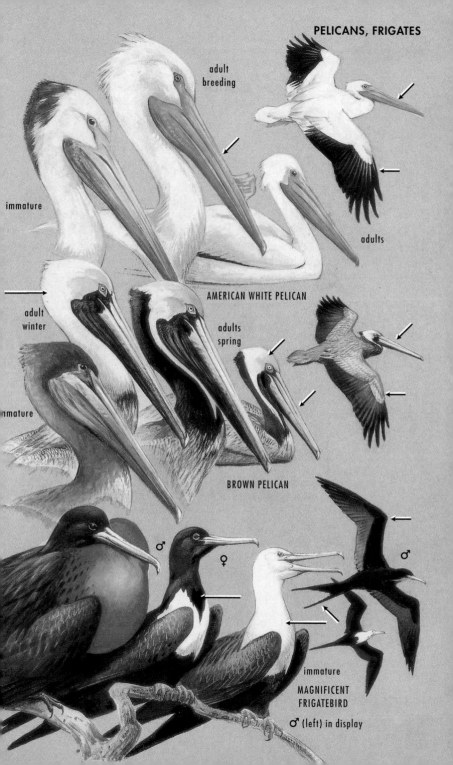

PELICANS, FRIGATES

adult
breeding

immature

adults

AMERICAN WHITE PELICAN

adult
winter

adults
spring

immature

BROWN PELICAN

♂   ♀

♂

immature
MAGNIFICENT
FRIGATEBIRD

♂ (left) in display

GANNETS, BOOBIES. Family Sulidae.

Seabirds with large, tapering bills, pointed tails ("pointed at both ends"). Larger than most gulls; necks longer. Sexes alike. **FOOD:** Fish, squid, taken by plunging from the air. **RANGE:** Gannets live in cold seas (N. Atlantic, S. Africa, Australia); boobies, tropical seas. **NO. OF SPECIES:** World, 9; East, 2 (+ 2 accidental).

NORTHERN GANNET *Morus bassanus*   Common

M 23

38" (95 cm) A goose-sized white seabird with extensive *black primaries*. Scales over ocean and plunges headlong for fish. Much larger than Herring Gull, with a *pointed tail*, longer neck, larger bill (often pointed toward water). Immature is dusky, note "pointed at both ends" shape. Young birds in transition may have a splotched piebald look. **VOICE:** In colony, a low barking *arrah*. **RANGE:** N. Atlantic. Oceanic; seen offshore regularly from land. Breeds colonially on sea cliffs.

MASKED BOOBY *Sula dactylatra*   Scarce

M 21

27" (68 cm) A white booby, smaller than Gannet, with a *black* tail and black along *entire rear edge* of wing. *Immature:* Dusky, with *whitish patch* on upper back and rump. **RANGE:** Tropical oceans. **EAST:** Occasional off Gulf Coast (sitting on buoys, oil rigs) and s. Fla. (regular off Dry Tortugas, where it nests).

BROWN BOOBY *Sula leucogaster*   Scarce, restricted

M 22

28–30" (70–75 cm) Sooty brown with a *white belly* in *clean-cut contrast* to its dark breast. Bill and feet yellowish. *Immature:* Brown above, paler belly; feet *yellowish*. **SIMILAR SPECIES:** (1) Immature Gannet lacks clean-cut breast contrast; feet are *dark* (not yellowish). (2) Immature Red-footed Booby more buffy and orange or reddish feet. (3) Immature Masked Booby resembles adult Brown Booby, but brown of head not clean cut off to paler underparts. **RANGE:** Tropical oceans.

TROPICBIRDS. Family Phaethontidae.

Although unrelated, tropicbirds resemble large terns with 2 greatly elongated *central* tail feathers and stouter, slightly decurved bills. Sexes alike. **FOOD:** Squid, crustaceans. **RANGE:** Tropical oceans of world. **NO. OF SPECIES:** World, 3; East, 1 (+ 1 accidental).

WHITE-TAILED TROPICBIRD *Phaethon lepturus*   Rare

M 20

32" (80 cm), including 16" (40 cm) tail streamers. Tropicbirds fly pigeonlike on strong quick wingbeats over the sea and dive ternlike. Note 2 *extremely long central tail feathers*. Bill yellow to orange-red. Young lack streamers; barred with black above; bill yellow. **SIMILAR SPECIES:** Red-billed Tropicbird (*Phaethon aethereus*) has finely barred back, deep red bill. **VOICE:** A harsh ternlike scream. Also *tik-et, tik-et*. **RANGE:** Pantropical oceans. **EAST:** Breeds in Bermuda. Occasionally seen in Gulf Stream off s. Atlantic Coast, Fla. Keys. Casual to n. Gulf Coast and N.S.

GANNETS, BOOBIES, TROPICBIRDS

adults

1st year

NORTHERN
GANNET

changing

diving

MASKED BOOBY

adults

immature

BROWN BOOBY

adult

adults

below

above

immature

immature

adult

WHITE-TAILED
TROPICBIRD

RED-BILLED TROPICBIRD

CORMORANTS. Family Phalacrocoracidae.

Large, blackish water birds that often stand erect on rocks or posts with neck in an S curve; may rest with wings spread. Adults may have colorful face skin, throat pouch; eyes usually green. Bill slender, hook-tipped. Sexes alike. Flocks fly in lines or wedges like geese (but are silent). Swims low like loon, but bill held tilted up at an angle. **FOOD:** Fish, crustaceans. **RANGE:** Nearly cosmopolitan. **NO. OF SPECIES:** World, 39; East, 3.

DOUBLE-CRESTED CORMORANT *Phalacrocorax auritus* (in flight p. 44)   Common

M 27

33" (83 cm) The one widespread cormorant of e. N. America; found both on coast and inland. Adults all black with erect posture. Bright orange-yellow gular pouch. Curled feather crests in breeding plumage. Lacks white flank patch. *Immature:* Brownish belly, pale throat and chest. **VOICE:** Silent, except for piglike grunts in nesting colony. **RANGE:** Most of N. America, winters to Belize. **HABITAT:** Coast, islands, bays, lakes, rivers; nests on ground or in trees.

GREAT CORMORANT *Phalacrocorax carbo* (in flight p. 44)   Uncommon

M 28

37" (93 cm) Larger than Double-crested; note *heavier* bill, *pale yellow* (not orangish) chin pouch, bordered by a *white throat strap*. In breeding plumage, has a *white patch* on flanks. Immature is *paler below* than most young Double-cresteds, which typically have a pale breast but a *dark* belly. **RANGE:** N. Atlantic, Eurasia, Africa, Australia, etc. **HABITAT:** Primarily coastal; nests on sea cliffs.

NEOTROPIC CORMORANT *Phalacrocorax brasilianus*   Fairly common

M 26

25" (63 cm) Similar to Double-crested Cormorant but smaller. Note duller (less orange) chin pouch and, in summer, *narrow white border to pouch*. At very close range, note lack of orange supraloral stripe of Double-crested. In nuptial plumage, white filoplumes on neck. **RANGE:** Gulf of Mexico to Argentina. **EAST:** Tex. and sw. La.; straggler farther north and east. **HABITAT:** Tidal waters, lakes near coasts.

ANHINGAS (OR DARTERS). Family Anhingidae.

The family is represented by the one U.S. species (below). **FOOD:** Fish, small aquatic animals. **RANGE:** N. and S. America, Africa, India, se. Asia, Australia. **NO. OF SPECIES:** World, 2; East, 1.

ANHINGA *Anhinga anhinga* (in flight p. 44)   Common

M 29

34" (85 cm) Similar to a cormorant, but neck *snakier*, bill *pointed*, tail much *longer*. Note large *silvery* wing patch. *Male* is black-bodied; *female* has a buffy neck and breast; *immature* is brownish. In flight, flaps and glides with neck extended, long tail spread. Often soars high, hawklike. Perches like a cormorant, often with wings half spread. May swim submerged, with only head emergent, appearing snakelike. **RANGE:** Se. U.S. to Argentina. **HABITAT:** Cypress swamps, rivers, wooded ponds.

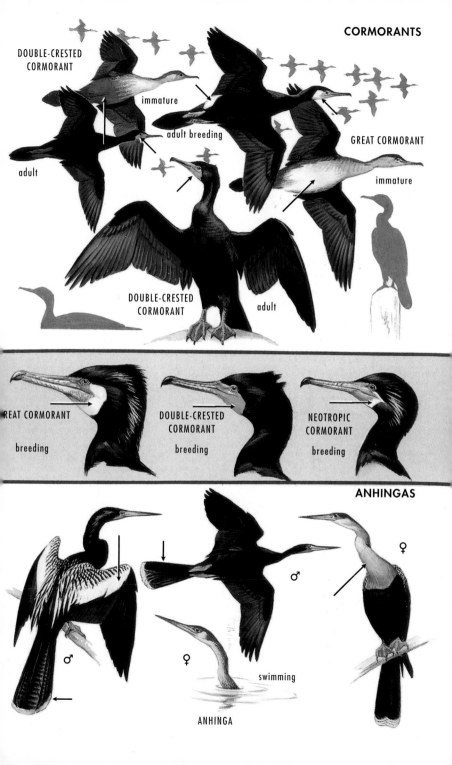

CORMORANTS

DOUBLE-CRESTED
CORMORANT

immature

adult breeding

adult

GREAT CORMORANT

immature

DOUBLE-CRESTED
CORMORANT

adult

REAT CORMORANT

breeding

DOUBLE-CRESTED
CORMORANT

breeding

NEOTROPIC
CORMORANT

breeding

ANHINGAS

♂

♂

♀

♀

swimming

ANHINGA

Airborne, loons are slower than most ducks; their outline is hunch-backed. Red-throated Loon flies with a sagging-neck look. The large webbed feet project rudderlike beyond the stubby tail.

COMMON LOON *Gavia immer*   **PP. 26–27**

More heavily built than the next two species. Look for especially large trailing feet and stout straight bill. In winter plumage, note irregular (half-collared) neck pattern.

RED-THROATED LOON *Gavia stellata*   **PP. 26–27**

Has a slimmer look than other loons; paler, with a slim, upturned bill. In winter, no strong demarcation between gray and white of head and neck. May be in large groups in winter and in migration.

PACIFIC LOON *Gavia pacifica*   **PP. 26–27**

Darker and more contrasty than Red-throated Loon; bill straight, not upturned. Head smaller and foot extension less than in Common Loon. In winter plumage, note well-defined, straight separation of blackish and white on neck. When seen overhead, *black bar across vent region* of underbelly (hard to see).

CORMORANTS IN FLIGHT

Cormorants often fly in lines or wedges, somewhat in the manner of geese, but are silent. Give the appearance of flying "uphill."

DOUBLE-CRESTED CORMORANT *Phalacrocorax auritus*   **PP. 42–43**

Note kink in neck and yellow or orange gular (throat) pouch. Neck thinner than Great Cormorant. Immature has dark underbelly when compared to an immature Great Cormorant.

GREAT CORMORANT *Phalacrocorax carbo*   **PP. 42–43**

Larger, heavier billed, and bulkier than Double-crested and Neotropic. Thick neck. Immature with very white underbelly, compared to dark underbelly of other two cormorants in region.

ANHINGA *Anhinga anhinga*   **PP. 42–43**

Often soars very high. Holds neck straight out and fans tail.

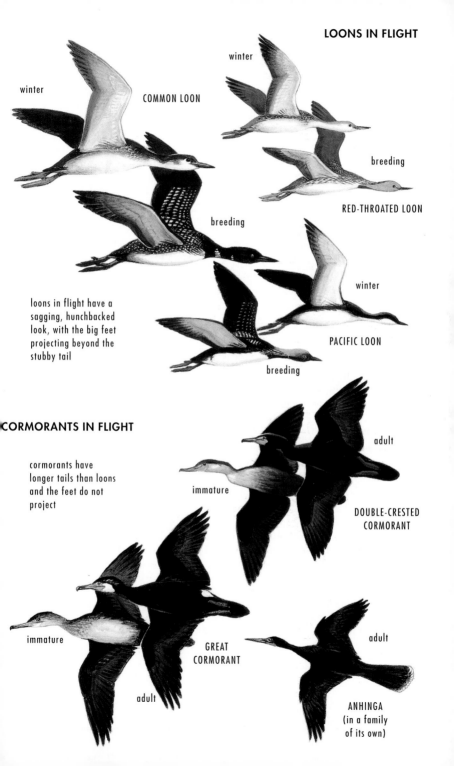

LOONS IN FLIGHT

winter

COMMON LOON

winter

breeding

RED-THROATED LOON

breeding

loons in flight have a
sagging, hunchbacked
look, with the big feet
projecting beyond the
stubby tail

winter

PACIFIC LOON

breeding

CORMORANTS IN FLIGHT

cormorants have
longer tails than loons
and the feet do not
project

immature

adult

DOUBLE-CRESTED
CORMORANT

immature

GREAT
CORMORANT

adult

adult

ANHINGA
(in a family
of its own)

HERONS, EGRETS, BITTERNS. Family Ardeidae.

Medium to large wading birds with long necks, spearlike bills. Stand with necks erect or with heads on shoulders. In flight, necks folded in an S-shape; the legs trail. May have plumes in breeding season. Sexes similar. **FOOD:** Fish, frogs, crayfish, other aquatic life; rodents, insects. **RANGE:** Worldwide except colder regions, some deserts and islands. **NO. OF SPECIES:** World, 63; East, 12 (+ 2 accidental).

GREAT BLUE HERON *Ardea herodius*   Common

M 33

42–52" (105–130 cm) A tall gray bird, often miscalled a crane; may stand 4 ft. tall. Its long legs, long neck, daggerlike bill, and, in flight, folded neck indicate a heron. Great size and blue-gray color and white about head (in adults) with long black plumes mark it as this species. **SIMILAR SPECIES:** See Sandhill Crane, pp. 56–57. **VOICE:** Deep harsh croaks, *frahnk, frahnk, frahnk.* **RANGE:** S. Canada to Mexico. Winters to n. S. America. **HABITAT:** Marshes, swamps, shores, tideflats.

"WURDEMANN'S" HERON *Ardea herodius* (in part)   Uncommon and restricted

Fla. Keys. Like Great Blue Heron, but its white head *lacks black plumes.* Presumably an intermediate color morph of the Great Blue–Great White Heron complex. See "Great White" Heron, p. 48.

LITTLE BLUE HERON *Egretta caerulea*   Uncommon

24" (60 cm) A slender, medium-sized heron. *Adult:* Bluish slate with a deep maroon-brown neck; legs dark. *Immature:* All-white with dusky wingtips; legs *dull olive*; bill blue-gray, tipped with black; greenish lores. Birds in transition are boldly pied with white and dark. See pp. 48–49. **SIMILAR SPECIES:** Snowy Egret has all-black bill, bright yellow feet; young Snowy has greenish yellow lores but may have yellowish stripe up rear of leg. **RANGE:** E. U.S. to Peru, Argentina. **HABITAT:** Marshes, swamps, rice fields, ponds, shores.

TRICOLORED HERON *Egretta tricolor*   Uncommon

M 38

26" (65 cm) *White belly* and *thin neck stripe* are key field marks of this very slender, dark heron. A white crown plume and pale rump plumes when breeding. **RANGE:** E. U.S. to Brazil. **HABITAT:** Marshes, swamps, streams, shores.

REDDISH EGRET *Egretta rufescens*   Uncommon

M 39

29" (73 cm) Note *pinkish* black-tipped bill in breeding season. Pale eye. Two color morphs: (1) neutral gray, with rusty head and neck; (2) *white* with *blue* legs (shown on p. 49). Loose-feathered; neck shaggy. When feeding, lurches about with spread wings. **SIMILAR SPECIES:** (1) Gray morph resembles adult Little Blue Heron, which is darker with bill *pale bluish* at base. (2) White morph suggests Great Egret, but legs bluish, bill pink. **RANGE:** Gulf states, W. Indies, Mexico. **HABITAT:** Coastal tidal flats, salt marshes, shores, lagoons.

DARK HERONS

herons fly with
necks pulled in

immature

herons' necks
may stretch or
be looped in

adult

adult

"WURDEMANN'S"
HERON

adult

GREAT BLUE HERON

LITTLE BLUE HERON

(white immature
on next plate)

adult

immature

adult

TRICOLORED
HERON

Reddish Egret
"dancing"
while feeding

adult

REDDISH
EGRET

gray morph

(white morph
on next plate)

GREAT EGRET *Ardea alba* Common

M 35

38" (95 cm) A large, stately, slender white heron with a *yellow bill* (orange with green lores when breeding). Legs and feet *black.* Straight plumes on back extend beyond tail. When feeding, assumes an eager, forward-leaning pose, neck extended. SIMILAR SPECIES: Snowy Egret has an *all-black* bill, *yellow* feet. VOICE: A low hoarse croak. Also, *cuk, cuk, cuk.* RANGE: Cosmopolitan. HABITAT: Marshes, ponds, shores, mudflats.

SNOWY EGRET *Egretta thula* Common

M 36

20–27" (50–68 cm) Note *"golden slippers."* A rather small white heron with a *slender black bill*, black legs, *yellow feet. Recurved plumes* on back during breeding season. A yellow loral area before eye (deep orange when breeding). When feeding, rushes about, shuffling feet to stir up food. SIMILAR SPECIES: (1) Great Egret has a largely yellow bill; (2) Cattle Egret has a yellow bill; (3) white immature Little Blue Heron has a blue-gray bill. VOICE: A low croak; in colony, a bubbling *wulla-wulla-wulla.* RANGE: N. U.S. to Argentina. HABITAT: Marshes, swamps, ponds, shores, tideflats.

LITTLE BLUE HERON *Egretta caerulea* (see adult on p. 46)

M 37

IMMATURE: *Blue-gray* bill, dull greenish legs. Also *pied pattern* with blue-gray plumage.

CATTLE EGRET *Bubulcus ibis* Common

M 40

20" (50 cm) Slightly smaller, stockier, thicker-necked than Snowy Egret. When breeding, shows *buff* on crown, breast, and back (but may appear whitish at a distance); little or no buff at other times. Bill *yellow* (orange-pink when nesting). Legs coral-pink (nesting); immature may have yellow, greenish, or dusky legs. SIMILAR SPECIES: (1) Snowy Egret has a *black* bill; (2) immature Little Blue Heron has a *blue-gray* bill; (3) Great Egret much larger. RANGE: S. Eurasia, Africa; immigrant N. and S. America, Australia. Introduced Hawaii. HABITAT: Farms, marshes, highway edges. Associates with cattle.

REDDISH EGRET *Egretta rufescens* (gray phase on p. 46)
WHITE PHASE: Note *flesh-pink* bill, bluish legs.

"GREAT WHITE" HERON *Ardea herodius* (in part) Uncommon and restricted

M 34

50" (125 cm) Our largest white heron, with the most restricted range. All white with a yellow bill and *yellowish legs,* the latter separating it positively from smaller Great Egret, which has blackish legs. Formerly believed to be (and may be) a distinct species (*A. occidentalis*); currently regarded as a white subspecies of Great Blue Heron (*A. herodius*), p. 46. RANGE: S. Fla., Cuba, coastal Yucatán. HABITAT: Mangrove keys, salt bays, marsh banks, open mudflats.

WHITE HERONS, EGRETS

SNOWY EGRET

GREAT EGRET

changing

immature

LITTLE BLUE
HERON

(adult on p. 47)

CATTLE EGRET

immature

breeding

REDDISH EGRET

(gray morph
on p. 47)

white morph

"GREAT WHITE"
HERON (regarded
as s. Florida color
morph of Great
Blue Heron)

BLACK-CROWNED NIGHT-HERON *Nycticorax nycticorax* Common

M 42

23–28" (58–70 cm) Stocky, thick-billed, short-legged. Usually hunched and inactive; most active at dusk. *Adult:* Note *blackish back and black cap* in contrast to pale gray or whitish underparts, gray wings. Eyes red; legs yellowish or yellow-green (pink when breeding), barely extend beyond tail tip in flight. Two long white head plumes when breeding. *Immature:* Brown, *spotted* and streaked with white and buff. Bill with *greenish base*, eyes small, reddish. **SIMILAR SPECIES:** See (1) immature Yellow-crowned Night-Heron; (2) American Bittern. **VOICE:** A flat *quok!* or *quark!* Most often heard at dusk. **RANGE:** S. Canada to Argentina; Eurasia, Africa, Pacific Is. **HABITAT:** Marshes, shores; roosts in trees.

YELLOW-CROWNED NIGHT-HERON *Nyctanassa violacea* Fairly common

M 43

22–28" (55–70 cm) A chunky *gray* heron; head black with a *whitish cheek patch and crown. Immature:* Very similar to young Black-crown, but grayer, *more finely speckled. Eyes large and orange.* Bill stouter and *entirely dark*; legs *longer*, yellower. In flight, *entire lower leg extends* beyond tail. **VOICE:** *Quark*, higher pitched than note of Black-crown. **RANGE:** E. U.S. to n. and e. S. America. **HABITAT:** Cypress swamps, mangroves, bayous, marshes, streams.

GREEN HERON *Butorides virescens* Common

M 41

16–22" (40–55 cm) A small dark heron that in flight looks crowlike (but flies with bowed wingbeats). When alarmed, it stretches its neck, elevates a shaggy crest, and jerks its tail nervously. Comparatively *short* legs are *greenish yellow* or *orange* (breeding). Back bluish green, neck deep chestnut. Immature has a streaked neck. **VOICE:** A series of *kuck's*; a loud *skyow* or *skewk*. **RANGE:** Nw. U.S., se. Canada to n. S. America. **HABITAT:** Lakes, ponds, marshes, swamps, streamsides.

LEAST BITTERN *Ixobrychus exilis* Uncommon and secretive

M 32

11–14" (28–35 cm) Very small, thin, furtive; straddles reeds. Note large *buff wing patch* (lacking in rails). An extremely rare dark chestnut color morph, "Cory's" Least Bittern. **VOICE:** A low, muted *coo-coo-coo* heard in the marsh. Also a loud, harsh contact note, *kiack-kack-kack.* **RANGE:** Se. Canada, U.S. to S. America. **HABITAT:** Fresh marshes, reedy ponds; not easy to flush.

AMERICAN BITTERN *Botaurus lentiginosus* Uncommon

M 31

23" (58 cm) A stocky brown heron; size of a young night-heron but warmer brown. In flight, entire trailing edge of wing is *black* and bill is held horizontal. At rest or when approached, often stands rigid, its bill pointing up. A *black stripe* shows on neck. **VOICE:** "Pumping" sound, a low, deep resonant *oong-ka´ choonk, oong-ka´ choonk, oong-ka´ choonk,* etc. Flushing note, *kok-kok-kok.* **RANGE:** Canada to Gulf states; winters to Panama. **HABITAT:** Marshes, reedy lakes. Unlike night-herons, seldom sits in trees.

adult

BLACK-CROWNED NIGHT-HERON

immature

adult

YELLOW-CROWNED
NIGHT-HERON

immature

typical

dark
morph
(rare)

LEAST
BITTERN

immature

adult
GREEN
HERON

AMERICAN
BITTERN

LIMPKINS. Family Aramidae.

A monotypic family, represented by one species. **FOOD:** Mostly large freshwater snails (mainly Apple Snails); a few insects, frogs. **RANGE:** Se. U.S., W. Indies, s. Mexico to Argentina. **NO. OF SPECIES:** World, 1; East, 1.

LIMPKIN *Aramus guarauna*   Uncommon and secretive

M 135

28" (70 cm) A large spotted swamp wader, a bit larger than an ibis. Its long legs and *drooping bill* give it an ibislike aspect, but no ibis is brown with *white spots and streaks.* Flight cranelike, with smart upward flaps. **SIMILAR SPECIES:** (1) Immature ibises, (2) night-herons, (3) American Bittern. **VOICE:** A piercing, repeated wail, *kree-ow, kra-ow,* etc., especially at night and on cloudy days. **RANGE:** Fla., W. Indies, s. Mexico to Argentina. **HABITAT:** Fresh swamps, marshes with large snails.

IBISES AND SPOONBILLS. Family Threskiornithidae.

Ibises are long-legged heronlike waders with slender *decurved* bills. Spoonbills have spatulate bills. Both fly in V's or lines and, unlike herons, with necks *outstretched.* **FOOD:** Small crustaceans, small fish, insects, etc. **RANGE:** Tropical and warm temperate regions. **NO. OF SPECIES:** World, 33; East, 4 (+ 1 introduced).

GLOSSY IBIS *Plegadis falcinellus*   Common

M 45

22–25" (55–63 cm) A medium-sized marsh wader with a long *decurved* bill; thin pale blue lines edge *dark face; deep glossy purplish chestnut;* at a distance it appears quite black, like a large black curlew. *Immature:* Browner with no gloss. Flies in lines with neck extended, flapping and gliding with quick wingbeats. **VOICE:** A guttural *ka-onk,* repeated; a low *kruk, kruk.* **SIMILAR SPECIES:** See White-faced Ibis. **RANGE:** E. U.S., W. Indies, s. Eurasia, Africa, Australia, etc. **HABITAT:** Marshes, rice fields, swamps.

WHITE-FACED IBIS *Plegadis chihi*   Common

M 46

22–25" (55–63 cm) Very similar to Glossy Ibis but has a dull *red eye* and, in summer, *reddish legs and lores,* and a more prominent *white stripe* around base of bill. Many Glossy Ibises' faces show a narrow line of pale bluish, but in White-faced, white goes in *back of eye and under chin* (lost in winter). **RANGE: EAST:** S. La. to s. Tex., Great Plains; very rare in Fla. and East Coast sites. **HABITAT:** Same as Glossy's.

WHITE IBIS *Eudocimus albus*   Common

M 44

22–27" (55–68 cm) Adult white. Note *red face,* long *decurved red bill,* and restricted black wingtips. Immature is dark; with *white belly, white rump,* curved red bill. Flies with neck outstretched; flocks fly in "roller-coasting" strings, flapping and gliding; often soar in circles. **SIMILAR SPECIES:** (1) Wood Stork is larger, with much more black in wing (p. 56). (2) Immature Glossy differs from immature White Ibis by its uniformly dark appearance. **RANGE:** Se. U.S. to n. S. America. **HABITAT:** Salt, brackish, and fresh marshes, rice fields, mangroves.

LIMPKIN

WHITE-
FACED IBIS

for facial
comparison in
breeding season

GLOSSY IBIS

GLOSSY IBIS
adult

GLOSSY IBIS
immature

WHITE IBIS
adult

WHITE IBIS
immature

SCARLET IBIS *Eudocimus ruber*   Escape

22–25" (55–63 cm) A *bright scarlet* ibis; same size, structure, and pattern (black wingtips) as White Ibis. **RANGE:** N. S. America. **U.S.:** Introduced into Fla. Escapes from zoos also reported. Hybridizes with White Ibis, and pink or splotched birds seen. Young hatched from eggs placed in White Ibis nests in Miami were reared to adulthood and released in local park. Hybrids resulted from this experiment.

ROSEATE SPOONBILL *Ajaia ajaja*   Fairly common

M 47

32" (80 cm) A *bright pink* wading bird with a long, flat spoonlike bill. Adults are *shell pink* with a blood red "strip" on shoulders, and an orange tail. Head is naked, greenish gray. *Immature:* Whitish, acquiring glow of pink as it matures. When feeding, sweeps bill rapidly from side to side. In flight, extends neck like that of an ibis, and it often glides between series of wing strokes. **VOICE:** About nesting colony, a low grunting croak. **RANGE:** Gulf states to Chile, Argentina. **HABITAT:** Coastal marshes, lagoons, mudflats, mangroves.

FLAMINGOES. Family Phoenicopteridae.

Pinkish white to vermilion wading birds with extremely long necks and legs. The thick bill is bent sharply down and lined with numerous lamellae for straining food. **FOOD:** Small mollusks, crustaceans, blue-green algae, diatoms. **RANGE:** W. Indies, Yucatán, Galapagos, S. America, Africa, s. Eurasia, India. **NO. OF SPECIES:** World, 5; East, 1.

GREATER FLAMINGO *Phoenicopterus ruber*   Rare and very restricted

45" (113 cm) W. Indian subspecies of this widespread flamingo is an extremely slim *rose-pink* wading bird as tall as a Great Blue Heron but much more slender. Note *thick, sharply bent bill.* Feeds with bill or head immersed. In flight, it shows much black in wings; its extremely long neck is extended droopily in front, and long legs trail behind, giving the impression that the bird might as easily fly backward as forward. Pale, washed-out birds may be escapes from zoos as color often fades under captive conditions. Immatures are also much paler than normal adults. **VOICE:** Gooselike calls, gabbling; *ar-honk,* etc. **RANGE:** W. Indies, Yucatán, Galapagos. **EAST:** Small fall-to-late-winter population has frequented Fla. Bay for years. Occasional on Fla. coast, especially after hurricanes; accidental elsewhere. It is difficult to determine whether some sightings are truly wild or escapes. Hialeah Race Track, Bok Sanctuary, Busch Gardens, etc., may be the sources of strays. **HABITAT:** Salt flats, saline lagoons.

PINK AND RED WADERS

SCARLET IBIS

adult

ROSEATE SPOONBILL

immature

adult

GREATER FLAMINGO

adult

STORKS. Family Ciconiidae.

Large, long-legged heronlike birds with long bills (straight, recurved, or decurved); some with naked heads. Sexes alike. Gait a sedate walk. Flight deliberate; neck and legs extended. **FOOD:** Frogs, crustaceans, lizards, rodents. **RANGE:** S. U.S., Cen. and S. America, Africa, Eurasia, E. Indies, Australia. **NO. OF SPECIES:** World, 19; East, 1.

WOOD STORK *Mycteria americana*   Uncommon

M 48

34–47" (85–118 cm) Very large (wingspread 5½ ft.); white, with a *dark naked head* and *much black* in wing; black tail. Bill long, *thick, decurved*. Immature has a yellow bill. When feeding, keeps head down and walks with bill open. In flight, alternately flaps and glides. Often soars very high on thermals. **SIMILAR SPECIES:** White Pelican, which also soars on thermals, has a similar wing pattern. **VOICE:** A hoarse croak; usually silent. **RANGE:** S. U.S. to Argentina. **HABITAT:** Cypress swamps (nesting colonies); marshes, ponds, lagoons.

CRANES. Family Gruidae.

Stately birds, more robust than herons, often with *red facial skin*. Note the *tufted or humped appearance* over the rump. In flight, neck extended; migrates in lines or V's rather like geese. Large herons are sometimes wrongly referred to as cranes. **FOOD:** Omnivorous. **RANGE:** Nearly cosmopolitan except Cen. and S. America and Oceania. **NO. OF SPECIES:** World, 15; East, 2 (+ 1 accidental).

WHOOPING CRANE *Grus americana*   Rare and restricted

50" (125 cm) Wingspread 7½ ft. Tallest N. American bird and one of rarest. A large *white* crane with a *red face*. Primary wing feathers *black*. Young birds are washed with rust color, especially about the head. **SIMILAR SPECIES:** (1) Wood Stork has a dark head, more black in wing; (2) egrets and (3) swans lack black in wings. See also (4) White Pelican, p. 38, and (5) Snow Goose, p. 60. **VOICE:** A shrill buglelike trumpeting *ker-loo! ker-lee-oo!* **RANGE:** Breeds in n. Alberta (Wood Buffalo Park); most migrate through Great Plains to coastal Tex. (Aransas National Wildlife Refuge). Introduction program established in Fla. **HABITAT:** Muskeg (summer); prairies, fields and pastures, coastal marshes.

SANDHILL CRANE *Grus canadensis*   Common, scarce in East

M 136

40–48" (100–120 cm) Wingspread 6–7 ft. Note *red crown*, tufted rear feathers. A long-legged, long-necked, gray bird, often stained with rust. Immature is browner. In flight, neck is extended and wings beat with an upward flick. **SIMILAR SPECIES:** Great Blue Heron (p. 46) is sometimes wrongly called a crane. **VOICE:** A shrill rolling *garooo-a-a-a*; repeated and bugled in flight. **RANGE:** Ne. Siberia, N. America. Winters to Mexico. **HABITAT:** Prairies, fields, marshes (summer); Lesser (subspecies) nests in tundra, Greater (subspecies) grasslands and bogs.

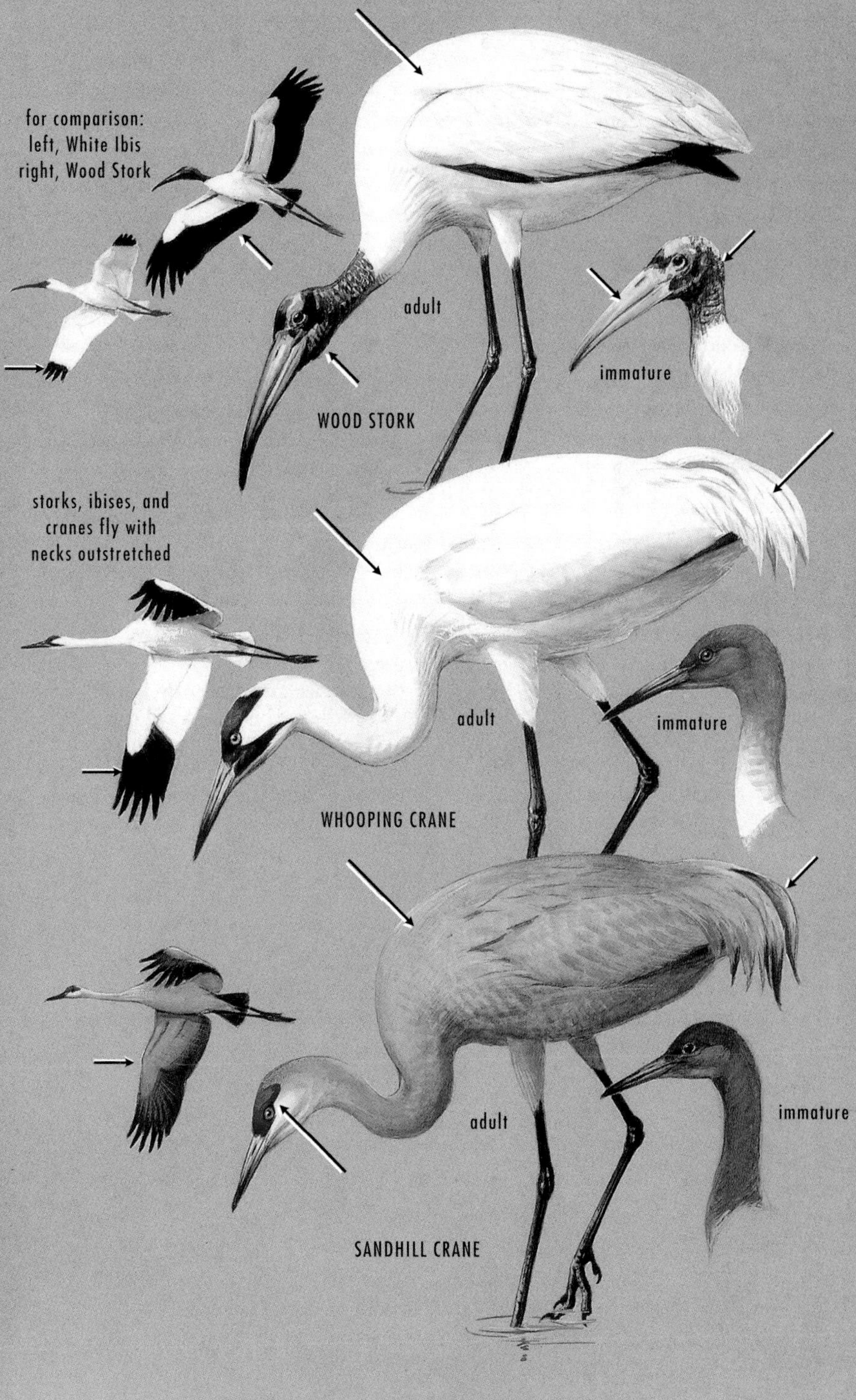

STORKS, CRANES

for comparison:
left, White Ibis
right, Wood Stork

storks, ibises, and
cranes fly with
necks outstretched

adult

immature

WOOD STORK

adult

immature

WHOOPING CRANE

adult

immature

SANDHILL CRANE

With greater coverage and careful observation, reports of species that in the past were unheard of in the U.S. and Canada are coming in with regularity. The rare-bird alert system that relays these finds brings birders in from all over the U.S. and Canada to glimpse these accidentals.

COMMON CRANE *Grus grus*

41" (103 cm) Eurasian. Note *black neck* and *white cheek stripe*. Feathers arching over rump are blacker than those of a Sandhill Crane. Inasmuch as this stray (probably from Asia) has been recorded in Alaska, Alberta, New Mexico, Nebraska, Indiana, and Quebec to date, it should be looked for among flocks of Sandhill Cranes traveling and feeding on the plains east of the 100th meridian. Some escapes have also occurred.

WESTERN REEF-HERON *Egretta gularis*

20–27" (50–68 cm) A notorious wanderer native from West Africa to India, this heron is regarded by some authorities to be conspecific with Little Egret. Dark morph can be told from Little Blue Heron by its darker color, *white throat,* and *yellow feet*. White morph is similar to Snowy Egret but bill is *heavier* and *yellow to brown*, not black. A stray bird was recorded on Nantucket Is., Mass., in September 1983 and stayed for some time, to the delight of hundreds of birders.

LITTLE EGRET *Egretta garzetta*

22" (56 cm) This Old World counterpart of Snowy Egret has turned up a number of times on our side of the Atlantic and recently was found breeding in Barbados. It has been recorded from Nfld., Que., N.S., N.H., Mass., Del., Va., and Fla. It differs from Snowy Egret by having 2 thin head plumes instead of a bushy crest, and back plumes are less recurved. Bill is heavier than a Snowy's. Legs of Little Egret are black and feet are dull yellow, not deep yellow of a Snowy. In several areas, birds showing features of both species imply hybridization may be occurring. Comparison studies of feeding methods show a decided posture like that of a Little Blue with arched neck, poised to strike.

JABIRU *Jabiru mycteria*

48–57" (144 cm) Widespread from s. Mexico to n. Argentina, this very large white stork has no black on wings. It is easily identified by its huge black bill and swollen neck with a broad red collar separating white body from bare black skin of upper neck and head. This rare stray has been found several times in s. Tex. and as far north as Okla. It is unmistakable even at a distance.

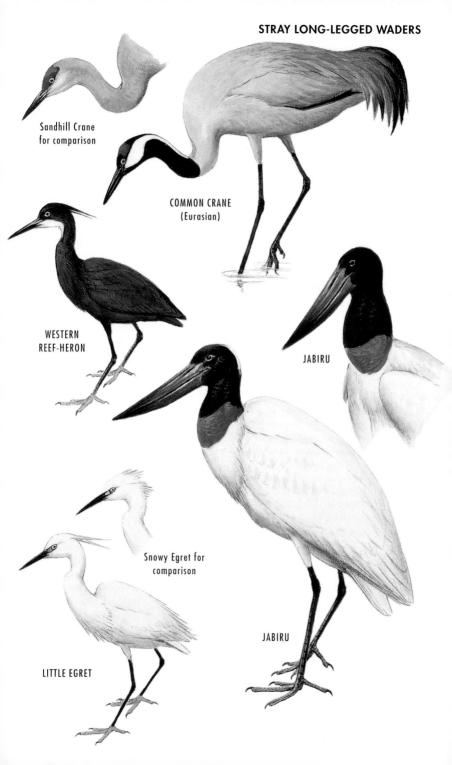

STRAY LONG-LEGGED WADERS

Sandhill Crane
for comparison

COMMON CRANE
(Eurasian)

WESTERN
REEF-HERON

JABIRU

Snowy Egret for
comparison

JABIRU

LITTLE EGRET

SWANS, GEESE, DUCKS. Family Anatidae.

Waterfowl; the subfamilies are discussed separately. **RANGE:** Cosmopolitan. **NO. OF SPECIES:** World, 157; East, 39 (+ 9 accidental, 1 introduced, 1 extinct).

SWANS. Subfamily Anserinae.

Huge, all-white swimming birds; larger, longer-necked than geese. Young tinged brown. Sexes alike. Migrate in lines or V's. Feed by immersing head and neck, or by "tipping up." **FOOD:** Aquatic plants, seeds.

MUTE SWAN *Cygnus olor* — Common, introduced

M 58

60" (150 cm) The ornamental park variety, now well-established in the wild; spreading. More graceful on water than Tundra Swan, often swimming with an S-curve in neck; wings arched. *Knobbed orange bill* points downward. Young bird dingy, with black at base of a pinkish bill. *Wingbeats* make a "whooshing" sound. **VOICE:** It is not mute but makes hissing and wheezing sounds. **RANGE:** Eurasia; introduced ne. U.S., elsewhere. **HABITAT:** Ponds, fresh and salt; coastal lagoons, salt bays.

TUNDRA SWAN *Cygnus columbianus* — Locally common

M 60

53" (133 cm) Wingspread 6–7 ft. America's widespread native swan. Often heard long before the ribbonlike flock high above can be spotted. *All-white* wings and very long necks mark them as swans. Bill *black*, often with a small yellow basal spot. Young bird, dingy with pinkish bill. **SIMILAR SPECIES:** Trumpeter Swan of the West is larger, deep-voiced. Reintroduced in Great Lakes region and spreading. **VOICE:** A mellow, high-pitched cooing: *woo-ho, woo-woo, woo-ho.* **HABITAT:** Lakes, large rivers, bays, estuaries, flooded fields, and cultivated fields. Breeds on tundra lakes.

M 59

GEESE. Subfamily Anserinae.

Large waterfowl; heavier-bodied, longer-necked than ducks; bills thick at base. Noisy in flight; some fly in line or V formation. Sexes alike. More terrestrial than ducks, grazing on land. Gregarious. **FOOD:** Grasses, seeds, aquatic plants; Brant prefers Eelgrass and the marine algae *Ulva* (Sea Lettuce).

SNOW GOOSE (WHITE MORPH) *Chen caerulescens* — Locally common

M 54

25–38" (63–95 cm) A *white* goose with *black primaries.* Often rust-stained on head from tundra waters. Bill and feet pink. Immature pale gray with a dark bill. Bill has black grin patch on side in all plumages. **VOICE:** A loud, nasal *whouk* or *houck* uttered in chorus. **HABITAT:** Marshes, grainfields, ponds, bays; tundra in summer.

ROSS'S GOOSE *Chen rossii* — Uncommon

M 55

23" (58 cm) Like a miniature Snow Goose. Bill decidedly stubbier, dark at base and *lacking* the black "lips" grin patch. Distinct steep forehead. Hybrids occur, "blue morphs" known. **EAST:** Local breeder northwest of Hudson Bay, with wintering birds in Tex. and s. Mississippi R. Valley. Small numbers found farther east.

immature

adult

SWANS, GEESE

immature

adult

TUNDRA SWAN

MUTE SWAN

adult

MUTE SWAN

immature

adult

TUNDRA SWAN

immature

adult

ROSS'S GOOSE

intergrade
between gray and
white morphs

SNOW GOOSE

white morph

SNOW GOOSE
(white morph)

ROSS'S

SNOW

SNOW GOOSE (BLUE MORPH) *Chen caerulescens* Common

M 54

25–30" (63–75 cm) The "Blue" Goose, dark with a *white head*, is now regarded as a color morph of the Snow Goose, with which it is usually associated. Intermediates are frequent (see p. 61). **SIMILAR SPECIES:** Dusky immature similar to young Greater White-fronted Goose, but feet and bill *dark*; wings paler, bluish. **RANGE:** Breeds in e. N. American Arctic, mainly in southern parts of white-morph Snow Goose range. Migrates through prairies to Gulf of Mexico. Smaller numbers to East Coast. **HABITAT:** Same as white-morph Snow Goose.

GREATER WHITE-FRONTED GOOSE *Anser albifrons* Fairly common

M 53

30" (75 cm) No other wild goose in our area has *yellow or orange feet*. A *brownish gray* goose with a *pink* bill, *white patch on front of face*, and variable *black bars* on belly. The Greenland subspecies has an *orange-yellow* bill. *Immature:* Dusky with a pale bill, yellow or orange feet; lacks belly bars of adult. **VOICE:** High-pitched yodeling, *kah-lah-a-luk*, in chorus. **RANGE:** Arctic; circumpolar; winters to Mexico, Gulf states, n. Africa, India. **HABITAT:** Marshes, prairies, fields, lakes, bays. Tundra in summer.

CANADA GOOSE *Branta canadensis* Common

M 56

25–43" (63–108 cm) The most widespread goose in N. America. Note black head and neck or "stocking" that contrasts strikingly with pale breast and *white patch* or *chinstrap* that runs onto side of head. Flocks travel in long strings in V formation, announcing their approach by musical honking or barking. Considerable variation in size among various races. **VOICE:** A deep musical honking or barking *ka-ronk* or *ka-lunk*; small races have higher-pitched calls. **RANGE:** Alaska, Canada, U.S. Winters to Mexico. **HABITAT:** Lakes, ponds, bays, marshes, fields. Nonmigratory groups released on ponds in parks and golf courses causing problems.

BRANT *Branta bernicla* Locally common

M 57

22–26" (55–65 cm) A small *black-necked* goose. Has a white belly and undertail, conspicuous when it upends, and streaks of white on neck (absent in immature). Travels in large irregular flocks. **SIMILAR SPECIES:** Breast of Canada Goose shows light above water, whereas foreparts of Brant are black *to waterline*. Canada Goose has a large white face patch. Brant is more strictly coastal. **VOICE:** A throaty *krrr-onk* — between a honk and a purr. **RANGE:** Arctic coasts of n. Eurasia, e. N. America. **HABITAT:** Mainly salt bays, estuaries; in summer, tundra.

BARNACLE GOOSE *Branta leucopsis* Vagrant

26" (65 cm) Similar in size to Brant. Has white sides and a black chest to waterline. Note *white face encircling eye*. Back is heavily scalloped. **RANGE:** Breeds in ne. Greenland, Spitzbergen, nw. Siberia. **EAST:** A casual or accidental visitor to northeast seaboard of N. America. Most reports likely represent aviary escapes.

GEESE

immature

adult

SNOW GOOSE blue morph
("Blue" Goose)

adult

immature

adult

GREATER WHITE-
FRONTED GOOSE

adult

Richardson's
race

Lesser
race

Atlantic
race

CANADA GOOSE

BARNACLE GOOSE

BRANT

Geese and swans fly in line
or "V" formation.

CANADA GOOSE *Branta canadensis*   PP. 62–63
    Light chest, black neck "stocking," white chinstrap.

BRANT *Branta bernicla*   PP. 62–63
    Small; black chest, black head and neck.

GREATER WHITE-FRONTED GOOSE *Anser albifrons*   PP. 62–63
    Adult: Gray-brown neck, black splotches on belly.
    Immature: Dusky, with light bill, light feet.

SNOW GOOSE (WHITE MORPH) *Chen caerulescens*   PP. 60–61
    Adult: White with black primaries.

SNOW GOOSE (BLUE MORPH), OR "BLUE" GOOSE *Chen caerulescens*   PP. 62–63
    Adult: Dark body, white head.
    Immature: Dusky, with a dark bill, dark feet.

TUNDRA SWAN *Cygnus columbianus*   PP. 60–61
    Very long neck; plumage entirely white.

GEESE, SWANS

CANADA GOOSE

below

above

BRANT

adult

immature

GREATER WHITE-
FRONTED GOOSE

immature

SNOW GOOSE
blue morph
("Blue" Goose)

adult

SNOW GOOSE
white morph

TUNDRA SWAN

adult

SNOW GOOSE
blue morph
("Blue" Goose)

WHISTLING-DUCKS. Subfamily Dendrocygninae.

Formerly called "tree ducks," these long-necked, erect-postured ducks are more closely related to geese than other ducks. They are named for their high-pitched calls. **FOOD:** Seeds of aquatic plants and grasses.

FULVOUS WHISTLING-DUCK *Dendrocygna bicolor*   Uncommon

18–21" (45–53 cm) *Long-legged*, gooselike. *Tawny* body, dark back, and *pale side stripe*. Flies with neck slightly drooped and feet trailing, showing *black* underwings, *white ring on rump*. **VOICE:** Squealing slurred whistle, *ka-whee-oo*. **HABITAT:** Coastal marshes. Rarely perches in trees.

M 52

BLACK-BELLIED WHISTLING-DUCK *Dendrocygna autumnalis*   Locally common

21" (53 cm) *Long-necked* duck with bright *pink legs*. Droops long neck downward when landing. Rusty with black belly, bright *coral red bill* and a very broad *white patch along forewing* when seen in flight. *Immature:* Gray bill, gray legs. Often found in large flocks. **VOICE:** Four-part high-pitched whistle. **HABITAT:** Ponds, resacas, fresh marshes. Frequently perches in trees. Sightings in East increasing.

M 51

DABBLING DUCKS. Subfamily Anatinae.

Surface-feeders on ponds, marshes. Feed by dabbling and upending; often feed on land. Take flight directly into air. Most species have an iridescent speculum on rear edge of wing. Sexes unlike in most; in late summer, males molt into drab "eclipse" plumage. **FOOD:** Aquatic plants, seeds, grass, small aquatic animals, insects.

AMERICAN BLACK DUCK *Anas rubripes* (in flight p. 82)   Common

21–25" (53–63 cm) In flight, *very dark* with flashing *silvery wing linings*. Sooty brown with a paler head and metallic violet wing patch not edged with white; feet may be *red/orange* or brown. Sexes similar; female's bill darker, greener. Increasing numbers of Black Ducks have Mallard characteristics due to hybridization. **VOICE:** Male, a low croak; female quacks like female Mallard. **HABITAT:** Marshes, bays, estuaries, ponds, rivers, lakes.

M 65

MOTTLED DUCK *Anas fulvigula*   Locally common

20" (50 cm) Like a pale brownish version of Black Duck. Note tan head, *unstreaked buffy throat* with black-tipped feathers and *unmarked yellow bill*. Sexes alike. Darker than female Mallard and lacking black on bill and broad white border to speculum. **HABITAT:** Marshes.

M 67

GADWALL *Anas strepera* (in flight p. 84)   Fairly common

19–23" (48–58 cm) *Male:* A *gray* duck with a *black rump*, *white patch* on rear edge of wing, and a dull ruddy patch on forewing. When swimming, wing patch may be concealed; then note black stern. Belly white, feet yellow, bill dark. *Female:* Brown, mottled; *white speculum*, yellow feet; bill darker and head rounder than in Mallard. **VOICE:** Male, low *bek*; a whistling call. Female quacks. **HABITAT:** Lakes, ponds, marshes.

M 62

MALLARD *Anas platyrhynchos* (in flight p. 82)   Common

20–28" (50–70 cm) *Male: Glossy-green head* and *white neck-ring*. Body grayish with a chestnut chest, white tail; *yellowish bill*, orange feet, violet-blue speculum edged with white. *Female:* Mottled brown; *whitish tail*. Bill orange with dark patch. **VOICE:** Male, *yeeb*; a low *kwek*; female, *noisy* quacking. **HABITAT:** Marshes, grainfields, ponds, rivers.

M 66

WHISTLING-DUCKS AND DABBLING DUCKS

Fulvous
Whistling-
Duck

Black-
bellied
Whistling-
Duck

sexes similar

FULVOUS
WHISTLING-
DUCK

BLACK-BELLIED
WHISTLING-DUCK

♂

♀

MOTTLED DUCK

AMERICAN BLACK DUCK

♀

♂

marsh ducks
tip up

GADWALL

marsh ducks
spring directly
from the water

♂

♀

♂

MALLARD

NORTHERN PINTAIL *Anas acuta* (in flight p. 84) Fairly common

M 71

26–30" (65–75 cm) *Male:* A slender, slim-necked, gray duck with a white breast and a *long needle-pointed tail.* A conspicuous *white point* runs from neck onto side of dark head. *Female:* Mottled brown; note rather pointed tail, slender neck, blue-gray bill. In flight, shows *one light border* on rear of rusty speculum. **SIMILAR SPECIES:** See (1) female Mallard; (2) female Gadwall. See also (3) Long-tailed Duck (not a "dabbler"). **VOICE:** Male utters a double-toned whistle, *prrip, prrip,* wheezy teal-like notes. Female, a low *quack.* **RANGE:** Northern parts of N. Hemisphere. Winters south to n. S. America, Africa, India. **HABITAT:** Marshes, prairies, fresh ponds, lakes, salt bays.

AMERICAN WIGEON *Anas americana* (in flight p. 84) Fairly common

M 64

18–23" (45–58 cm) In flight, drake is recognized by *large white patch* on front part of wing. (Similarly placed blue patches of Northern Shoveler and Blue-winged Teal may also appear whitish.) On water, it rides high, picking at surface like a coot. Often grazes on land. *Male:* Brownish; head gray with deep green cheek patch. Note distinct *white or creamy crown. Female:* Brown with gray head and neck; belly and forewing whitish. **SIMILAR SPECIES:** Female can be confused with (1) female Gadwall and (2) female pintail, but note whitish patch on forewing, bluish bill, and contrasting gray head. (3) See Eurasian Wigeon. **VOICE:** Male, a whistled two-note *whee-whew.* Female, *qua-ack.* **RANGE:** Alaska, w. Canada, n. U.S. Winters to Cen. America, W. Indies. **HABITAT:** Marshes, lakes, bays, fields, grassy lawns, golf courses, parks, etc.

EURASIAN WIGEON *Anas penelope* Rare

M 63

18–20" (45–50 cm) *Male:* Note *red-brown* head, *buff crown.* A *gray* wigeon with a vinaceous breast. *Female:* Very similar to female American Wigeon, but head often brown tinged with rust. A key point when visible is the *dusky* (not white) axillars, or "wingpits." **VOICE:** Male, a whistle, *whee-oo.* Female, a *purr* or a *quack.* **RANGE:** Breeds in Eurasia, Iceland. **EAST:** Rare visitor, chiefly near coast.

WOOD DUCK *Aix sponsa* (in flight p. 84) Fairly common

M 61

17–20" (43–51 cm) Highly colored; often perches in trees. In flight, white belly contrasts with dark breast and wings. Note also *long square dark tail,* short neck, and angle at which bill points downward in flight. *Male:* Bizarre face pattern, swept-back crest, and rainbow iridescence are unique. *Female:* Dull-colored; note dark crested head and *white eye patch.* **VOICE:** Male, a high whistled *jeee,* with rising inflection. Female, a loud distressed *whoo-eek.* **RANGE:** S. Canada, U.S., Cuba. Winters to Mexico. **HABITAT:** Wooded swamps, rivers, ponds.

♀
♂
NORTHERN PINTAIL

♂
♀
AMERICAN WIGEON

♂
♀
EURASIAN WIGEON

♀
♂ in eclipse
(autumn)
♂
WOOD DUCK

POSTURES OF DUCKS ON LAND

Dabbling Ducks
(dabblers)

Sea and Bay
Ducks (divers)

Mergansers
(divers)

Ruddy Duck
(diver)

Whistling-Ducks
(dabblers)

NORTHERN SHOVELER *Anas clypeata* (in flight p. 84)   Fairly common

M 70

1 7–2 0" (43–50 cm) Note *spoon-shaped bill.* A medium-sized duck; in flight, long bill makes wings seem well back on body. Swims low, bill pointed toward water. *Male:* Much black and white; with *rufous belly and sides,* pale *blue patch* on forewing, *orange feet. Female:* Brown; large bill, *blue wing patch,* orange feet. **VOICE:** Male, a low *took, took, took;* female, a light *quack.* **HABITAT:** Fresh marshes, ponds, sloughs; in winter, also salt bays.

BLUE-WINGED TEAL *Anas discors* (in flight p. 84)   Common

M 68

1 5–1 6" (38–40 cm) A half-sized dabbling duck. *Male:* Note *white facial crescent* and large *chalky-blue* patch on forewing. Male holds eclipse plumage late in year and may resemble female. *Female:* Brown, mottled; with a blue patch on forewing. **SIMILAR SPECIES:** See (1) Green-winged Teal; (2) Northern Shoveler. **VOICE:** Male utters *peeping* notes; female, a soft, atonal *quack.* **HABITAT:** Fresh ponds, marshes. Likes muddy-edge areas.

GREEN-WINGED TEAL *Anas crecca carolinensis* (in flight p. 84)   Common

M 72

1 4" (35 cm) In flight, teal are recognized by their small size; fly in tight flocks. Green-wing lacks pale blue wing patch of Blue-wing (speculum is *deep iridescent green*). *Male:* A small gray duck with a *chestnut* head (green around eye patch in sunlight). *Vertical white mark* in front of wing evident when swimming. Yellow spot near side of tail base. *Female:* A small speckled brown duck with a green speculum. **SIMILAR SPECIES:** Blue-winged Teal (male and female) has light-blue wing patch and is longer-billed. In flight, male Blue-wing shows dark belly; Green-wing, a white belly. Female Blue-wing is larger than female Green-wing. **VOICE:** Male, a whistle, froglike peeping; female, a *quack.* **HABITAT:** Marshes, rivers, bays.

GREEN-WINGED TEAL (EURASIAN RACE) *Anas crecca crecca*   Rare

1 3–1 5" (33–39 cm) Considered conspecific with American Green-winged Teal by some taxonomists. *Male:* Note *longitudinal white stripe on scapulars.* Bolder buffy "frame" to eye patch. *Female:* Indistinguishable from female American Green-wing. **RANGE:** Iceland, n. Europe, Asia, Aleutians. **EAST:** Rare visitor to N. Atlantic ponds and marshes along coast.

CINNAMON TEAL *Anas cyanoptera*   Uncommon

M 69

1 5–1 7" (38–43 cm) *Male:* A small, dark chestnut duck; large chalky-blue patch on front part of wing. Male with red eye, which it retains in eclipse plumage. In flight, suggests Blue-winged Teal. *Female:* Like female Blue-wing, but browner head, slightly longer and broader bill. **HABITAT:** Ponds.

MUSCOVY DUCK *Cairina moschata*   Local, scarce

Male 3 2" (80 cm); Female 2 5" (63 cm) Native of tropical America (Mexico to n. Argentina). *Black,* gooselike duck with *large white wing patch* and underwing coverts. *Male:* Has a *bare, knobby, red face. Female:* Duller, may lack facial knobs. Recent colonizer of the lower Rio Grande Valley, Tex. Widespread domestic Muscovy vary in pattern.

DABBLING DUCKS AND MUSCOVY

NORTHERN SHOVELER
♀
♂

BLUE-WINGED TEAL
♂ ♀

GREEN-WINGED TEAL
♂ ♀

GREEN-WINGED TEAL
Eurasian race
♂

CINNAMON TEAL
♂

ancestral form

domestic
variation

MUSCOVY DUCK
(a frequent escape
from captivity)

DIVING DUCKS. Subfamily Aythyinae.

Also called "sea ducks" and "bay ducks," but many are found on lakes and rivers and breed in marshes. All dive; surface-feeding ducks rarely do. Legs close to the tail; hind toe with a paddlelike flap (lacking in surface feeders). In taking wing, they must patter on the surface of the water while getting underway. Sexes unlike. **FOOD:** Small aquatic animals and plants. Seagoing species eat mollusks and crustaceans.

WHITE-WINGED SCOTER *Melanitta fusca* (in flight p. 86)   Fairly common

M 82

21" (53 cm) Scoters are heavy blackish ducks seen coastwide, flying in thin line formation. White-wing is largest. On water, *white wing patch* is often concealed (wait for bird to flap or fly). *Male:* Black with a white "teardrop" below eye; bill orange with a black basal knob. *Female:* Sooty with a white wing patch and 2 light patches on the face (sometimes obscure; more pronounced on young birds). **SIMILAR SPECIES:** See Surf Scoter and Black Scoter. **VOICE:** In flight, a low bell-like whistle in a series of 6–8 notes (Kortright) believed to be produced by wings. **RANGE:** Alaska, n. Canada; winters to s. U.S. (both coasts) and Great Lakes. **HABITAT:** Salt bays, ocean; in summer, lakes.

SURF SCOTER *Melanitta perspicillata* (in flight p. 86)   Common

M 81

19" (48 cm) The "Skunkhead" of duck hunters. *Male:* Black, with 1 or 2 *white patches on crown and nape.* Bill patterned with orange, black, and white. *Female:* Dusky brown; 2 light spots on side of head (sometimes obscured). **SIMILAR SPECIES:** Female White-wing has similar head pattern though neither white patch is vertical in shape as in Surf. Note female Surf's bill pattern and rear head smudge. White patch in wing of White-wing. **VOICE:** Usually silent. A low croak; grunting sounds. **RANGE:** Alaska, n. Canada. Winters to s. U.S. (both coasts) and Great Lakes. **HABITAT:** Ocean surf, salt bays; in summer, fresh, arctic lakes, tundra.

BLACK SCOTER *Melanitta nigra* (in flight p. 86)   Common

M 83

18½" (46 cm) *Male:* A sea duck with entirely black plumage *and a bright orange-yellow knob on bill* ("butter-nose"). In flight, underwing shows a two-toned effect, more pronounced than in other scoters. *Female:* Sooty; *light cheeks* contrast with *dark cap.* **SIMILAR SPECIES:** (1) Coot is dark, but has a white bill and white patches under tail. (Hunters often call scoters "coots.") (2) Some young male Surf Scoters may lack head patches and appear all black but have round black spot at base of higher-sloping bill. (3) Female and immature scoters of other 2 species have light spots on side of head. (4) Female Black Scoter may suggest winter Ruddy Duck (p. 78). **VOICE:** Male, melodious cooing notes; female, growls. **RANGE:** Alaska, ne. Canada, Iceland, n. Eurasia. Winters to s. U.S. and Great Lakes. **HABITAT:** Seacoast; in summer, coastal tundra.

SEA DUCKS (SCOTERS)
(Divers)

scoters fly in line
or V formation

Surf

White-winged

Black

immature

♂

♀

immature

WHITE-WINGED SCOTER

♂

♂

♀

immature

♂

SURF SCOTER

inset
LABRADOR
DUCK extinct
♂

1878

1st winter

♂

♀

BLACK SCOTER

diving ducks (sea ducks and bay ducks)
raft on water, skitter when taking wing

LONG-TAILED DUCK *Clangula hyemalis* (in flight p. 86) Common

M 84

Male 21" (53 cm); Female 16" (40 cm) The only sea duck combining much *white on body and unpatterned dark wings*. Often flies in bunched, irregular flocks. Rocks side to side in flight. *Male, winter:* Note *needlelike tail, pied pattern,* dark cheek. *Female, winter:* Dark wings, white face, dark cheek spot. *Male, summer:* Dark with white flanks and belly. Pink on bill. Note white eye patch. *Female, summer:* Similar to male but darker; also lacks pink on bill. **VOICE:** Talkative; a musical *ow-owdle-ow,* or *owl-omelet.* **RANGE:** Arctic; circumpolar. Winters to s. U.S., cen. Europe, cen. Asia. **HABITAT:** Ocean, large lakes; in summer, tundra pools and lakes.

HARLEQUIN DUCK *Histrionicus histrionicus* (in flight p. 86) Scarce

M 80

18" (45 cm) Spectacular pattern. *Male:* A small slaty duck with *chestnut sides* and white facial crescent, patches, and spots. In flight, has stubby shape of goldeneye, but appears uniformly dark. *Female:* Dusky with 3 round white spots on each side of head; no wing patch. **SIMILAR SPECIES:** (1) Female Bufflehead has a white wing patch and only 1 face spot. (2) Female scoters are larger, have larger bills. **VOICE:** Male, a squeak; also *gwa gwa gwa.* Female, *ek-ek-ek-ek.* **HABITAT:** Turbulent mountain streams in summer; rocky coastal waters in winter.

KING EIDER Common breeder, scarce winter
Somateria spectabilis (in flight p. 86)

M 78

21–24" (53–60 cm) *Male:* A stocky sea duck; on water, foreparts appear white, rear parts black. Note *orange bill-shield.* Large white wing patch. *Female:* Stocky; warm golden brown or pale sandy brown, with heavy dark bars. Note distinct forehead and thin line running back and downward from eye. *Immature male:* Dusky, with light breast, dark brown head. **SIMILAR SPECIES:** (1) Male Common Eider has *white* back. Female Common Eider has a sloped-head profile, with longer bill lobe before eye. (2) Immature male King Eider has darker head than immature Common and lacks white shoulder stripe of immature Common. **VOICE:** Courting male, a low crooning phrase; female, grunting croaks. **RANGE:** Breeds in arctic regions of N. Hemisphere. **HABITAT:** Coasts, ocean. Summer, nests on tundra.

COMMON EIDER *Somateria mollissima* (in flight p. 86) Common

M 79

23–27" (58–68 cm) Large sea duck, living about shoals; bulky, thick-necked. Flight sluggish and low, usually in a line. *Male:* The only duck in our area with a *black belly and white back.* Forewing white; head white, with a black crown, greenish nape. *Female:* Large, rich brown or gray brown, *closely barred;* long flat head profile. *Immature male:* At first grayish brown; later dusky with white collar; may develop a chocolate head or breast; patchy white areas. **SIMILAR SPECIES:** (1) Male King Eider has a *black* back; female King has a different facial profile than female Common. (2) Female scoters are smaller and darker, lack heavy black barrings of female eiders. **VOICE:** Male, a slurred moaning *ow-ooo-urr;* female, a drawn-out cooing: *kor-r-r.* **RANGE:** Northern parts of N. Hemisphere. **HABITAT:** Rocky coasts, shoals; in summer, also islands, tundra.

SEA DUCKS
(Divers)

♀ breeding

♂ breeding

♂ winter

♀ winter

LONG-TAILED
DUCK

♂

♀

HARLEQUIN DUCK

♂ immature

♀

bill of ♀
King Eider

♂

KING EIDER

♂ immature

♀

bill of ♀
Common Eider

♂

COMMON EIDER

Common Eider

King Eider

eiders raft in large flocks

CANVASBACK *Aythya valisineria* (in flight p. 88)   Fairly common

M 73

20–24" (50–60 cm) Note *long sloping head profile* (both sexes). White-bodied duck with dark head and chest. Flocks travel in lines or V formation. *Male:* Tan/white back and white sides with a *chestnut-red* head and neck, black chest, and a long *blackish* bill. *Female:* Grayish brown, with a suggestion of pale rust on head and neck. **VOICE:** Male, a low croak; growling notes; female, a *quack*. **RANGE:** Alaska, w. Canada, nw. U.S. Winters to Mexico, Atlantic and Gulf coasts. **HABITAT:** Fresh marshes (summer), lakes, salt bays, estuaries.

REDHEAD *Aythya americana* (in flight p. 88)   Uncommon

M 74

18–23" (45–58 cm) *Male:* Gray with a black chest and a *round rufous head;* bill bluish with a black tip. *Female:* Brownish; note *suffused light patch* near base of bill. Both sexes have a *gray* wing stripe. **SIMILAR SPECIES:** (1) Male Canvasback is much whiter with a sloping forehead and a black bill. (2) See female Ring-necked Duck and (3) Lesser and Greater Scaup. **VOICE:** Male, a harsh catlike *meow*; deep purr; female, *squawk.* **RANGE:** W. Canada, w. and n.-cen. U.S. Winters to Mexico, W. Indies. **HABITAT:** Fresh marshes (in summer), lakes, saltwater bays, estuaries.

RING-NECKED DUCK *Aythya collaris* (in flight p. 88)   Fairly common

M 75

15–18" (38–45 cm) *Male:* Scauplike in appearance with a black back. Note *vertical white mark* before wing; bill crossed by a white ring. In flight, a broad *gray* (not white) wing stripe. *Female:* Shaped like female Lesser Scaup but has an *indistinct* light face patch, dark eye, white eye-ring, and *ring on bill.* Wing stripe is *gray.* **SIMILAR SPECIES:** Male **Tufted Duck** (*A. fuligula*), rare in e. U.S., has a wispy *crest, white sides, white wing stripe.* Male scaup has pale gray back, female scaup distinct white face. **RANGE:** Canada, n. U.S. Winters to Panama. **HABITAT:** Wooded lakes, ponds; in winter, also rivers, bays.

LESSER SCAUP *Aythya affinis* (in flight p. 88)   Common

M 77

15–18" (38–45 cm) Both species of scaup are our only ducks with a broad white stripe on trailing edge of wing extending into primaries. *Male:* On water, black at both ends, white in middle. Bill *blue;* head with "peaked" appearance, glossy with *dull purple.* Flanks and back finely barred. *Female:* Dark brown, with a clean-cut white patch near base of bill. Wing stripe shorter than in Greater, being confined to secondaries. **VOICE:** A loud *quack* or *scaup;* purring notes. **RANGE:** Alaska, w. Canada. Winters to n. S. America. **HABITAT:** Marsh ponds (summer), lakes, bays, estuaries.

GREATER SCAUP *Aythya marila* (in flight p. 88)   Common

M 76

16–20" (40–50 cm) Very similar to Lesser Scaup but male whiter; head rounder, less peaked, mainly with *dull green* rather than *dull purple.* **SCAUP COMPARISONS:** *Head:* Greater rounded; Lesser peaked. Head color is not 100 percent reliable. *Bill:* At close range, Greater, wider bill and large dark nail; Lesser, bill tapers and small nail; female Greater often has larger white patch at base of bill. *Wings:* Greater, white wing stripe extends to primaries; Lesser, white wing stripe only on secondaries. **RANGE:** Alaska, Canada, n. Eurasia. Winters to Mexico, se. U.S., Mediterranean, India. **HABITAT:** Lakes, rivers, salt bays, estuaries, tundra ponds (summer).

BAY DUCKS
(Divers)

CANVASBACK

diving ducks
run and patter

REDHEAD

TUFTED DUCK (accidental)

RING-NECKED DUCK

Lesser

Greater

Greater

Lesser

GREATER SCAUP

LESSER SCAUP

COMMON GOLDENEYE *Bucephala clangula* (in flight p. 88)   Fairly common

M 86

20" (50 cm) *Male:* Note large *round white spot* before eye. A white-looking duck with a black back and puffy dark green-glossed head. In flight, short-necked; wings whistle in flight and show large white patch. *Female:* Gray with a white collar and a dark rusty brown head; wings with large square white patch (showing also on closed wing), bill mostly dark with some yellow. **SIMILAR SPECIES:** (1) Barrow's Goldeneye; (2) Scaup (males have black chests). **VOICE:** Courting male has a harsh nasal double note, suggesting *pee-ik* of Common Nighthawk; Female, a harsh *quack*. **RANGE:** Northern parts of N. Hemisphere. Winters to Gulf Coast, s. Eurasia. **HABITAT:** Forested lakes, rivers; in winter, also salt bays, ocean coasts.

BARROW'S GOLDENEYE *Bucephala islandica*   Scarce

M 87

21" (53 cm) *Male:* Similar to Common Goldeneye (hybrids are known), blacker above; head glossed with *purple* (not green); nape more puffy. Note *white crescent* in front of eye. Distinct black shoulder stripe across white to near water level. *Female:* Very similar to female Common Goldeneye; bill shorter and deeper, forehead more abrupt. Bill more yellow than dark and, as spring advances, bill increasingly *yellow or yellow-orange.* **VOICE:** Courting male, a mewing cry; female, a hoarse *quack*. **RANGE:** Alaska, Canada, nw. U.S., sw. Greenland, Iceland. **HABITAT:** Wooded lakes, beaver ponds; in winter, coastal waters, a few on inland rivers.

BUFFLEHEAD *Bucephala albeola* (in flight p. 88)   Common

M 85

13–15" (33–38 cm) Small duck. *Male:* Mostly white with a black back; puffy head with a *large bonnetlike white patch.* In flight, shows a large white wing patch. *Female:* Dark, compact, with a *white cheek spot,* small bill, white wing patch. **SIMILAR SPECIES:** (1) Male Hooded Merganser has a spikelike bill, dark flanks. (2) See winter Ruddy Duck. **VOICE:** Male, a hoarse rolling note; female, a harsh *quack*. **RANGE:** Alaska, Canada. Winters to Gulf Coast, Mexico. **HABITAT:** Lakes, ponds, rivers; in winter, also salt bays.

STIFF-TAILED DUCKS. Subfamily Oxyurinae.

Small, chunky; nearly helpless on land. Spiky tail has 18 or 20 feathers. Sexes unlike. **FOOD:** Aquatic life, insects, water plants.

RUDDY DUCK *Oxyura jamaicensis* (in flight p. 88)   Common

M 91

15–16" (38–40 cm) Small, chubby. Often cocks tail vertically. Flight "buzzy." *Male, breeding plumage:* Rusty red with *white cheek,* black cap, large blue bill. *Fall/winter:* Gray with *white cheek,* dull grayish bill. *Female:* Similar to winter male but cheek crossed by a dark line. **SIMILAR SPECIES:** See Masked Duck (p. 90). **VOICE:** Courting male, a sputtering *chick-ik-ik-ik-k-k-krrrr.* **RANGE:** Canada locally to n. S. America. **HABITAT:** Fresh marshes, ponds, lakes; in winter, also salt bays.

BAY DUCKS
(Divers)

COMMON GOLDENEYE

♂

♀

BARROW'S GOLDENEYE

♂

♀ breeding

♀ winter

BUFFLEHEAD

♂

♀

RUDDY DUCK

♂ breeding

♂ winter

♀

Long-lined, slender-bodied, diving ducks with spikelike bills, saw-edged mandibles. Most species have crests. In flight, bill, head, neck, and body are on a horizontal axis. Duck hunters often call them "saw-bills." Sexes unlike. **FOOD:** Chiefly fish.

COMMON MERGANSER *Mergus merganser* (in flight p. 82)   Common

M 89

22–27" (55–68 cm) In flight, lines of these slender ducks follow the winding courses of streams and rivers. Whiteness of males and merganser shape (bill, neck, head, and body held horizontally) identify this species. *Male:* Note long whitish body, black back, green-black head. Bill and feet red; breast tinged delicate peach. *Female:* Gray with a crested rufous head with *sharp delineation to clean white chest,* large square white wing patch. **SIMILAR SPECIES:** Female Red-breasted Merganser very similar to female Common. Note distinct cut-off of rusty head and neck to breast in Common, diffuse in Red-breasted. Female mergansers, which are rusty headed, suggest male Canvasbacks or Redheads, but these have black chests and no crests. **VOICE:** Male, low staccato croaks; female, a guttural *karrr.* **RANGE:** Northern parts of N. Hemisphere. Winters to cen. U.S., n. Africa, s. China. **HABITAT:** Wooded lakes, ponds, rivers; in winter, open lakes, rivers, rarely coastal bays.

RED-BREASTED MERGANSER *Mergus serrator* (in flight p. 82)   Common

M 90

20–26" (50–65 cm) *Male:* Rakish; head black, glossed with green and *conspicuously crested;* breast at waterline *dark rusty,* separated from head by *wide white* collar; bill and feet red. *Female:* Gray; crested rusty head, large white wing patch, red bill and feet. **SIMILAR SPECIES:** Male Common Merganser is whiter, without collar and breast-band effect; lacks crest. In the female Common, white chin and white chest are *sharply defined* (in Red-breasted, rufous of head is paler, *blending* into throat and neck). **VOICE:** Usually silent or a hoarse croak; female, *karrr.* **RANGE:** Northern parts of N. Hemisphere. Winters to Mexico, Gulf of Mexico, n. Africa, s. China. **HABITAT:** Lakes; in winter, coastal bays, ocean edge.

HOODED MERGANSER *Lophodytes cucullatus* (in flight p. 82)   Fairly common

16–19" (40–48 cm) *Male:* Note vertical *fan-shaped white crest* that may be raised or lowered. Breast white with 2 black bars on each side. Wing with a white patch; flanks *brown. Female:* Recognized as a merganser by its silhouette and spikelike bill, small size, dusky appearance, *dark head, bill, and chest.* Note loose *tawny crest.* **SIMILAR SPECIES:** (1) Male Bufflehead; chubbier with *white* sides. See also female Bufflehead. (2) Other female mergansers are larger, with rufous heads, red bills. (3) In flight, male Hooded separated from male Wood Duck by white wing patch and silhouette. **VOICE:** Low grunting or croaking notes. **RANGE:** Se. Alaska, Canada, n. U.S. Winters to n. Mexico, Gulf. **HABITAT:** Wooded lakes, ponds, rivers; in winter, tidal creeks and estuaries.

M 88

mergansers fly
with bill, head,
body, and tail
on the same
horizontal axis

MERGANSERS
(Divers)

saw-edged mandibles
of merganser

♂

♀

COMMON MERGANSER

♂

♀

RED-BREASTED MERGANSER

♂ crest up

♂ crest
down

♀

♂ in eclipse

HOODED MERGANSER

Common

Red-breasted

Hooded

FLIGHT PATTERNS OF DABBLING DUCKS
AND MERGANSERS

NOTE: Males are diagnosed below. Females are somewhat similar. Mergansers have a distinctive flight silhouette with bill, head, neck, body, and tail all on a horizontal axis. The top panel shows birds as they appear overhead. The lower panel shows birds as their backs appear. Names in parentheses are nicknames often used by hunters.

MALLARD (GREENHEAD) *Anas platyrhynchos* PP. 66–67
Overhead: Dark chest, light belly, white neck-ring.
Topside: Dark head, neck-ring, 2 white borders on speculum.

AMERICAN BLACK DUCK *Anas rubripes* PP. 66–67
Overhead: Dusky body, silvery wing linings.
Topside: Dusky body, paler head.

FULVOUS WHISTLING-DUCK (MEXICAN SQUEALERS) *Dendrocygna bicolor* PP. 66–67
Overhead: Tawny, with blackish wing linings.
Topside: Dark unpatterned wings, white "U" on rump.

COMMON MERGANSER (SAWBILL) *Mergus merganser* PP. 80–81
Overhead: Long, thin, fast flying; black head, white body, white wing linings.
Topside: Long, thin; white chest, large wing patch.

RED-BREASTED MERGANSER (SAWBILL) *Mergus serrator* PP. 80–81
Overhead: Long, thin, fast flying; dark chest band.
Topside: Long, thin, fast flying; dark chest, large wing patch.

HOODED MERGANSER *Lophodytes cucullatus* PP. 80–81
Overhead: Small head, humpbacked, fast flying, dusky wing lining.
Topside: Small head, drooping neck, fast flying; small wing patch.

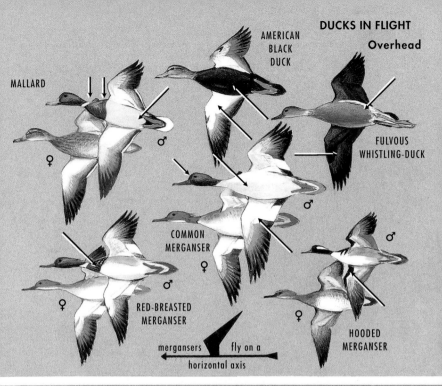

MALLARD

AMERICAN
BLACK
DUCK

♂

FULVOUS
WHISTLING-DUCK

♀

COMMON
MERGANSER

♂

♀

RED-BREASTED
MERGANSER

♂

HOODED
MERGANSER

♀

mergansers   fly on a
horizontal axis

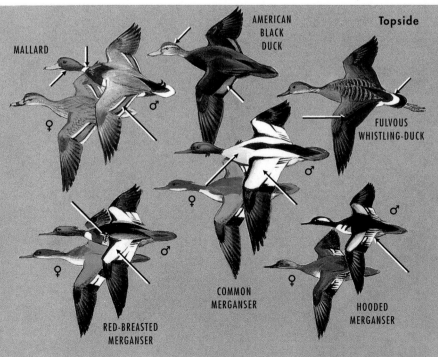

Topside

MALLARD

AMERICAN
BLACK
DUCK

♀

♂

FULVOUS
WHISTLING-DUCK

♂

♀

RED-BREASTED
MERGANSER

COMMON
MERGANSER

♀

♂

HOODED
MERGANSER

NOTE: Males are diagnosed below. Females are somewhat similar. The top panel shows birds as they appear overhead. The lower panel shows birds as their backs appear. Names in parentheses are nicknames often used by hunters.

NORTHERN PINTAIL (SPRIG) *Anas acuta*   **PP. 68–69**
Overhead: Needle tail, white breast, thin neck. Long, slender profile.
Topside: Needle tail, neck stripe, thin white border on rear edge of wing (speculum).

WOOD DUCK *Aix sponsa*   **PP. 68–69**
Overhead: White belly, dusky wings, long square tail.
Topside: Stocky; overall dark long tail, white border on dark wing.

AMERICAN WIGEON (BALDPATE) *Anas americana*   **PP. 68–69**
Overhead: White belly, dark pointed tail.
Topside: Large white shoulder patch.

NORTHERN SHOVELER (SPOONBILL) *Anas clypeata*   **PP. 70–71**
Overhead: Dark belly, white chest, spoon bill.
Topside: Large bluish shoulder patch, spoon bill.

GADWALL *Anas strepera*   **PP. 66–67**
Overhead: White belly, square white patch on rear edge of wing (speculum).
Topside: White patch on rear edge of wing (speculum).

GREEN-WINGED TEAL *Anas crecca*   **PP. 70–71**
Overhead: Small; light belly, dark head.
Topside: Small; dark-winged; green speculum

BLUE-WINGED TEAL *Anas discors*   **PP. 70–71**
Overhead: Small; dark belly.
Topside: Small; large bluish shoulder patch.

Wing of a dabbling duck showing the iridescent speculum.

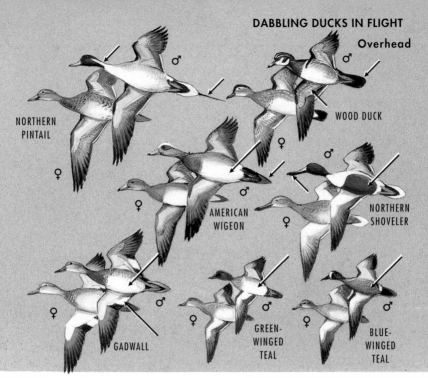

DABBLING DUCKS IN FLIGHT

Overhead

NORTHERN PINTAIL ♂ ♀

WOOD DUCK ♂ ♀

AMERICAN WIGEON ♂ ♀

NORTHERN SHOVELER ♂ ♀

GADWALL ♀ ♂

GREEN-WINGED TEAL ♀ ♂

BLUE-WINGED TEAL ♀ ♂

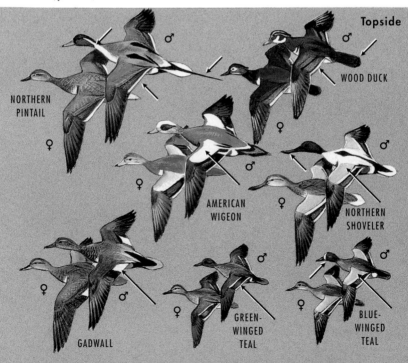

Topside

NORTHERN PINTAIL ♂ ♀

WOOD DUCK ♂ ♀

AMERICAN WIGEON ♀ ♂

NORTHERN SHOVELER ♂ ♀

GADWALL ♀ ♂

GREEN-WINGED TEAL ♀ ♂

BLUE-WINGED TEAL ♂ ♀

NOTE: Only males are diagnosed below. Top panel shows birds as they appear overhead. Lower panel shows birds as they appear from above. Names in parentheses are nicknames often used by hunters.

LONG-TAILED DUCK (OLDSQUAW) *Clangula hyemalis*   PP. 74–75
Overhead: Dark unpatterned wings, white belly; rocks side to side in flight.
Topside: Dark unpatterned wings, much white on body.

HARLEQUIN DUCK *Histrionicus histrionicus*   PP. 74–75
Overhead: Solid dark below, white head spots, small bill.
Topside: Stocky, dark with white marks, small bill.

SURF SCOTER (SKUNKHEAD) *Melanitta perspicillata*   PP. 72–73
Overhead: Black body, white head patches (not readily visible from below).
Topside: Black body, white head patches.

BLACK SCOTER (OCEAN COOT) *Melanitta nigra*   PP. 72–73
Overhead: Black plumage, paler flight feathers.
Topside: All-black plumage (pale flight feathers may be visible).

WHITE-WINGED SCOTER *Melanitta fusca*   PP. 72–73
Overhead: Black body, white wing patch.
Topside: Black body, white wing patch.

COMMON EIDER *Somateria mollissima*   PP. 74–75
Topside: White back, white forewing, black belly.

KING EIDER *Somateria spectabilis*   PP. 74–75
Topside: Whitish foreparts, black rear parts.

SEA DUCKS IN FLIGHT

Overhead

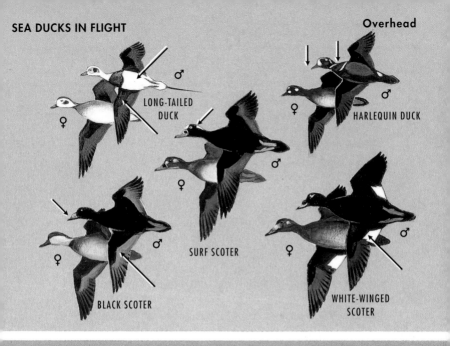

LONG-TAILED DUCK ♂ ♀

HARLEQUIN DUCK ♀ ♂

SURF SCOTER ♂ ♀

BLACK SCOTER ♂ ♀

WHITE-WINGED SCOTER ♂ ♀

Topside

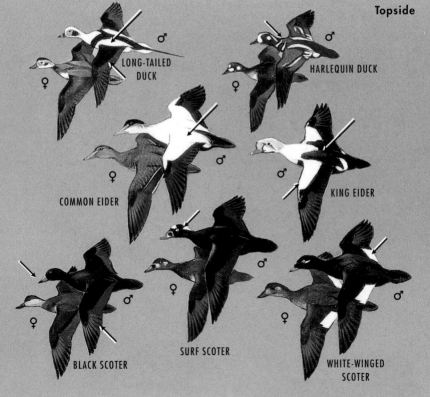

LONG-TAILED DUCK ♂ ♀

HARLEQUIN DUCK ♂ ♀

COMMON EIDER ♂ ♀

KING EIDER ♂

BLACK SCOTER ♂ ♀

SURF SCOTER ♂ ♀

WHITE-WINGED SCOTER ♂ ♀

NOTE: Only males are diagnosed below. The first five all have black chests. The top panel shows birds as they appear overhead. The lower panel shows birds as their backs appear. Names in parentheses are nicknames often used by hunters.

CANVASBACK *Aythya valisineria*   PP. 76–77
  Overhead: Black chest, long forehead on rufous head.
  Topside: White back, long forehead on rufous head.

REDHEAD *Aythya americana*   PP. 76–77
  Overhead: Black chest, roundish rufous head.
  Topside: Gray back, broad gray wing stripe.

RING-NECKED DUCK *Aythya collaris*   PP. 76–77
  Overhead: Similar to scaup. Note grayer sides and underwings.
  Topside: Black back, broad gray wing stripe.

GREATER SCAUP (BLUEBILL) *Aythya marila*   PP. 76–77
  Overhead: Black chest, white stripe showing through wing.
  Topside: Broad white wing stripe (extending onto primaries).

LESSER SCAUP (BLUEBILL) *Aythya affinis*   PP. 76–77
  Topside: Wing stripe shorter than that of Greater Scaup.

COMMON GOLDENEYE (WHISTLER) *Bucephala clangula*   PP. 78–79
  Overhead: Blackish wing linings, white wing patch.
  Topside: Large white wing-square, short neck, black head.

RUDDY DUCK (STIFF-TAIL) *Oxyura jamaicensis*   PP. 78–79
  Overhead: Stubby; white face, dark chest.
  Topside: Small; dark with white cheek.

BUFFLEHEAD (BUTTERBALL) *Bucephala albeola*   PP. 78–79
  Overhead: Like small goldeneye; note head patch.
  Topside: Small; large wing patch, white head patch.

SILHOUETTES OF DUCKS ON LAND

Dabbling and Pond Ducks (Dabblers)

Bay and Sea Ducks (Divers)

Mergansers (Divers)

Ruddy Duck (Diver)

Whistling-Ducks (Dabblers)

BAY DUCKS IN FLIGHT

Overhead

CANVASBACK

REDHEAD

♀

♂

♀

RING-NECKED
DUCK

♂

♀

GREATER
SCAUP

♂

♂

COMMON
GOLDENEYE

♀

RUDDY
DUCK

BUFFLEHEAD

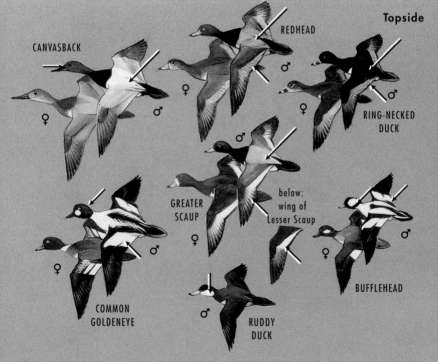

Topside

CANVASBACK

REDHEAD

♂

♀

♂

♀

RING-NECKED
DUCK

GREATER
SCAUP

below:
wing of
Lesser Scaup

♀

♂

♀

COMMON
GOLDENEYE

♂

RUDDY
DUCK

BUFFLEHEAD

Field marks of the Eurasian strays listed below can be found in *A Field Guide to the Birds of Britain and Europe*. Some have been substantiated by specimens or photographs; others are convincing sight records. Many are suspected aviary or zoo escapes.

1. **GRAYLAG GOOSE** *Anser anser* Handful of sighting in East, but origin in question.

2. **BEAN GOOSE** *Anser fabalis* Alaskan and Canadian sightings.

3. **PINK-FOOTED GOOSE** *Anser brachyrhynchus* Handful of eastern sightings.

4. **LESSER WHITE-FRONTED GOOSE** *Anser erythropus* Handful of eastern sightings.

5. **BARNACLE GOOSE** *Branta leucopsis* Many sightings from Canada south along East Coast and westward. Origin of many in question.

6. **RED-BREASTED GOOSE** *Branta ruficollis* (Escape).

7. **WHOOPER SWAN** *Cygnus cygnus* Formerly bred sw. Greenland. Very early records from Northeast. Now escapes occur regularly.

8. **GARGANEY** *Anas querquedula* Many records from Maritimes and East Coast as well as inland.

9. **BAIKAL TEAL** *Anas formosa* (Escape).

10. **TUFTED DUCK** *Aythya fuligula* Now regular in U.S. (see p. 76).

11. **RED-CRESTED POCHARD** *Netta rufina* (Escape).

12. **SMEW** *Mergellus albellus* Many sightings (origin of some in question).

13. **SHELDUCK** *Tadorna tadorna* Many sightings. (Escape).

14. **RUDDY SHELDUCK** *Tadorna ferruginea* (Origin in question).

ACCIDENTALS FROM THE TROPICS

15. **MASKED DUCK** *Nomonyx dominicus* Rare
13" *Male:* Rusty striped body with an all-black face and blue bill. Stiff tail feathers held upright at times. *Female:* buffy with black crown and two distinct face stripes. Heavily barred back. **SIMILAR SPECIES:** See Ruddy Duck (p. 78). **HABITAT:** Ponds and resacas with weedy edges.

16. **WHITE-CHEEKED PINTAIL** *Anas bahamensis* (West Indies) Numerous reports from Fla. Some birds are likely escapes.

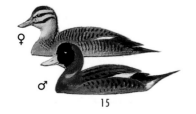

NEW WORLD VULTURES. Family Cathartidae.

Blackish, eaglelike birds often seen soaring high in wide circles. Their naked heads are relatively smaller than those of hawks and eagles. Often incorrectly called buzzards. Sexes alike. **FOOD:** Carrion. **RANGE:** S. Canada to Cape Horn. **NO. OF SPECIES:** World, 7; East, 2.

TURKEY VULTURE *Cathartes aura*   Common

M 50

26–32" (65–80 cm) Nearly eagle-sized (wingspread 6 ft.). When overhead, note two-toned wings (dark coverts, silver flight feathers). Soars with wings in a slight dihedral (a shallow V) rocking and tilting unsteadily. At close range, small naked *red head* of adult is evident; immature bird has dark head (like a Black Vulture). **RANGE:** S. Canada to Cape Horn. Migratory in north. **HABITAT:** Usually seen soaring in the sky or perched on dead trees or posts, at carrion, or on the ground sunning with wings outstretched.

BLACK VULTURE *Coragyps atratus*   Common

M 49

23–27" (58–68 cm) Wingspan under 5 ft. This large blackish scavenger is readily identified by the short tail that barely projects from rear edge of wings and by a silver patch restricted to outer wing. Pale feet sometimes project beyond tail. Note quick shallow flapping flight alternating with short glides. **SIMILAR SPECIES:** Turkey Vulture has a longer tail; flaps less, soars unsteadily with a rocking motion. *Caution:* Young Turkey Vulture has dark head. **RANGE:** Cen. and e. U.S. to n. Chile, n. Argentina. Range is extending north. **HABITAT:** Similar to Turkey Vulture's.

KING VULTURE *Sarcoramphus papa*

32" (80 cm) A whitish vulture with black flight feathers, gaudy head and neck. A rare resident of tropical America. Recorded by John and William Bartram on St. Johns R. in Fla. in 1765–1766, but this species has not been seen in the U.S. since.

CARACARAS AND FALCONS. Family Falconidae.

CARACARAS. Subfamily Caracarinae.

Large, long-legged birds of prey with naked faces. Sexes alike. **FOOD:** Our only U.S. species eats chiefly carrion and insects. **RANGE:** S. U.S. to Tierra del Fuego, Falklands. **NO. OF SPECIES:** World, 10; East, 1.

CRESTED CARACARA *Caracara cheriway*   Fairly common, restricted

M 110

20–25" (50–63 cm) A large, long-legged, big-headed, dark bird of prey often seen feeding with vultures or hunting on foot in pasturelands; its *black crest* and *red face* are distinctive. In flight, its underbody presents alternating areas of light and dark; white chest, black belly, and whitish, dark-tipped tail. Note combination of *pale* wing patch and *white chest*. Young bird is browner, streaked below. **RANGE:** Sw. U.S., Tex., and Fla. to S. America. **HABITAT:** Prairies, rangeland, desert.

SCAVENGERS

adult

immature

TURKEY VULTURE

BLACK VULTURE

adult

immature

adult

above, King Vulture
(formerly in Florida)

CRESTED CARACARA

We tend to lump all the diurnal (day-flying) raptors with hooked beaks and hooked talons as "birds of prey." Actually, they fall into quite separate families.

The **HAWK GROUP** (Accipitridae) — kites, eagles, buteos, accipiters, and harriers. There are 236 species in the world, 19 in the East, + 4 accidentals.

The **FALCON GROUP** (Falconidae) — falcons and caracaras. These are shown on pp. 116–119. There are 62 species in the world, 4 in the East, + 1 accidental.

The illustrations on the following pages present the obvious field marks. For a more in-depth treatment of variable plumages, see *A Field Guide to the Hawks,* by William S. Clark and Brian K. Wheeler. For subtleties of "jizz" (general impression and shape) at a distance, study *Hawks in Flight,* by Pete Dunne, Clay Sutton, and David Sibley.

The various groups of raptors can be sorted out by their basic shapes and flight styles. When not flapping, they may alternate between soaring, with wings fully extended and tails fanned, and gliding, with wings slightly pulled back and tails folded. These two pages show some basic silhouettes.

full soar

glide

BUTEOS are stocky, with broad wings and wide rounded tails. They soar and wheel high in the open sky, often on warm rising air thermals.

full soar

glide

ACCIPITERS (bird hawks) have small heads, short rounded wings, and long tails. They fly with several rapid wingbeats followed by a glide.

glide

full soar

HARRIERS are elongate, with slim, round-tipped wings and long tails. They fly in open country and glide low, often with a rocking motion and with wings held in an uplifted dihedral.

full soar

glide

KITES (except for the Snail Kite and Hook-billed Kite) are falcon-shaped, but unlike falcons they are buoyant gliders, not power flyers.

glide

full soar

FALCONS have long pointed wings and long tails. Their wing strokes are strong and rapid.

HAWKS, KITES, ACCIPITERS, HARRIERS, AND EAGLES. Family Accipitridae.

Diurnal birds of prey, with hooked beaks, hooked talons. Several sub-families are presented separately. Though persecuted and misunderstood by many, they are very important in the ecosystem. **RANGE:** Almost worldwide. **NO. OF SPECIES:** World, 236; East, 17 (+ 5 accidental).

KITES. Subfamilies Elaninae and Milvinae.

Graceful birds of prey of southern distribution. U.S. species (except Snail Kite and Hook-billed Kite) are falcon-shaped with pointed wings. **FOOD:** Large insects, reptiles, rodents. Snail Kite and Hook-billed Kite specialize in snails.

SWALLOW-TAILED KITE *Elanoides forficatus* — Uncommon

M 93

24" (60 cm) A sleek, elegant, black-and-white hawk that flies with in-comparable grace. Note black upperparts, clean white head and un-derparts, and long, mobile, *deeply forked* tail. **VOICE:** A shrill, keen *ee-ee-ee* or *pee-pee-pee*. **HABITAT:** Wooded river swamps and pine lands, where it feeds mainly on snakes. Leaves U.S. in winter.

MISSISSIPPI KITE *Ictinia mississippiensis* — Fairly common

M 96

14" (35 cm) Falcon-shaped, graceful, mainly gray. Dark above, lighter below; head *very pale gray;* tail and underwing blackish. No other fal-conlike bird has a black unbarred tail. In flight, shows a broad *pale patch* on rear of wing (not visible when bird is overhead). Immature is heavily streaked below; tail shows banding. **VOICE:** *Phee-phew;* a clear *kee-ee*. **HABITAT:** Wooded streams; groves, shelterbelts.

WHITE-TAILED KITE *Elanus leucurus* — Scarce and restricted

M 94

15–17" (38–43 cm) This whitish kite is falcon-shaped with long pointed wings and a *long white tail.* Soars and glides like a small gull; *often hovers. Adult:* Pale gray with white head, underparts, and tail. Note *large black patch* toward fore edge of upperwing. *Immature:* Rec-ognized by rusty breast, brown back, and a narrow band near tip of pale tail. **HABITAT:** Open groves, river valleys, marshes.

SNAIL KITE *Rostrhamus sociabilis* — Scarce and restricted

M 95

17–19" (43–48 cm) Suggests Northern Harrier at distance, but with-out gliding, tilting flight; flies more floppily, with head looking down, searching for snails. *Male:* All black except for a broad white band across base of tail; legs *red. Female:* Heavily streaked on buffy body; white stripe over eye and white band across black tail. **VOICE:** A cackling *kor-ee-ee-a, kor-ee-ee-a*. **HABITAT:** Fresh marshes and canals with Apple (*Pomacea*) Snails.

HOOK-BILLED KITE *Chondrohierax uncinatus* — Scarce and restricted

16" (41 cm) A scarce resident in s. Tex. Bill has a *long hooked tip.* Legs *yellow.* Plumage varies from blackish in some adults to pale in imma-tures. Most adults have *barred underparts* (dark in male, rusty in fe-male).

KITES

overhead flight patterns on p. 119

SWALLOW-TAILED KITE

immature

adult

MISSISSIPPI KITE

adult

immature

immature

adult

WHITE-TAILED KITE

adult

immature

immature

black phase

HOOK-BILLED KITE

♀

SNAIL KITE

♂

♂

♀

ACCIPITERS (BIRD HAWKS). Subfamily Accipitrinae.

Long-tailed woodland raptors with short, rounded wings, adapted for hunting among the trees. Typical flight consists of several quick beats and a glide. Sexes similar; females larger. Size can help distinguish the species but not always reliable in the field. **FOOD:** Chiefly birds, some small mammals. **RANGE:** Almost cosmopolitan. **NO. OF SPECIES:** World, 57; East, 3.

SHARP-SHINNED HAWK *Accipiter striatus*   Fairly common

M 99

10–14" (25–35 cm) A small, slim-bodied woodland hawk with a slim tail and *short, rounded wings.* Flies with several quick wingbeats and then a glide. Adult has a slate-gray back, rusty-barred breast. Folded tail is *slightly notched* or *square* (may seem a bit rounded when spread) and *narrowly tipped with white.* Head and neck proportionately *smaller* than a Cooper's. Immature is dark brown above, *heavily streaked* with dark brown below, *streaking onto underbelly.* **SIMILAR SPECIES:** Female Cooper's Hawk is obviously larger with a *well-rounded* tail; but male Cooper's and female Sharp-shinned may approach each other in size and tail shape. Compare descriptions of immatures. In flight, notice "flickering" of rapid wingbeats and tiny-headed appearance with virtually no neck. **VOICE:** Like Cooper's Hawk's, but shriller; a high *kik, kik, kik.* **RANGE:** Tree limit in Canada to Gulf states; winters from n. U.S. south. **HABITAT:** Mixed woods, evergreen forests, and thickets.

COOPER'S HAWK *Accipiter cooperii*   Fairly common

M 100

14–20" (35–50 cm) A short-winged, long-tailed hawk very similar to Sharp-shinned Hawk but larger; female usually distinctly larger than male. Tail is *well-rounded,* even when folded, and more *broadly tipped with white.* Adult Cooper's shows a more distinct contrast between blackish crown and gray nape. In flight, notice slower, stiffer wingbeats, longer neck, and larger head when compared to a "Sharpie." *Immature:* Brown, with *thin brown streaks* on breast, *lacks streaking* on underbelly. Face and nape often have a warm cast. No strong white supercilium as in Northern Goshawk. **VOICE:** About nest, a rapid *kik, kik, kik;* suggests Northern Flicker. **RANGE:** S. Canada to n. Mexico. **HABITAT:** Mature forests, open woodlands, wood edges, river groves.

NORTHERN GOSHAWK *Accipiter gentilis*   Uncommon to scarce

M 101

20–26" (50–65 cm) *Adult:* A large, robust hawk with a long tail, rounded wings, bulging secondaries. White undertail coverts often puff out and wrap to give white rump appearance. Crown and cheek blackish, a *broad white stripe over eye.* Underparts *pale gray, finely barred;* back paler and grayer than in Cooper's or Sharp-shinned. *Immature:* Like immature Cooper's; usually larger; note bolder pale stripe over eye and irregular tail-banding. Broad striping on underparts covers both breast and belly. **VOICE:** Fast, rapidly increasing *kak, kak, kak* or *kuk, kuk, kuk,* heavier than Cooper's. **RANGE:** Eurasia, n. N. America. **HABITAT:** Coniferous and deciduous forests, especially in mountains; forest edges. Periodic irruptions in fall and winter to south.

NORTHERN HARRIER *Circus cyaneus*   SEE P. 108

(For comparison.)

ACCIPITERS

overhead flight
patterns on p. 119

Accipiters
(true hawks)
have small heads,
short rounded
wings, long tails

immature

adult

SHARP-SHINNED
HAWK

immature

adult

COOPER'S HAWK

NORTHERN
GOSHAWK

immature

adult

Northern
Harrier

immature

♂

♀

NORTHERN
HARRIER

BUTEOS (BUZZARD HAWKS).
Subfamily Buteoninae (in part).

Large thick-set raptors with broad wings and wide rounded tails. They habitually soar high in wide circles. Much variation; sexes similar, females larger. Young birds are usually *streaked* below. Dark morphs often occur. **FOOD:** Rodents, rabbits; sometimes small birds, reptiles, grasshoppers. **RANGE:** Cosmopolitan. **NO. OF SPECIES:** World, 69; East, 13.

RED-TAILED HAWK *Buteo jamaicensis*   Common

M 106

19–25" (48–63 cm) The common hawk of roadsides and woodland edges. While soaring, shows *rufous* on upperside of tail (in adult). From below, tail is pale but may transmit a hint of red. Immatures have brownish gray tails that show pale banding. Underparts of typical Red-tails are "zoned" (whitish breast, broad band of streaks across belly). There is much variation westward, where one might encounter the pale *krideri* form, the blackish *harlani*, as well as various melanistic and rufous birds. **VOICE:** A drawn-out scream, *keeer-r-r* (slurring downward). **HABITAT:** Open country, woodlands, prairie groves, mountains, plains, roadsides, field edges.

"KRIDER'S" RED-TAILED HAWK *Buteo jamaicensis krideri*   Restricted

A pale prairie race or form of the Red-tail with a white tail that may be tinged with pale rufous. **RANGE:** Prairie provinces of Canada and northern prairie states. In winter, south through southern plains to Tex., La.

"HARLAN'S" RED-TAILED HAWK *Buteo jamaicensis harlani*   Restricted

A variable and usually blackish race of Red-tail; formerly regarded as a distinct species. Tail never solid red but usually dirty white with a *longitudinal* mottling and freckling of black merging into a dark subterminal band, giving a *white-based* effect. Similar to other melanistic Red-tails. **RANGE:** Breeds in e. Alaska and nw. Canada. Winters in central plains to Tex. and the lower Mississippi Valley.

SWAINSON'S HAWK *Buteo swainsoni*   Common

M 105

19–22" (48–55 cm) A buteo of the plains; slimmer than a Red-tail with wings a bit more pointed. When gliding, *wings are held slightly above horizontal*. Typical adult has a *dark chest-band*. Overhead, *buffy wing linings* contrast with *dark* flight feathers. Tail gray above, often shading to white at base. There are confusing individuals with light breasts and dark-morph birds, but note underwing with its dark flight feathers and light wing linings. **VOICE:** A shrill plaintive whistle, *kreeeeeeer.* **HABITAT:** Plains, range, open hills. Rare in fall to East Coast.

FERRUGINOUS HAWK *Buteo regalis*   Uncommon

M 107

23–25" (58–63 cm) A large buteo of the plains, *rufous above* and whitish below, with a *whitish or pale rufous tail* and a light patch on upper surface of wing. Head often quite light. Overhead, typical adults show a *dark V* formed by rufous thighs. Straggler east of Great Plains.

BUTEOS

overhead patterns on
pp. 107, 109, 111

immature

Buteos have
stocky build,
wide tail

adult

RED-TAILED HAWK

"HARLAN'S"
RED-TAILED HAWK

"Harlan's"
Red-tailed

"KRIDER'S"
RED-TAILED
HAWK

immature

dark
morph

light
morph

SWAINSON'S HAWK

FERRUGINOUS HAWK

ROUGH-LEGGED HAWK *Buteo lagopus*   Uncommon

M 108

19–24" (48–60 cm) When hunting, this hawk of open country often *hovers* on beating wings. A buteo by shape but with longer tail and wings than a Red-tail. Typically shows a *dark or blotched belly* and a *black patch* at "wrist" of underwing. Tail *white with a broad black band or bands* toward the tip. Dark morph lacks extensive white on upper tail, but shows much white on flight feathers of underwing. **SIMILAR SPECIES:** (1) Northern Harrier (white rump) has slimmer wings, slim tail. See (2) Golden Eagle, (3) Red-tailed Hawk. **RANGE:** Arctic; circumpolar. Winters to s. U.S., cen. Eurasia. **HABITAT:** Tundra escarpments, arctic coasts; in winter, open fields, plains, marshes.

RED-SHOULDERED HAWK *Buteo lineatus*   Uncommon (common in Fla.)

M 102

17–24" (43–60 cm) *Adult:* Recognized as a buteo by the ample tail and broad wings; as this species by narrow white bands set on a dark tail. Adult has *rufous shoulders* (not always visible in flight) and pale robin-red underparts (very pale in South Florida form). In flight, note also a translucent crescent or "window" near tip of wing. *Caution:* Other buteos may show pale patches along trailing edge of wing. *Immature:* Streaked below; can be recognized by proportions, tail banding and, in flight overhead, by wing "windows." **SIMILAR SPECIES:** (1) Adult Broad-winged Hawk has paler wing linings, broader white bands on tail. (2) Red-tailed Hawk. **VOICE:** A series of two-syllabled screams, *kee-yer* (dropping inflection). **RANGE:** Se. Canada, e. U.S., Calif., Mexico. **HABITAT:** Woodlands, wooded rivers, timbered swamps.

BROAD-WINGED HAWK *Buteo platypterus*   Common

M 103

14–19" (35–48 cm) A small chunky buteo, size of a crow. Often seen migrating in spiraling flocks called "kettles." Note tail banding of adult — white bands are *about as wide* as black bands. Wing linings are whitish and edge trimmed with black. *Immature:* Heavily streaked along sides of neck, breast, and belly. Chest often unmarked; tail has several narrow dark bands. Terminal dark band twice as wide as the rest. **SIMILAR SPECIES:** Young Red-shouldered Hawk is similar to immature Broad-wing, but latter is chunkier, streaking is heaviest on breast. Underwing is usually whiter in Broad-wing. **VOICE:** A high-pitched shrill, two-parted downward *pweeeeeee*. **RANGE:** S. Canada, e. U.S. to Gulf states. Winters mainly in Cen. and S. America, few in s. U.S. especially Fla. **Habitat:** Woods, groves.

SHORT-TAILED HAWK *Buteo brachyurus*   Uncommon and restricted

M 104

17" (43 cm) A small black or black-and-white buteo, size of a crow. Two morphs: (1) black body and black wing linings, and (2) black above, white below, with white wing linings. No other Fla. buteo would be jet-black or clear white below. **RANGE:** Fla., Mexico to Chile, Bolivia, n. Argentina. **HABITAT:** Pines, woodland edges, cypress swamps, mangroves.

dark morph

light morph

immature

BUTEOS

overhead patterns on p. 107

ROUGH-LEGGED HAWK

adult

RED-SHOULDERED HAWK

immature

pale s. Florida form

immature

immature

adult

adult

immature

BROAD-WINGED HAWK

light morph immature

dark morph

light morph

light morph adult

SHORT-TAILED HAWK

dark morph

HARRIS'S HAWK *Parabuteo unicinctus*　　　　　Locally common

19–22" (48–56 cm); wingspread 3½'. A dark brown hawk with a flashing *white rump* and *white band* at tip of its black tail. *Chestnut thighs and shoulders* distinguish it from other black or melanistic buteos. Juvenile has light, streaked underparts and *rusty shoulders;* might be confused with Red-shouldered Hawk except for conspicuous *white* at base of tail. **RANGE:** Resident of s. and cen. Tex. Strays to coastal plains, upper Gulf Coast. **HABITAT:** Riverine woods, mesquite, brush, cactus deserts.

ZONE-TAILED HAWK *Buteo albonotatus*　　　　　Scarce and restricted

18½–21" (47–54 cm); wingspread 4'. A dull *black* hawk, with more slender wings than most buteos. Easily mistaken for Turkey Vulture because of its shape and wing dihedral along with the two-toned underwing, but the feathered, hawk-shaped head and *white tail-bands* (pale gray on topside) identify the adult. The immature has narrower tail-bands and a scattering of *small white spots* on its black body. **RANGE:** In Tex., found east to Edwards Plateau and along Rio Grande casually to Brownsville. **HABITAT:** Riverine woods, dry mountains, canyons.

COMMON BLACK-HAWK *Buteogallus anthracinus*　　　Rare and very restricted

20–23" (50–58 cm); wingspread 4'. (See overhead, p. 111.) A black hawk with exceptionally wide wings and *long, yellow legs.* Identified by chunky shape and broad white *band* crossing middle of tail. In flight, a whitish spot shows near tip of wing at base of primaries. *Immature:* Dark-backed with a heavily striped *buffy* head and underparts; tail is narrowly banded with 5 or 6 dark bands. **SIMILAR SPECIES:** Whereas slimmer-winged Zone-tailed Hawk bears a superficial resemblance to a Turkey Vulture, broader-winged Common Black-Hawk suggests a Black Vulture. **RANGE:** Very rare visitor to lower Rio Grande Valley, Tex. **HABITAT:** Wooded stream bottoms.

WHITE-TAILED HAWK *Buteo albicaudatus*　　　Fairly common but restricted

23–24" (58–60 cm); wingspread 4'. A long-winged, short-tailed buteo with clear white underparts contrasting with dark flight feathers and a *white tail* with a black band near tip. Upperparts are dark gray, shoulders rusty red. *Immature:* Heavily streaked, almost blackish below but shows a white breast patch. Tail is pale gray, marked with a dark tip on two-year-old birds; flies with marked dihedral. **RANGE:** In Tex., local from Rio Grande to upper coast, formerly farther inland. **HABITAT:** Coastal prairie, brushlands.

GRAY HAWK *Asturina nitida*　　　　　Scarce and very restricted

16–18" (40–45 cm); wingspread 3'. A small buteo. *Adult:* gray back, and *densely barred gray* underparts, white band on rump, and *widely banded* tail (similar to Broad-winged Hawk's). *Immature:* Has a narrowly barred tail, striped buffy underparts. Note relatively short wings, barred thighs, bold pale supercilium, buffy face, *white bar* across rump. **HABITAT:** Wooded bottoms, along rivers and streams and mesquite lands. Rare during fall and winter in lower Rio Grande Valley. Has bred.

BUTEOS
SOUTHWESTERN
SPECIALTIES
overhead
patterns
on pp.
109, 111

immature

adult

HARRIS'S HAWK

immature

adult

ZONED-TAILED HAWK

mature

adult

WHITE-TAILED HAWK

immature

GRAY HAWK

adult

BUTEOS are chunky, with broad wings and broad, rounded tails. They soar and wheel high in the air.

RED-TAILED HAWK *Buteo jamaicensis*   PP. 100–101
The *dark patagial bar* at fore-edge of wing is best marked from below. Light chest, streaked belly (often forming belly band); tail plain, with hint of red and little or no banding. Immature is streaked below and has light tail-banding. Note always *patagial bar*.

SWAINSON'S HAWK *Buteo swainsoni*   PP. 100–101
Adult has a dark chest band. Note also contrast between *light wing linings* and *dark flight feathers*. Immature has a similar look, but has streaks on underbody.

RED-SHOULDERED HAWK *Buteo lineatus*   PP. 102–103
Tail is strongly banded (white bands are *narrower* than dark ones). Adult is *strongly barred with rusty* on body and wing linings. Immature has a heavily streaked chest and belly. There is a *light crescent "window"* on outer wing of adult as well as immature.

BROAD-WINGED HAWK *Buteo platypterus*   PP. 102–103
Smaller and chunkier, with a widely banded tail (*white bands wide*); underwing pale with dark rear margin and tip. *Immature:* Body striped, tail narrowly banded. Pale underwings may show lighter "windows" near wingtips.

ROUGH-LEGGED HAWK *Buteo lagopus*   PP. 102–103
Note *black carpal patch* contrasting with *white* flight feathers. A *broad, blackish band* or cummerbund across belly is distinctive in female and immature. Tail light, with a broad, dark subterminal band. Adult male is darker-chested, has multiple bands on tail and less bold belly-patch.

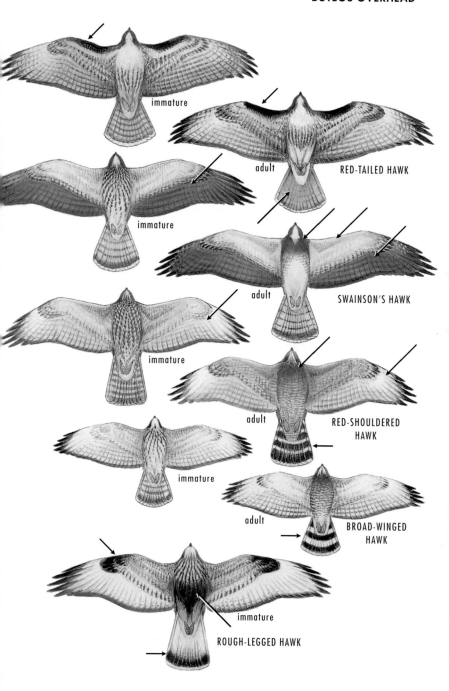

BUTEOS OVERHEAD

immature

adult   RED-TAILED HAWK

immature

adult   SWAINSON'S HAWK

immature

adult   RED-SHOULDERED
HAWK

immature

adult   BROAD-WINGED
HAWK

immature

ROUGH-LEGGED HAWK

FERRUGINOUS HAWK *Buteo regalis*   **PP. 100–101**
Whitish underparts, with a dark V formed by reddish thighs in adult. Wings and tail long for a buteo. A bird of western plains and open range.

GRAY HAWK *Asturina nitida*   **P. 104–105**
Stocky. Broadly banded tail (suggestive of a Broad-wing); gray-barred underparts. Uncommon resident of the Rio Grande Valley. Has nested.

WHITE-TAILED HAWK *Buteo albicaudatus*   **PP. 104–105**
Whitish underparts, gray head. White tail with a black band near tip. Soars with marked dihedral. Resident of coastal prairie of Tex.

HARRIERS. Subfamily Circinae.

Slim hawks with slim wings, long tails. Flight low, languid, gliding, with wings in a shallow V (dihedral). Sexes dissimilar. They hunt in open country. One species in N. America.

NORTHERN HARRIER *Circus cyaneus*   Common
17½–24" (44–60 cm) Note *white rump*. A slim hawk. *Male:* Pale gray above, white below, with a gray hooded appearance. *Female:* Brown with streaking below. *Immature:* Russet to orangy below with some streaking. Glides and flies buoyantly low over ground with wings slightly above horizontal, suggesting Turkey Vulture's dihedral. **VOICE:** A weak, nasal whistle, *pee, pee, pee.* **RANGE:** Alaska, Canada to s. U.S.; n. Eurasia. Winters to n. S. America, n. Africa. **HABITAT:** Marshes, fields, prairies, salt marshes, dumps, etc.

M 98

BUTEOS OVERHEAD

FERRUGINOUS HAWK

GRAY HAWK

WHITE-TAILED HAWK

HARRIERS

♂ overhead

♀ overhead

immature

♂

♀

NORTHERN HARRIER

CRESTED CARACARA *Caracara cheriway*   PP. 92–93
   Whitish chest, black belly, large *pale patch* in primaries. Elongate neck, stiff-winged flight.

ROUGH-LEGGED HAWK *Buteo lagopus* (dark morph)   PP. 102–103
   Dark body and wing linings; *whitish flight feathers;* tail light from below, with 1 broad *black terminal band* in female; additional bands in male.

FERRUGINOUS HAWK *Buteo regalis* (dark morph)   PP. 100–101
   Similar to dark morph of Rough-leg, but tail whitish, *without dark banding.* Note also white wrist marks, or *"commas."*

SWAINSON'S HAWK *Buteo swainsoni* (dark morph)   PP. 100–101
   In dark morph, wings are usually dark throughout, including flight feathers, tail narrowly banded. Rufous morph may be rustier, with lighter rufous wing linings.

RED-TAILED HAWK *Buteo jamaicensis* (dark morph)   PP. 100–101
   Chunky; tail reddish above, pale tinged with rusty below; variable. May not always be safely distinguishable underneath from "Harlan's" form of Red-tail.

"HARLAN'S" HAWK *Buteo jamaicensis* (in part)   PP. 100–101
   Similar to dark morph of Red-tail, breast is mottled white; tail is streaked gray and white; lacks red.

SNAIL KITE *Rostrhamus sociabilis*   PP. 96–97
   Flight is buoyant, floppy, with head looking down, searching for snails. Wide, paddlelike wings. Blackish with broad white band across base of tail. Female streaked on buffy underparts, white band across black tail.

ZONE-TAILED HAWK *Buteo albonotatus* (immature)   PP. 104–105
   Longish, *two-toned wings* (resembles a Turkey Vulture). Three white tail-bands.

HARRIS'S HAWK *Parabuteo unicinctus*   PP. 104–105
   Chestnut wing linings. A very broad white band at base of black tail, with a narrow white terminal band.

COMMON BLACK-HAWK *Buteogallus anthracinus*   PP. 104–105
   Broad black wings; *light patch* near wingtips. A broad *white band at midtail* and a very broad, black subterminal band. Whereas Zone-tailed Hawk resembles Turkey Vulture, chunkier Common Black-Hawk more suggestive of Black Vulture.

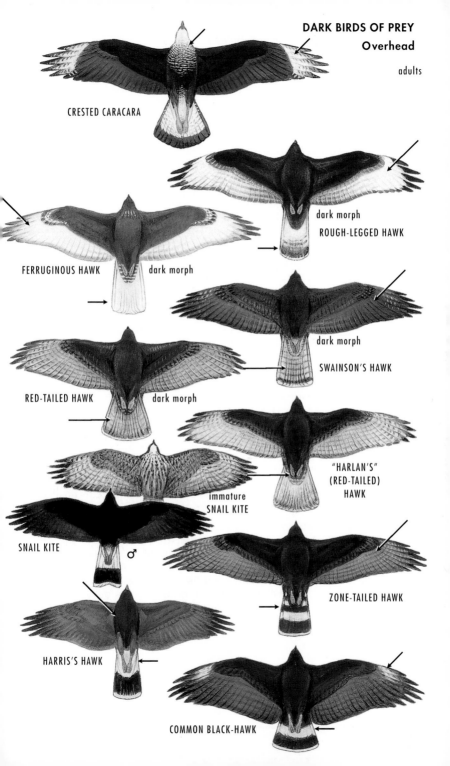

DARK BIRDS OF PREY
Overhead

adults

CRESTED CARACARA

dark morph
ROUGH-LEGGED HAWK

FERRUGINOUS HAWK   dark morph

dark morph
SWAINSON'S HAWK

RED-TAILED HAWK   dark morph

"HARLAN'S"
(RED-TAILED)
HAWK

immature
SNAIL KITE

SNAIL KITE   ♂

ZONE-TAILED HAWK

HARRIS'S HAWK

COMMON BLACK-HAWK

EAGLES. Subfamily Buteoninae (in part).

Eagles are distinguished from buteos, to which they are related, by their much greater size and proportionately longer wings. Very large, powerful bill. **FOOD:** Golden Eagle eats chiefly rabbits and large rodents; Bald Eagle, chiefly fish or carrion.

BALD EAGLE *Haliaeetus leucocephalus* Uncommon

M 97

30–43" (75–108 cm); wingspread 7–8'. The national bird of the U.S. Adult, with its all-white head and white tail, is "all field mark." Bill yellow, massive. Most immatures are all dark except for whitish underwings and base of the tail. Older (two- and three-year-old) birds are very mottled with white on underwings, belly, flight feathers, tail, and back. Wings held flat when soaring. **SIMILAR SPECIES:** See Golden Eagle. **VOICE:** A sharp, pleading, creaking cackle, *kleek-kik-ik-ik-ik,* or a lower *kak-kak-kak.* **RANGE:** Alaska, Canada to s. U.S. **HABITAT:** Coasts, rivers, large lakes.

GOLDEN EAGLE *Aquila chrysaetos* Uncommon

M 109

30–40" (75–100 cm); wingspread 7'. Majestic. The Golden Eagle glides and soars with a slight dihedral. Its greater size and longer wings set it apart from large buteos. *Adult:* Uniformly dark below, or with a slight lightening at base of obscurely banded tail. On hindneck, a *wash of gold. Immature:* In flight, more readily identified than adult, showing a *white flash in wings* at base of primaries, and a *white tail with a broad dark terminal band.* **SIMILAR SPECIES:** (1) Immature Bald Eagle usually has white in wing linings and often on body. Dark morphs of (2) Rough-legged Hawk and (3) Ferruginous Hawk are smaller, have white flight feathers. **VOICE:** Seldom heard; a yelping bark, *kya;* drawn-out whistled notes. **RANGE:** Mainly mountain regions and plains of N. Hemisphere. **HABITAT:** Open mountains, foothills, plains, open country, coastal marshes.

OSPREYS. Family Pandionidae.

A monotypic family comprising a single large bird of prey that plunges feet-first for fish. Sexes alike. **RANGE:** Cosmopolitan. (Occurs on all continents except Antarctica.) **NO. OF SPECIES:** World, 1; East, 1.

OSPREY *Pandion haliaetus* Locally common

M 92

21–24½" (53–61 cm) Our only raptor that plunges *into* the water. Large (wingspread to 6 ft.) brownish black above, *black-and-white below.* Head largely white, suggesting Bald Eagle, but with a *broad black patch through eye.* Flies with a gull-like crook in wing, showing a *black "wrist" patch* from below. Hovers on beating wings and plunges feet-first for fish. *Immature* with *whitish spotting* above. **VOICE:** A series of sharp, annoyed, strained whistles, *cheep, cheep,* or *yewk, yewk,* etc. Near nest, a frenzied *cheereek!* **RANGE:** Cosmopolitan. **HABITAT:** Rivers, lakes, coasts.

EAGLES

overhead
patterns
on p. 114

BALD EAGLE
adult

BALD EAGLE
immature

GOLDEN EAGLE
adult

GOLDEN EAGLE
immature

OSPREY

hovering

OSPREY

adult

BALD EAGLE *Haliaeetus leucocephalus* PP. 112–113
> *Adult:* White head and tail.
> *Immature:* Some white in wing linings, often on body.

GOLDEN EAGLE *Aquila chrysaetos* PP. 112–113
> *Adult:* Almost uniformly dark; wing linings dark.
> *Immature:* White patch at base of primaries and tail; no white on body.

OSPREY *Pandion haliaetus* PP. 112–113
> White body and coverts; black wrist patch; crooked wing

TURKEY VULTURE *Cathartes aura* PP. 92–93
> Two-toned wings held in a distinct dihedral. Small head, red in adults, gray in immatures. Longish tail.

BLACK VULTURE *Coragyps atratus* PP. 92–93
> Silver wing patch. Wings held flat or with very slight dihedral. Rapid shallow wingbeats. Stubby tail.

Where the Bald Eagle, Turkey Vulture, and Osprey all are found, they can be separated at a great distance by their manner of soaring: the Bald Eagle with flat wings; the Turkey Vulture with a dihedral; the Osprey often with a kink or crook in its wings.

TURKEY VULTURE

BLACK VULTURE

EAGLES, OSPREY, Overhead

BALD EAGLE   adult

BALD EAGLE   immature

GOLDEN EAGLE   adult

GOLDEN EAGLE   immature

OSPREY

FALCONS. Family Falconidae.

Falcons are streamlined birds of prey with pointed wings, longish tails.
FOOD: Birds, rodents, insects. **RANGE:** Almost cosmopolitan. **NO. OF SPECIES:**
World, 42; East, 5 (+ 1 accidental)

AMERICAN KESTREL *Falco sparverius* Fairly common

M 111

9–12" (23–30 cm) A swallowlike falcon, size of a jay. No other *small* hawk has a *rufous back or tail*. Males have blue-gray wings. Both sexes have a mustached black-and-white face pattern. *Hovers* for prey, kingfisher-like, on rapidly beating wings. Sits fairly erect, with an occasional lift of the tail. **SIMILAR SPECIES:** (1) Sharp-shinned Hawk has rounded wings. Sharp-shinned and (2) Merlin have gray or brown backs and tails. **VOICE:** A rapid, high *klee klee klee* or *killy killy killy*. **HABITAT:** Open country, farmland, cities, wood edges, dead trees, wires.

MERLIN *Falco columbarius* Uncommon

M 112

10–13½" (25–34 cm) A small compact falcon, length of a jay, with a mustache less distinct than peregrine or kestrel. *Male:* Blue-gray above, with broad black bands on a gray tail. *Female and immature:* Dusky brown to chocolate brown with a banded tail. Both adults and immature are boldly streaked below and appear overall dark at a distance. **SIMILAR SPECIES:** (1) Sharp-shinned Hawk has rounded wings. (2) American Kestrel has a rufous tail, rufous back. **HABITAT:** Open conifer woodlands; in migration, also foothills, marshes, open country, coastal shoreline.

PRAIRIE FALCON *Falco mexicanus* Accidental in East

17" (43 cm) Like a sandy-colored peregrine with *narrower mustache* and white behind eye. In flight overhead, shows *blackish* underwing linings. **SIMILAR SPECIES:** Adult peregrine has blacker sideburns, slaty back. Some may be escapes from falconers.

PEREGRINE FALCON *Falco peregrinus* Uncommon

M 114

15–20" (38–50 cm) Recognized as a falcon by its pointed wings, long tail, and quick, powerful, fluid wingbeats. Size, slightly longer than that of crow, and strong mustache mark help identify this species. *Adult:* Slaty-backed, barred and spotted below. *Immature:* Brown, heavily streaked. **VOICE:** At eyrie, a repeated *we'chew*; a rapid *kek kek kek kek*. **HABITAT:** Mainly open country (mountains to coast); locally in cities, where reestablishment efforts work well.

GYRFALCON *Falco rusticolus* Rare

M 113

20–25" (50–63 cm) A very large arctic falcon. Larger, more robust than Peregrine; slightly broader tailed and wider-winged. Wingbeats slower, stiffer than peregrine. More uniformly colored than peregrine and lacks bold facial mustache. Three color morphs: dark brown, gray, and white. Darker immature birds are more prone to wander south. **HABITAT:** Arctic barrens, seacoasts, open mountains. Wanders south in winter to northern states. Open coastal area favored.

FALCONS

overhead patterns on p. 118

falcons have long, pointed wings, long tails

♀ ♂

Kestrel

AMERICAN KESTREL

♀ ♂

MERLIN

♂ Merlin

Peregrine

PRAIRIE FALCON

immature adult

PEREGRINE FALCON

dark morph

gray morph

white morph

GYRFALCON

ACCIPITERS (bird hawks) have short rounded wings, long tails. They fly with several rapid beats and a short glide. They are better adapted to hunting in the woodlands than most other hawks. Females are larger than males. Immatures (not shown) have streaked breasts.

COOPER'S HAWK *Accipiter cooperii*   PP. 98–99
Underparts rusty. Near the size of an American Crow. Tail well-rounded and tipped with a broad white terminal band. Note long neck and large head.

NORTHERN GOSHAWK *Accipiter gentilis*   PP. 98–99
Larger than American Crow; bold facial pattern, underbody heavily barred with pale gray.

SHARP-SHINNED HAWK *Accipiter striatus*   PP. 98–99
Small; a bit larger than a jay; when folded, tail *square or notched*, with narrow white tip. Fanned tail slightly rounded. Note small head and flickering wingbeats.

FALCONS have long, pointed wings and relatively long tails. Wing strokes are typically rapid and continuous.

PEREGRINE FALCON *Falco peregrinus*   PP. 116–117
Falcon shape; larger than an American Crow; bold face pattern.

AMERICAN KESTREL *Falco sparverius*   PP. 116–117
Small size; banded rufous tail.

MERLIN *Falco columbarius*   PP. 116–117
Small size, near that of a jay; banded gray tail.

GYRFALCON *Falco rusticolus*   PP. 116–117
Larger than Peregrine; grayer, without that bird's contrasting facial pattern. Dark and white morphs also occur.

WHITE-TAILED KITE *Elanus leucurus*   PP. 96–97
Falcon-shaped; white body, whitish tail.

MISSISSIPPI KITE *Ictinia mississippiensis*   PP. 96–97
Falcon-shaped. *Adult:* Black tail, blackish wings, gray body. *Immature:* Streaked breast; banded square-tipped or notched tail.

KITES (except Snail Kite) are falcon-shaped but, unlike falcons, are buoyant gliders, not power fliers. All are southern.

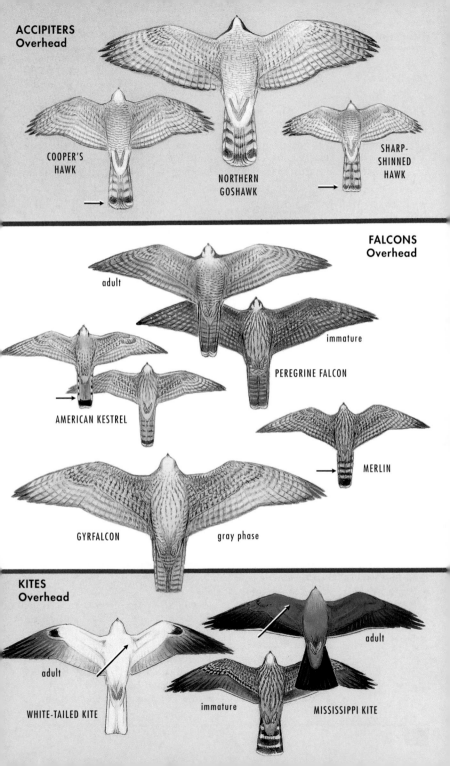

**ACCIPITERS
Overhead**

COOPER'S HAWK

NORTHERN GOSHAWK

SHARP-SHINNED HAWK

**FALCONS
Overhead**

adult

immature

PEREGRINE FALCON

AMERICAN KESTREL

MERLIN

GYRFALCON

gray phase

**KITES
Overhead**

adult

WHITE-TAILED KITE

immature

adult

MISSISSIPPI KITE

PHEASANT, GROUSE, TURKEY, AND ALLIES. Family Phasianidae.

Medium to large fowl. Classification of groups subject to revision. Mainly ground-dwelling. **FOOD:** Insects, seeds, buds, fruits. **RANGE:** Nearly cosmopolitan. **NO. OF SPECIES:** World, 143; East, 9 (+ 2 introduced).

TURKEYS. Subfamily Meleagridinae.

Very large fowl, iridescent, naked-headed; male with tail erected fanwise in display; female smaller. **FOOD:** Berries, acorns, nuts, seeds, insects. **RANGE:** Scattered throughout U.S., south to Mexico, Guatemala. Domesticated throughout much of world. **NO. OF SPECIES:** World, 2; East, 1.

WILD TURKEY *Meleagris gallopavo*   Fairly common

M 123

Male 48" (120 cm); female 36" (90 cm) A streamlined version of the barnyard Turkey, with *rusty* instead of white tail tips. Head naked; bluish with red wattles, intensified in male's display. Tail of male erected like a fan in display. Bronzy iridescent body; barred wings (primaries and secondaries); prominent "beard" on breast. Female and immature smaller, with a smaller head; less iridescent; less likely to have a beard. **VOICE:** "Gobbling" of male like domestic Turkey's. Alarm, *pit!* or *put-put!* Flock call, *keow-keow.* Hen clucks to her chicks. **RANGE:** Scattered throughout U.S., south to n. Mexico. Reintroduced to many areas. **HABITAT:** Woods, mountain forests, wooded swamps, clearings. Introduced birds adapting very well to being near people.

GROUSE, ETC. Subfamily Tetraoninae (in part).

RUFFED GROUSE *Bonasa umbellus*   Uncommon, cyclic

M 117

16–19" (40–48 cm) Note fan-shaped tail with a broad black band near tip. A large *red-brown* or *gray-brown* chickenlike bird of brushy woodlands, usually not seen until it flushes with a startling whir. Two color morphs occur: "rusty" with rufous tails, and "gray" birds with gray tails. Rusty birds are in preponderance in southern parts of range, gray birds northward. **VOICE:** Sound of drumming male suggests a distant motor starting up. Low muffled thumping starts slowly, accelerating into a whir: *Bup. . .bup. . .bup. . .bup. . .bup bup up r-rrrrr.* **RANGE:** Alaska, Canada, n. U.S. **HABITAT:** Ground and understory of deciduous or mixed woodlands.

PHEASANTS. Subfamily Phasianinae.

RING-NECKED PHEASANT *Phasianus colchicus*   Fairly common

M 116

Male 30–36" (75–90 cm); female 21–25" (53–63 cm) Note long, sweeping, pointed tail. A large chickenlike or gamecocklike bird. Runs swiftly; flight strong (takeoff noisy). *Male:* Highly colored and iridescent, with scarlet wattles on its face and a *white neck-ring* (not always present). *Female:* Mottled brown, with a moderately long, pointed tail. **VOICE:** Crowing male utters a loud double squawk, *kork-kok,* followed by a brief whir of wing flapping. When flushed, harsh croaks. Roosting call, a two-syllabled *kutuck-kutuck,* etc. **RANGE:** Introduced from Eurasia widely in N. America. **HABITAT:** Farms, fields, marsh edges, brush.

MISCELLANEOUS FOWL-LIKE BIRDS

display ♂

♂

♀

WILD TURKEY

♂

RUFFED GROUSE

♂

gray

red

♂

display

♀

♂

♀

♂

RING-NECKED PHEASANT

GROUSE, ETC. Subfamily Tetraoninae.

Ground-dwelling chickenlike birds; larger than quail, lacking long tails of pheasants. **FOOD:** Insects, seeds, buds, berries, etc. **RANGE:** N. America, Europe, Asia. **NO. OF SPECIES:** World, 18; East, 7.

SPRUCE GROUSE *Falcipennis canadensis*   Scarce

M 118

15–17" (38–43 cm) Look for this very tame, dusky grouse in dark conifer forests of the North. *Male:* Sharply defined *black breast*, *white barring* on sides and a chestnut band on tail tip. A comb of red skin above eye is visible at close range. *Female:* Dark rusty brown, thickly barred; tail short and dark, with a rusty tip. **RANGE:** Alaska, Canada, n. U.S. **HABITAT:** Conifer forests, Jack Pines, muskeg, blueberry bogs, dirt roadsides for dusting areas.

SHARP-TAILED GROUSE *Tympanuchus phasianellus*   Uncommon

M 121

15–20" (38–50 cm) Note the *short pointed tail*, which in flight shows *white at sides*. A pale speckled brown grouse of the prairie grasslands. Displaying male inflates *purplish* neck sacs. **SIMILAR SPECIES:** (1) Female Ring-necked Pheasant (p. 120) has a *long* pointed tail that lacks white sides. (2) Prairie-chicken has short, *rounded, dark tail.* (3) Ruffed Grouse (p. 120) has a larger fan-shaped tail. **VOICE:** A cackling *cac-cac-cac,* etc. Courting note, a single low *coot* or *coo-oo,* accompanied by tail vibrating and foot shuffling. **RANGE:** Alaska, Canada, nw. and n.-cen. U.S. **HABITAT:** Prairies, brushy groves, open thickets, forest edges, clearings, coulees, open burns in coniferous forests.

GREATER PRAIRIE-CHICKEN *Tympanuchus cupido*   Uncommon, restricted

M 122

17–18" (43–45 cm) Note short *rounded dark tail* (black in males, barred in females). A brown henlike bird of prairies; heavily barred. Courting males in communal "dance" inflate orange neck sacs and erect hornlike pinnae (blackish neck feathers). **SIMILAR SPECIES:** (1) Female Ring-necked Pheasant (p. 120) has a long pointed tail. (2) Sharp-tailed Grouse (often mistakenly called "Prairie Chicken") has a whitish-edged pointed tail. (3) Ruffed Grouse (p. 120) lives in woods, has a large fan-shaped tail. (4) See Lesser Prairie-Chicken. **VOICE:** "Booming" male in dance makes a hollow *oo-loo-woo,* suggesting sound made by blowing across top of a bottle. **RANGE:** Northern plains to coastal Tex. (where very rare). **HABITAT:** Tall-grass prairie; now very local.

LESSER PRAIRIE-CHICKEN *Tympanuchus pallidicinctus*   Scarce, restricted

16" (40 cm) A small, pale prairie-chicken; best identified by its range (see below). Male's gular sacs are *dull purplish red or plum-colored* (not orange as in Greater Prairie-Chicken). **VOICE:** Courtship "booming" not as rolling or as loud as Greater Prairie-Chicken's. Both have clucking, cackling notes. **RANGE:** Resident locally in se. Colo., e. N.M., and n. Tex. Panhandle, entering our area in extreme w. Kans. and Okla., just west of range of Greater Prairie-Chicken as shown on Map 122. **HABITAT:** Sandhill country (sagebrush and bluestem grass, "shrubby" oaks).

GROUSE

♀

♂

SPRUCE GROUSE

♂ display

SHARP-TAILED
GROUSE

♂

♂ display

GREATER
PRAIRIE-CHICKEN

♂

LESSER
PRAIRIE-CHICKEN

♂

display

WILLOW PTARMIGAN *Lagopus lagopus*   Fairly common

M 119

16" (40 cm) Ptarmigan are arctic grouse that change their brown summer plumage to white in winter. The 2 eastern species are similar; in breeding plumage variable, brown to rufous with white wings; in winter, white with black tails. In summer, Willow Ptarmigan is usually more deeply chestnut than Rock Ptarmigan. **SIMILAR SPECIES:** Some races of Rock Ptarmigan are decidedly gray, finely barred. Bill is smaller, more slender. In winter, most Rocks have a black mark between eye and bill. Habitats differ in summer, with Rock preferring higher, more barren hills. **VOICE:** Deep raucous calls, *go-out, go-out*; male, a staccato crow; *kwow, kwow, tobacco, tobacco*, etc., or *go-back, go-back*. **RANGE:** Arctic regions; circumpolar. **HABITAT:** Tundra, willow scrub, muskeg; in winter, sheltered valleys.

ROCK PTARMIGAN *Lagopus mutus*   Uncommon

M 120

13" (33 cm) See Willow Ptarmigan (above) for comparisons. **RANGE:** Arctic and alpine regions of N. Hemisphere. **HABITAT:** Above timberline in mountains (to lower levels in winter); also bleak tundra of northern coasts.

GRAY PARTRIDGE *Perdix perdix*   Uncommon

M 115

12–14" (30–35 cm) In flight, note short rufous tail. A rotund gray and brown partridge, larger than Northern Bobwhite; has a *dark U-shaped splotch* on belly, rusty face, chestnut bars on flanks. **SIMILAR SPECIES:** Chukar (*Alectoris chukar*), another Old World partridge, has been introduced successfully in the West, unsuccessfully in the East, except on hunting preserves for short term (see p. 328). **VOICE:** A hoarse *kar-wit, kar-wit*. When flushed, a cackle. **RANGE:** Eurasia; introduced in N. America. **HABITAT:** Open farmland, grainfields.

NEW WORLD QUAILS. Family Odontophoridae.

Quails are smaller than grouse. Sexes alike or unlike. **FOOD:** Insects, seeds, buds, berries. **RANGE:** Nearly cosmopolitan. **NO. OF SPECIES:** World, 155; East, 2 (+ 2 introduced successfully; others have failed).

NORTHERN BOBWHITE *Colinus virginianus*   Fairly common

M 125

8½–10½" (21–26 cm) A small, rotund fowl, near size of a meadowlark. Ruddy, with a short, dark tail. Male has a conspicuous white throat and white brow stripe. On female these are buff. **SIMILAR SPECIES:** Ruffed Grouse is larger with a fanlike tail. **VOICE:** A clearly whistled *bob-white!* or *poor, bob-whoit!* Covey call, *ka-loi-kee?* Answered by *whoil-kee!* **RANGE:** Cen. and e. U.S. to Guatemala, Cuba. **HABITAT:** Farms, brushy open country, roadsides, wood edges.

SCALED QUAIL *Callipepla squamata*   Fairly common but restricted

M 124

10–12" (25–30 cm) A gray, scaly "cotton-topped" quail of the arid Southwest that just crosses the 100th meridian into our area in extreme sw. Kansas, sw. Okla., and sw. Tex. See inset of head.

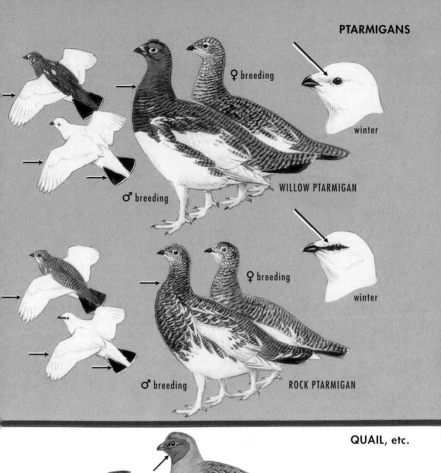

PTARMIGANS

♀ breeding

winter

♂ breeding

WILLOW PTARMIGAN

♀ breeding

winter

♂ breeding

ROCK PTARMIGAN

QUAIL, etc.

GRAY PARTRIDGE

sexes similar

SCALED QUAIL

NORTHERN BOBWHITE

♂

♀

DUCKLIKE SWIMMERS (COOTS, GALLINULES).
Family Rallidae (in part; see p. 128).

Coots and gallinules belong to the same family as the rails (see further family discussion on p. 128). Whereas the rails are more chickenlike and are basically secretive wading birds of the marshes, coots and gallinules are superficially more ducklike except for their smaller heads, forehead shields, foot structure, and rather chickenlike bills. They spend most of their time swimming, although they may also feed on shores. Often vocal with loud squawks, grunts, and peeps.

AMERICAN COOT *Fulica americana* — Common

M 134

13–16" (33–40 cm) A slaty ducklike bird with a blackish head and neck, *white bill*, and divided white patch under tail. No side striping. Its big feet are lobed ("scallops" on toes). Gregarious. Swimming, it pumps its head back and forth (like a moorhen). Dabbles but also dives from surface. Taking off, it skitters; flight is labored; big feet trail beyond short tail; a narrow white border shows on rear of wing. *Immature:* Paler with a slightly duller bill. Downy young has "hairy" *orange-red* head and shoulders. **SIMILAR SPECIES:** Common Moorhen is smaller, has a red bill with yellow tip. Browner above, sides with white line. Coots are more ducklike than moorhens and flock more on open water. "Caribbean" Coot, formerly judged to be a valid species, is now regarded as a questionable subspecies. **VOICE:** A grating *kuk-kuk-kuk-kuk; kakakakakaka*, etc.; also a measured *ka-ha, ha-ha;* various cackles, croaks. **RANGE:** Canada to Ecuador. **HABITAT:** Ponds, lakes, marshes; in winter, also fields, park ponds, salt bays.

COMMON MOORHEN *Gallinula chloropus* — Fairly common

M 133

13" (33 cm) Note rather chickenlike red bill with yellow tip, *red forehead shield,* and white stripe on flanks. Legs green. When walking, it flicks white undertail coverts; when swimming, pumps head. **SIMILAR SPECIES:** (1) American Coot is stockier, shorter-necked; has a gray back, white bill, no side stripe. **VOICE:** A croaking *kr-r-ruk,* repeated; a froglike *kup;* also *kek, kek, kek* and loud, complaining piping notes. **RANGE:** S. Canada to Argentina; Eurasia, Africa. **HABITAT:** Fresh marshes, cattail and reedy ponds.

PURPLE GALLINULE *Porphyrula martinica* — Uncommon

M 132

13" (33 cm) Very colorful; swims, wades, and climbs bushes. Size of Common Moorhen but head and underparts *deep violet-purple,* back bronzy green, no side stripe. Shield on forehead *pale blue;* bill red with a yellow tip. Legs *yellow,* conspicuous in flight. *Immature:* Duller; dark greenish above, pale buffy below; *no side stripes;* bill dark. **SIMILAR SPECIES:** (1) Common Moorhen has a *red* frontal shield, greenish legs, white side stripes; young Common Moorhen also has whitish side stripes. (2) Young American Coot has a pale bill; black divides white patch under tail. **VOICE:** A chickenlike cackling *kek, kek, kek,* given when flying; also guttural notes. **RANGE:** Se. U.S. to n. Argentina. Winters mainly south of U.S. **HABITAT:** Fresh swamps, marshes, ponds.

DUCKLIKE SWIMMERS

Coots skitter on takeoff

lobed foot of Coot

immature

Coot chick

Gallinule chick

adult

adult

AMERICAN COOT

immature

adult

COMMON MOORHEN

COMMON MOORHEN

immature

adult

PURPLE GALLINULE

PURPLE GALLINULE

RAILS, GALLINULES, AND COOTS. Family Rallidae.

Rails are compact, rather chicken-shaped marsh birds of secretive habits and mysterious voices; more often heard than seen. Flight, when flushed, brief and reluctant, with legs dangling. Gallinules and coots swim (rails can also); they resemble ducks except for smaller heads, forehead shields, and chickenlike bills. They are treated separately on pp. 126–127. Sexes in all the Rallidae are alike. **FOOD:** Aquatic plants, seeds, buds, insects, frogs, crustaceans, mollusks. **RANGE:** Widespread in nonpolar regions. **NO. OF SPECIES:** World, 134; East, 9 (+ 5 accidental).

VIRGINIA RAIL *Rallus limicola*   Fairly common but secretive

M 130

9" (23 cm) A small *rusty* rail with *gray cheeks*; black bars on flanks and a long, slightly decurved reddish bill. The only small rail, near size of a meadowlark, with a *long slender* bill. Full-grown young in late summer overall darker with black underparts. **SIMILAR SPECIES:** Sora has small stubby bill and unbarred undertail coverts. See King Rail, below. **VOICE:** *Wak-wak-wak,* etc., descending; also *kidick, kidick,* etc., and various "kicking" and grunting sounds. **RANGE:** S. Canada to s. S. America. Winters mainly from s. U.S. south. **HABITAT:** Mainly fresh and brackish marshes; in winter, also salt marshes.

KING RAIL *Rallus elegans*   Uncommon, secretive

M 129

15–19" (38–48 cm) A large, *rusty* rail with a long, slender bill; twice the size of a Virginia Rail, or about that of a small chicken. Similar to Clapper Rail but note *rusty/chestnut cheeks* and black and white flanks, more rusty overall with bolder back pattern; prefers fresh marshes. **SIMILAR SPECIES:** (1) Clapper Rail grayer with gray cheeks. (2) Virginia Rail is half the size and has slaty gray cheeks. *Note:* Hybrids between Clapper and King occur in coastal areas from N.J. to Mass. and along Gulf Coast. **VOICE:** A low, slow, grunting *bup-bup, bup-bup-bup,* etc., or *chuck-chuck-chuck* (deeper than Virginia Rail; not descending). **RANGE:** E. U.S., to Cuba, Mexico (rarely). Migrant from northern areas in winter. **HABITAT:** Fresh and brackish marshes, rice fields, swamps. In winter, also salt marshes.

CLAPPER RAIL *Rallus longirostris*   Common

M 128

14–16" (35–40 cm) The large gray-brown "marsh hen" of coastal marshes. Note chickenlike appearance, strong legs, long, slightly decurved bill, barred flanks, and white patch under short tail, which is usually cocked or flicked. Cheeks are gray. Clapper sometimes swims. **SIMILAR SPECIES:** King Rail prefers fresh (sometimes brackish) marshes and averages larger, has blacker stripes on back and flanks, *rusty brown* on wings. Its breast is cinnamon, but Clappers along Gulf Coast show similar warm tawny tones. Clapper has *grayer cheeks.* In fact, where these 2 rails occur in adjacent salt and fresh marshes, they occasionally hybridize. **VOICE:** A clattering *kek-kek-kek-kek,* etc., or *cha-cha-cha,* etc. **RANGE:** Coasts of e. U.S. and Calif. to n. S. America. **HABITAT:** Salt marshes, rarely brackish; locally in mangroves.

adult

immature

VIRGINIA RAIL

KING RAIL

chick

CLAPPER RAIL

Limpkin for comparison

SORA *Porzana carolina*   Common

M 131

8–9½" (20–24 cm) Note *short yellow* bill. *Adult:* A small plump gray-brown rail with a *black patch on face and throat* (which may be somewhat obscured in winter). The short cocked tail reveals white or buff undertail coverts. *Immature:* Buffy brown; lacks black throat patch. **SIMILAR SPECIES:** (1) Immature Sora may be confused with smaller and rarer Yellow Rail, which sports large white wing patches and blacker-centered feathers above. (2) Virginia Rail has a slender bill. **VOICE:** A descending whinny. In spring, a plaintive whistled *ker-wee?* When alarmed or surprised, a sharp *keek.* **HABITAT:** Fresh marshes, wet meadows; in winter, also salt marshes.

CORN CRAKE *Crex crex*   Extremely rare vagrant

9–10" (23–25 cm) From Europe; about 15 records. With population crash of this species in Europe, chances for sightings in N. America diminish. An upland field rail of the short-billed Sora type, but larger; *yellowish buff* with conspicuous *rufous* wings.

BLACK RAIL *Laterallus jamaicensis*   Scarce, local, secretive

M 127

5–6" (13–15 cm) A tiny *blackish* rail with small *black* bill; about the size of a bobtailed young sparrow. Nape deep chestnut. Very difficult to flush or glimpse, but may be attracted at night by judicious use of tape recording of its calls. **SIMILAR SPECIES:** *Caution:* All young rails in downy plumage are glossy black (but lack bars on flanks). **VOICE:** Male at night, *kiki-doo* (or *"kitty-go"*); *dee-dee-drrr.* **HABITAT:** Tidal marshes, *Salicornia* and *Spartina* (coast); grass marshes on coast and inland; fresh marshes (inland).

YELLOW RAIL *Coturnicops noveboracensis*   Scarce, local, secretive

M 126

7" (18 cm) Bold *white wing patch* (in flight). A small buffy rail, suggesting a week-old chicken. Bill very short, greenish. Back striped and checkered with buff and black. Mouselike; difficult to flush, but can be attracted at night by judicious use of a tape recording or tapping coins or pebbles together. **SIMILAR SPECIES:** Immature Sora is larger, not as buffy below; lacks wing patch. Note very different back pattern. **VOICE:** Nocturnal ticking notes, often in long series: *tic-tic, tic-tic-tic, tic-tic, tic-tic-tic,* etc. (groups of 2 and 3). Compared to hitting 2 small stones together. **HABITAT:** Grassy fresh marshes, meadows; wild-rice marshes in fall movement; in winter, also open grainfields, upland edges of salt marshes.

PAINT-BILLED CRAKE *Porzana erythrops*

7½" (19 cm) (South America) Virginia and Texas records.

SPOTTED RAIL *Pardirallus maculatus*

10" (25 cm) (Mexico) Pennsylvania and Texas records.

NORTHERN JACANA *Jacana spinosa* **FAMILY JACANIDAE**   Rare vagrant

9" (23 cm) Gallinule- or rail-like in appearance. Chestnut body with dark head. Spectacularly long toes for walking on lily pads. Yellow bill and forehead frontal shield. Striking yellow of wing primaries and secondaries when it flies. Holds wings over head when it lands. Immature with white underparts, distinct line behind eye. **RANGE:** Mexico. Rarely wanders into s. Tex. Frequents ponds with emergent vegetation.

SHORT-BILLED RAILS

SORA
adult
chick
immature
SORA
SORA

BLACK RAIL

CORN CRAKE
(accidental)

YELLOW RAIL

PAINT-BILLED
CRAKE

NORTHERN
JACANA

SPOTTED
RAIL

PLOVERS. Family Charadriidae.

Wading birds, more compactly built, thicker-necked than most sand-pipers, with shorter bills and larger eyes. Call notes assist identification. Unlike most sandpipers, plovers run in short starts and stops. Sexes alike. **FOOD:** Small marine life, insects, some vegetable matter. **RANGE:** Nearly worldwide. **NO. OF SPECIES:** World, 66; East, 8 (+ 4 accidental).

BLACK-BELLIED PLOVER *Pluvialis squatarola*   Common

M 137

10½–13½" (26–34 cm) A large plover; in breeding plumage with *black face, chest, and underbelly.* Pale gray speckled back. Winter birds and immatures are gray and lack black underparts. Many birds seen in transition patterns. In flight in any plumage, note *black axillars* ("wingpits") and white rump and tail. Recognized as a plover by stocky shape, hunched posture, short pigeonlike bill and hesitant walk-then-pause movement. **SIMILAR SPECIES:** American Golden-Plover browner, lacks black axillars and lacks white in wing and rump. **VOICE:** A plaintive slurred whistle, *pee-ooo-wheee* or *tlee-oo-eee* (middle note lower). **HABITAT:** Mudflats, open marshes, beaches; in summer, tundra.

AMERICAN GOLDEN-PLOVER *Pluvialis dominica*   Scarce in East

M 138

9½–11" (24–28 cm) Size of a Killdeer. Breeding adults are *golden brown with golden spots* above; *underparts black.* A broad *white stripe* runs from over eye, down side of neck to shoulder. Young birds and winter adults are gray-brown tinged with golden, darker above than below, with a distinct capped appearance. In flight, *underwing dusky and no white rump.* **SIMILAR SPECIES:** (1) Black-bellied Plover (see above). (2) European Golden-Plover in breeding plumage has white extending down side of body along folded wing. White extensive on breast sides (see next account). Underwing white. **VOICE:** A whistled *queed-leee* dropping at the end. **HABITAT:** Prairies, mudflats, shores, turf farms; in summer, nests on tundra.

EUROPEAN GOLDEN-PLOVER *Pluvialis apricaria*   Casual vagrant

11" (28 cm) A very similar species to American Golden-Plover except larger. Breeding adults with golden brown upperparts with small golden spots. White extends from eye down neck onto sides to rear. *White on breast sides extensive,* causing black of underbelly to taper into a narrow line. *Underwings pale to almost white.* No white rump. Young and winter adults lack dark underbelly. **SIMILAR SPECIES:** See comparisons with two species above. **VOICE:** Melodic drawn-out whistle. **RANGE:** Breeds in Iceland and Greenland. **EAST:** Casual spring vagrant to Nfld. More numerous sightings in recent years.

MOUNTAIN PLOVER *Charadrius montanus*   Scarce and restricted

8–9½" (20–24 cm) White forehead and line over eye, contrasting with dark crown. Winter plumage may be told from winter golden-plovers by its tan-brown back devoid of mottling and its tan, unmarked breast. Has pale blue-gray legs, a light wing stripe, and a dark tail-band. **VOICE:** A low whistle, variable. **HABITAT:** Plowed fields and short-grass plains to just east of 100° w. **RANGE:** Winters in s. Tex. Summers in plains from Tex. panhandle to Mont.

PLOVERS

winter

breeding

immature

BLACK-BELLIED
PLOVER

breeding

winter

AMERICAN
GOLDEN-PLOVER

breeding

winter

MOUNTAIN
PLOVER

breeding

winter

EUROPEAN
GOLDEN-PLOVER

SEMIPALMATED PLOVER *Charadrius semipalmatus* Common

M 141

6½–7½" (1 6–1 9 cm) A plump, brown-backed plover, half the size of a Killdeer, with a *single dark breast-band*. Bill yellow to orange-yellow with black tip, or (in winter) all-dark. Legs orange or yellow. **SIMILAR SPECIES:** Piping Plover is pale, the color of dry sand. (Semipalmated is darker, like wet sand or mud.) **VOICE:** A plaintive upward-slurred *chi-we* or *too-li*. **RANGE:** Arctic America. Winters from Virginia and the Carolinas to S. America. **HABITAT:** Shores, tideflats; nests on tundra.

COMMON RINGED-PLOVER *Charadrius hiaticula* Casual vagrant

7" (1 9 cm) Very similar to Semipalmated Plover, replacing it in Greenland and n. Baffin, Devon, and Ellesmere Is. Migrates to Europe. Best distinguished by flutelike *pooo-lee* call. Distinguished in hand by lack of basal webs between inner and middle toes. Black near eyes, over bill, and breast-band is wider than in Semipalmated, bill slightly thinner.

PIPING PLOVER *Charadrius melodus* Scarce

M 142

6–7½" (1 5–1 9 cm) As pallid as a sand crab, the *color of dry sand*. A complete or incomplete dark ring around neck. Legs yellow; bill yellow with a black tip. In winter, bill dark, legs pale. Performs stiff-winged "bat-flight" on breeding territory. **VOICE:** A plaintive whistle; *peep-lo* (first note higher). **RANGE:** S. Canada to ne. and cen. U.S. Winters southern U.S. coasts south to Mexican Gulf Coast. Federally endangered. **HABITAT:** Sand beaches, cobble and shell areas, tidal flats.

SNOWY PLOVER *Charadrius alexandrinus* Uncommon

M 139

6½" (1 6 cm) A pale plover of the Gulf Coast and southern plains. Similar to Piping Plover, but with a *slim black bill, dark legs,* and a *dark ear patch*. **SIMILAR SPECIES:** Immature and winter-plumaged adult Piping Plovers may have dark bills, but they have *white rumps* and yellowish legs whereas immature Snowy has brownish rump and grayish legs. **VOICE:** A musical whistle; *pe-wee-ah* or *o-wee-ah*. **RANGE:** Local on western and southern U.S. coast and inland U.S. south to northern Venezuela and through West Indies. Eurasia (called Kentish Plover), Africa, Australia, etc. **HABITAT:** Beaches, sand flats.

WILSON'S PLOVER *Charadrius wilsonia* Uncommon

M 140

7–8" (1 8–2 0 cm) A "ringed" plover, larger than Semipalmated, with a wider breast-band and a longer and *heavier black bill*. Legs flesh-gray. **VOICE:** An emphatic whistled *whit!* or *wheet!* **RANGE:** Va. to n. S. America. **HABITAT:** Open beaches, tidal flats, sandy islands.

KILLDEER *Charadrius vociferus* Common

M 143

9–1 1 " (2 3–2 8 cm) The common noisy breeding plover of the farm country. Note the 2 *black breast-bands* (chick has 1 band). In flight, displays a *golden orange rump,* longish tail, white wing stripe. **VOICE:** Noisy; a loud insistent *kill-deeah* or *killdeer*, repeated; a plaintive *dee-ee* (rising); *dee-dee-dee,* etc. Also a low trill. **RANGE:** Canada to cen. Mexico, W. Indies; also coastal Peru. Migrant in the North. **HABITAT:** Fields, airports, lawns, river banks, shores; will nest on flat roofs.

BELTED PLOVERS

COMMON RINGED-PLOVER

SEMIPALMATED PLOVER

winter

breeding

PIPING PLOVER

belted form

breeding

winter

immature ♀

♂

SNOWY PLOVER

♂

WILSON'S PLOVER

KILLDEER

chick

Common Ringed-

Piping

Snowy

Semipalmated

Wilson's

Killdeer

Learn the distinctive flight calls.

PIPING PLOVER *Charadrius melodus*   PP. 134–135
Pale sand color, wide black tail spot, *whitish rump*.
Note, a plaintive whistle; *peep-lo* (first note higher).

SNOWY PLOVER *Charadrius alexandrinus*   PP. 134–135
Pale sand color; tail with a dark center, white sides; *rump not white*.
Note, a musical whistle; *pe-wee-ah* or *o-wee-ah*.

SEMIPALMATED PLOVER *Charadrius semipalmatus*   PP. 134–135
Mud brown; dark tail with white borders.
Note, a plaintive upward-slurred *chi-we* or *too-li*.

WILSON'S PLOVER *Charadrius wilsonia*   PP. 134–135
Similar in pattern to Semipalmated; larger with a *big bill*.
Different note; an emphatic whistled *whit!* or *wheet!*

KILLDEER *Charadrius vociferus*   PP. 134–135
Tawny-orange rump, longish tail.
Noisy; a loud *kill-deeah* or *killdeer*; also *dee-dee-dee,* etc.

BLACK-BELLIED PLOVER *Pluvialis squatarola*   PP. 132–133
Spring: Black below, *white* undertail coverts. Pattern above as in fall.
Fall: Black axillars ("wingpits"), white in wing and tail.
Note, a plaintive slurred whistle, *pee-ooo-wheee* or *tlee-oo-eee*.

AMERICAN GOLDEN-PLOVER *Pluvialis dominica*   PP. 132–133
Spring: Black below, *black* undertail coverts. Pattern above as in fall.
Fall: Speckled brown above and grayish below; underwing grayer than
Black-bellied's; *no black in axillars*.
Call, a querulous whistled *queed-leee*.

RUDDY TURNSTONE *Arenaria interpres*   PP. 150–151
Harlequin pattern in breeding plumage is distinctive.
Call, a low chuckling *tuk-a-tuk* or *kut-a-kut*.

PLOVERS AND TURNSTONE
in flight

PIPING
PLOVER

SNOWY
PLOVER

KILLDEER

SEMIPALMATED
PLOVER

WILSON'S
PLOVER

breeding

winter

winter

BLACK-
BELLIED
PLOVER

BLACK-
BELLIED
PLOVER

winter

winter

breeding

AMERICAN
GOLDEN-
PLOVER

AMERICAN
GOLDEN-
PLOVER

RUDDY
TURNSTONE

breeding

The shorebirds (or "waders") are often real puzzlers to the novice. There are a dozen plovers possible in the U.S. and nearly 60 sandpipers and their allies, not to mention the very obvious oystercatchers, stilts, and avocets. To start with, here are a few things to look for:

PLOVERS VS. SANDPIPERS

Plovers are usually more compact and thicker-necked than most sandpipers, with pigeonlike bills and larger eyes. They run in short starts and stops.

Plover

Sandpiper

BILL SHAPES OF SHOREBIRDS
SOME BASIC BODY SHAPES AND ACTIONS OF SANDPIPERS

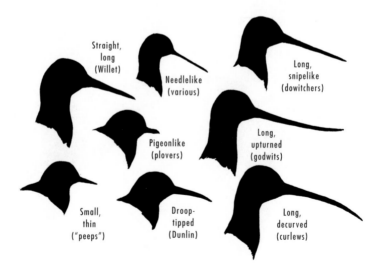

Straight, long (Willet)

Needlelike (various)

Long, snipelike (dowitchers)

Pigeonlike (plovers)

Long, upturned (godwits)

Small, thin ("peeps")

Droop-tipped (Dunlin)

Long, decurved (curlews)

Sanderlings run.

If it swims, and spins, it is a phalarope.

Does it teeter like a Spotted Sandpiper?

Or does it nod like a Solitary?

Is it slim like a yellowlegs?

Or is it squat like a turnstone?

Does it probe with a sewing-machine motion like a dowitcher?

AMERICAN WOODCOCK *Scolopax minor* — Fairly common

M 173

11" (28 cm) Near size of Northern Bobwhite, with an extremely long bill and large bulging eyes placed high on head. Rotund, almost neck-less, with a leaflike camouflage pattern, *broadly barred crown*. When flushed from a thicket, rises vertically, producing a whistling sound with wings. **VOICE:** At dusk in spring, a nasal *beezp* (suggesting nighthawk). Aerial "song," a chipping trill made by wings as bird ascends, changing to a bubbling twittering on descent. **RANGE:** Se. Canada to Gulf states. Winters mainly in se. U.S., depending on severity of winter. **HABITAT:** Wet thickets, moist woods, brushy swamps. Nocturnal display high over semi-open fields, pastures.

COMMON SNIPE *Gallinago gallinago* — Fairly common

M 172

11" (28 cm) A tight-sitting bog wader; brown with *buff stripes on back, striped head, extremely long bill*. Flies off in a *zigzag pattern* when flushed, showing a *short orange tail*. **VOICE:** A rasping *scaip* when flushed. Song, a measured *chip-a, chip-a, chip-a*, etc. In aerial display, a winnowing *woowoowoowoooo* made by fanning tail. **RANGE:** N. N. America, n. Eurasia. Winters to Brazil, cen. Africa. **HABITAT:** Marshes, bogs, springs, wet meadows.

SHORT-BILLED DOWITCHER *Limnodromus griseus* — Common

M 170

10½–12" (26–30 cm) A snipelike bird of open *mudflats*. Note very long bill and *long white wedge* up the back. In breeding plumage, under-parts are orange with some barring on flanks. Underbelly in Atlantic subspecies shows some white, which helps separate from lookalike Long-billed Dowitcher. Bill length is not a dependable separation. By fall, adult is gray. Face, neck, and underparts more speckled and mottled than in Long-billed. Underparts more extensive white and spotted on flanks (barred in Long-billed). Juveniles with orange-edged feath-ers above and on chest. Also note distinct tiger-striped tertials of juve-nile Short-billed compared to mainly gray color in juvenile Long-billed. Many birds best separated by voice. Dowitchers feed with a sewing-machine motion. **VOICE:** A staccato *tu-tu-tu*; pitch of Lesser Yel-lowlegs. **RANGE:** S. Alaska, Canada. Winters s. U.S. to Brazil. **HABITAT:** Mudflats, tidal marshes, infrequently pond edges.

LONG-BILLED DOWITCHER *Limnodromus scolopaceus* — Fairly common

M 171

11–12½" (28–31 cm) Bill lengths of the 2 dowitcher species overlap, but many Long-billed with very long bills (3") usually females, may be recognized by bill length. In breeding plumage, underparts *reddish to lower belly*, dark bars on tail broader, giving tail a *dark look*. Sides of breast *barred* rather than spotted (see comparison above with Short-billed Dowitcher and for juveniles). Adults in winter more uniform gray with barred sides. Often, best clue is voice. **VOICE:** A single sharp *keek*, occasionally doubled or trebled but higher pitched than Short-bill's notes. **RANGE:** Ne. Siberia to nw. Canada. Winters s. U.S. to Guatemala. **HABITAT:** Mudflats, shallow pools, freshwater ponds, and lake margins. More partial to fresh water than is Short-bill. Tends to be a later fall migrant than Short-billed Dowitcher.

SNIPE-LIKE WADERS

AMERICAN
WOODCOCK

COMMON
SNIPE

juvenile

juvenile

SHORT-
BILLED
DOWITCHER

winter

breeding

snipe

juvenile

winter

LONG-
BILLED
DOWITCHER

breeding

dowitcher
probing

HUDSONIAN GODWIT *Limosa haemastica* — Scarce

M 155

13–16" (33–40 cm) Note pattern in flight. Rather large size and long *slightly upturned* bill mark this wader as a godwit; black tail, *ringed broadly with white,* proclaims it this species. Underwing is *blackish,* separating it from vagrant Black-tailed Godwit, which has white underwings. In spring, male is ruddy-breasted, female duller; in fall, they are gray-backed, pale breasted. **VOICE:** *Tawit!* (or *godwit!*); higher pitched than Marbled's. **RANGE:** Mainly arctic Canada; winters in S. America. Migrates through Great Plains in spring, Atlantic Coast in fall. **HABITAT:** Tidal mudflats, prairie pools; tundra in summer.

MARBLED GODWIT *Limosa fedoa* — Uncommon in East

M 156

16–20" (40–50 cm) Godwits are large shorebirds with very long, *slightly upturned* bills. Rich mottled *buff-brown* color identifies this species. Linings of raised wing are *cinnamon.* **SIMILAR SPECIES:** Hudsonian Godwit has white on wings and tail. **VOICE:** An accented *kerwhit!* (*godwit!*); also *raddica, raddica.* **RANGE:** N. Great Plains. Winters s. U.S. to n. S. America. **HABITAT:** Prairies, pools, shores; tideflats.

LONG-BILLED CURLEW *Numenius americanus* — Rare in East

M 154

20–26" (50–65 cm) Note *very long sickle-tipped bill* (4–8½ in.; 10–21 cm). Much larger than Whimbrel, more buffy; *lacks* bold crown stripes. Overhead, shows *cinnamon wing linings.* In young birds, bill may be scarcely longer than that of Whimbrel. **VOICE:** A loud *cur-lee* (rising inflection); a rapid, whistled *kil-li-li-li.* "Song," a trilled, liquid *curleeeeeeeeeuuu.* **RANGE:** Sw. Canada, w. U.S. Winters s. U.S. to Guatemala. **HABITAT:** High plains, rangeland. In winter, also cultivated land, airports, tideflats, beaches, salt marshes.

ESKIMO CURLEW *Numenius borealis* — Probably extinct

12–14" (30–35 cm) Last documented record in early 1960s. Much smaller than Whimbrel. Bill shorter, thinner, *only slightly curved.* More patterned above than Whimbrel, more like Long-billed Curlew, strong buff interspersed with black. Linings of raised wing, *cinnamon-buff* with unbarred primaries. Legs slate gray. **SIMILAR SPECIES:** See (1) Whimbrel, below; (2) Long-billed Curlew, above; (3) Upland Sandpiper, p. 154. **VOICE:** Call has been variously described as *tee-dee-dee* or a repeated *tee-dee* or a note suggestive of Common Tern. **RANGE:** Formerly arctic America. Wintering in s. S. America. Migrated along East Coast in fall, through Great Plains in spring. Last sight records from Tex. coast.

WHIMBREL *Numenius phaeopus* — Fairly common

M 153

15–19" (38–48 cm) A large gray-brown wader with a long *decurved bill.* Grayer than Long-billed Curlew; bill shorter (2½–4 in.; 6–10 cm), crown *striped.* European race (*N. p. phaeopus*) a vagrant to the East Coast, shows white rump and underwings. **VOICE:** Five to 7 short rapid whistles: *to-to-to-to-to.* **RANGE:** Arctic; circumpolar. Winters s. U.S. to s. S. America. **HABITAT:** Beaches, mudflats, marshes; in summer, tundra.

LARGE SANDPIPERS

breeding

winter

HUDSONIAN
GODWIT

winter

♂ breeding

MARBLED
GODWIT

LONG-
BILLED
CURLEW

underwing

ESKIMO
CURLEW

WHIMBREL

Learn to know their flight calls, which are diagnostic.

HUDSONIAN GODWIT *Limosa haemastica*   PP. 142–143
Upturned bill, white wing stripe, ringed tail.
Overhead, shows blackish wing linings.
Flight call, tawit!, higher-pitched than Marbled Godwit's call.

WILLET *Catoptrophorus semipalmatus*   PP. 148–149
Contrasty black, gray, and white wing pattern.
Overhead, wing pattern is even more striking.
Flight call, a whistled *whee-wee-wee,* or *pill-will-willet.*

MARBLED GODWIT *Limosa fedoa*   PP. 142–143
Long upturned bill, tawny brown color.
Overhead, shows cinnamon wing linings.
Flight call, an accented *kerwhit!* (or *godwit!).*

WHIMBREL *Numenius phaeopus*   PP. 142–143
Decurved bill, gray-brown color, striped crown.
Overhead, grayer than next species; lacks cinnamon wing linings.
Flight call, 5–7 short rapid whistles: *to-to-to-to-to.*

LONG-BILLED CURLEW *Numenius americanus*   PP. 142–143
Very long, sicklelike bill; no head striping.
Overhead, shows bright cinnamon wing linings.
Flight call, a rapid, whistled *cur-lee.*

WADERS IN
FLIGHT

HUDSONIAN
GODWIT

breeding

WILLET
winter

winter

HUDSONIAN
GODWIT

MARBLED
GODWIT

WHIMBREL

bill of juvenile
Long-bill

LONG-BILLED
CURLEW

OYSTERCATCHERS. Family Haematopodidae.

Large waders with long, laterally flattened, chisel-tipped, red bills. Sexes alike. **FOOD:** Mollusks, crabs, marine worms. **RANGE:** Widespread on coasts of world; inland in some areas of Europe and Asia. **NO. OF SPECIES:** World, 11; East, 1.

AMERICAN OYSTERCATCHER *Haematopus palliatus*　　　　Fairly common

M 144

17–21" (43–53 cm) A very noisy, thick-set, black-headed shorebird with a dark back, white belly, large white wing and tail patches. The outstanding feature is the *large straight red bill*, flattened laterally. Legs pale pink. **SIMILAR SPECIES:** See Black Skimmer, pp. 190–191. **VOICE:** A piercing *wheep!* or *kleep!*; a loud *pic, pic, pic.* **RANGE:** Isolated sites in N.S. and Me., then shores of Cape Cod south to Chile and Argentina. **HABITAT:** Coastal beaches, tidal flats.

AVOCETS AND STILTS. Family Recurvirostridae.

Slim waders with very long legs and very slender bills (curved upward in avocets). Sexes alike. **FOOD:** Insects, crustaceans, other aquatic life. **RANGE:** U.S., Cen. and S. America, Africa, s. Eurasia, Australia, Pacific region. **NO. OF SPECIES:** World, 10; East, 2.

BLACK-NECKED STILT *Himantopus mexicanus*　　　　Fairly common

M 145

13–17" (33–43 cm) A tall, extremely slim wader; black above, white below. Note *exceptionally long pink legs,* needlelike bill. In flight, it has black *unpatterned* wings, which contrast with white rump, tail, and underparts. **VOICE:** A sharp yipping *kyip, kyip, kyip.* **RANGE:** W. and se. U.S. to Peru. Winters mainly south of U.S. **HABITAT:** Grassy marshes, mudflats, pools, shallow lakes (fresh or alkaline).

AMERICAN AVOCET *Recurvirostra americana*　　　Common; rare in Northeast

M 146

16–20" (40–50 cm) A large slim shorebird with a very slender, *up-turned,* somewhat godwitlike bill. This and striking white-and-black pattern make it unique. In breeding plumage, *head and neck are pinkish tan*; in winter, this color is replaced with pale gray. Avocets feed with a scythelike sweep of head and bill. **VOICE:** A sharp *wheek* or *kleet,* excitedly repeated. **RANGE:** Breeds sw. Canada, w. U.S. Winters from s. U.S. to Guatemala. **HABITAT:** Marshes, flats, shallow lakes, prairie ponds.

OYSTERCATCHER, STILT, AVOCET

AMERICAN
OYSTERCATCHER

BLACK-NECKED STILT

breeding

breeding

winter

AMERICAN AVOCET

SANDPIPERS. Family Scolopacidae (in part) see p. 150.

WILLET *Catoptrophorus semipalmatus* — Fairly common

M 150

14–17" (35–43 cm) Stockier than Greater Yellowlegs; has a grayer look, heavier bill, bluish gray legs. In flight, note *striking black-and-white wing pattern.* At rest, when banded wings cannot be seen, this large wader is nondescript; gray above, somewhat barred below in summer, unmarked below in fall and winter. *Note:* Western breeding population differs from Eastern breeding population in being larger, longer billed, and paler in overall color. **VOICE:** In breeding season, a ringing repetitious *pill-will-willit.* Also a loud *kay-ee* (second note lower) and a rapidly repeated *kip-kip-kip,* etc. In flight, *whee-wee-wee.* **RANGE:** Cen.-s. Canada to Gulf of Mexico, W. Indies. Winters from s. U.S. to Brazil. **HABITAT:** Marshes, wet meadows, mudflats, beaches.

GREATER YELLOWLEGS *Tringa melanoleuca* — Common

M 147

14" (35 cm) Note *bright yellow legs* (shared with next species, but leg joints thicker). A slim gray sandpiper; back checkered with gray, black, and white. Flying, it appears *dark-winged* (no stripe) with a *whitish rump and tail.* Bill is long and slightly upturned, paler at base. **VOICE:** A 3-note whistle, *whew-whew-whew,* or *dear! dear! dear!* **RANGE:** Alaska, Canada. Winters U.S. to Tierra del Fuego. **HABITAT:** Open marshes, mudflats, streams, ponds; in summer, wooded muskeg, spruce bogs.

LESSER YELLOWLEGS *Tringa flavipes* — Common

M 148

10–11" (25–28 cm) Like Greater Yellowlegs but noticeably smaller when seen in direct comparison. Its shorter, slimmer, all-black bill is straight; that of Greater often appears slightly upturned. Readily identified by voice. **SIMILAR SPECIES:** (1) Stilt Sandpiper and (2) Wilson's Phalarope (fall) have flight patterns similar to that of a yellowlegs. **VOICE:** *Yew* or *yu-yu* (usually 1 or 2 notes); softer, less forceful than clear 3-note whistle *whew-whew-whew* of Greater Yellowlegs. **RANGE:** Alaska, Canada. Winters from s. U.S. to Argentina. **HABITAT:** Marshes, mudflats, shores, pond edges; in summer, wet areas of open boreal woods.

SOLITARY SANDPIPER *Tringa solitaria* — Uncommon

M 149

8–9" (20–23 cm) Note dark wings and conspicuous *white sides of tail* (crossed by bold black bars). A dark-backed sandpiper, whitish below, with a *white eye-ring* and *greenish legs.* Bobs nervously as it walks. Usually feeds alone rather than in groups. **SIMILAR SPECIES:** (1) Lesser Yellowlegs has yellow (not greenish) legs and a white (not dark) rump. (2) Spotted Sandpiper teeters more; has a white wing stripe; has a stiff, shallow wing arc in flight. Solitary, a darting, almost swallowlike wing stroke. **VOICE:** *Peet!* or *peet-wee-weet!* (higher than Spotted's call). **RANGE:** Alaska, Canada. Winters Gulf of Mexico to Argentina. **HABITAT:** Streamsides, wooded swamps and ponds, fresh marshes.

STILT SANDPIPER *Calidris himantopus* — SEE P. 154

FALL: Droop-tipped bill, long yellow-green legs, white rump, light eyebrow stripe.

WILSON'S PHALAROPE *Phalaropus tricolor* — SEE P. 164

FALL: Needle bill, clear white underparts, dull yellow legs.

SANDPIPERS

breeding

winter

WILLET

LESSER YELLOWLEGS

GREATER YELLOWLEGS

SOLITARY
SANDPIPER

STILT
SANDPIPER

winter

WILSON'S
PHALAROPE

winter

SANDPIPERS, PHALAROPES. Family Scolopacidae.

Small to medium-sized waders. Bills more slender than those of plovers. Sexes similar, except in phalaropes (swimmers that were formerly regarded as a separate family). **FOOD:** Insects, crustaceans, mollusks, worms, etc. **RANGE:** Cosmopolitan. **NO. OF SPECIES:** World, 87; East, 31 (+ 14 accidental).

RUDDY TURNSTONE *Arenaria interpres*   Common

M 157

8–10" (20–25 cm) A squat, robust, *orange-legged* shorebird with a *harlequin pattern*. In breeding plumage, with its russet back and curious face and breast pattern, the bird is unique; in flight it is equally striking. Winter adults and young birds are duller, but retain enough of the basic pattern to be recognized. **VOICE:** A staccato *tuk-a-tuk* or *kut-a-kut*; also a single *kewk*. **RANGE:** Arctic, sub-Arctic; circumpolar. Winter coastal U.S., Hawaii, s. Eurasia to S. Hemisphere. **HABITAT:** Beaches, mudflats, jetties, rocky shores; in summer, tundra.

PURPLE SANDPIPER *Calidris maritima*   Uncommon

M 166

8–9" (20–23 cm) Stocky, dark sandpipers on rocks, jetties, or breakwaters along our northern Atlantic coasts in winter are likely to be this hardy species. Slate gray to brown with a white belly. At close range, note short yellow-orange legs, yellowish base of bill, and white eye-ring. In summer, the bird is much browner, more heavily streaked above and below with purplish sheen to some back feathers. **SIMILAR SPECIES:** See winter Dunlin, which differs in having a black bill and black legs. **VOICE:** A low *weet-wit* or *twit*. **RANGE:** E. Arctic, Greenland, Iceland; winters along East Coast, occasionally on Great Lakes and to Gulf Coast. **HABITAT:** Wave-washed rocks, jetties, rare on sandy shoreline (often quite tame). Coastal tundra on breeding grounds.

RED KNOT *Calidris canutus*   Uncommon

M 158

10–11" (25–28 cm) Larger than Sanderling (p. 152). Stocky, with medium-length bill and short legs. *Breeding:* Face and underparts *pale robin red*; back mottled with black, gray, and russet. *Fall:* A stocky wader with a washed-out gray look; medium-length bill, pale rump, greenish legs. Juvenile bird at close range shows *conspicuous scaly feather edgings* on back. **VOICE:** A low *knut*; also a low, mellow *tooit-wit* or *wah-quoit*. **RANGE:** Arctic; circumpolar. Winters to S. Hemisphere. A well-studied species that has very specific stopping spots for feeding and staging during migration. **HABITAT:** Sandy beaches, mudflats, tidal flats and shores; breeds on tundra.

SANDPIPERS

winter

breeding

RUDDY
TURNSTONE

PURPLE
SANDPIPER

winter

breeding

winter

juvenile

winter

breeding

RED KNOT

SPOTTED SANDPIPER *Actitis macularia* Common

M 151

7½" (19 cm) Most widespread sandpiper along shores of small lakes and streams. Teeters up and down as if a bit too delicately balanced. In breeding plumage, note *round breast spots.* In winter plumage, no spots; brown above with a white line over eye. A *dusky smudge* on each side of breast enclosing a *white wedge* near shoulder is a good mark. Flight is distinctive: Wings beat in a *shallow arc,* giving a stiff, bowed appearance. Underwing shows a bold wing stripe. **VOICE:** A clear *peet* or *peet-weet!* or *peet-weet-weet-weet!* **RANGE:** Alaska, Canada south to northern half of U.S. Winters from s. U.S. to n. Argentina. **HABITAT:** Lakeshores, ponds, streamsides, marshes; also rock jetties.

DUNLIN *Calidris alpina* Common

M 167

8–9" (20–23 cm) Slightly larger than Sanderling, with a *downward droop* toward tip of its rather long bill. When it feeds, posture is hunched. *Breeding plumage: Rusty red above,* with *black patch across belly. Winter plumage:* Unpatterned gray-brown above, with a grayish wash across breast (not clean white as in Sanderling or Western Sandpiper). Juvenile is rusty above, with a buffy breast and streaked flanks. In all plumages, note longish droop-tipped bill. **VOICE:** A nasal, rasping *cheezp* or *treezp.* **RANGE:** Arctic; circumpolar. Winters from coasts of U.S., s. Eurasia to Mexico, n. Africa, India. **HABITAT:** Tidal flats, beaches, muddy pools, breakwaters; in summer, wet tundra.

CURLEW SANDPIPER *Calidris ferruginea* Very rare visitor

7–9" (18–23 cm) In breeding plumage, *rich rufous red,* with slim *downcurved bill, blackish legs, white rump* in flight. *Winter plumage:* Very similar to Stilt Sandpiper because of bill shape and white rump, but longer-legged, less streaked and bill curves downward throughout its length. Curved bill plus white rump in flight clinches identification. **VOICE:** A liquid *chirrip,* less grating than a Dunlin. **RANGE:** E. arctic, Asia. Migrant to Africa. Straggler to e. N. America. **HABITAT:** Tidal flats, muddy pools, mudflats.

SANDERLING *Calidris alba* Common

M 159

7–8" (18–20 cm) A plump active sandpiper of the outer beaches, where it chases retreating waves like a wind-up toy. Note bold *white wing stripe* in flight. *Breeding plumage:* Bright rusty about head, back, and breast. *Winter plumage:* Palest sandpiper; *chalk white* below, plain gray back, *black shoulders.* Juvenile bird differs from winter adult by having a strong pattern of black flecking on back. **VOICE:** A short *twick* or *quit* is distinctive. **RANGE:** Arctic; circumpolar. Winters from U.S., Britain, China to S. Hemisphere. **HABITAT:** Outer beaches, tidal flats; uncommon on lakeshores. Nests on stone-covered tundra.

SANDPIPERS

winter

breeding

SPOTTED SANDPIPER

winter

CURLEW
SANDPIPER

breeding

winter

DUNLIN   juvenile

breeding

juvenile
winter

adult
winter

breeding   SANDERLING

STILT SANDPIPER *Calidris himantopus*   Uncommon

M 168

8" (20 cm) In spring, heavily marked below with *transverse bars*. Note *rusty cheek-patch*. In fall, similar to yellowlegs, with which it often associates. Gray above, white below; dark winged and white rumped; note *greenish legs* and *white eyebrow stripe*. Bill long, with slight droop at the tip. Feeds like dowitcher with a sewing-machine motion. **VOICE:** A single *whu* (like Lesser Yellowlegs but lower, hoarser). **RANGE:** N. American Arctic. Winters s. U.S. to Argentina. **HABITAT:** Shallow pools, mudflats, marshes; tundra in summer.

BUFF-BREASTED SANDPIPER *Tryngites subruficollis*   Scarce

M 169

7½" (19 cm) No other shorebird is as buff below (paling to whitish on undertail coverts). A tame, buffy wader, with an erect stance, small head, short bill, and yellowish legs. Dark eye stands out on a plain face. In flight or in "display," buffy body contrasts with underwing, which is *white* with a *marbled tip. Juveniles are very scaly above,* pale on belly. **VOICE:** A low, trilled *pr-r-r-eet,* a sharp *tik.* **RANGE:** Breeds in nw. Arctic. Winters in Argentina. Migrant mainly through cen. U.S. in spring and fall. Scattered birds (usually juveniles) on coast in fall. **HABITAT:** Short-grass prairies, fresh-cut fields, airports, sod farms, shoreline; in summer, tundra.

UPLAND SANDPIPER *Bartramia longicauda*   Uncommon to scarce

M 152

11½" (29 cm) A brown "pigeon-headed" sandpiper; larger than a Killdeer. Short bill, *small head*, large eyes, thin neck, and long tail are helpful marks. *Erect posture.* On nesting grounds, often perches on fence posts or poles, holding wings elevated upon alighting. **VOICE:** A mellow liquid *quidi-quit.* Song a tremulous cascade of yodeling whistles: *whoooleeee, wheeeloooooooo.* **RANGE:** Mainly Canada and n.-cen. and e. U.S. Winters on pampas of Argentina. **HABITAT:** Mid- and tallgrass prairies, open meadows, fields, airports, and freshly mowed or plowed fields. Declining.

RUFF *Philomachus pugnax*   Very rare visitor

Male (Ruff) 12" (30 cm); female (Reeve) 9" (23 cm) *Male, spring and summer:* Unique with *erectile neck ruff* and *ear tufts* that may be black, brown, rufous, buff, white, or barred or various combinations. Often seen either lacking ruff or only in partial ruff plumage. Legs may be greenish, yellow, or orangish. In molt, dabbled spotting on underparts and around head. *Female:* Lacks ruff and variable in dappling below. Both show a bull-necked appearance, upright posture, and small head. Bill usually dark with a pale yellowish brown base. Often runs about, then pauses in erect stance. In flight, distinct *oval white patch* on each side of tail. Winter birds pale, scaly brown back and breast, and plain face. **VOICE:** Usually silent when not on breeding grounds but when flushed gives a *too-i* or *tu-whit* call. **RANGE:** N. Eurasia; winters in s. Eurasia and Africa. **EAST:** Scattered records throughout eastern portion of U.S. with regular occurrence along Atlantic Seaboard.

SANDPIPERS

juvenile

winter

breeding

STILT
SANDPIPER

UPLAND
SANDPIPER

BUFF-BREASTED
SANDPIPER

winter ♀
("Reeve")

winter ♂
("Ruff")

breeding
dress of ♂
variable

♂

RUFF

♀ ("Reeve")

♂

♂

WHITE-RUMPED SANDPIPER *Calidris fuscicollis* Uncommon

M 163

7–8" (18–20 cm) Larger than Semipalmated Sandpiper, smaller than Pectoral. The only small streaked sandpiper with a completely *white rump*, conspicuous in flight. In spring, adult may be quite rusty; in fall, grayer than other "peeps." Long wings extend beyond tail end at rest and, in adults, side shows distinct *triangular marks* below folded wing down to flank. **SIMILAR SPECIES:** Adult Baird's lacks flank marks. Juvenile and fall-plumaged White-rumps tend to be grayer and with more distinct supercilium than Baird's. In flight, white rump quickly separates the two. **VOICE:** A high, thin mouselike *jeet* or *tink* like striking two quarters together. **RANGE:** N. American Arctic. Winters in s. S. America. **HABITAT:** Prairies, shores, mudflats; tundra in summer.

BAIRD'S SANDPIPER *Calidris bairdii* Scarce in East

M 164

7–7½" (18–19 cm) Larger than Semipalmated or Western with a more *elongated look*. Note crossed wingtips extend a good ½ in. *beyond tail tip*. Browner, buffier across breast. Suggests a large Least Sandpiper with long wings and black legs. Back of immature has *scaled* appearance. **VOICE:** A low *kreep* or *kreee*, a rolling trill. **RANGE:** Ne. Siberia and N. American Arctic. Migrates largely through Plains, a few to East Coast in fall. Winters in w. and s. S. America. **HABITAT:** Rainpools, pond margins, mudflats, shorelines.

PECTORAL SANDPIPER *Calidris melanotos* Fairly common

M 165

8–9" (20–23 cm) Note heavy breast streaks *ending abruptly*, like a corduroy bib. Medium-sized. Neck longer than in smaller "peeps." Dark back is *lined* snipelike with white; wing stripe faint or lacking; crown rusty. Legs and bill base dull yellow. **VOICE:** A reedy *krik, krik* or *trrip-tr-rip*. **RANGE:** Ne. Siberia, N. American Arctic. **HABITAT:** In migration, grassy pools, muddy shores, fresh and tidal marshes. In summer, tundra.

SHARP-TAILED SANDPIPER *Calidris acuminata* Casual vagrant

8½" (21 cm) Similar to Pectoral Sandpiper, but in fall the breast is rich buff (juvenile) or pale gray-buff (adult), spotted lightly on the sides and breast. Crissum is streaked. In no plumage is there the sharp contrast between the white belly and streaked breast, as in the Pectoral. The juvenile is especially distinctive, with its rich orange-buff breast and *rufous cap* and *distinct supercilium*. **VOICE:** A low, trilled *preeet* or *tr-rit-trit*, sometimes twittered. **RANGE:** Breeds in n. Siberia. **HABITAT:** Grassy borders of salt marshes, muddy shores, wet fields. **EAST:** Scattered records throughout East.

SANDPIPERS

fall

WHITE-RUMPED
SANDPIPER

breeding

juvenile

breeding

BAIRD'S
SANDPIPER

♂
breeding

juvenile

PECTORAL
SANDPIPER

juvenile

breeding

SHARP-TAILED
SANDPIPER

Collectively the small, streaked sandpipers of N. America are nicknamed "peeps." In Britain and Europe, related species are called "stints."

LEAST SANDPIPER *Calidris minutilla*   Common

M 162

5–6½" (1 3–1 6 cm) A small "peep"; *brown* (not gray) coloration (plain brown in winter plumage), *yellowish or greenish* (not black) legs, small bill with droop to tip. **VOICE:** A thin *kreet* or *kree-eet,* with more of an *eet* sound than the *chirt* of a Semipalmated. **RANGE:** Alaska and Canada. Winters s. U.S. to Brazil. **HABITAT:** Mudflats, grassy marshes, rainpools, shoreline.

SEMIPALMATED SANDPIPER *Calidris pusilla*   Common

M 160

5½–6½" (1 4–1 6 cm) Coastally, the most numerous "peep" in migration. Compared to Least, it has relatively *stouter* bill and may be slightly larger, grayer above; usually has *blackish* legs. **SIMILAR SPECIES:** Aside from Least Sandpiper, it is most often confused with Western Sandpiper (see next species). **VOICE:** Note, *chirt* or *cheh* (lacks *ee* sound of Least or Western). **RANGE:** N. American Arctic. Winters mainly in n. S. America. **HABITAT:** Marshes, mudflats; tundra in summer.

WESTERN SANDPIPER *Calidris mauri*   Fairly common

M 161

6–7" (1 5–1 8 cm) Very similar to Semipalmated Sandpiper but a trifle larger. Summer adults are rusty on back and crown and have *rusty scapulars.* In typical adult female, bill is definitely thicker at base and longer than Semipalmated's and droops near tip. Fall birds often show trace of rust on scapulars and show paler facial region than Semipalmated. Perhaps palest of the "peeps" in winter. Can be fairly common on East Coast in fall; winters in U.S. (Semipalmated does not). **VOICE:** A distinct high-pitched *jeet* or *cheet,* unlike lower, soft *chirt* of Semipalmated. **RANGE:** Breeds in Alaska; winters from coastal U.S. to Peru. **HABITAT:** Shores, beaches, mudflats.

SMALL "PEEP" SANDPIPERS

winter

juvenile

breeding

LEAST
SANDPIPER

winter

juvenile

breeding

SEMIPALMATED
SANDPIPER

♀
juvenile
winter

♀ winter

juvenile

♀ breeding

WESTERN
SANDPIPER

HEADS AND BILLS OF "PEEPS"

LEAST

SEMIPALMATED

WESTERN

These species and the shorebirds on the next plate show their basic flight patterns. Most of these have unpatterned wings, lacking a pale stripe. All are shown in full color on previous plates. Learn their distinctive flight calls.

COMMON SNIPE *Gallinago gallinago*   PP. 140–141
Long bill, pointed wings, tawny orange tail, zigzag flight.
Flight call, when flushed, a rasping *scaip.*

AMERICAN WOODCOCK *Scolopax minor*   PP. 140–141
Long bill, rounded wings, chunky shape. Wings whistle in flight.
At night, an aerial flight "song."

SOLITARY SANDPIPER *Tringa solitaria*   PP. 148–149
Dark unpatterned wings, conspicuous bars on white sides of tail.
Flight call, peet! or *peet-weet-weet!* (higher than Spotted Sandpiper's).

LESSER YELLOWLEGS *Tringa flavipes*   PP. 148–149
Similar to Greater Yellowlegs (next), but smaller, with a smaller bill and finer markings on breast. Distinctive call, 1 or 2 notes (rarely 3).
Flight call, yew or *yu-yu,* softer than Greater's call.

GREATER YELLOWLEGS *Tringa melanoleuca*   PP. 148–149
Dark unpatterned wings, whitish rump and tail.
Flight call, a forceful 3-note whistle, *whew-whew-whew.*

WILSON'S PHALAROPE *Phalaropus tricolor*   PP. 164–165
Fall: Suggests Lesser Yellowlegs; smaller, whiter, bill needlelike.
Flight call, a low nasal *wurk.*

STILT SANDPIPER *Calidris himantopus*   PP. 154–155
Suggests Lesser Yellowlegs, but legs greenish.
Flight call, a single *whu,* lower than Lesser Yellowleg's.

UPLAND SANDPIPER *Bartramia longicauda*   PP. 154–155
Brown; small head, long tail. White line on trailing edge of wing.
Often flies "on tips of wings," like Spotted Sandpiper.
Flight call, a mellow whistled *quidi-quit.*

BUFF-BREASTED SANDPIPER *Tryngites subruficollis*   PP. 154–155
Evenly buff below, contrasting with white wing linings.
Flight call, a low trilled *pr-r-r-reet;* usually silent.

PECTORAL SANDPIPER *Calidris melanotos*   PP. 156–157
Like double-sized Least Sandpiper. Wing stripe faint or lacking.
Flight call, a low reedy *krik, krik.*

WADERS
in flight

COMMON SNIPE

AMERICAN
WOODCOCK

SOLITARY
SANDPIPER

GREATER
YELLOWLEGS

LESSER
YELLOWLEGS

WILSON'S
PHALAROPE
winter

STILT
SANDPIPER
winter

UPLAND
SANDPIPER

BUFF-BREASTED
SANDPIPER

PECTORAL
SANDPIPER

DOWITCHERS *Limnodromus* spp.   PP. 140–141
Snipelike bill and long wedge of white up back.
Flight call of Short-billed Dowitcher, a staccato mellow *tu-tu-tu*; that
of Long-billed Dowitcher, a single sharp *keek*, occasionally doubled or
trebled.

DUNLIN *Calidris alpina*   PP. 152–153
Fall: Gray-brown, slightly larger than "peep," darker than Sanderling.
Flight call, a nasal rasping *cheezp* or *treezp*.

RED KNOT *Calidris canutus*   PP. 150–151
Fall: Washed-out gray look, pale rump.
Flight call, a low *knut*.

PURPLE SANDPIPER *Calidris maritima*   PP. 150–151
Slaty color. Inhabits rocks, jetties, etc.
Flight call, a low *weet-wit* or *twit*.

WHITE-RUMPED SANDPIPER *Calidris fuscicollis*   PP. 156–157
White rump; only "peep" so marked.
Flight call, a mouselike squeak, *jeet*.

CURLEW SANDPIPER *Calidris ferruginea*   PP. 152–153
Fall: Suggests Dunlin, but rump white.

RUFF *Philomachus pugnax*   PP. 154–155
If seen well, oval white patch on each side of dark tail. Usually silent.

SPOTTED SANDPIPER *Actitis macularia*   PP. 152–153
The shallow wing stroke gives a stiff, bowed effect.
Flight call, a clear *peet* or *peet-weet*.

SANDERLING *Calidris alba*   PP. 152–153
The most contrasting wing stripe of any small shorebird.
Flight call, a sharp metallic *twick* or *quit*.

RED PHALAROPE *Phalaropus fulicaria*   PP. 164–165
Fall: Seagoing. Paler above than Red-necked Phalarope; bill thicker.

RED-NECKED PHALAROPE *Phalaropus lobatus*   PP. 164–165
Fall: Seagoing, Sanderling-like, but with dark eye patches.
Flight call (both phalaropes), a sharp *whit or kit*.

LEAST SANDPIPER *Calidris minutilla*   PP. 158–159
Very small, brown; faint wing stripe.
Flight call, a thin *kree-eet*.

SEMIPALMATED SANDPIPER *Calidris pusilla*   PP. 158–159
Grayer than Least; identify by voice.
Flight call, a soft *chirt* (lacks *ee* sound of Least).

BAIRD'S SANDPIPER *Calidris bairdii*   PP. 156–157
Larger than above two. Size of White-rump but rump dark.
Flight call, a low *kreep* or *kreee*.

WADERS
in flight

SHORT-BILLED
DOWITCHER
(Long-billed has
similar pattern)

winter

DUNLIN

winter

RED KNOT

PURPLE
SANDPIPER

WHITE-RUMPED
SANDPIPER

winter

CURLEW
SANDPIPER

winter

RUFF

winter

SPOTTED
SANDPIPER

winter

RED
PHALAROPE

SANDERLING

winter

RED-NECKED
PHALAROPE

LEAST
SANDPIPER

SEMIPALMATED
SANDPIPER

BAIRD'S
SANDPIPER

PHALAROPES. Subfamily Phalaropodinae.

Sandpiper-like birds with lobed toes; equally at home wading or swimming. Placed by some taxonomists in a family of their own, Phalaropodidae. When feeding, phalaropes often spin like tops, rapidly dabbling at the disturbed water for plankton, brine shrimp, and other fresh and marine invertebrates, mosquito larvae, and insects. Females larger and more colorful than males. Two of the 3 species are circumpolar, wintering at sea; the other (Wilson's Phalarope) breeds on the N. American plains and winters in S. America.

WILSON'S PHALAROPE *Phalaropus tricolor*　　　　Scarce in East

M 174

9" (23 cm) This trim phalarope is *dark-winged* (*no wing stripe*), with a white rump. Breeding female is unique, with a *broad black face and neck stripe blending into cinnamon.* Male is duller, with just a wash of cinnamon on side of neck and a white spot on hindneck. *Fall:* Suggests a Lesser Yellowlegs (dark wings, white rump), but whiter below, with no breast streaking; bill needlelike; legs greenish or straw colored (not canary yellow). **VOICE:** A low nasal *wurk*; also *check, check, check.* **RANGE:** Sw. Canada, w. U.S., and Great Lakes. Winters in s. S. America. **HABITAT:** Seen spinning in water to bring up food on shallow prairie lakes, fresh marshes, and pools. Also running about on shores and mudflats, snapping up flies. In migration, also salt marshes.

RED-NECKED PHALAROPE *Phalaropus lobatus*　　　Common offshore, scarce inland

M 175

7–8" (18–20 cm) A Sanderling-like bird at sea is most likely to be a phalarope. Of the 2 seagoing phalaropes, this is the more common one and is more likely to occur inland than Red Phalarope. Breeding female is striped above, with a patch of rufous on neck and a white throat. Male is duller, but similar in pattern. In fall, both sexes are gray above (strongly streaked) and white below. Note dark "phalarope patch" through eye and needlelike black bill. **VOICE:** A sharp *kit* or *whit,* similar to note of Sanderling. **RANGE:** Circumpolar. Winters at sea, s. U.S. to S. Hemisphere. **HABITAT:** Ocean, bays, lakes, ponds; tundra in summer.

RED PHALAROPE *Phalaropus fulicaria*　　　Uncommon offshore, very rare inland

M 176

8–9" (20–23 cm) The seagoing habits (swimming buoyantly like a tiny gull) distinguish this as a phalarope; in breeding plumage, the deep *chestnut underparts* and *white face* and yellow bill designate it as this species. Male duller than female. In fall and winter, both sexes are plain gray above, white below; in flight suggests a Sanderling, but with a *dark patch* through eye. **SIMILAR SPECIES:** Fall Red-necked Phalarope is darker, with a more strongly striped back, darker crown. Its wing stripe contrasts more; its bill is more needlelike. Slightly thicker bill of Red Phalarope in fall may be yellowish at base. Immature has a black bill. **VOICE:** Similar to Red-necked Phalarope's *whit* or *prip.* **RANGE:** Arctic; circumpolar. Winter range at sea poorly known; from s. U.S. to S. Hemisphere. **HABITAT:** More strictly pelagic than Red-necked. In summer, tundra.

PHALAROPES

♀ breeding

winter

juvenile

WILSON'S PHALAROPE

winter

♂ breeding

phalaropes spin

winter

RED-NECKED PHALAROPE

juvenile

winter

♀ breeding

♂ breeding

♀ breeding

winter

RED PHALAROPE

juvenile

winter

lobed foot of phalarope

♂ breeding

N. America and Europe share many species of waders. A number of others have found their way across the Atlantic from Europe, casually or accidentally. Several species (Ruff, Curlew Sandpiper, Whimbrel [European race], Little Egret, Common Crane, and Corn Crake) are covered in their respective groups in the text. Sample locations of sightings are given. For additional field marks of most of the species below, see *A Field Guide to the Birds of Britain and Europe*, by Roger Tory Peterson, Guy Mountfort, and P. A. D. Hollom.

1. **EUROPEAN GOLDEN-PLOVER** *Pluvialis apricaria* (see text p. 132)

2. **NORTHERN LAPWING** *Vanellus vanellus* Baffin Is., Lab., Nfld., Que., N.B., N.S., Me., Mass., R.I., N.Y., N.J., N.C., S.C., Fla., Ohio, etc.

3. **MONGOLIAN PLOVER** *Charadrius mongolus*
   Slightly smaller with a decidedly smaller bill than Wilson's Plover. Has rufous breast-band, black mask in summer but not in winter. La., R.I., N.J., Ont.

4. **EUROPEAN WOODCOCK** *Scolopax rusticola* Que., Nfld., Ohio, Pa., N.J., Va., Ala. (all records old and many questioned).

5. **GREAT SNIPE** *Gallinago media* N.J., Va. (recorded, but record in question).

6. **JACK SNIPE** *Limnocryptes minimus* Lab.

7. **COMMON GREENSHANK** *Tringa nebularia* N.S., N.Y.

8. **COMMON REDSHANK** *Tringa totanus* Nfld.

9. **SPOTTED REDSHANK** *Tringa erythropus* Ont., Nfld., Conn., Mass., R.I., Pa., N.Y., N.J.

10. **BLACK-TAILED GODWIT** *Limosa limosa* Nfld., Me., R.I., Conn., N.Y., N.J., Del., N.C., etc.

11. **BAR-TAILED GODWIT** *Limosa lapponica* Nfld., Miquelon Is., Mass., N.Y., N.J., N.C., Fla., etc.

12. **EURASIAN CURLEW** *Numenius arquata* Nfld., N.S., Mass., N.Y. Has white rump.

13. **WHIMBREL (EUROPEAN RACE)** *Numenius phaeopus* (see text p. 142)

winter

1 winter

2

3 breeding

4

5

6

7

8

breeding   winter

9

10

11 winter

winter

12

13

Predatory seabirds related to skuas (shown on the following plate) but are smaller than those broad-winged, hump-backed birds (although dark Pomarine Jaegers can be skualike). These dark falconlike or hawklike seabirds with slightly hooked beaks harass gulls and terns, forcing them to disgorge their food. Parasitic and Pomarine Jaegers occur in light, intermediate, and dark morphs; their diagnostic tail points not always evident. All have a *flash of white* in the primaries. Jaegers have 2 projecting central tail feathers, lacking or diminished in immatures. Skuas lack elongate tail points. Immatures have stubbier central tail feathers and pose more of a problem in identification. Relative size of the 3 jaegers can help with identification. Many articles and chapters in books have been written on jaeger identification. Don't expect to identify every jaeger you see at first. Partial competence comes only with time. Sexes alike. **FOOD:** In Arctic, lemmings, eggs, young birds. At sea, food taken from other birds or from water. **RANGE:** Seas of world, breeding in subpolar regions. **NO. OF SPECIES:** World, 3; East, 3.

PARASITIC JAEGER *Stercorarius parasiticus*   Uncommon

M 180

18" (45 cm) In adult, *sharp tail points* project up to 3½ in. Parasitic is the jaeger most frequently seen from shore; plumage is most variable of any jaeger, ranging from light to dark morphs. Immature may show less white in outer wing than larger Pomarine Jaeger. **RANGE:** Arctic; circumpolar. Winters at sea from latitude of s. U.S. to Tierra del Fuego. **HABITAT:** Open ocean, coastal bays, large lakes (rarely); tundra in summer.

POMARINE JAEGER *Stercorarius pomarinus*   Uncommon

M 179

22" (55 cm) Larger-, heavier-, and broader-winged than other jaegers. Flanks and undertail often prominently barred. Broad breast-band. In adult, note *broad and twisted* central tail feathers (projecting 2–7 in.) and large hooked bill. In both adults and immatures, more white in primaries and their undersurface than other jaegers. Immature lacks blunt tail projections. **RANGE:** Arctic; circumpolar. Winters at sea from s. U.S. to S. Hemisphere. **HABITAT:** Open sea, coasts (offshore); tundra in summer.

LONG-TAILED JAEGER *Stercorarius longicaudus*   Scarce

M 181

20–23" (51–58 cm) *Long tail streamers* of adults may project 9–10 in. (usually 3–6 in.). Smallest, trimmest, and palest of the 3 jaegers. Whiter below with no breast-band. Black cap is well separated from pale gray back by a *broad white collar. Grayish mantle* contrasting with darker trailing edge to flight feathers is distinctive, as is more ternlike flight. Adult lacks whitish patch on dark underwing and from above shows only 2 whitish feather shafts in outer primaries. Dark morph very rare. Bill short; legs blue-gray (Parasitic's are black). Immature typically somewhat grayer than other two species. **RANGE:** Arctic; circumpolar. Winters at sea in S. Hemisphere. **HABITAT:** Open ocean; tundra in summer.

JAEGERS

PARASITIC

POMARINE

LONG-TAILED

light morph

PARASITIC JAEGER

dark morph

PARASITIC JAEGER

intermediate

dark morph juvenile (Parasitic)

dark morph

immature

POMARINE JAEGER

POMARINE JAEGER

light morph

LONG-TAILED JAEGER

juvenile

dark-immature (Long-tail)

The skuas are the largest and most powerful of the Stercorariidae. They dominate the ocean when in the vicinity of other birds and are powerful predators on their breeding grounds. Their size, bulk, and powerful flight make then fairly easy to identify.

GREAT SKUA *Catharacta skua*   Scarce

M 177

21–24" (53–60 cm) Note *conspicuous white wing patch.* Near size of Herring Gull but stockier. Dark brown, with rusty and streaked underparts and a short, slightly wedge-shaped tail. Flight strong and swift; harasses other seabirds. **SIMILAR SPECIES:** Dark and immature jaegers may lack distinctive tail-feather extensions. However, Skuas' wings are wider, less falconlike, white wing patches more striking, and flight more powerful. **RANGE:** N. Hemisphere. Breeds locally in colder parts of e. N. Atlantic. Wanders south well off coast of s. Europe to coastal West Africa.

SOUTH POLAR SKUA *Catharacta maccormicki*   Scarce

M 178

21" (53 cm) Very similar to Great Skua with bold white wing patches; bill and legs shorter. "Blond" form is much paler on head and nape, as well as underparts, than Great Skua. Dark form lacks scattered rusty feathers of Great Skua. **RANGE:** Breeds Antarctica. Wanders widely in Pacific and into Atlantic (as far north as Greenland). Summer skuas off East Coast are usually this species.

TAIL SHAPE

When in breeding plumage, skuas and jaegers show distinct tail shapes. Skua has a wedge-shaped tail compared to the three jaegers, with elongate central tail feathers. In prime condition, the twisted central plumes of the large-bodied Pomarine separate it from the trimmer Parasitic, with sharp central feathers. The Long-tailed, sleekest of the jaegers, sports the longest central tail feathers. However, the central tail plumes of younger birds are not so developed, so other characters must be used to separate the three species — often a difficult task!

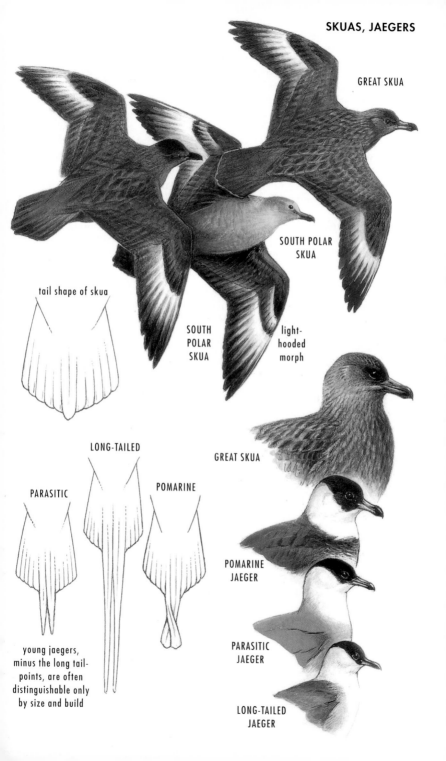

GREAT SKUA

SOUTH POLAR SKUA

tail shape of skua

SOUTH POLAR SKUA

light-hooded morph

LONG-TAILED

PARASITIC

POMARINE

GREAT SKUA

POMARINE JAEGER

PARASITIC JAEGER

LONG-TAILED JAEGER

young jaegers, minus the long tail-points, are often distinguishable only by size and build

GULLS. Family Laridae.

Long-winged swimming birds with superb flight. More robust, wider-winged, longer-legged than terns. Bills often slightly hooked in the larger gulls. Tails square or rounded (terns usually have forked tails). They seldom dive (terns hover, plunge headfirst). **FOOD:** Omnivorous; marine life, plant and animal food, refuse, carrion. **NO. OF SPECIES:** World, 51; East, 17 (+ 3 accidental).

SEQUENCE OF PLUMAGES IN A FOUR-YEAR GULL

On the opposite page, the well-known Herring Gull, a widespread species inland and coastally, illustrates the transition of plumages from juvenile to adult. It is often important to properly age a gull before identifying it.

The **HERRING GULL**, a four-year gull, does not obtain full breeding plumage until it is at least 3½ years old or as late as 4½. However, identification in the first-year plumage will help sort out all the intermediate stages until adult plumage.

In this field guide, intended for identification on the species level, I have not given similar full-page treatment to any other four-year gulls. That is the province of a larger handbook or text specifically on gulls. However, on pp. 174, I have given similar breakdowns of a widespread three-year gull, the Ring-billed Gull, and a two-year gull, the Bonaparte's Gull. Should you wish in-depth analysis of other species, I recommend Peter Grant's *Gulls: A Guide to Identification*, which devotes several pages per species. Study also Kenn Kaufman's *Field Guide to Advanced Birding*, in which Kevin Zimmer devotes 17 pages to the point-counterpoint puzzles of the Herring Gull/Thayer's Gull/Iceland Gull/ Kumlien's Gull complex, which is beyond the scope of this field guide.

IN SUMMARY

FOUR-YEAR GULLS: This category includes most of the larger species, including Great Black-backed and Lesser Black-backed, Herring, Thayer's, California, Glaucous, and Iceland, which attain full maturity in 3½ to 4½ years.

THREE-YEAR GULLS: Medium-sized species, including Ring-billed and Laughing.

TWO-YEAR GULLS: Mostly the smaller species, including Franklin's, Bonaparte's, Black-headed, Little, Ross's, Sabine's, and Ivory, and the kittiwakes.

HERRING GULL
Plumage Transition
of a 4-year Gull

juvenile

1st winter

2nd winter

3rd winter

adult

adult breeding

winter

SEQUENCE OF PLUMAGES IN A THREE-YEAR GULL

On the opposite page, the RING-BILLED GULL, widespread and abundant both coastally and inland, has been chosen to illustrate the transition of plumages from juvenile to adult. A bird hatched in the summer will be in a dusky juvenal plumage in July. By August and September, it will already be changing to its first-winter plumage with much gray on the back and a narrow black tail-band and bicolored bill. By the second winter, it is much like an adult except for the trace of a black tail-band, somewhat darker eyes, a bit more black on the bill, and possibly still a small amount of brown in the wing. By the third summer, it is in full adult plumage with yellow eyes and a clear-cut ring on the bill. From then on, it remains the same except for the streaking on the head and neck during the nonbreeding season.

Another eastern three-year gull is the Laughing Gull, a coastal species.

SEQUENCE OF PLUMAGES IN A TWO-YEAR GULL

On the bottom of the opposite page, the BONAPARTE'S GULL, widespread and common on the coast and on inland lakes, has been chosen to illustrate the transition of plumages from juvenile to adult.

Other two-year gulls that occur in the East are Franklin's, Black-headed, Little, Ross's, Sabine's, and Ivory Gulls and Black-legged Kittiwake.

CAUTION: Do not feel defeated if you cannot name every gull you see. There is considerable variation due to age, season, molt, feather wear, occasional hybridization, and even albinism. The true expert puts a question mark after an observation if he or she is not sure.

RING-BILLED GULL
Plumage Transition of a 3-year Gull

1st winter

a gull that attains adult plumage in its 3rd year

2nd winter

3rd winter

breeding

adult winter

adult

BONAPARTE'S GULL
A 2-year Gull

1st winter

adult winter

adult breeding

GLAUCOUS GULL *Larus hyperboreus* Uncommon

M 193

26–32" (65–80 cm) Note "frosty" wingtips. A large pale gull, size of Great Black-backed. Adults have a pale gray mantle and *unmarked white primaries. Immature:* See pp. 182–183. **SIMILAR SPECIES:** Iceland Gull is size of a Herring Gull or smaller; bill is smaller than that of Glaucous; head rounder; wing proportionately longer and narrower. Adult has a narrow *red* ring around eye (Glaucous, *yellow*), but this is hard to see. **RANGE:** Arctic; circumpolar. Winters to U.S., Britain, n. China. **HABITAT:** Mainly coastal; some inland.

ICELAND GULL *Larus glaucoides glaucoides* (In part) Very rare

M 191

23–26" (58–65 cm) A pale ghostly gull, slightly smaller than a Herring Gull. Adult has a pale gray mantle and *whitish or pure white primaries without dark markings* that extend well beyond tail. *Immature:* See pp. 182–183. "Kumlien's" Gull *(Larus glaucoides kumlieni),* a sub-species that breeds in e. arctic Canada, is the one most often seen in U.S.; differs by having *gray or dark markings,* variable in extent, toward tips of whitish primaries (not black with white "mirrors" as in Herring Gull). Wings extended well beyond tail. Bill dark and thin. **SIMILAR SPECIES:** (1) Glaucous Gull has a more massive bill. (2) Thayer's Gull has a darker mantle, blacker primaries, dark eyes. **RANGE:** Breeds in Greenland. **HABITAT:** Coastal, less frequent inland.

IVORY GULL *Pagophila eburnea* Very rare

M 197

15–17" (38–43 cm) The only *all-white* gull with *black* legs. Pigeon-sized with dovelike head; wings long, flight quite ternlike. Bill black with a yellow tip. *Immature:* See pp. 184–185. **SIMILAR SPECIES:** (1) Ice-land and (2) Glaucous Gulls are larger with pinkish legs. Perhaps more likely to be confused with a white pigeon! **VOICE:** Harsh shrill tern-like cries: *keeeer,* etc. **RANGE:** High Arctic; circumpolar. **EAST:** Breeds lo-cally on arctic islands of northernmost Canada (NWT). Winters from pack ice south to Gulf of St. Lawrence and Nfld., casually to New England. Accidental south to N.J. and on Great Lakes to Tenn.

ROSS'S GULL *Rhodostethia rosea* Very rare

12½–14" (31–35 cm) A rare gull of the drift ice. *Summer:* Note *wedge-shaped tail*, rosy underparts, *fine black collar*, blue-gray wing linings. *Winter:* Loses black collar. *Immature:* See p. 184–185. **RANGE:** Breeds mainly in Siberia. **EAST:** Rare breeder to arctic Canada and casual south of that region.

"WHITE-WINGED" GULLS
Adults

GLAUCOUS GULL

ICELAND GULL

"Kumlien's" form

typical form

IVORY GULL

winter

breeding

ROSS'S GULL

MEW GULL *Larus canus* (shown on p. 36) — Vagrant

16–18" (40–45 cm) (Called Common Gull in Europe.) Smaller than Ring-billed Gull, with a small, short *unmarked, greenish yellow* bill; darker back. Legs greenish. *Immature:* Looks like a "pint-sized" young Herring Gull with ploverlike bill. (N. Eurasia, nw. N. America.)

HERRING GULL *Larus argentatus* — Common

M 189

23–26" (58–65 cm) The common large "seagull." *Adult:* A big gray-mantled gull with *pinkish legs.* Wingtips black with white spots; large yellow bill with a red spot. *Immature:* See pp. 182–183. **VOICE:** A loud *hiyak . . . hiyah . . . hyiah-hyak* or *yuk-yuk-yuk-yuk-yuckle-yuckle.* Mewing squeals. Anxiety note, *gah-gah-gah.* **RANGE:** Northern parts of N. Hemisphere. **HABITAT:** Coasts, bays, beaches, lakes, rivers, piers, farms, dumps, sewage outlets.

THAYER'S GULL *Larus thayeri* — Rare

M 190

23–25" (58–63 cm) Very similar to Iceland Gull. Adult has *pale to dark brown* (not yellow) eyes, narrow red (not yellow) eye-ring, slate gray primaries, slightly darker mantle, *pinker* legs. **RANGE:** Arctic Canada in summer.

RING-BILLED GULL *Larus delawarensis* — Common

M 187

19" (48 cm) *Adult:* Similar to Herring Gull but smaller, more buoyant, and dovelike. Note *black ring* encircling bill and *yellowish* or *pale greenish* (not pink or pinkish-gray) legs of adult. Shows more black on *underside* of primaries. *Immature:* See pp. 182–183. **VOICE:** Notes higher pitched than Herring Gull's. **RANGE:** Canada, n. U.S. Winters to Mexico, Cuba. **HABITAT:** Lakes, bays, coasts, piers, dumps, plowed fields, sewage outlets, shopping malls, fast-food restaurants.

CALIFORNIA GULL *Larus californicus* — Vagrant in East

M 188

20–23" (50–58 cm) *Adult:* Resembles Ring-billed Gull (both have yellowish green legs), but note larger size, darker mantle, *dark eye,* and *red and black spot* on longer bill. Shows more white in wingtips. *Immature:* See pp. 182–183.

BLACK-LEGGED KITTIWAKE *Rissa tridactyla* — Uncommon

M 196

17" (43 cm) A small buoyant oceanic gull. In adults, black on wingtips are *cut straight across,* as if dipped in ink. Small, pale yellow bill is unmarked. Legs *black.* *Immature:* See p. 184–185. **VOICE:** At nesting colony, a raucous *kaka-week* or *kitti-waak.* **RANGE:** Oceans of N. Hemisphere.

GREAT BLACK-BACKED GULL *Larus marinus* — Common

M 194

28–31" (70–78 cm) Larger than Herring Gull. *Adult:* Unmistakable; black back and wings, snow-white underparts. *Immature:* See pp. 182–183. **SIMILAR SPECIES:** See Lesser Black-backed Gull. **VOICE:** A harsh deep *kyow* or *owk.* **RANGE:** Mainly coasts of N. Atlantic, wintering to mid-Atlantic states, and Great Lakes, Mediterranean. **HABITAT:** Mainly coastal waters, estuaries; a few on large lakes and rivers.

LESSER BLACK-BACKED GULL *Larus fuscus* — Scarce

M 192

23" (58 cm) Similar to Great Black-backed Gull but smaller (size of small Herring Gull). Distinguished by *yellow* (not pink) legs and dark (but not black) mantle. Extensive head streaks in winter plumage. Pale eye. **RANGE:** N. Europe, wintering to Mediterranean. **EAST:** Regular at sites from e. Canada to s. Fla. in fall and winter. Few stay entire year.

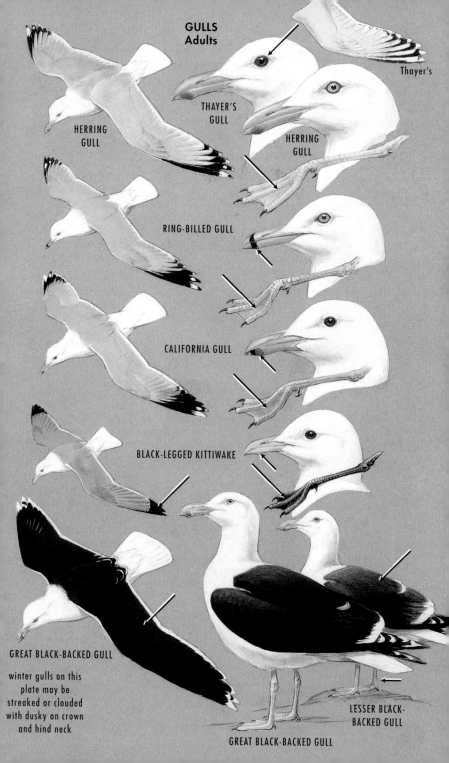

GULLS
Adults

Thayer's

THAYER'S
GULL

HERRING
GULL

HERRING
GULL

RING-BILLED GULL

CALIFORNIA GULL

BLACK-LEGGED KITTIWAKE

GREAT BLACK-BACKED GULL

winter gulls on this
plate may be
streaked or clouded
with dusky on crown
and hind neck

LESSER BLACK-
BACKED GULL

GREAT BLACK-BACKED GULL

LAUGHING GULL *Larus atricilla* Common

M 182

16–17" (40–43 cm) A small coastal gull. Dark mantle blends into black wingtips. White border shows on rear edge of wing. In summer, head is black with a deep reddish bill; in winter, head white with dark nape smudge. *Immature:* See p. 184–185. **VOICE:** A strident laugh, *ha-ha-ha-ha-ha-haah-haah-haah,* etc. **RANGE:** Coast, N.S. to Venezuela, also locally in se. Calif., w. Mexico. Winters from s. U.S. south. **HABITAT:** Salt marshes, coastal bays, piers, beaches, ocean, plowed fields.

FRANKLIN'S GULL *Larus pipixcan* Scarce in East

M 183

14–15" (35–38 cm) Note *white wing band* separating black at tips from gray. In summer, breast has a rosy bloom, head is black with bold *white eyelids* and a dark reddish bill. In fall, head white with dark cheek and nape. *Immature:* See pp. 184–185. **VOICE:** A shrill *kuk-kuk-kuk;* also mewing, laughing cries. **RANGE:** Breeds in w. Canada and nw. and n.-cen. U.S. Winters in Pacific from Guatemala to Chile. **HABITAT:** Prairies, inland marshes, lakes; in winter, coasts, ocean.

SABINE'S GULL *Xema sabini* Very rare

M 195

13–14" (33–35 cm) Our only gull with a *well-notched tail.* Note black outer primaries and *triangular white wing patch,* slaty hood. Bill black with *yellow tip,* feet black. *Immature:* See p. 184–185. **RANGE:** Arctic; circumpolar. Winters in Pacific to Peru; very rare in w. Atlantic. **HABITAT:** Ocean; tundra in summer.

BLACK-HEADED GULL *Larus ridibundus* Scarce

M 185

14–15" (35–38 cm) Similar in pattern to Bonaparte's Gull and associates with it; slightly larger. Adult in summer has *brown* (not black) hood. In winter, loses dark hood. Bill *dark red,* not black. Shows extensive *blackish on underside of primaries. Immature:* See p. 184–185. **RANGE:** Eurasia, Iceland. **EAST:** Regular along northeast coast of N. America, especially in Maritimes; less frequent in s. U.S., Great Lakes. Has bred in Nfld.

BONAPARTE'S GULL *Larus philadelphia* Common

M 186

13" (33 cm) A petite, almost ternlike gull. Note *long wedge of white* on fore edge of wing. In summer, has a blackish head. Legs red; bill small, black. In winter, adults have a white head with a *black ear spot.* Often in flocks. *Immature:* See pp. 184–185. **VOICE:** A nasal *cheer* or *cherr.* Some notes ternlike. **RANGE:** Alaska, w. and cen. Canada. Winters n. U.S. to Mexico, Cuba. **HABITAT:** Ocean bays, coastal waters, sewage treatment ponds, lakes; muskeg in summer.

LITTLE GULL *Larus minutus* Scarce

M 184

11" (28 cm) The smallest gull. Note *blackish undersurface* of *rather rounded wing* and absence of black above. Head black in summer, *capped* in winter. Legs red, short. In summer, bill dark red, breast pinkish. In winter, bill black. *Immature:* See p. 184–185. **RANGE:** Eurasia, wintering to Mediterranean. **EAST:** Regular on Great Lakes and along East Coast. Has bred in Ont., Que., Man., Mich., Wisc. **HABITAT:** Lakes, rivers, bays, coastal waters, sewage treatment plants; often with Bonaparte's Gulls.

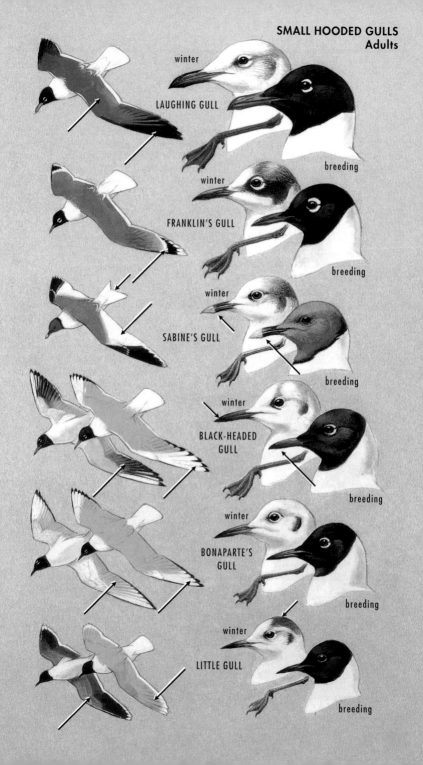

SMALL HOODED GULLS
Adults

winter

LAUGHING GULL

breeding

winter

FRANKLIN'S GULL

breeding

winter

SABINE'S GULL

breeding

winter

BLACK-HEADED
GULL

breeding

winter

BONAPARTE'S
GULL

breeding

winter

LITTLE GULL

breeding

Immature gulls usually are more difficult to identify than adults. They are darkest the first year, lighter the second, and, in the larger species, may not be fully adult until the third or fourth year. Leg and bill colors of most immatures are not as diagnostic as in adults. Go mainly by pattern and size. The most typical plumages are shown opposite; intermediate stages can be expected. Do not feel you must identify *every* immature gull. Because of variables such as stage of molt, wear, age, individual variation, and even occasional albinism and hybridization, some birds may remain a mystery even to the expert.

GLAUCOUS GULL *Larus hyperboreus*   **ADULT, PP. 176–177**
FIRST WINTER: Recognized by its larger size (size of a Great Black-backed Gull), mottled pale tan to *off-whitish* coloration, and unmarked *whitish primaries*, a shade lighter than rest of wing. Wingtips usually fall short of tail end, are equal to it, or slightly beyond. Bill *pale pink* with a dark tip sharply delineated. **SECOND YEAR:** Body very pale overall, pale eye, beginning of pale gray mantle.

ICELAND GULL *Larus glaucoides*   **ADULT, PP. 176–177**
Sequence of plumages is similar to Glaucous Gull's but Iceland is smaller (size of Herring Gull) with a smaller bill and proportionately longer wings (projecting beyond tail when at rest). Flight more buoyant. Bill of first-year Iceland Gull is mostly dark (pink with dark tip in Glaucous).

HERRING GULL *Larus argentatus*   **ADULT, PP. 178–179**
FIRST WINTER: Brown to marbled tan; the common dusky gull. No other young gull is quite as variable in appearance. **SECOND AND THIRD WINTERS:** Paler. Head and underparts whiter; tail feathers dark tipped, contrasting with white rump, pale gray mantle, and pale eye. See Sequence of Plumages in a Four-Year Gull, pp. 172–173.

CALIFORNIA GULL *Larus californicus*   **ADULT, PP. 178–179**
FIRST WINTER: As *dark* as Herring Gull in its first winter but with a shorter *bicolored bill.*

GREAT BLACK-BACKED GULL *Larus marinus*   **ADULT, P. 178–179**
Young birds are larger and more salt-and-pepper patterned than first-year Herring Gulls. They show more contrast, being paler on head, rump, and underparts; first-year birds more checkered looking than Herring, the "saddle-back" pattern is suggested in second-year birds. They may resemble later immature stages of Herring Gull, but back is darker and head and bill are larger.

RING-BILLED GULL *Larus delawarensis*   **ADULT, PP. 178–179**
Immatures may be confused with second- or third-winter Herring Gull, which has a semblance of a ring near tip of bill, which is longer. (*Note:* Like second-year Ring-bills, second- and third-year Herring Gulls have pale eyes.) In Herring Gull, tail terminates in a *broad* ill-defined band. Subterminal band in Ring-bill is narrower (a little over 1 in. wide) and usually (but not always) well defined. Leg color in most instances is not useful, as first-winter Ring-bills have pinkish or pinkish-gray legs not unlike those of young Herring Gulls. See Sequence of Plumages in a Three-Year Gull, pp. 174–175.

GULLS
Immature

GLAUCOUS
1st winter

GLAUCOUS
1st winter

ICELAND
1st winter

GLAUCOUS
2nd winter

1st winter

HERRING

2nd winter

ICELAND
1st winter

CALIFORNIA
1st winter

ICELAND
2nd winter

GREAT BLACK-BACKED
1st winter

HERRING
1st winter

RING-BILLED
1st winter

HERRING
2nd winter

RING-BILLED
2nd winter

LAUGHING GULL *Larus atricilla* ADULT, PP. 180–181

A three-year gull. **FIRST YEAR:** Very *dark,* with a *white rump* and a *broad white border* on trailing edge of dark wing. Brown breast and brown forehead. Distinct black tail-band. **FIRST WINTER:** Pale gray wash on chest and forehead (see Franklin's Gull). **SECOND WINTER:** Similar to winter adult, but with a trace of black in tail.

FRANKLIN'S GULL *Larus pipixcan* ADULT, PP. 180–181

A two-year gull. **FIRST WINTER:** Very similar to first-winter Laughing Gull, but smaller-billed and more petite. It perhaps may best be distinguished by *white outer tail feathers.* Note also *darker cheek* and *more distinctly hooded* effect. Juvenile Laughing Gull is separated from Franklin's by its brown breast and brown forehead, which become whiter as fall progresses. Franklin's mainly inland, compared to coastal Laughing.

SABINE'S GULL *Xema sabini* ADULT, PP. 180–181

A two-year gull. **FIRST WINTER:** Medium brown on back, feathers present a scaled pattern but with adult's bold *triangular wing pattern.* Note weakly *forked* tail with black terminal band. Young kittiwake is similar, but is grayer and has a dark bar on nape and a diagonal bar across wing.

BLACK-LEGGED KITTIWAKE *Rissa tridactyla* ADULT, PP. 178–179

A two-year gull. **FIRST WINTER:** Note *dark bar on nape,* black outer primaries, and dark bar across inner wing. Tail may seem slightly notched with black terminal band. See Plumages in a Two-Year Gull, pp. 174–175.

BONAPARTE'S GULL *Larus philadelphia* ADULT, PP. 180–181

A two-year gull. Petite, ternlike. **FIRST WINTER:** Note cheek spot, narrow black tail-band, brown band across inner wing, and pattern of black and white in outer primaries. See Plumages in a Two-Year Gull, pp. 174–175.

BLACK-HEADED GULL *Larus ridibundus* ADULT, PP. 180–181

A two-year gull. **FIRST WINTER:** Similar in pattern to immature Bonaparte's Gull, with which it associates, but slightly larger and less ternlike; bill is longer, orange to dull red at base, black at tip. Sooty underwing.

IVORY GULL *Pagophila eburnea* ADULT, PP. 176–177

A two-year gull. **FIRST WINTER:** A ternlike white gull with irregular *dark smudges on face*, a *sprinkling of black spots* above, and a narrow black border on rear edge of its white wings.

LITTLE GULL *Larus minutus* ADULT, PP. 180–181

A two-year gull. **FIRST WINTER:** Smaller than young Bonaparte's, with a *blacker M pattern* formed by outer primaries and darker band across wing than in Bonaparte's. Note especially *dusky cap.*

ROSS'S GULL *Rhodostethia rosea* ADULT, PP. 176–177

A two-year gull. **FIRST WINTER:** Upperwing pattern similar to immature Little Gull or Black-legged Kittiwake, but note *wedge-shaped* tail (not square or notched) and pale underwing. Lacks dark nape of immature kittiwake.

SMALL GULLS
Immature

1st winter

2nd winter

1st winter

2nd winter

LAUGHING

LAUGHING

FRANKLIN'S

1st winter

1st winter

FRANKLIN'S

SABINE'S

BLACK-LEGGED
KITTIWAKE

BONAPARTE'S

BLACK-HEADED

IVORY

LITTLE

ROSS'S

Graceful water birds, more streamlined than gulls. Bill sharp-pointed, often tilted toward the water when tern is flying. Tail usually forked. Most terns are whitish with black caps; in winter, the black of the forehead is replaced by white. Sexes alike. Terns often hover and plunge beak-first for fish. Normally they do not swim (whereas gulls do). **FOOD:** Small fish, marine life, large insects. **RANGE:** Almost worldwide. **NO. OF SPECIES:** World, 44; East, 14 (+ 2 accidental).

GULL-BILLED TERN *Sterna nilotica* — Uncommon

M 198

14" (35 cm) Note stout, almost *gull-like black* bill. Stockier and paler than Common Tern; tail much less forked; feet *black*. In winter, head is nearly white. *Immature:* Pale gray outer wing and a notched tail. Swoops more than dives, snatching prey from surface. Occasionally hawks for insects over land. **VOICE:** A throaty, rasping *za-za-za*; also *kay-weck, kay-weck*. **RANGE:** Breeds locally, wanders widely in many parts of world. **HABITAT:** Salt marshes, fields, coastal bays.

SANDWICH TERN *Sterna sandvicensis* — Fairly common

M 201

16–18" (40–45 cm) Larger than Common Tern. Note *long black bill* with its *yellow tip* "as though dipped in mayonnaise" (often obscure in young birds). Adult breeding, all-black cap; white forehead in non-breeding plumage; feathers on back of crown elongated, forming a crest. Feet black. **SIMILAR SPECIES:** See Gull-billed Tern (stout black bill). **VOICE:** A grating *kirr-ick* (higher than Gull-bill's *kay-weck*). **RANGE:** Coasts of se. U.S., British Isles, Europe. Winters to S. America, Africa. **HABITAT:** Coastal waters, jetties, beaches. Often seen with Royal Terns.

ROYAL TERN *Sterna maxima* — Common

M 200

18–21" (45–53 cm) A large tern, slimmer than Caspian Tern, with a large *orange* bill (Caspian's is redder with a small dark tip). Tail deeply forked. Although some Royal Terns in spring show a solid cap, they more often have white on the forehead, the black crown feathers forming a crest. **VOICE:** *Keer*, higher than Caspian's note; also *kaak* or *kak*. **RANGE:** Coasts of se. U.S., nw. Mexico, W. Indies, w. Africa. Winters s. U.S. to Argentina; w. Africa. **HABITAT:** Coasts, sandy beaches, salt bays.

CASPIAN TERN *Sterna caspia* — Uncommon

M 199

19–23" (48–58 cm) The large size and large red bill set Caspian apart from all other terns except slimmer Royal. Caspian ranges inland, whereas Royal does not. Tail of Caspian is shorter; bill is stouter, *red* rather than orange. Royal has a more *crested* look and usually a *clear white* forehead. (In similar plumage, Caspian has clouded, *streaked* forehead.) Caspian shows much more black under primaries, whereas Royal is darker on *upper* surface of primaries. **VOICE:** A hoarse, low *kraa-uh* or *karr*; also repeated *kaks*. **RANGE:** Breeds locally, wanders widely. **HABITAT:** Large lakes, coastal waters, beaches, bays.

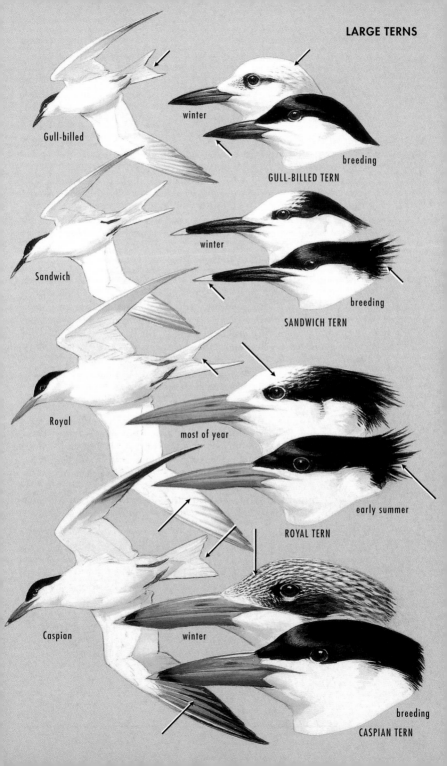

LARGE TERNS

Gull-billed

winter

Gull-billed

breeding

GULL-BILLED TERN

Sandwich

winter

Sandwich

breeding

SANDWICH TERN

Royal

most of year

early summer

ROYAL TERN

Caspian

winter

Caspian

breeding

CASPIAN TERN

LEAST TERN *Sterna antillarum* Locally common

M 206

9" (23 cm) A *very small* pale tern with *yellow* bill and feet, white forehead. Quicker wingbeats than other terns. *Immature:* Dark bill; dark nape; much dark on forewing. In fall, all birds may have dark bills, but feet show yellow. **VOICE:** A sharp repeated *kit*; a harsh squealing *zree-eek* or *zeek*; also a rapid *kitti-kitti-kitti.* **RANGE:** Temperate and tropical oceans. Winters south of U.S. **HABITAT:** Sea beaches, bays; large rivers.

ARCTIC TERN *Sterna paradisaea* Uncommon

M 204

14–17" (35–43 cm) Very similar to Common Tern but underparts slightly *grayer; white cheeks* contrasting with grayish throat and breast. Shorter bill is usually *blood-red* to tip. Legs shorter. Overhead, note *translucent* effect of primaries and *narrow* black-edged border. Adults in fall are more difficult to identify (bill and feet become dark). **VOICE:** *Kee-yah*, similar to Common Tern's cry; less slurred, higher. A high *keer-keer* is characteristic. **RANGE:** Northern parts of N. Hemisphere; circumpolar. Winters in sub-Antarctic seas. **HABITAT:** Open ocean, rocky coasts, islands; tundra lakes in summer.

COMMON TERN *Sterna hirundo* Common

M 203

13–16" (33–40 cm) A graceful small *black-capped* slim bird with a *deeply forked tail. Summer:* White with a pale gray mantle and black cap; bill red-orange with a black tip; feet orange-red. Slight gray wash to underparts. *Immature and winter adult:* Black cap incomplete; bill blackish; dark bar on shoulder. **VOICE:** A drawling *kee-arr* (downward inflection); also *kik-kik-kik*; a quick *kirri-kirri.* **RANGE:** Temperate zone of N. Hemisphere. Winters to S. Hemisphere. **HABITAT:** Lakes, ocean, bays, beaches; nests colonially on sandy beaches and small islands.

FORSTER'S TERN *Sterna forsteri* Common

M 205

14–15" (35–38 cm) A tern with *frosty wingtips.* Very similar to Common Tern, but primaries lighter than rest of wing on some birds (darker in Common), tail grayer; bill more orange. In fall and winter, adult and immature Forster's Terns have a *black mask through eye and ear* (not around nape), *lack* dark bar on shoulder. **VOICE:** A harsh, nasal *za-a-ap* and a nasal *kyarr.* **RANGE:** W. Canada, w. U.S., and cen. Atlantic Coast to Tamaulipas. Winters s. U.S. to Guatemala. **HABITAT:** Marshes (fresh, salt), lakes, bays, beaches, ocean. Nests in marshes.

ROSEATE TERN *Sterna dougallii* Scarce

M 202

14–17" (35–43 cm) Similar to Common Tern but paler above, with longer tail points. At rest, tail extends well beyond wingtips. In spring and summer, thin, long *black bill* sets it apart from similar terns, all of which have reddish bills at that time of year. When breeding, Roseate may acquire rosy blush to breast and varying amounts of red at base of bill; then rely on other points such as wingbeats more shallow and rapid to separate from Common. **VOICE:** A rasping *ka-a-ak*; a soft two-syllabled *chu-ick* or *chiv-ick.* **RANGE:** Breeds locally and wanders widely along Atlantic Coast and Indian Ocean coasts. **HABITAT:** Coastal; salt bays, estuaries, ocean.

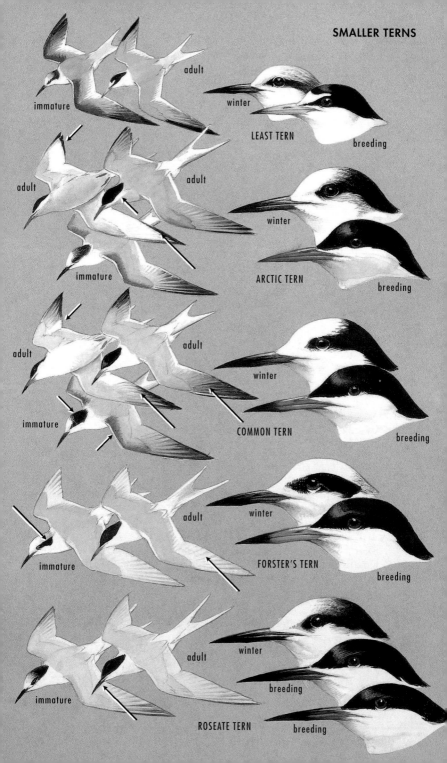

SMALLER TERNS

immature

adult

winter

LEAST TERN

breeding

adult

adult

immature

winter

ARCTIC TERN

breeding

adult

adult

immature

winter

COMMON TERN

breeding

adult

immature

winter

FORSTER'S TERN

breeding

adult

immature

winter

breeding

ROSEATE TERN

breeding

BLACK TERN *Chlidonias niger* Uncommon

M 209

9–10" (23–25 cm) A *black-bodied* tern. *Breeding:* Head and under-parts black; back, wings, and tail dark gray. Molting birds by midsummer have black largely replaced by white. Then note pied head and smudge on side of breast. Immature similar. **SIMILAR SPECIES:** White-winged Tern (next). **VOICE:** A sharp *kik, keek,* or *klea.* **HABITAT:** Fresh marshes, lakes; in migration, coastal waters.

WHITE-WINGED TERN *Chlidonias leucopterus* Casual vagrant

9" (23 cm) In summer, underwing lining black, upperwing mostly white and paler tail. In winter, paler than Black Tern; lacks dark shoulder spot of Black Tern. Numerous eastern sightings. European.

BROWN NODDY *Anous stolidus* Uncommon and restricted

15" (38 cm) A sooty *brown tern* with a whitish cap. *Wedge-shaped tail.* Immature has duller cap. **SIMILAR SPECIES:** Black Noddy (*A. minutus*) occurs occasionally with Brown Noddies at Dry Tortugas. It is smaller (12 in.), blacker, with a whiter cap and slightly larger bill. **VOICE:** A ripping *karrrrk* or *arrrrowk.* A harsh *eye-ak.* **EAST:** Breeds in Dry Tortugas off Fla. Keys. Rarely carried northward by tropical hurricanes. Casual stray to Tex.

SOOTY TERN *Sterna fuscata* Uncommon and restricted

M 208

15–17" (38–43 cm) A cleanly patterned tern that is *black above and white below.* Cheeks and patch on forehead white; bill and feet black. *Immature:* Dark brown; back spotted with white; tail forked. **VOICE:** A nasal *wide-a-wake* or *wacky-wack.* **EAST:** A large colony in Dry Tortugas off Fla. Keys. Also breeds off Gulf Coast of La. and Tex. Regularly carried northward along coast and inland by hurricanes.

BRIDLED TERN *Sterna anaethetus* Uncommon and restricted

M 207

14" (35 cm) A tern of warm oceans and farther north after hurricanes. **SIMILAR SPECIES:** Resembles Sooty Tern, but back grayer; note wide *whitish collar* separating black cap from back; white forehead patch extends *behind eye* (in Sooty, *to* eye). Sooty also is darker in tail and has paler underside of primaries. **EAST:** Carried by tropical storms well north along Atlantic Coast. Regular in Gulf Stream north to Cape Hatteras and in Gulf of Mexico, smaller numbers north to N.J. coast.

SKIMMERS. Family Rynchopinae.

Slim, short-legged relatives of gulls and terns. Unequal mandible lengths of their knifelike red bills is unique. **FOOD:** Small fish, crustaceans. **RANGE:** Coasts, large rivers, lakes. **NO. OF SPECIES:** World, 3; East, 1.

BLACK SKIMMER *Rynchops niger* Locally common

16–20" (40–50 cm) This species skims low, dipping its knifelike lower mandible into water. Black above and white below; more slender than a gull, with long wings. Bright red bill (tipped with black) is long and flattened side to side; lower mandible juts a third beyond upper. *Immature:* Brownish, speckled; slightly smaller bill. **VOICE:** Soft, short, barking notes. Also *kaup, kaup.* **HABITAT:** Ocean beaches, salt bays, tidewater; in Fla., also inland lakes.

DARK TERNS, SKIMMER

winter

molting

breeding

BLACK TERN

WHITE-WINGED
TERN

BROWN NODDY

BLACK NODDY

immature
SOOTY TERN

SOOTY TERN
adult

BRIDLED TERN

immature

adult

BLACK SKIMMER

adult

AUKS, ETC. Family Alcidae.

Auks ("alcids") are black-and-white seabirds that suggest penguins, replacing the latter in the N. Hemisphere. Sexes alike. They dive expertly, using their wings underwater, flipperlike, as penguins do, but they also use them to propel themselves through the air in a rapidly whirring flight. In flight, they are given to much veering and spread their webbed feet wide as brakes before landing. Swimming, they are ducklike but have short necks and pointed, stubby, or laterally flat bills. On rocky islands, where most species nest in crowded colonies, they stand nearly erect, penguinlike. Birds of the open sea, they very rarely appear on fresh water, descending to the latitudes of n. U.S. in fall or winter. Watch for them from coastal points during nasty weather. **FOOD:** Fish, crustaceans, mollusks, algae. **RANGE:** N. Atlantic, N. Pacific, Arctic Ocean. **NO. OF SPECIES:** World, 23; East, 6 (+ 2 accidental, 1 extinct).

RAZORBILL *Alca torda* Uncommon

M 214

16–18" (40–45 cm) Size of a small duck. Black above and white below; characterized by a rather heavy head, thick neck, and *flat bill* that is crossed midway by a white mark. On the water, *cocked-up pointed tail* is often characteristic. **SIMILAR SPECIES:** Immature Razorbill has a smaller bill than the adult, and it lacks white mark (hence resembling Thick-billed Murre), but bill is stubby and rounded enough to suggest bird's parentage. **VOICE:** A weak whirring whistle; a deep growling *hey Al.* **RANGE:** N. Atlantic (both sides) from Arctic south to Me. in summer, British Isles. **HABITAT:** Open ocean; sea cliffs when nesting.

THICK-BILLED MURRE *Uria lomvia* Scarce

M 213

17–19" (43–48 cm) Similar to Common Murre but a bit larger, *blacker above;* bill slightly thicker, with a *whitish line* along gape. Note also sharper peak of the white on throat. In winter, black extends *below eye;* no dark stripe through white ear coverts; white bill mark less evident. **VOICE:** Very similar to Common Murre. **RANGE:** Cold oceans of N. Hemisphere. **HABITAT:** Open ocean; sea cliffs when nesting.

COMMON MURRE *Uria aalge* Scarce

M 212

16–17" (40–43 cm) Size of a small duck, with a *slender* pointed bill. *Breeding:* Head, back, and wings dark brown; underparts and line on rear edge of wing white. *"Ringed"* morph: A few birds have a narrow white eye-ring and white line behind it. More common in the Far North. *Winter:* Similar, but throat and cheeks white. A *black mark* extends from eye onto white cheek. Murres raft on water, fly in lines. They are very gregarious in nesting colonies. **VOICE:** Hoarse, deep growls, *arrr* or *arra.* **RANGE:** N. parts of N. Pacific, N. Atlantic. **HABITAT:** Sea cliffs (breeding), ocean.

ALCIDS (AUKS)

immature

breeding

RAZORBILL

winter

winter

THICK-BILLED MURRE

breeding

winter

breeding

COMMON MURRE

"bridled" form

COMMON
MURRE
breeding

THICK-BILLED
MURRE
breeding

RAZORBILL
breeding

1844

GREAT AUK
extinct

DOVEKIE *Alle alle*   Scarce

M 211

7½–9" (19–23 cm) The smallest auk, about the size of a European Starling; chubby and seemingly neckless. In flight, flocks bunch tightly, starlinglike. Contrasting alcid pattern, *black above, white below,* together with *small size and very stubby bill,* separates it quickly from other alcids. By far the smallest winter alcid in the East. It is black-hooded in summer, white-chested in winter. **SIMILAR SPECIES:** Young of other alcids are larger (size is deceptive on the ocean); all have *larger bills.* **VOICE:** A shrill chatter. Noisy on nesting grounds. **RANGE:** Breeds coastal Greenland, n. Iceland, Spitzbergen, etc. Winters at sea to e. U.S. **EAST:** Winters offshore in N. Atlantic from ice line south to Va., irregularly to Fla. Accidental inland when "wrecked" by November storms. **HABITAT:** Offshore, open ocean. Nests on seacliffs.

BLACK GUILLEMOT *Cepphus grylle*   Fairly common

M 215

12–14" (30–35 cm) A mid-sized *black* bird with large *white* wing patch, *bright red* feet, and pointed bill in breeding plumage. Inside of mouth is *red. Winter:* Pale with whitish underparts and barred back. Wings black with a white patch as in summer. *Immature:* Darker above than winter adult, with a dingier, mottled wing patch. **SIMILAR SPECIES:** No other Atlantic alcid has a white wing patch (although others show a narrow line of white on trailing edge of wing). In winter, much larger White-winged Scoter (which has a white wing patch) is black, whereas Black Guillemot is usually whitish. Wing patch of White-winged Scoter is positioned at rear of wing. **VOICE:** A wheezing or hissing *peeeee;* very high-pitched. **RANGE:** N. Atlantic sector of Arctic south to New England, British Isles. **HABITAT:** Inshore waters of ocean; breeds in small groups or singly in holes in ground or under rocks on rocky shores, islands. Less pelagic than other auks.

ATLANTIC PUFFIN *Fratercula arctica*   Scarce

M 216

12" (30 cm) *Colorful triangular bill* is most striking feature of the chunky little "Sea Parrot." On the wing, it is a stubby, short-necked, thick-headed bird with a buzzy flight. No white border on wing. *Breeding:* Upperparts black, underbody white, cheeks *pale gray;* triangular bill broadly tipped with *red.* Feet bright orange. *Winter:* Cheeks grayer; bill smaller, duller; but obviously a puffin. *Immature:* Bill much smaller, mostly dark, but both mandibles well curved. Chunky shape and gray cheeks are unmistakably those of a puffin. **SIMILAR SPECIES:** Immature puffin may be mistaken for young Razorbill, but note gray cheeks, all-dark underwing. **VOICE:** Usually silent. When nesting, a low growling *ow* or *arr.* **RANGE:** N. Atlantic from s. Greenland and Iceland to New England, British Isles. **HABITAT:** Coastal and offshore waters, open sea (very rarely seen from shore except near breeding colonies). Colonial; breeds in holes in turf and among the rocks of sea islands.

ALCIDS (AUKS)

winter

DOVEKIE

breeding

winter

breeding

BLACK GUILLEMOT

winter

breeding

breeding

immature

ATLANTIC PUFFIN

winter

adults
breeding

ATLANTIC
PUFFIN

BLACK GUILLEMOT
breeding

DOVEKIE
breeding

PIGEONS AND DOVES. Family Columbidae.

Plump, fast-flying birds with small heads; low cooing voices. Two types: (1) with fanlike tails (e.g., Rock Dove) and (2) smaller, brownish, with rounded or pointed tails (e.g., Mourning Dove). Sexes similar. **FOOD:** Seeds, waste grain, fruits, insects. **RANGE:** Nearly worldwide. **NO. OF SPECIES:** World, 308; East, 4 (+ 5 accidental, 3 introduced, 1 extinct).

MOURNING DOVE *Zenaida macroura* — Common

12" (30 cm) The common wild dove in the East. Brown; smaller and slimmer than Rock Dove. Note *pointed tail* with large white spots. **VOICE:** A hollow mournful *coah, cooo, cooo, coo.* At a distance only the 3 *coo's* are audible. **RANGE:** Se. Alaska, s. Canada to Panama. **HABITAT:** Farms, towns, open woods, scrub, roadsides, grassland.

M 221

EURASIAN COLLARED-DOVE *Streptopelia decaocto* — Locally common

12½" (32 cm) Like a Mourning Dove without pointed tail and slightly stockier, *pale buffy gray* with distinct *black collar*. Note *squared-off tail* with *broad pale terminal band*. Arrived in Fla. from the Bahamas, where it was introduced. Population in Fla. is booming, and is rapidly spreading north and west. **HABITAT:** Towns, field edges, cultivated land.

M 219

COMMON GROUND-DOVE *Columbina passerina* — Uncommon

6½" (16 cm) A very small dove, *not much larger than a sparrow.* Note *stubby black tail* and rounded wings that flash *rufous* in flight. **SIMILAR SPECIES:** Juvenile Mourning Doves may have short tails and scaly-appearing plumage. **VOICE:** A soft, monotonously repeated *woo-oo, woo-oo,* etc. May sound monosyllabic, *wooo,* with rising inflection. **HABITAT:** Farms, orchards, wood edges, roadsides, waste places, coastal dunes.

M 223

INCA DOVE *Columbina inca* — Locally common

7½" (19 cm) A very small slim dove with a *scaly* appearance; *rufous* in primaries. Differs from Common Ground-Dove by its *comparatively long* square-ended tail that *flashes white on sides.* **SIMILAR SPECIES:** Juvenile Mourning Dove may have short tail and scaly plumage. **HABITAT:** Towns, parks, farms.

M 222

WHITE-WINGED DOVE *Zenaida asiatica* — Locally common

11–11½" (28–29 cm) In flight, note large white patch on wing, black primaries. Tail blunt, not pointed; white corners. **RANGE:** Sw. U.S. to Peru. Strays north. **HABITAT:** Mesquite, citrus groves, towns, riparian woodlands.

M 220

WHITE-CROWNED PIGEON *Columba leucocephala* — Fairly common, local

13" (33 cm) A stocky, wild pigeon, size and build of Rock Dove; *completely dark* except for an immaculate *white crown.* **VOICE:** A low owl-like *wof, wof, wo, co-woo.* **RANGE:** W. Indies locally to s. Fla. and Keys, mainly in summer. **HABITAT:** Mangrove keys, thickets, hardwood hammocks. Perches on power lines.

M 218

RINGED TURTLE-DOVE *Streptopelia risoria*

12" (30 cm) Escaped cagebirds appear at feeders.

ROCK DOVE *Columba livia* — Common

13" (33 cm) Typical birds are gray with a *whitish rump,* 2 *black wing bars,* and a broad dark tail-band. Many color variants. **VOICE:** A soft gurgling *co-roo-coo.* **RANGE:** Worldwide.

M 217

PASSENGER PIGEON

extinct

PIGEONS, DOVES
Sexes similar

COMMON
GROUND-
DOVE

INCA DOVE

MOURNING
DOVE

EURASIAN
COLLARED-
DOVE

WHITE-
CROWNED
PIGEON

WHITE-WINGED
DOVE

RINGED
TURTLE-DOVE

plumages
variable

ROCK DOVE
(Domestic or
Feral Pigeon)

EURASIAN
COLLARED-DOVE

typical or
ancestral form

PARROTS, PARAKEETS. Family Psittacidae.

Compact, short-necked birds with stout hooked bills. Feet zygodactyl (2 toes fore, 2 aft). Noisy and gaudily colored. **RANGE:** Most of S. Hemisphere; also Tropics and Subtropics of N. Hemisphere. **NO. OF SPECIES:** World, 331; East, only 1 endemic, the Carolina Parakeet, *Conuropsis carolinensis*, now extinct (last reported 1920 in Fla.). A number of exotic species have been released or have escaped, especially around Miami, where species such as the Yellow-chevroned and White-winged Parakeets are well established. Monk Parakeet is doing well in several states. At least a score of other species have been observed in a free-flying state. Most species unable to withstand winter in northern areas. Below is a sampling; new species occur yearly! (Indigenous location given in parentheses.)

MONK PARAKEET *Myiopsitta monachus*   Locally common
(Argentina) 11" (29 cm) Pale gray face and chest, buff band across belly. Has become established in spots from Conn. to Fla. and west to Ill. and Tex. Nest of sticks (only parrot to build a stick nest), massive with several compartments. Has become a nuisance in many areas. Raucous calls. Comes to feeders.

WHITE-WINGED PARAKEET *Brotogeris versicolurus*   Local
(S. America) 9" (23 cm) White and yellow wing patch. Established in Miami area. Now outnumbered by Yellow-chevroned *Brotogeris chiriri*, which is very similar but lacks white in wings. Numbers on decline.

BUDGERIGAR *Melopsittacus undulatus*   Local
(Australia) 7" (18 cm) Scalloped back. The classic parakeet. Usually green; a small minority may be blue, yellow, or white. Thousands were established along the west coast of Fla.; lesser numbers on the southeast coast of Fla. Recent years have seen dramatic decline. Escapes many areas.

RED-CROWNED PARROT *Amazona viridigenalis*   Locally established
12" (30 cm) Large, with red crown (blue nape in first year), red wing panels. Established in many southern cities from introductions. S. Tex. population may be from Mexican vagrants.

1. **YELLOW-HEADED PARROT** *Amazona oratrix* (Tropical America) 14" (35 cm)

2. **BLACK-HOODED PARAKEET** *Nandayus nenday* (S. America) 12" (30 cm)

3. **BLOSSOM-HEADED PARAKEET** *Psittacula roseata* (Himalayas) 12" (30 cm)

4. **ROSE-RINGED PARAKEET** *Psittacula krameri* (Africa, India) 16" (40 cm)

5. **YELLOW-COLLARED LOVEBIRD** *Agapornis personatus* (E. Africa) 6" (15 cm)

6. **HISPANIOLAN PARAKEET** *Aratinga chloroptera* (Hispaniola) 12" (31 cm)

7. **GREEN PARAKEET** *Aratinga holochlora* (Mexico) 10–12" (25–30 cm)

8. **ORANGE-FRONTED PARAKEET** *Aratinga canicularis* (Mexico) 9" (23 cm)

9. **ORANGE-CHINNED PARAKEET** *Brotogeris jugularis* (C. America) 7" (18 cm)

10. **COCKATIEL** *Nymphicus hollandicus* (Australia) 12–13" (30–33 cm)

PARROTS
(Escapes)

CAROLINA PARAKEET
(formerly endemic to
N. America, now extinct)

WHITE-WINGED
PARAKEET

MONK PARAKEET

RED-CROWNED
PARROT

BUDGERIGAR
some individuals
may be blue or
yellow

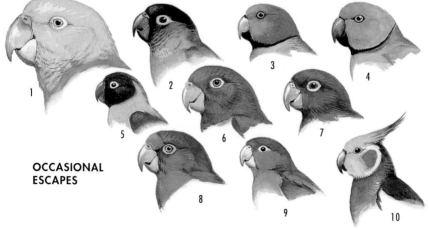

OCCASIONAL
ESCAPES

1

2

3

4

5

6

7

8

9

10

CUCKOOS. Family Cuculidae.

Slender, long-tailed birds; feet zygodactyl (2 toes forward, 2 aft). Sexes alike. **FOOD:** Caterpillars, insects; roadrunners eats reptiles; anis eat seeds, fruits. **RANGE:** Warm and temperate regions of world. **NO. OF SPECIES:** World, 138; East, 6.

YELLOW-BILLED CUCKOO *Coccyzus americanus* Fairly common

M 225

11–13" (28–33 cm) Recognized as a cuckoo by slim sinuous look, brown back, plain white breast. *Rufous* in wings, *large white* spots at tips of black tail feathers (most noticeable from below), narrow yellow eye-ring, and *yellow* lower mandible on slightly curved bill. Secretive. **VOICE:** Song, a rapid throaty *ka-ka-ka-ka-ka-ka-ka-ka-ka-ka-ka-ka-kow-kow-kowlp-kowlp-kowlp-kowlp* (slowing toward end). **RANGE:** S. Canada to Mexico, W. Indies. Winters to Argentina. **HABITAT:** Woodlands, thickets, orchards.

BLACK-BILLED CUCKOO *Coccyzus erythropthalmus* Fairly common

M 224

11–12" (28–30 cm) Similar to Yellow-billed Cuckoo: bill black; narrow *red* eye-ring (in adult). *Little or no rufous in wing*; small tail spots. **VOICE:** A fast rhythmic *cucucu, cucucu, cucucu,* etc. Grouped rhythm (3 or 4) is typical. May sing at night. Secretive. **RANGE:** S. Canada, cen. and ne. U.S. Winters in n. S. America. **HABITAT:** Wood edges, groves, thickets.

MANGROVE CUCKOO *Coccyzus minor* Uncommon, local

M 226

12" (30 cm) Similar to Yellow-billed Cuckoo (both live in s. Fla.), but belly *creamy buff*; no rufous in wing. Note *black ear patch*. **RANGE:** S. Fla., W. Indies, Mexico, to n. Brazil. **HABITAT:** In our area, mangroves and hardwood woodlands.

SMOOTH-BILLED ANI *Crotophaga ani* Scarce, restricted

M 228

12½" (31 cm) A coal-black grackle-sized bird with a long "loose-jointed tail," short wings, and huge bill with a *high curved* ridge and noticeable *angle* to lower mandible (giving a puffinlike profile). Flight weak; alternately flaps and sails. Often moves in groups. **VOICE:** A whining whistle. A querulous *que-lick.* **RANGE:** S. Fla., W. Indies, Caribbean coastal islands to Argentina. Recent serious declines in Fla. **HABITAT:** Brushy edges, thickets.

GROOVE-BILLED ANI *Crotophaga sulcirostris* Uncommon, restricted

M 229

13" (33 cm) Very similar to Smooth-billed Ani but with 3 grooves on upper mandible; *lacks hump* on ridge of bill. **VOICE:** A repeated *whee-o* or *chik bereek,* first note slurring up. **RANGE:** S. Tex. and Gulf Coast to Argentina. Scattered records east, west, and north to Great Lakes and Mid-Atlantic. **HABITAT:** Brushy edges, thickets, weedy fields.

GREATER ROADRUNNER *Geococcyx californianus* Fairly common

M 227

20–24" (50–60 cm) The cuckoo that runs on the ground. Large, slender, streaked, with a long white-tipped tail, shaggy crest, long legs. In flight, a white crescent on open wing. **VOICE:** 6 to 8 low dovelike *coo's* descending in pitch. **RANGE:** Sw. and s. Central U.S. to cen. Mexico. **HABITAT:** Dry open country with scattered cover, brush.

CUCKOOS, etc.
Sexes similar

YELLOW-BILLED
CUCKOO

adult

immature

BLACK-BILLED
CUCKOO

MANGROVE CUCKOO

adult

GROOVE-
BILLED
ANI

SMOOTH
BILLED
ANI

GREATER ROADRUNNER

OWLS. Families Strigidae (True Owls) and Tytonidae (Barn Owls).

Chiefly nocturnal birds of prey, with large heads, flattened faces forming facial disks, and large forward-facing eyes. Hooked bills, hooked talons, and usually feathered feet (outer toe reversible). Flight silent, often mothlike. Some species have "horns" or "ears" of feather tufts. Sexes similar; female larger. **FOOD:** Rodents, birds, reptiles, fish, large insects. **RANGE:** Nearly cosmopolitan. **NO. OF SPECIES:** True Owls, World, 188; East, 11 (+ 1 accidental); Barn Owls, World, 16; East, 1.

SHORT-EARED OWL *Asio flammeus* — Uncommon

M 239

13–17" (33–43 cm) A pale owl of open country, often abroad by day. Streaked tawny brown color and bounding, mothlike flight. Large buffy wing patch shows in flight; on underwing, a black carpal ("wrist") patch. *Dark face disks* emphasize yellow eyes. **SIMILAR SPECIES:** Long-eared Owl in flight is nearly identical. Short-eared deep wingbeats. Long-eared rarely breaks the horizontal. **VOICE:** An emphatic sneezy bark, *kee-yow!, wow!,* or *waow!* **RANGE:** Nearly worldwide. In N. America breeds from Arctic to cen. U.S. Winters south to Mexico. **HABITAT:** Prairies, marshes (fresh and salt), dunes, tundra. Nests on ground.

EASTERN SCREECH-OWL *Otus asio* — Common

M 231

7–10" (18–25 cm) Our only *small* eastern owl with ear tufts. Two color morphs: foxy red and gray. No other eared owl is bright foxy red. Young bird may lack conspicuous ear tufts. **VOICE:** A mournful whinny or wail; tremulous, descending in pitch. Sometimes a series on a single pitch. **RANGE:** S. Canada to cen. Mexico. **HABITAT:** Woodlands, farm groves, shade trees.

LONG-EARED OWL *Asio otus* — Uncommon

M 238

13–16" (33–40 cm) A slender crow-sized owl with long ear tufts. Usually seen "frozen" close to trunk of dense tree for camouflage. In winter, often roosts in *groups*. Smaller than Great Horned Owl (see also Short-eared Owl). Underparts streaked *lengthwise,* not barred crosswise. Ears closer together, erect. **VOICE:** A low moaning *hooooo.* Also a catlike whine and a doglike bark. **RANGE:** Canada to sw. and s.-cen. U.S.; Eurasia, n. Africa. **HABITAT:** Woodlands, thickets, tangles, conifer groves; hunts open areas.

GREAT HORNED OWL *Bubo virginianus* — Common

M 232

18–25" (45–63 cm) A very *large* owl with ear tufts or "horns." Often active before dark. Heavily *barred* beneath; has a conspicuous *white bib or "beard"* on throat. In flight, as large as a buteo; shallow wingbeats; looks neckless, large headed. In Canada, races vary from very dark in the Maritimes to almost as pale as Snowy Owl around Hudson Bay. **SIMILAR SPECIES:** Long-eared Owl is smaller (crow-sized in flight), with lengthwise streaking rather than crosswise barring beneath. Ears closer together; lacks white bib. **VOICE:** A resonant hooting of 3–8 hoots. Male usually 4 or 5, in this rhythm: *hoo, hoo-oo, hoo, hoo.* Female lower in pitch, 6–8: *hoo, hoo-hoo-hoo, hoo-oo, hoo-oo.* Young birds make catlike screams, especially when separated from adults in late summer and fall. **RANGE:** Tree limit in Canada to Tierra del Fuego. **HABITAT:** Forests, woodlands, streamsides, open country.

EARED OWLS

SHORT-EARED OWL

rufous morph

EASTERN SCREECH-OWL

gray morph

LONG-EARED OWL

subarctic form

GREAT HORNED OWL

typical

BARRED OWL *Strix varia* Locally common

M 236

17–24" (43–60 cm) A large gray-brown, puffy-headed woodland owl. Note big *brown* eyes. Barred pattern *across* chest and streaked *lengthwise* on belly. Whitish spots on back. Often active before dark. **SIMILAR SPECIES:** Other owls, except Barn Owl, have yellow eyes. **VOICE:** Usually consists of 8 accented hoots, in 2 groups of 4: *hoohoo-hoohoo, hoohoo-hoohooaw.* The *aw* at the close is characteristic. **RANGE:** Canada to Honduras. **HABITAT:** Woodlands, wooded river bottoms, wooded swamps.

BARN OWL *Tyto alba* Uncommon

M 230

14–20" (35–50 cm) Our only owl with a *white, heart-shaped face.* A long-legged, knock-kneed, pale, monkey-faced owl. *Dark eyes,* no ear tufts. Distinguished in flight as an owl by the large head and light mothlike flight; unstreaked whitish or pale cinnamon underparts (ghostly at night), and golden-buff or rusty upper plumage. **SIMILAR SPECIES:** Short-eared Owl (marshes) is streaked, has darker face and underparts, yellow eyes, shorter legs. **VOICE:** A shrill rasping hiss or snore: *kschh* or *shiiish.* **RANGE:** Nearly worldwide in tropical and temperate regions; in New World from s. Canada to Tierra del Fuego, S. America. **HABITAT:** Open country, groves, farms, barns, towns, cliffs.

GREAT GRAY OWL *Strix nebulosa* Scarce

M 237

24–33" (60–83 cm) Largest N. American owl; dusky gray, heavily striped *lengthwise* on underparts. It is round-headed, without ear tufts; *concentrically lined facial disks* are very large and prominent, dwarfing yellow eyes. Note *black chin spot* bordered by 2 broad white patches like *white mustaches.* Tail is long for an owl (12 in.). Often hunts by day. Very tame. **SIMILAR SPECIES:** Barred Owl is smaller, browner, with *brown* (not yellow) eyes, smaller face disks, shorter tail. **VOICE:** A deep booming *whoo-hoo-hoo.* Also deep single *whoo's.* **RANGE:** Boreal forests of N. Hemisphere. An irruptive species. Invasion south one year, and then may be rare for many years. **HABITAT:** Dense conifer forests, adjacent meadows, bogs, field edges.

SNOWY OWL *Nyctea scandiaca* Scarce

M 233

20–27" (50–68 cm) A large *white* owl; variously flecked or barred. Round head, *yellow* eyes. Males tend to be much whiter than heavily streaked or barred female and immature. Perches on dunes, posts, haystacks, buildings, etc. **SIMILAR SPECIES:** (1) Barn Owl is whitish on underparts only; has dark eyes; nocturnal. (2) Young owls of all species are whitish when in the downy stage. (3) See Gyrfalcon (white morph), p. 116. **VOICE:** Usually silent. On nesting territory, a deep booming *hooo.* Flight note when breeding, a loud repeated *krow-ow;* also a repeated *rick.* **RANGE:** Arctic; circumpolar. Has cyclic winter irruptions southward into U.S. **HABITAT:** Prairies, fields, marshes, beaches, dunes; in summer, arctic tundra.

LARGE OWLS
Without ear tufts

BARRED OWL

BARN OWL

GREAT GRAY OWL

SNOWY OWL

BOREAL OWL *Aegolius funereus*   Scarce

M 240

9–10" (23–25 cm) A small, flat-headed, earless owl. Very tame. Similar to Northern Saw-whet Owl but a bit larger; facial disks pale grayish white *framed with black. Note:* Bill *pale horn* or *yellowish;* forehead *thickly spotted* with white. *Juvenile:* Similar to young Northern Saw-whet but duskier; eyebrows dirty whitish or gray; belly obscurely blotched, not tawny ocher. **SIMILAR SPECIES:** (1) Northern Saw-whet Owl is smaller. Adult has a black bill, lacks black facial frames, and has fine white *streaks* on forehead rather than spots. (2) Hawk Owl is larger, grayer, *long-tailed;* it is *barred below.* **VOICE:** A series of high-pitched "tooting" notes in a rapid series. At a distance, almost like a winnowing snipe. Ventriloquial quality makes it hard to locate. **RANGE:** Boreal forests of W. Hemisphere. Sporadic irruptive years when species appears south of normal range. **HABITAT:** Mixed-wood and conifer forests, muskeg.

NORTHERN SAW-WHET OWL *Aegolius acadicus*   Uncommon

M 241

7–8½" (18–21 cm) A very tame little owl; smaller than Eastern Screech-Owl, lacking ear tufts. Underparts have soft blotchy brown streaks. *Note:* Bill is black. Young bird in summer is chocolate brown, with conspicuous white eyebrows forming a broad V over bill. Belly *tawny ocher.* **SIMILAR SPECIES:** Boreal Owl is somewhat larger, has black facial frames and a yellowish or pale horn-colored bill. **VOICE:** Song, a mellow whistled toot repeated mechanically in endless succession, often 80–100 times per minute: *too, too, too, too, too,* etc. **RANGE:** Se. Alaska, Canada, w. and ne. U.S. to cen. Mexico. **HABITAT:** Forests, conifers, groves.

BURROWING OWL *Athene cunicularia*   Uncommon

M 235

9–11" (23–28 cm) A small owl of open country, often seen by day standing erect on ground near nest hole or on posts. About size of Eastern Screech-Owl; barred and spotted, white chin stripe, round head, stubby tail. Note *long legs* (for an owl). Bobs and bows when agitated. **VOICE:** A rapid chattering *quick-quick-quick.* At night, a mellow *co-hoo,* higher than Mourning Dove's *coo.* Young in burrow rattle like rattlesnake to deter predators. **RANGE:** Sw. Canada, w. U.S., Fla. to s. Argentina. Migratory in North. Rarely wanders, especially in fall. **HABITAT:** Open grassland, prairies, farmland, airfields, golf courses, etc.

NORTHERN HAWK OWL *Surnia ulula*   Scarce

M 234

14–17½" (36–44 cm) A medium-sized, hawklike, day-flying owl, with a *long, rounded tail and completely barred underparts.* Note *broad black sideburns* framing its pale face. Does not sit as erect as other owls; often perches at tip of a tree and jerks tail like a kestrel. Flight is shrikelike, flying low, then rising abruptly to its perch. **VOICE:** A chattering *kikikiki,* more like a falcon than an owl. A kestrel-like *illy-illy-illy-illy.* Also a harsh scream. **RANGE:** Boreal forests of N. Hemisphere. Sporadic irruptive years when it appears south of normal range. **HABITAT:** Conifer forests, birch scrub, tamarack bogs, muskeg, field edges.

SMALL OWLS

BOREAL OWL

NORTHERN
SAW-WHET
OWL
juvenile

adult

NORTHERN
SAW-WHET
OWL

BURROWING
OWL

NORTHERN HAWK OWL

NIGHTHAWKS, NIGHTJARS. Family Caprimulgidae.

Nocturnal birds with ample tails, large eyes, tiny bills, large bristled gapes, very short legs. By day they rest horizontally on limbs or on ground, camouflaged by "dead leaf" feather pattern. Most easily identified at night by voice. Nighthawks are an aberrant goatsucker, often abroad by day. **FOOD:** Insects. **RANGE:** Nearly worldwide in temperate and tropical regions. **NO. OF SPECIES:** World, 89; East, 6 (+ 1 accidental).

WHIP-POOR-WILL *Caprimulgus vociferus* — Uncommon

M 245

9½" (24 cm) A voice of the night woods. When flushed by day, flutters away on *rounded* wings like a large brown moth. Male shows large white tail patches; in female, these are buffy. Note, when sitting, wingtip well short of tail end. **VOICE:** At night, a rolling, tiresomely repeated *whip´ poor-weel´* or *pur´ple-rib´*, etc.; accent on first and last syllables. If close, listen for introductory *chuck* note. **RANGE:** Cen. and e. Canada to Honduras. Winters from Gulf states to Honduras. **HABITAT:** Deciduous woodlands, field edges, open ridges.

CHUCK-WILL'S-WIDOW *Caprimulgus carolinensis* — Uncommon

M 244

12" (30 cm) Similar to Whip-poor-will; larger, much browner, with a *brown* (not blackish) throat. Identify by size (flat, bull-headed appearance), brownish look, more restricted white areas in tail of male; also by voice, range. **VOICE:** Call, *chuck-will´-wid´-ow* (less vigorous than efforts of Whip-poor-will); four-syllabled, *chuck* often very low and difficult to hear. **RANGE:** S. U.S. Winters south to Colombia. **HABITAT:** Pine forests, river woodlands, groves.

COMMON POORWILL *Phalaenoptilus nuttallii* — Uncommon

M 243

7–8" (18–20 cm) Best known by its plaintive night call from arid hillsides. It appears smaller than a Common Nighthawk, has more rounded wings (no white bar), and its short rounded tail has *white corners.* **VOICE:** At night, a loud repeated *poor-will* or *poor-jill-ip.* **RANGE:** S. B.C., w. U.S. to cen. Mexico. Winters sw. U.S. south into Mexico. Known to hibernate. **HABITAT:** Dry hills, open brush.

COMMON PAURAQUE *Nyctidromus albicollis* — Uncommon

12" (30 cm) Larger than Whip-poor-will with white wing-bands as well as white in tail. Recognized by its call. **VOICE:** A hoarse slurred whistle, *pur-wi´eeeeer* or *we´eeeeer.* **RANGE:** S. Tex. to n. Argentina.

GOATSUCKERS

WHIP-POOR-WILL

COMMON POOR-WILL

CHUCK-WILL'S-WIDOW

COMMON PAURAQUE

NIGHTHAWKS. Family Caprimulgidae.

These goatsuckers are part of the same family treated on the previous pages.

COMMON NIGHTHAWK *Chordeiles minor*   Uncommon

M 242

9½" (24 cm) A slim-winged gray-brown bird often seen high in the air; flies erratically with deep stiff strokes; glides with wings on a dihedral. Prefers evening and night activity. More numerous and active in day over prairie habitat than in eastern forest areas. Note *broad white bar* across pointed wings. Male has a white bar across its notched tail and a white throat. When sitting, note wingtips well beyond tail tip. **SIMILAR SPECIES:** (1) Antillean Nighthawk regular, in Fla. Keys. Best distinguished by its voice, which is a dry four-syllabled *pity-pit-pit* or *killy-kadick*. (2) Lesser Nighthawk white on wing closer to tip, wings rounded. Juvenile is browner and less barred. **VOICE:** A nasal *peent* or *pee-ik*. In aerial display, male dives, then zooms up sharply with a sudden deep whir of wings. **RANGE:** Canada to Panama. Winters S. America. **HABITAT:** Open country to mountains; open pine woods; often seen in air over cities or towns. Sits on ground, posts, rails, roof-tops, and wires. Marked decline in East since 1970s.

LESSER NIGHTHAWK *Chordeiles acutipennis*   Fairly common, restricted

8–9" (20–23 cm) Slightly smaller than Common Nighthawk with shorter, more rounded wingtips, which in male have white bar (buffy in female) closer to wingtip. A more prominent white tail-band than in Common Nighthawk. Does not power dive. A bird of lowlands, not mountains. **VOICE:** A low *chuck, chuck* and a soft purring or pulsating sound, much like the trill of a toad. **RANGE:** Sw. U.S. to n. Chile, Brazil. **HABITAT:** Arid scrub, dry grassland, fields, prairies. Occurs east of 100° in Tex., very rarely east to Fla.

ANTILLEAN NIGHTHAWK *Chordeiles gundlachii*   Scarce, very restricted

8½" (22 cm) This W. Indian species is a regular spring and summer visitor to Fla. Keys and Dry Tortugas. Somewhat tawnier than Common Nighthawk but is more readily distinguished from it by call, a katydid-like *killy-kadick* or *pity-pit-pit*.

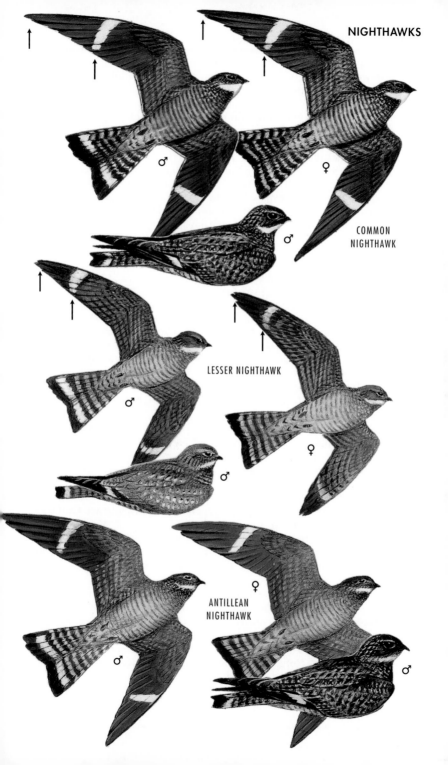

NIGHTHAWKS

COMMON
NIGHTHAWK

♂

♀

♂

LESSER NIGHTHAWK

♂

♀

♂

ANTILLEAN
NIGHTHAWK

♀

♂

♂

HUMMINGBIRDS. Family Trochilidae.

The smallest birds. Iridescent, with needlelike bills for sipping nectar. Jewel-like gorgets (throat feathers) adorn most adult males. Most females have whitish throats with dark spotting. Hover when feeding and can fly backward. Pugnacious. **FOOD:** Nectar (red flowers favored), small insects, spiders. Readily come to hummingbird feeders. **RANGE:** W. Hemisphere; most in Tropics. **NO. OF SPECIES:** World, 335; East, 1 (+10 accidental).

RUBY-THROATED HUMMINGBIRD *Archilochus colubris* Common

M 248

3–3¾" (8–9 cm) The male Ruby-throat has a *fiery red throat,* iridescent green back, forked tail. Female lacks red throat; tail blunt, with white spots. The *only widespread species in the East;* a number of other hummers may turn up as strays (usually at feeders), especially in the Gulf states in late fall and winter. Some day-flying sphinx moths (Sphingidae) might be mistaken for hummers when they hover to feed at flowers. **VOICE:** Male's wings hum while in courtship display. Chase notes high, squeaky. Other note a soft *chew.* **HABITAT:** Flowers, gardens, wood edges, over streams, edges of bogs.

RUFOUS HUMMINGBIRD *Selasphorus rufus* Rare in East

M 250

3½" (9 cm) *Male:* No other N. American hummingbird has a rufous back. Upperparts bright red-brown; throat orange-red. *Female and immature:* Green-backed; dull rufous on sides and at base of tail (no rufous in tail of Ruby-throated). Any *late hummingbird* visiting feeders in late October, November, and December in the East should be checked for this species.

ALLEN'S HUMMINGBIRD *Selasphorus sasin* Casual vagrant

3½" (9 cm) *Male:* Combination of green back, rufous sides and tail.

ANNA'S HUMMINGBIRD *Calypte anna* Casual vagrant

3½–4" (9–10 cm) *Male:* Red crown, red throat, dingy underparts.

BROAD-TAILED HUMMINGBIRD *Selasphorus platycercus* Casual vagrant

4–4½" (10–11 cm) Male has a red throat but lacks deeply forked tail of Ruby-throated. Wings *hum* and *buzz* in flight. Very rare in winter along w. Gulf Coast, casual farther east.

CALLIOPE HUMMINGBIRD *Stellula calliope* Casual vagrant

3" (7 cm) Throat of male purple rays on white. Strays reach Gulf states.

BLACK-CHINNED HUMMINGBIRD *Archilochus alexandri* Very rare vagrant

3½" (9 cm) *Male:* Black throat with violet blue patch. (*Note:* Most Eastern records have been immatures with spotted throats.) Western U.S. east to cen. and s. Tex. Vagrant elsewhere in East.

M 249

BAHAMA WOODSTAR *Calliphlox evelynae* Accidental to Fla.

3½" (9 cm) *Male:* Ocher belly, white breast, purple throat, forked tail.

GREEN VIOLET-EAR *Colibri thalassinus* Casual vagrant

4¾" (12 cm) Green with violet ear patch, bluish tail. Stray from Mexico.

BUFF-BELLIED HUMMINGBIRD *Amazilia yucatanensis* Uncommon, restricted

4¼" (11 cm) Note combination of buff underparts, rufous tail, and green throat. Bill red. Sexes similar.

M 247

RUBY-THROATED
HUMMINGBIRD

♂

♀

RUFOUS

♂

♀

CALLIOPE

♂

sphinx
moths resemble
hummingbirds

BROAD-
TAILED

♂

♀

ALLEN'S

♂

BLACK-
CHINNED

♂

♀

ANNA'S

♂

♀

BAHAMA
WOODSTAR

♂

♀

BUFF-
BELLIED

GREEN
VIOLET-EAR

♂

Solitary birds with large heads, large bills, and small syndactyl feet (2 toes partially joined). Most are fish-eaters, perching above the water, or hovering and plunging headfirst. **FOOD:** Mainly fish; some species eat insects, lizards. **RANGE:** Almost worldwide. **NO. OF SPECIES:** World, 93; East, 3.

GREEN KINGFISHER *Chloroceryle americana*   Uncommon, restricted

7½–8½" (18–21 cm) Kingfisher shape, *small size*; flight rapid, direct. Upperparts deep green with white spots; collar and underparts white, sides spotted. Male has a *rusty* breast-band; female has 1 or 2 greenish bands. (Note: Female Belted Kingfisher has a rusty band.) **VOICE:** A sharp clicking, *tick, tick, tick*; also a sharp squeak. **RANGE:** S. Tex. to Argentina. Resident in Tex. north to s. Edwards Plateau and along lower Rio Grande. **HABITAT:** Rivers, streams, ponds.

RINGED KINGFISHER *Ceryle torquata*   Uncommon, restricted

15–16" (38–40 cm) Larger than Belted Kingfisher; bill very large. Male has a *chestnut breast and belly*. Female has a broad blue-gray band across breast, separated from its chestnut belly by a narrow white line. **VOICE:** A rusty *cla-ack* or *wa-ak* or rolling rattle after a loud *chack*. **RANGE:** S. Tex. south to Tierra del Fuego. Uncommon resident along lower Rio Grande north to Webb Co., Tex.

BELTED KINGFISHER *Ceryle alcyon*   Fairly common

13" (33 cm) Hovering on rapidly beating wings in readiness for the plunge, or flying with uneven wingbeats (as if changing gear), rattling as it goes, the Belted Kingfisher is easily recognized. Perched, it is big headed and big billed, larger than a robin; blue-gray above, with a ragged bushy crest and a broad blue-gray breast-band. Female has an additional rusty breast-band. **VOICE:** A loud dry rattle. **RANGE:** Alaska, Canada to s. U.S. Winters to n. S. America. **HABITAT:** Streams, lakes, bays, coasts; nests in sand or clay banks; often perches on wires.

M 251

KINGFISHERS

GREEN KINGFISHER

♀

♂

RINGED KINGFISHER

♀

hovering

males lack the upper breast-band

♀

plunging

BELTED KINGFISHER

♂

WOODPECKERS. Family Picidae.

Chisel-billed, wood-boring birds with strong zygodactyl feet (usually 2 toes front, 2 rear), remarkably long tongues, and stiff spiny tails that act as props when climbing. Flight usually undulating. Most males have some red on head. **FOOD:** Tree-boring insects; some species eat ants, flying insects, berries, acorns, sap. **RANGE:** Mainly wooded parts of world, but absent in Australian region, Madagascar, most oceanic islands. **NO. OF SPECIES (INCLUDING ALLIES):** World, 217; East, 10 (+ 1 accidental).

RED-HEADED WOODPECKER *Melanerpes erythrocephalus*   Uncommon

M 252

8½–9½" (21–24 cm) The only eastern woodpecker with the *entire head red* (others may have a patch of red). Back *solid black,* rump white. Large square *white patch* is conspicuous on wing (making lower back look white when bird is at rest). Sexes similar. *Juvenile:* Dusky-headed; large white wing patch with black markings. **VOICE:** A loud *queer* or *queeah,* louder and higher pitched than *churr* of Red-bellied Woodpecker. **RANGE:** East of Rockies from s. Canada to Gulf states. Partial migrant in North. **HABITAT:** Groves, farm country, orchards, shade trees in towns, large scattered trees.

PILEATED WOODPECKER *Dryocopus pileatus*   Uncommon

M 261

16–19½" (40–49 cm) A spectacular *crow-sized* black woodpecker with a *flaming red crest.* Female has a blackish forehead, lacks red on mustache. Great size, sweeping wingbeats, and flashing white underwing areas identify it in flight. The diggings, large *oval* or *oblong* holes, indicate its presence. **VOICE:** Call resembles that of Northern Flicker, but louder, irregular: *kik-kik-kikkik — kik-kik,* etc. Also a more ringing, hurried call that may rise or fall slightly in pitch. **RANGE:** Canada to s. U.S. **HABITAT:** Conifer, mixed, and hardwood forests; woodlots.

IVORY-BILLED WOODPECKER *Campephilus principalis*   Probably extinct

20" (50 cm) Separated from Pileated Woodpecker by its slightly larger size, ivory-white bill, large *white wing patch visible at rest,* underwing pattern all white with black line through it. Female has a *black* crest. **VOICE:** Call unlike that of Pileated, a single loud tooting note constantly uttered as the bird forages about — a sharp nasal *kent* suggesting to some the note of a big nuthatch. Audubon wrote it as *pait,* resembling high false note of a clarinet. **RANGE:** Formerly river-bottom forests of se. U.S. and Cuba. Unsubstantiated reports still persist.

WOODPECKERS

immature

adult

RED-HEADED
WOODPECKER

sexes similar

♂

♀

under

PILEATED WOODPECKER

♀

♂

under

IVORY-BILLED
WOODPECKER

presumably
extinct

upper

NORTHERN "YELLOW-SHAFTED" FLICKER *Colaptes auratus* ✓ Common

M 260

12–14" (30–35 cm) Note conspicuous *white rump*, visible when bird flies. Flight is undulating. Overhead, it flashes *golden yellow* under wings and tail. Close up, it displays a black patch across chest and a red crescent on nape. Male has a black mustache. Flicker often hops awkwardly on ground while feeding on ants. **VOICE:** Song, a loud *wick wick wick wick wick*, etc. Notes, a loud *klee-yer,* and a squeaky *flick-a, flick-a,* etc. **RANGE:** Tree limit in Alaska, Canada south to Gulf states, Cuba. Migrant in northern parts of range. **HABITAT:** Open forests, woodlots, groves, farms, towns, semi-open country.

NORTHERN "RED-SHAFTED" FLICKER *Colaptes auratus* Common

12–14" (30–35 cm) Similar to "Yellow-shafted" (above), but with yellow of wing and tail linings replaced by *salmon red.* Both sexes lack red crescent on nape. Male has a *red* (not black) mustache. Where their ranges overlap (western edge of Great Plains), intergrades occur. These may have orange wing linings or a combination of other characters. **RANGE:** Se. Alaska, sw. Canada, w. U.S. to Guatemala. **EAST:** Migrants, usually intergrades, may occur in western part of our area.

RED-BELLIED WOODPECKER *Melanerpes carolinus* Common

M 253

9–10½" (23–26 cm) A *zebra-backed* woodpecker with a *red cap,* white rump. Red covers both crown and nape in male, only nape in female. Juvenile is also zebra-backed but has a brown head, devoid of red. **VOICE:** Note, *kwirr, churr,* or *chaw;* also *chiv, chiv.* Also a muffled flickerlike series. **RANGE:** S. Great Lakes area and s. New England to Gulf states. **HABITAT:** Woodlands, groves, orchards, towns.

RED-COCKADED WOODPECKER *Picoides borealis* Rare and local

M 257

8½" (21 cm) *Zebra-backed,* with a *black cap. White cheek* is an obvious field mark. Male's tiny red cockade is hard to see. Endangered. **VOICE:** A rough rasping *sripp* or *zhilp* (suggests flock note of young starling). Sometimes a higher *tsick.* Form colonial "clans." **RANGE:** Se. U.S. **HABITAT:** Open pine woodland that has trees with heartwood disease. Numbers continue to decline.

YELLOW-BELLIED SAPSUCKER *Sphyrapicus varius* Fairly common

M 254

8–9" (20–23 cm) Note longish white wing stripe and red forehead patch. Male has all-red throat patch, female a white chin. Young bird is brown, but note distinctive white wing stripe. Sapsuckers drill orderly rows of small holes in trees for sap. **VOICE:** A nasal mewing note, or squeal: *cheerrrr,* slurring downward. On nesting grounds, distinctive drumming; several rapid thumps followed by several slow rhythmic ones. **RANGE:** Canada south to s. Appalachians. Migrant in most of its range. Winters to Cen. America, W. Indies. **HABITAT:** Woodlands; in winter, also orchards, other trees.

GOLDEN-FRONTED WOODPECKER *Melanerpes aurifrons* Common

8½–10½" (21–26 cm) *Male:* Separated patches of bright color on the head (yellow near bill, poppy red on crown, orange nape). Zebra-backed, light underparts, white rump. White wing patches in flight. *Female:* Lacks red crown patch. **VOICE:** A tremulous *churrrr.* Flickerlike *kek, kek, kek, kek,* etc. **HABITAT:** Mesquite, stream woodlands, groves. **RANGE:** Resident from s. Tex. north to sw. Okla.

Yellow-shafted

Red-shafted

Red-shafted
form

♂

♂

♀

Yellow-shafted

immature

NORTHERN FLICKER
Yellow-shafted
form

♀

♂

RED-BELLIED
WOODPECKER

♀

♂

GOLDEN-FRONTED
WOODPECKER

RED-COCKADED
WOODPECKER

♂

immature

♂

YELLOW-BELLIED
SAPSUCKER

DOWNY WOODPECKER *Picoides pubescens*   Common

M 255

6½" (16 cm) Note *white* back and *small* bill. Outer tail feathers spotted, red nape patch of male in unbroken square. *Note:* In rare occasions, red nape patch can be yellow in juvenile birds. **SIMILAR SPECIES:** Hairy Woodpecker is larger, has a large bill, white outer tail feathers, and red nape of male divided by black line. **VOICE:** A rapid whinny of notes, descending in pitch. Call note, a flat *pick*, not as sharp as Hairy's *peek!* **RANGE:** Alaska, Canada to s. U.S. **HABITAT:** Forests, woodlots, willows, river groves, orchards, shade trees. Comes to suet feeders.

HAIRY WOODPECKER *Picoides villosus*   Fairly common

M 256

9½" (24 cm) Note *white* back (Maritime race has partly barred back) and *large* bill. Other woodpeckers may have white rumps or white bars on back, but Downy and Hairy are our only woodpeckers with *white backs* without markings. Male has a small red patch on back of head divided by a black line, absent in female. **SIMILAR SPECIES:** (1) See Downy Woodpecker; Hairy has larger bill. (2) Three-toed Woodpecker has a barred back but has side stripes and a yellow crown. **VOICE:** A kingfisher-like rattle, run together more than call of Downy and not descending at end. Call note, a sharp *peek!* (Downy says *pick*.) **RANGE:** Alaska, Canada to Panama. **HABITAT:** Forests, woodlands, river groves, shade trees. Comes to suet feeders.

THREE-TOED WOODPECKER *Picoides tridactylus*   Scarce

M 258

8–9½" (20–24 cm) Males of this and the next species are our only woodpeckers that normally have *yellow* caps. Both have *barred sides.* The "ladder" back distinguishes this species from Black-backed. Female lacks yellow cap and suggests Hairy Woodpecker, but note *barred sides.* **SIMILAR SPECIES:** (1) Black-backed Woodpecker has a solid *black* back. (2) Rarely, juvenile Hairy or Downy Woodpecker has a yellowish or orange cap, but either would lack bars on flanks and have more white on face. Maritime race of Hairy has a barred back. **VOICE:** Call, a *kik* or *chik.* **RANGE:** Boreal forests of N. Hemisphere. Rarely wanders south of normal range. **HABITAT:** Conifer forests.

BLACK-BACKED WOODPECKER *Picoides arcticus*   Scarce

M 259

9–10" (23–25 cm) Note combination of *solid black back, barred sides.* This and preceding species (both have 3 toes) inhabit boreal forests of the North. Their sides are heavily barred; males have *yellow* caps. Their presence can often be detected by patches of bark scaled from dead conifers. **SIMILAR SPECIES:** Three-toed Woodpecker (*barred* back). **VOICE:** A short flat *kuk.* Also in series. **RANGE:** Boreal forests of n. N. America. **HABITAT:** Firs and spruces.

WOODPECKERS

DOWNY
WOODPECKER

♀

♂

HAIRY
WOODPECKER

southern
form

♀

♂

♂

THREE-TOED
WOODPECKER

♀

♂

BLACK-BACKED
WOODPECKER

♀

♂

TYRANT FLYCATCHERS. Family Tyrannidae.

Most flycatchers perch quietly upright on exposed branches and sally forth to snap up insects or glean them from leaves. Bills flattened, with bristles at base. **FOOD:** Flying insects and larvae. **RANGE:** New World; majority in Tropics. **NO. OF SPECIES:** World, 425; East, 17 (+14 accidental).

SCISSOR-TAILED FLYCATCHER *Tyrannus forficatus* Common

M 277

11–15" (28–38 cm) A beautiful bird; pale pearly gray, with an *extremely long scissorlike tail*, usually folded. Sides orangy buff and wing linings salmon pink. Young bird with a short tail may suggest Western Kingbird. **VOICE:** A harsh *keck* or *kew*; a repeated *ka-leep*; also shrill kingbirdlike bickerings and squealings. **RANGE:** Central and southern plains. Strays wander to East. **HABITAT:** Semi-open country, ranches, farms, roadsides, wires, golf courses, airports, etc.

EASTERN KINGBIRD *Tyrannus tyrannus* Common

M 275

8" (20 cm) *White band* across tail tip identifies this species. Red crown mark is concealed and rarely seen. Often seems to fly quiveringly on "tips of wings." Harasses crows, hawks. **VOICE:** A rapid sputter of high bickering notes: *dzee-dzee-dzee*, etc., and *kit-kit-kitter-kitter*, etc. Also a nasal *dzeeb*. **RANGE:** Cen. Canada to Gulf of Mexico. Winters Peru to Bolivia. **HABITAT:** Wood edges, river groves, farms, shelterbelts, orchards, roadsides, fencerows, wires.

WESTERN KINGBIRD *Tyrannus verticalis* Common

M 274

8" (20 cm) Size of Eastern Kingbird, but with a *paler* head and back, *yellowish* belly. Western's black tail has a *narrow white edging* on each side, but no white band across tip. **VOICE:** Shrill bickering calls; a sharp *whit* or *whit-ker-whit*. **RANGE:** Sw. Canada, w. U.S., upper Mississippi Valley to n. Mexico. Strays regularly wander east in fall. **HABITAT:** Farms, open country with scattered trees, roadsides, wires.

GRAY KINGBIRD *Tyrannus dominicensis* Fairly common, restricted

M 276

9" (23 cm) Resembles Eastern Kingbird, but larger and very much paler. Conspicuously *notched tail* has *no white band*. *Very large bill* gives a large-headed look. Dark ear patch. **VOICE:** A rolling *pi-teer-rrry* or *pe-cheer-ry*. **RANGE:** S. Fla., W. Indies. Very rarely wanders north. **HABITAT:** Roadsides, wires, mangroves, edges.

GREAT CRESTED FLYCATCHER *Myiarchus crinitus* Common

M 273

8–9" (20–23 cm) A kingbird-sized flycatcher with *cinnamon wings and tail*, a gray breast, and a bright yellow belly. Often erects a bushy crest. **SIMILAR SPECIES:** Brown-crested Flycatcher (*Myiarchus tyrannulus*, not shown). Equal in size but bulkier than Great Crested. *Distinctly larger, all-dark bill.* Paler yellow underbelly. Summer in s. Tex.; winter Gulf Coast records. **VOICE:** A loud whistled *wheeep!* Also a rolling *prrrrrreet!* **RANGE:** S. Canada, e. and cen. U.S. **HABITAT:** Woodlands, groves.

ASH-THROATED FLYCATCHER *Myiarchus cinerascens* Rare vagrant

M 272

8" (20 cm) A western stray; suggests a small washed-out Great Crested Flycatcher with a white throat, yellow wash on belly, less rufous. **VOICE:** Calls all year with a distinctive *prrrt*. Rare along Gulf Coast east to Fla.; very rare northward. A *Myiarchus* flycatcher in late fall or winter in the East may be this species.

LARGE FLYCATCHERS
Sexes similar

EASTERN KINGBIRD

SCISSOR-TAILED
FLYCATCHER

ASH-
THROATED
FLYCATCHER

WESTERN
KINGBIRD

GREAT CRESTED
FLYCATCHER

GRAY KINGBIRD

EASTERN PHOEBE *Sayornis phoebe*   Common

M 269

6½–7" (16–18 cm) Note *downward tail-bobbing*. A gray-brown sparrow-sized flycatcher without an eye-ring or strong wing bars (but may have dull ones, especially young bird). Bill is *all black*. Young bird in fall somewhat yellowish below. **SIMILAR SPECIES:** Eastern Wood-Pewee and the small *Empidonax* flycatchers have conspicuous wing bars. Their bills are yellowish or whitish on lower mandible. Eastern *Empidonax* flick tail *upward*. **VOICE:** Song, a well-enunciated *phoe-be*, or *fibree* (second note alternately higher or lower). Note, a sharp *chip*. **RANGE:** East of Rockies; cen. Canada to s. U.S. Winters to s. Mexico. **HABITAT:** Streamsides, bridges, farms, roadsides, towns.

EASTERN WOOD-PEWEE *Contopus virens*   Fairly common

M 263

6–6½" (15–16 cm) About the size of Eastern Phoebe, but with 2 *narrow white wing bars*, no eye-ring, and pale orangish lower mandible. Immature lacks distinct wing bars. Similar to but slightly larger than *Empidonax* flycatchers, but with *no eye-ring*. Wings extend a bit farther down the tail. Does not flick tail. **SIMILAR SPECIES:** Eastern Phoebe lacks white wing bars; bobs its tail. **VOICE:** A sweet plaintive whistle: *pee-a-wee*, slurring down, then up. Also *pee-ur*, slurring down. **RANGE:** S. Canada, e. U.S. Winters Costa Rica to Peru. **HABITAT:** Woodlands, groves.

LEAST FLYCATCHER *Empidonax minimus* (shown for comparison)   **SEE P. 226**

OLIVE-SIDED FLYCATCHER *Contopus cooperi*   Uncommon

M 262

7–8" (18–20 cm) A rather large, large-headed flycatcher; often perches at top of a dead tree. Note largish bill and *dark chest patches* with a narrow strip of white between (suggesting an unbuttoned jacket). A *cottony tuft* may poke out from behind wing. **SIMILAR SPECIES:** Eastern Wood-Pewee is smaller, has light wing bars. **VOICE:** Note, a trebled *pip-pip-pip*. Song, a spirited whistle: *quick-three-beers*, middle note highest, last sliding. **RANGE:** Alaska, Canada, w. and ne. U.S. Winters Colombia to Peru. **HABITAT:** Conifer forests, bogs, burns. In migration, usually seen on tips of dead trees.

SAY'S PHOEBE *Sayornis saya*   Very rare vagrant in East

M 270

7–8" (18–20 cm) Midsized gray-brown flycatcher with a pale *rusty orange* belly. *Black tail*, rusty belly give it the look of a small robin. **VOICE:** A plaintive *pee-ur* or *pee-ee*; also a trilling note. **RANGE:** W. N. America; east to about 100th meridian on Plains (boundary of area covered by guide).

VERMILION FLYCATCHER *Pyrocephalus rubinus*   Rare vagrant

M 271

6" (15 cm) *Male:* Crown and underparts *flaming vermilion*; upperparts and tail dusky to blackish. *Female and immature:* Underparts whitish, narrowly streaked; belly and undertail coverts washed with pinkish or yellow. **SIMILAR SPECIES:** Male Scarlet Tanager has a *scarlet back*. See Say's Phoebe. **VOICE:** A slightly phoebelike *p-p-pit-zee* or *pit-a-zee*. **RANGE:** Sw. U.S. to Argentina. In winter, a few wander eastward along Gulf Coast from La. to Fla. Very rare vagrant farther north.

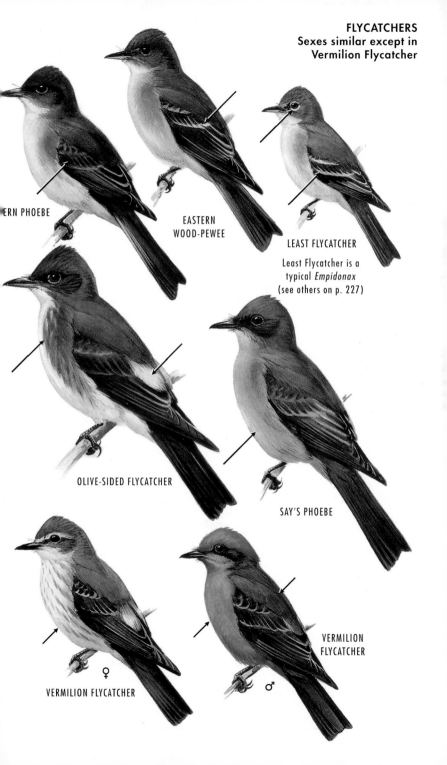

FLYCATCHERS
Sexes similar except in
Vermilion Flycatcher

ERN PHOEBE

EASTERN
WOOD-PEWEE

LEAST FLYCATCHER

Least Flycatcher is a
typical *Empidonax*
(see others on p. 227)

OLIVE-SIDED FLYCATCHER

SAY'S PHOEBE

VERMILION FLYCATCHER

♀

VERMILION
FLYCATCHER

♂

Genus *Empidonax*. Five small flycatchers in our area share the characters of *light eye-ring* and 2 *whitish wing bars*. (Note: Not all Willows and Alders show the eye-ring.) When breeding, they are readily separated by voice, habitat, and way of nesting (see *A Field Guide to Birds' Nests*, by Hal Harrison). In migration, they seldom sing, so we are forced to let many of them go simply as *Empidonax* flycatchers.

ACADIAN FLYCATCHER *Empidonax virescens* — Fairly common

M 265

5¾" (14 cm) The only breeding *Empidonax* in most of the South. A greenish *Empidonax* with a yellowish wash on sides and a shadow vest across breast, thin eye-ring, extensively paler lower mandible. Best separated from others of the genus by habitat, range, and voice. **VOICE:** "Song," a sharp explosive *pit-see!* or *wee-see!* (sharp upward inflection); also a thin *peet*. **RANGE:** E. U.S. Winters Costa Rica to Ecuador. **HABITAT:** Deciduous forests, ravines, swampy woods, beech and hemlock groves.

YELLOW-BELLIED FLYCATCHER *Empidonax flaviventris* — Uncommon

M 264

5½" (14 cm) Decidedly *yellowish* underparts (including throat) separate this northern flycatcher from other small eastern flycatchers. Others of this group may have a tinge of yellow, especially in fall, but none has a wash of yellow from throat to belly. Eye-ring also is yellowish. Some Acadians in fall resemble Yellow-bellies. **VOICE:** A simple spiritless *per-wee* or *chu-wee*. Also *killik*. **RANGE:** Canada, ne. U.S. Winters Mexico to Panama. **HABITAT:** Woods; in summer, boreal forests, muskeg, bogs.

LEAST FLYCATCHER *Empidonax minimus* — Common

M 268

5¼" (13 cm) Whiter below than other *Empidonax* flycatchers. Distinct white eye-ring. Short bill mostly pale beneath. Nervously flicks its tail. Best told by its voice coming from the open groves it inhabits. **VOICE:** A sharply snapped dry *che-bek´!* Emphatic. Call, a sharp *whit*. **RANGE:** Canada, east of Rockies; n.-cen. and ne. U.S. Winters Mexico to Panama. **HABITAT:** Open woods, aspen groves, orchards, shade trees.

WILLOW FLYCATCHER *Empidonax traillii* — Fairly common

M 267

5¾" (14 cm) Alder and Willow Flycatchers are almost identical in appearance, a bit larger and browner than Least Flycatcher. They may be separated from each other mainly by voice and breeding habitat. Willow has less distinct eye-ring than Alder and back is not as green. **VOICE:** Song, a sneezy *fitz-bew*, unlike *fee-bee´-o* of Alder. Call, a soft *whit*. **RANGE:** Alaska, w. Canada to sw. and e.-cen. U.S. Winters s. Mexico to Argentina. **HABITAT:** Bushes, willow thickets, etc.; often in drier situations (brushy fields, upland copses, etc.) than Alder, but found side by side in some areas.

ALDER FLYCATCHER *Empidonax alnorum* — Fairly common

M 266

5¾" (14 cm) This species and Willow Flycatcher (formerly lumped) can be separated in the field mainly by voice and at times by habitat but occur in some areas side by side. Alder's eye-ring more distinct; back slightly darker. **VOICE:** Song, an accented *fee-bee´-o*. Call, *peep* or *bik*. **RANGE:** Canada, ne. U.S. Winters in tropical America. **HABITAT:** Willows, alders, brushy swamps, swales, usually in moister areas than Willow.

EMPIDONAX FLYCATCHERS
Sexes similar

pit-see!

All 5 Empidonax flycatchers have eye-rings and wing bars. (See text.) Identify by habitat and voice.

chu-wee

eciduous woods, esp.
eech trees; wooded
umps; s. and cen. U.S.

conifer woods, bogs; Canada, n. edge of U.S.

ACADIAN

eener than Least,
Alder, or Willow

YELLOW-BELLIED

breast washed with yellow

che-BEK or chebek

farms, orchards, groves, open woods; n. U.S. and Canada

fitz-bew

fee-bee'-o

LEAST

grayest of the group

wet and dry thickets, brushy pastures, old orchards, willows; n. and cen. U.S.

alder swamps, wet thickets, usually near water; n. U.S., Canada

WILLOW

ALDER

The New World Flycatchers, or Tyrant Flycatchers, make up the largest family of birds in the world, with 425 known species. They dominate in the Neotropics. A large number are very similar and require attention to fine points to separate them. Some species still need documentation. Other members of this family are sure to wander north.

GREENISH ELAENIA *Myiopagus viridicata*

5½" (14 cm) Yellow belly, no distinct wing bars, yellow crown (often concealed). **RANGE:** N. Mexico to S. America. Accidental to Tex.

CARIBBEAN ELAENIA *Elaenia martinica*

5½" (14 cm) Similar to preceding species, but *lacks strong yellowish* belly and eye-ring. Has bold wing bars, whitish crown-patch. **RANGE:** Greater and Lesser Antilles. Accidental to Fla.

CUBAN PEWEE *Contopus caribaeus*

6¼" (16 cm) A dark, olive-gray flycatcher with crown darker than back. Upperparts grayish olive and underparts buffy gray. Pale base to large flat bill. Often shakes tail side to side while perched. **VOICE:** Staccato *pit-pit-pit* or *wheeet-weet*. At times a drawn-out *eee-oooo*. **RANGE:** N. Bahamas, Cuba, Jamaica, Hispaniola. Several Fla. records.

LA SAGRA'S FLYCATCHER *Myiarchus sagrae*

7½–8¼" (18–20 cm) Similar to Ash-throated Flycatcher with only a hint of yellow on belly. Tail brownish, not rufous. Short primaries. Often "droopy" behavior. **VOICE:** High, rapid double *wick-wick*. **RANGE:** Resident of Bahamas, Grand Cayman Is., and Cuba. Rare winter and spring visitor to s. Fla. One Alabama record.

VARIEGATED FLYCATCHER *Empidonomus varius*

7" (18 cm) Suggestive of a small Sulphur-bellied Flycatcher of the West. Bold brown-and-white head *streaks*. Underbelly *tinted yellow with heavy streaks*. *Rufous* in tail and wings. **VOICE:** A piercing *seeeeep*. **RANGE:** S. America, east of Andes. Accidental to Me., Ont.

PIRATIC FLYCATCHER *Legatus leucophaius* (Not shown)

6" (15 cm) Similar to Variegated Flycatcher but plain-backed with distinct eye line running to back of head creating a brown-capped appearance. White throat, small all-dark bill. Below pale yellowish with indistinct streaks. **VOICE:** *Weee-see* or a sharp rising *pireee*. **RANGE:** Mexico to n. Argentina. **NOTE:** Upon reexamination, several early records of Variegated Flycatcher have proven to be this species (Fla., Tenn.).

MASKED TITYRA *Tityra semifasciata*

7½–8" (18–20 cm) Male is distinctive. Pale gray with black mask and red facial skin. Black wings. Female similar but with brown mask. **VOICE:** Like a squeaking wheel that needs oiling. **RANGE:** N. Mexico to cen. S. America. Tex. record.

LOGGERHEAD KINGBIRD *Tyrannus caudifasciatus*

9½–10" (24–25 cm) Like a Gray Kingbird but cap blacker, tail not notched. Underbelly slight yellowish wash. **RANGE:** Bahamas and Greater Antilles. Unconfirmed Fla.

SOCIAL FLYCATCHER *Myiozetetes similis*

7" (18 cm) Like a small Kiskadee flycatcher with a small bill. Rounded head with vermilion crown patch often concealed. **RANGE:** Neotropics. Unconfirmed Tex.

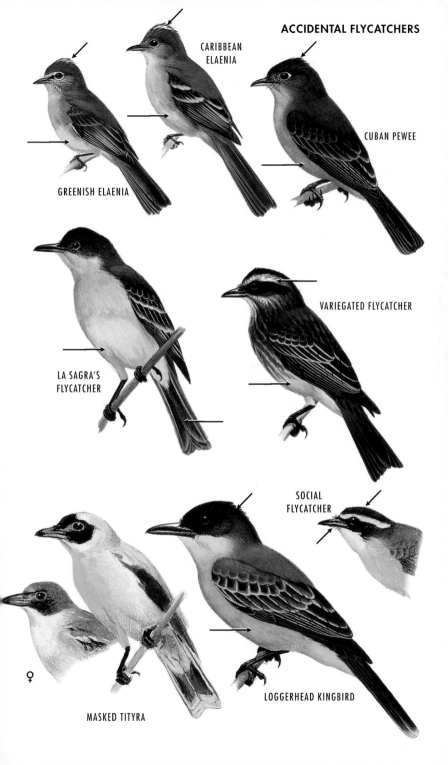

ACCIDENTAL FLYCATCHERS

CARIBBEAN
ELAENIA

GREENISH ELAENIA

CUBAN PEWEE

LA SAGRA'S
FLYCATCHER

VARIEGATED FLYCATCHER

SOCIAL
FLYCATCHER

MASKED TITYRA

LOGGERHEAD KINGBIRD

♀

LARKS. Family Alaudidae.

Brown terrestrial birds. Their hindclaws are elongated, almost straight. Songs are musical; frequently given high above ground in display flight. Larks are often gregarious. Sexes usually similar. **FOOD:** Mainly seeds, insects. **RANGE:** Old World (except for Horned Lark). **NO. OF SPECIES:** World, 91; East, 1.

HORNED LARK *Eremophila alpestris* Common

M 297

7–8" (18–20 cm) Note head pattern. A brown ground bird, larger than a sparrow, with black sideburns, 2 small black feathered *"horns"* (not always noticeable), and a black breast-band. *Walks*, does not hop. Overhead, pale with a *black* tail; folds wings after each wingbeat. Eye line ranges from bright yellow to pale, depending on subspecies. Female and immature are duller, but with basic pattern. **VOICE:** Song, tinkling, irregular, high pitched, often prolonged; from ground or high in air. Note, a clear *tsee-titi.* **RANGE:** Breeds widely in N. Hemisphere (south locally to n. S. America, n. Africa); some migration. **HABITAT:** Prairies, open fields, golf courses, airports, shores, tundra.

PIPITS. Family Motacillidae.

Streaked brown ground birds with white outer tail feathers, long hindclaws, thin bills. They walk briskly instead of hopping. **FOOD:** Insects, seeds. **RANGE:** Nearly cosmopolitan. **NO. OF SPECIES** (including relatives): World, 48; East, 2.

AMERICAN PIPIT *Anthus rubescens* Common

M 338

6–7" (15–18 cm) A slender, brown, sparrow-sized bird of open country. Bill *slender;* underparts buffy with streaks; *outer tail feathers are white. Dark legs.* Walks; bobs its tail almost constantly. Up-and-down flight. Learn note *pippipit,* as most are detected as they fly over. **SIMILAR SPECIES:** Vesper Sparrow (p. 300) and longspurs (p. 308) have thicker bills, do not bob tails. See Sprague's Pipit below. **VOICE:** Note, a thin *peet* or *pee-eet.* In aerial song flight, *chwee chwee chwee chwee chwee chwee chwee.* **RANGE:** Northern areas of N. Hemisphere. Winters to Cen. America, n. Africa, s. Asia. **HABITAT:** Tundra, alpine slopes; in migration and winter, plains, bare fields, shores. In e. U.S., nests atop Mt. Katahdin, Me., and Mt. Washington, N.H.

SPRAGUE'S PIPIT *Anthus spragueii* Uncommon

M 339

6½" (16 cm) Note *pale pinkish or yellowish legs. Plain buffy face with beady dark eye.* A buffy sparrowlike bird with *scaly back* with buffy lines and white outer tail feathers. Suggests a Vesper Sparrow or longspur with a *thin bill.* Back streaked with *buff and black.* More solitary than American Pipit and more secretive; does not bob tail; when flushed, often towers high in aimless flight, then drops straight down to ground. **SIMILAR SPECIES:** American Pipit has faintly streaked back, more heavily streaked breast. Legs brown to black. Stronger face pattern. **VOICE:** Sings high in the air, a sweet thin jingling series descending in pitch: *tshling, tshling, tshling.* Also a sharp *sleet.* **RANGE:** Prairie provinces of Canada, n. prairie states. Accidental visitor farther east. **HABITAT:** Plains, short-grass prairies.

LARKS, PIPITS
Sexes similar

immature

prairie race

overhead

northern race

HORNED LARK

topside

overhead

tail wagging

breeding

AMERICAN PIPIT

winter

towering flight

overhead

SPRAGUE'S PIPIT

SWALLOWS. Family Hirundinidae.

Slim, streamlined form and graceful flight characterize this family. Tiny feet, long pointed wings, and short bills with very wide gapes. **FOOD:** Flying insects; Tree Swallows also take bayberries. **RANGE:** Cosmopolitan. **NO. OF SPECIES:** World, 90; East, 7.

PURPLE MARTIN *Progne subis*   Fairly common, local

M 298

7½–8½" (18–21 cm) Largest N. American swallow. Male is uniformly deep blue (often appearing black) *above and below*; no other swallow is dark-bellied. Female is light-bellied; throat and breast grayish, often with a faint collar above. Glides in circles, alternating quick flaps and glides; often spreads tail. **SIMILAR SPECIES:** (1) Tree Swallow is much smaller than female Purple Martin; immaculate white, can have slight gray wash on breast. (2) Starling in flight may suggest Purple Martin because of its triangular wings, but note long bill. **VOICE:** Throaty and rich *chew-wew*, etc., or *pew, pew*. Song gurgling, ending in a succession of low rich gutturals. **Range:** S. Canada to n. Mexico, Gulf states. Winters in S. America. **HABITAT:** Towns, farms, open or semi-open country, often near water. Attracted to martin houses, especially with water and large open areas nearby.

CLIFF SWALLOW *Petrochelidon pyrrhonota*   Common, local

M 302

5–6" (13–15 cm) Note rusty or buffy rump. Overhead, bird appears square-tailed, with a *dark throat*. Glides in a long ellipse, often ending in an upward climb. **SIMILAR SPECIES:** (1) Cave Swallow has pale buffy throat, rusty forehead, and buffy collar. (2) Barn Swallow lacks rump patch and has elongated tail feathers. **VOICE:** *Zayrp;* a low *chur.* Alarm note, *keer!* Song, creaking notes and guttural gratings; harsher than Barn Swallow's song. **RANGE:** Alaska, Canada to Mexico. Winters Brazil, Argentina, Chile. **HABITAT:** Open to semi-open land, farms, cliffs, river bluffs, lakes. Nests colonially on cliffs, barns, bridges, rock faces, constructing "mud jugs" from individual mud balls.

CAVE SWALLOW *Petrochelidon fulva* See p. 326   Uncommon, restricted

5½" (14 cm) Very similar to Cliff Swallow, with square tail and buffy rump. Note *pale buffy throat* and *pale collar.* Up close, forehead is rusty, not buff as in Cliff Swallow. *Caution:* Southwestern race of Cliff Swallow has rusty forehead. **RANGE:** S. Tex. and Mexico, W. Indies. W. Indian subspecies nests in s. Fla. Tex. population range expanding. In recent years, many records of wanderers in late fall north and east of normal range.

M 303

BARN SWALLOW *Hirundo rustica*   Common

M 304

6–7½" (15–19 cm) Our only swallow that is truly *swallow-tailed*; also the only one with *white tail spots*. Blue-black above, cinnamon-buff below, with a darker throat. Flight direct, close to ground; wingtips pulled back at end of stroke; not much gliding. **SIMILAR SPECIES:** Most other N. American swallows have notched (not deeply forked) tails. **VOICE:** A soft *vit* or *kvik-kvik, vit-vit.* Also *szee-szah* or *szee.* Anxiety note around nesting barns, a harsh *ee-tee* or *keet.* Song, a long musical twitter interspersed with guttural notes. **RANGE:** Cosmopolitan. **HABITAT:** Open or semi-open land; farms, fields, marshes, usually near habitation.

Martin
house

PURPLE MARTIN

♂

♀

CAVE SWALLOW

CLIFF SWALLOW
juglike nests under eaves
or on cliffs; colonial

immature

nests on beams
inside barns

BARN SWALLOW

TREE SWALLOW *Tachycineta bicolor* Common

M 299

5–6" (13–15 cm) Steely blue-green-black above, *clear white below.* Immature with dusky brown back and faint breast-band may be confused with Northern Rough-winged Swallow (dingy throat) or Bank Swallow (dark well-defined breast-band). Tree Swallow glides in circles, often ending in glide. **VOICE:** Note, *cheet* or *chi-veet.* A liquid twitter. Song, *weet, trit, weet,* repeated with variations. **RANGE:** Alaska, Canada to Calif., cen.-e. U.S. Winters from s. U.S. to Cen. America. **HABITAT:** Open country near water; marshes, meadows, streams, lakes, wires. Roosts in reed beds in fall and winter. Nests in holes in dead trees, snags, birdhouses.

NORTHERN ROUGH-WINGED SWALLOW Fairly common
Stelgidopteryx serripennis

M 300

5–5½" (13–14 cm) A *brown-backed* swallow, lighter brown than Bank Swallow; *no* breast-band; note *dusky throat.* Flight not fluttering like Bank Swallow's, more gliding like Barn Swallow's; wings pulled back at end of stroke. **VOICE:** A harsh *trrrit,* rougher than Bank Swallow's. **RANGE:** S. Canada to Argentina. Winters mostly south of U.S. **HABITAT:** Near streams, lakes, riverbanks; holes in cement, brick, and stone structures.

BANK SWALLOW *Riparia riparia* Locally common

M 301

4½–5½" (11–14 cm) A small *brown-backed* swallow. Note distinct *dark breast-band on white underparts.* Flight irregular, more fluttery than other swallows'. **SIMILAR SPECIES:** Northern Rough-winged Swallow lacks breast-band, is usually a solitary nester (Bank Swallow is colonial). **VOICE:** A dry trilled chitter or rattle, *brrt* or *trr-tri-tri.* **RANGE:** Widespread in N. Hemisphere. Winters in S. America, Africa, s. Asia. **HABITAT:** Near water and over fields, marshes, lakes. Nest colonies in sand banks.

SWIFTS. Family Apodidae.

Swallowlike, but structurally distinct. Flight very rapid, "twisting," sailing between spurts; wings often stiffly *bowed.* Sexes similar. **FOOD:** Flying insects. **RANGE:** Nearly worldwide. **NO. OF SPECIES:** World, 98; East, 1 (+ 1 accidental).

CHIMNEY SWIFT *Chaetura pelagica* Common

M 246

5–5½" (12–14 cm) Like a cigar with wings. A blackish swallowlike bird with long, slightly curved, stiff wings and stubby tail. It appears to beat its wings not in unison but alternately (actually this is an illusion); effect is more batlike, unlike skimming of swallows. They seem to fairly twinkle, gliding between spurts, holding wings *bowed* in a *crescent.* **VOICE:** Loud, rapid, ticking or twittering notes. **RANGE:** S. Canada to Gulf of Mexico. Winters in Peru. **HABITAT:** Open sky, especially over cities, towns; nests and roosts in chimneys (originally in large hollow trees and cliff crevices).

VAUX'S SWIFT *Chaetura vauxi* Rare stray

4½" (11 cm) Like Chimney Swift, but slightly smaller, and paler on underparts. **RANGE:** W. N. America. Very rare, but probably regular stray to Tex., La., and Fla., November to March.

SWALLOWS, SWIFTS
Sexes similar

TREE SWALLOW

adult

nests in tree holes
or bird boxes

TREE SWALLOW

immature

ank Swallow
colony

BANK SWALLOW

NORTHERN
ROUGH-WINGED
SWALLOW

VAUX'S
SWIFT

CHIMNEY SWIFT

roosting swifts

♂

Purple Martin

Barn

Cliff

Tree

Rough-winged

Bank

SWALLOWS ON A WIRE

CHICKADEES AND TITMICE. Family Paridae.

Small, plump, small-billed birds; acrobatic when feeding. Often roam in little bands. Sexes usually alike. **FOOD:** Insects, seeds, acorn mast, berries. At feeders, suet, sunflower seeds. **RANGE:** Widespread in N. America, Eurasia, Africa. **NO. OF SPECIES:** World, 55; East, 4.

BLACK-CAPPED CHICKADEE *Poecile atricapilla* — Common

M 306

4½–5½" (12–14 cm) This small tame acrobat is distinctively patterned with a combination of *black cap and bib, white cheeks.* White area in wing, sides buffy. **SIMILAR SPECIES:** See Carolina Chickadee (below). **VOICE:** A clearly enunciated *chick-a-dee-dee-dee* or *dee-dee-dee.* Song, a clear whistle, *fee-bee-ee* or *fee-bee,* first note higher. **RANGE:** Alaska, Canada, northern half of U.S. **HABITAT:** Mixed and deciduous woods; willow thickets, groves, shade trees. Visits feeders, where it eats suet, sunflower seeds. Often tame, inquisitive, and trusting.

CAROLINA CHICKADEE *Poecile carolinensis* — Common

M 305

4½" (11 cm) Nearly identical to Black-capped Chickadee, slightly smaller and lacking conspicuous white area in wing created by white feather edges. Bib area smaller and more sharply defined. Song is notably different. **SIMILAR SPECIES:** Replaced by Black-cap northward. In summer, the two are best distinguished by locality and voice. Amount of white in Black-cap's wing is usually a good distinction, but may not always be reliable because of season, wear, angle of light, etc. Hybrids are known. **VOICE:** "Chickadee" call of this species is higher pitched and more rapid than that of Black-cap. Two-noted whistle is replaced by a four-syllabled *fee-bee, fee-bay.* **RANGE:** In border areas with Black-capped, check local or state publications for details. In some winters, Black-caps penetrate range of Carolina.

BOREAL CHICKADEE *Poecile hudsonica* — Uncommon

M 307

5–5½" (13–14 cm) Note *dull brown* cap, rich brown to pinkish brown flanks. Small size, black bib, whitish cheeks, and tiny bill mark it as a chickadee, but general color is *brown* rather than gray. **VOICE:** A wheezy *chick-che-day-day;* notes, slower, more raspy and drawling than lively *chick-a-dee-dee-dee* of Black-cap. **RANGE:** Boreal forests of Alaska, Canada, n. New England. Rarely wanders southward during some winters. **HABITAT:** Conifer forests, evergreen plantations.

TUFTED TITMOUSE *Baeolophus bicolor* — Common

M 308

6" (15 cm) A small, gray, mouse-colored bird with a *tufted crest.* Its flanks are rusty. The form occurring in s. Tex. has a *black crest* (and may be a full species). **VOICE:** A clear whistled chant: *peter, peter, peter* or *here, here, here, here.* Notes similar to those of chickadees, but more drawling, nasal, wheezy, and complaining. **RANGE:** S. Ont. south through e. U.S. to Gulf states. **HABITAT:** Woodlands, shade trees, groves; feeders. Very inquisitive and loudly vocal.

VERDIN *Auriparus flaviceps* FAMILY REMIZIDAE — Uncommon

4–4½" (10–11 cm) Tiny, gray with yellowish head, rufous at bend of wing (often hidden). Juveniles lack these marks. **SIMILAR SPECIES:** Bushtits have long tails, prefer oak hillsides. **VOICE:** Song, *tsee, seesee.* Call, *see-lip* or rapid chipping. **HABITAT:** Brushy desert valleys, mesquite, semiarid plains. **RANGE:** Sw. U.S. into cen. and s. Tex.

CHICKADEES AND TITMICE
Sexes alike

CAROLINA
CHICKADEE

BLACK-CAPPED
CHICKADEE

BOREAL
CHICKADEE

Black-crested
race

west + central
Texas

TUFTED
TITMOUSE

immature

adult

VERDIN

NUTHATCHES. Family Sittidae.

Small stout tree-climbers with strong bills. Stubby square-cut tails not used to brace like woodpeckers' in climbing. Habitually go down trees headfirst. Sexes similar. **FOOD:** Bark insects, seeds, nuts; attracted to feeders by suet, sunflower seeds. **RANGE:** Most of N. Hemisphere. **NO. OF SPECIES:** World, 24; East, 3.

WHITE-BREASTED NUTHATCH *Sitta carolinensis*   Common

M 310

5–6" (13–15 cm) Nuthatches climb down trees *headfirst*. This, the most widespread species, is known by its black cap (gray in female) and beady black eye on a white face. Undertail coverts are chestnut. **VOICE:** Song, a rapid series of low, nasal, whistled notes on one pitch: *whi, whi, whi, whi, whi, whi* or *who, who, who,* etc. Note, a nasal *yank, yank, yank;* also a nasal *tootoo.* **RANGE:** S. Canada to s. Mexico. **HABITAT:** Forests, woodlots, groves, river woods, shade trees; visits feeders.

RED-BREASTED NUTHATCH *Sitta canadensis*   Common

M 309

4½" (11 cm) A small nuthatch with a *broad black line* through eye and a white line above it. The underparts *rusty.* **VOICE:** Call higher, more nasal than that of White-breast; *ank* or *enk,* sounding like a baby nuthatch or a small tin horn. **RANGE:** Se. Alaska, Canada, w. U.S., ne. U.S. Winters irregularly to s. U.S. **HABITAT:** Conifer forests; in winter, also other trees; may visit feeders.

BROWN-HEADED NUTHATCH *Sitta pusilla*   Common

M 311

4½" (11 cm) A small nuthatch of the Southern pinelands. Smaller than White-breast, with a *brown cap coming down to eye* and a pale or whitish spot on nape. Travels in groups. **VOICE:** Unlike a nuthatch; a high rapid *kit-kit-kit;* also a squeaky piping *ki-day* or *ki-dee-dee,* constantly repeated, sometimes becoming an excited twitter or chatter. **RANGE:** Se. U.S. **HABITAT:** Open pine woods.

CREEPERS. Family Certhiidae.

Small, slim, stiff-tailed birds with slender, slightly curved bills used to probe the bark of trees. **FOOD:** Bark insects. **RANGE:** Cooler parts of N. Hemisphere. **NO. OF SPECIES:** World, 7; East, 1.

BROWN CREEPER *Certhia americana*   Fairly common

M 312

5" (13 cm) A very small, slim, well-camouflaged tree-climber. Brown above with streaking, white below, with a *slender decurved bill,* and a stiff tail used to brace when climbing. Ascends trees spirally from the base. **VOICE:** Note, a single high thin *seee,* similar to quick-trebled note (*see-see-see*) of Golden-crowned Kinglet. Song, a thin musical *see-ti-wee-tu-wee* or *see-see-see-sisi-see.* **RANGE:** Eurasia, s. Alaska, Canada to Nicaragua. **HABITAT:** Woodlands, groves, shade trees. In winter, often moves with titmice and chickadees. Nests under hanging bark flaps.

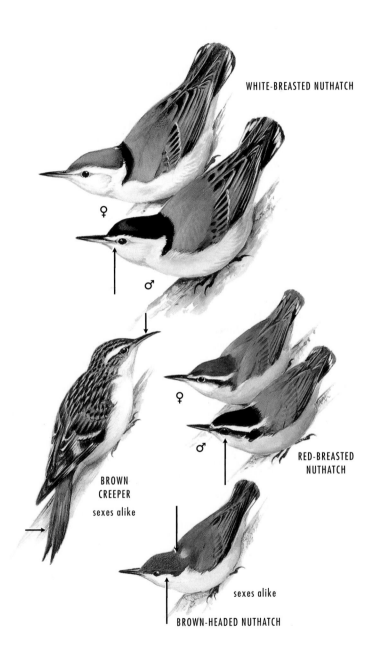

WHITE-BREASTED NUTHATCH

♀

♂

BROWN
CREEPER

sexes alike

♀

♂

RED-BREASTED
NUTHATCH

sexes alike

BROWN-HEADED NUTHATCH

WRENS. Family Troglodytidae.

Small, stumpy, energetic brown birds; slender, slightly decurved bills; tails often cocked. **FOOD:** Insects, spiders. **RANGE:** N., Cen., and S. America; only one (Winter Wren) in Eurasia. **NO. OF SPECIES:** World, 79; East, 9.

HOUSE WREN *Troglodytes aedon* — Common

M 316

4½–5" (11–13 cm) A small energetic gray-brown wren distinguished by a light eye-ring and lack of facial striping. **VOICE:** A choppy, gurgling sound, rising in a musical burst, then falling at the end. **RANGE:** S. Canada to Argentina. Migratory in the North. **HABITAT:** Open woods, thickets, towns, gardens; nests in bird boxes.

WINTER WREN *Troglodytes troglodytes* — Fairly common, secretive

M 317

4" (10 cm) A very small, roundish dark wren known from House Wren by a *much stubbier tail*, a light line over eye, and *dark heavily barred sides and flanks*. Often bobs body and flicks wings. Mouselike, it stays near ground. **VOICE:** Song, a rapid succession of high tinkling warbles and trills, prolonged, often ending on a *very high* light trill. Note, a hard two-syllabled *kip-kip* (suggests Song Sparrow's *chip*). **RANGE:** Northern parts of N. Hemisphere. **HABITAT:** Woodland underbrush; in summer, conifer forests.

BEWICK'S WREN *Thryomanes bewickii* — Common in West, scarce in East

M 315

5½" (13 cm) Note long tail with *white corners. White stripe over eye.* **VOICE:** Song suggests Song Sparrow's, but thinner, starting on 2 or 3 high notes, dropping lower, ending on a thin trill. **RANGE:** S. Canada to Mexico. **HABITAT:** Thickets, underbrush, gardens. Often nests in bird boxes. Population decline in some areas.

CAROLINA WREN *Thryothorus ludovicianus* — Common

M 314

5½" (14 cm) A large wren; *warm reddish brown* above, buff below. Has a conspicuous *white eyebrow stripe.* **VOICE:** A clear three-syllabled chant. Variable; *tea-kettle, tea-kettle, tea-kettle, tea* or *chirpity, chirpity, chirpity, chirp.* Variety of *chips* and *churrs.* **RANGE:** Resident e. U.S., e. Mexico. **HABITAT:** Tangles, brushy undergrowth, suburban gardens, towns.

MARSH WREN *Cistothorus palustris* — Fairly common, local

M 319

5" (13 cm) Conspicuous *white stripes on back* and white eyebrow stripe identify this marsh dweller. **VOICE:** Song, reedy, gurgling, ending in a guttural rattle: *cut-cut-turrrrrrrrrr-ur;* often heard at night. Note, a low *tsuck.* **RANGE:** S. Canada to nw. Mexico. Winters s. U.S. to cen. Mexico. **HABITAT:** Marshes (cattail, bulrush, brackish).

SEDGE WREN *Cistothorus platensis* — Uncommon, secretive

M 318

4–4½" (10–11 cm) Overall paler and buffier than Marsh Wren; streaked crown. Both have streaked backs. **VOICE:** Song, a dry staccato chattering, *chap chap chap chap chap chap chap chapper-rrrrr.* Call note, *chap.* **RANGE:** S. Canada locally to S. America. **HABITAT:** Grassy marshes, sedgy meadows; scarce, local on eastern seaboard.

ROCK WREN *Salpinctes obsoletus* — Vagrant in East

M 313

5½–6½" (14–16 cm) A gray Western wren with a *finely streaked breast,* rusty rump, and *buffy terminal tail-band.* **VOICE:** Song, a harsh chant. A loud dry trill; also *ti-keer.* **HABITAT:** Rocky slopes, canyons, rubble. Casual east of Mississippi R.

WRENS
Sexes similar

HOUSE WREN

WINTER WREN

BEWICK'S WREN

CAROLINA WREN

SEDGE WREN

MARSH WREN

CACTUS WREN

text for Cactus
and Canyon Wrens
on p. 242

ROCK WREN

CANYON WREN

CANYON WREN *Catherpes mexicanus*   Fairly common
5¾" (14 cm) White bib and chest, dark rufous brown belly. **VOICE:** A cadence of clear curved notes tripping down the scale: *te-you, te-you, tew tew.* **HABITAT:** Cliffs, canyons, rockslides. **RANGE:** Western, to 100th meridian in Tex.

CACTUS WREN *Campylorhynchus brunneicapillus*   Common
7–8¾" (18–22 cm) Very large wren of arid country. Chest and underparts heavily spotted. White supercilium and chestnut cap. Spotted outer tail feathers. **VOICE:** Monotonous *chu-chu-chu-chu* gaining speed. **HABITAT:** Arid areas of cactus, mesquite, and yucca. **RANGE:** Sw. to cen. and s. Tex.

GNATCATCHERS (Subfamily Polioptilinae) AND
KINGLETS (Family Regulidae).

Tiny active birds with small slender bills. Gnatcatchers have long mobile tails; kinglets short tails, bright crowns. **FOOD:** Insects, larvae. **RANGE:** Most large forested areas and scrub hillsides of world. **NO. OF SPECIES:** Gnatcatchers, World 15; East, 1; Kinglets, World, 6; East, 2.

RUBY-CROWNED KINGLET *Regulus calendula*   Common
4" (10 cm) A tiny stub-tailed birdlet; olive-gray above, with strong wing bars; male with a *scarlet crown patch* (usually concealed; visible when excited). A conspicuous *broken white eye-ring* gives a big-eyed look. Any kinglet without a crown patch and supercilium is this species. Both kinglets flick wings, although this species does so with greater regularity. **VOICE:** Call a husky *ji-dit*. Song, quite loud; 3 or 4 high notes, several low notes, and a chant, *tee tee tee, tew tew te tew, ti-dadee, ti-dadee, ti-dadee.* Variable. **RANGE:** Canada, Alaska, w. U.S. Winters to Gulf, Cen. America. **HABITAT:** Conifers; in winter, other woodlands, thickets. Inquisitive.

M 321

GOLDEN-CROWNED KINGLET *Regulus satrapa*   Fairly common
3½" (9 cm) Note bright crown patch (*yellow* in female, *orange* in male) *bordered by black*, and *whitish supercilium*. Kinglets are tiny olive-gray birds, smaller than most warblers, with 2 wing bars. Often give upward flick of wings. **VOICE:** Call note, a high wiry *see-see-see*. Song, a series of high thin notes ascending, then dropping into a little chatter. **RANGE:** S. Alaska, cen. Canada, south in western mountains to Guatemala. **HABITAT:** Conifers; in winter, also other trees.

M 320

BLUE-GRAY GNATCATCHER *Polioptila caerulea*   Fairly common
4½" (11 cm) Suggests a miniature mockingbird. A tiny slender mite, body smaller than a chickadee's; blue-gray above and whitish below, with a narrow *white eye-ring* and a *long black-and-white tail*, which is often cocked like a wren's and flipped about. **VOICE:** Note, a thin, explosive *spit-chee*. Song, a thin, squeaky, wheezy bubbly series of notes; easily overlooked. **RANGE:** Oregon, s. Ont. to Guatemala. Winters to Honduras. **HABITAT:** Open woods, oaks, thickets.

M 322

BULBULS. Family Pycnonotidae.   Introduced in Fla.

RED-WHISKERED BULBUL *Pycnonotus jocosus*   Uncommon, restricted
7" (18 cm) Note *black crest, red cheek patch*, and red undertail coverts. Se. Asia. Established locally in s. Miami, Fla., in early 1960s, where it still forms a small breeding population.

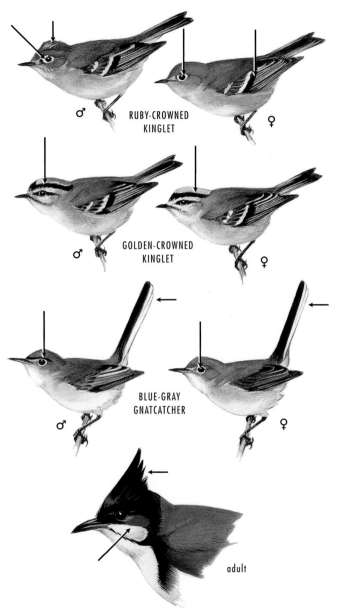

RUBY-CROWNED
KINGLET

♂   ♀

GOLDEN-CROWNED
KINGLET

♂   ♀

BLUE-GRAY
GNATCATCHER

♂   ♀

adult

RED-WHISKERED BULBUL

Large-eyed, slender-billed songbirds. The eastern species that bear the name "thrush" are brown-backed with *spotted* breasts. Robins, bluebirds, etc., betray their relationship through their spot-breasted young. Often fine singers. **FOOD:** Insects, worms, snails, berries, fruits. **RANGE:** Nearly worldwide. **NO. OF SPECIES:** World, 175; East, 8 (+ 3 accidental).

EASTERN BLUEBIRD *Sialia sialis*
Fairly common

7" (18 cm) A *blue* bird with a *rusty red* breast; appears round-shouldered when perched. Female duller than male; young bird is speckle-breasted, grayish, devoid of red, but always with some telltale blue in wings and tail. **VOICE:** Note, a musical *chur-wi* or *tru-ly.* Song, 3 or 4 soft gurgling notes. **RANGE:** East of Rockies; s. Canada to Gulf states, also se. Arizona to Nicaragua. Migrant in North. **HABITAT:** Open country with scattered trees; farms, roadsides. Uses nesting boxes.

M 324

MOUNTAIN BLUEBIRD *Sialia currocoides*
Vagrant

7" (18 cm) *Male: Turquoise-blue*, paler below; belly whitish. *Female:* Dull gray with a touch of blue on rump, tail, and wings. **RANGE:** Alaska, w. Canada to sw. U.S. **EAST:** Very rare wanderer east of 100th meridian.

M 325

AMERICAN ROBIN *Turdus migratorius*
Common

9–11" (23–28 cm) One of our most familiar birds, often seen walking with an erect stance on lawns. Recognized by its brick-red breast, dark gray back. Head and tail of male are blackish; female's grayer. Young bird has a speckled breast, but rusty wash identifies it. **SIMILAR SPECIES:** Clay-colored and Rufous-backed Robins are casual strays into s. Tex. (see p. 320). **VOICE:** Song, a clear caroling; short phrases, rising and falling, often prolonged. Notes, *tyeep* and *tut-tut-tut.* **RANGE:** Alaska, Canada to s. Mexico. Winters mainly south of Canada. **HABITAT:** Cities, towns, farmland, lawns, shade trees, forests; in winter, feeds on apple and berry trees.

M 333

VARIED THRUSH *Ixoreus naevius*
Vagrant

9–10" (23–25 cm) A casual winter straggler from the Northwest. Similar to American Robin; distinguished by *orangish eye stripe* and *wing bars,* and wide black (male) or gray (female) *band* across the rusty breast. **RANGE:** Alaska, w. Canada, nw. U.S. **EAST:** Many recent winter records at feeders, mostly from Maritime Canada and n. U.S.

NORTHERN WHEATEAR *Oenanthe oenanthe*
Casual stray

(FAMILY MUSCICAPIDAE: OLD WORLD FLYCATCHERS. Placed in this family by most classification systems instead of with the thrushes. I have retained its position on the plate with the thrushes based on its similarity in form.) 6" (15 cm) A dapper sparrow-sized ground bird of arctic barrens. Restless, flitting from rock to rock, fanning its tail, and bobbing. Note conspicuous *white rump and sides of tail.* Black of tail forms a *broad inverted T.* Breeding male has a blue-gray back, black wings, black ear patch, buff underparts. Autumn male is buffier with a brownish back. Female resembles autumn male. *Immature:* rich cinnamon buff below and pale on back. **VOICE:** Note, a hard *chak-chak* or *chack-weet, weet-chack.* **RANGE:** Eurasia, Alaska, nw. and ne. Canada, Greenland. Migrates to Africa, India. **HABITAT:** In summer, rocky tundra, barren slopes. As a stray, open areas, beaches, rock piles, etc.

M 323

♀

♂

juvenile

EASTERN BLUEBIRD

♂

MOUNTAIN BLUEBIRD

♂

♀

juvenile

AMERICAN ROBIN

♂

VARIED THRUSH

breeding

winter

NORTHERN WHEATEAR

GRAY-CHEEKED THRUSH *Catharus minimus*   Uncommon

M 328

7–8" (18–20 cm) A dull gray-brown thrush, distinguished from Swainson's Thrush by its *grayish* cheeks and less conspicuous eye-ring. **VOICE:** Song, thin and nasal; suggests Veery's: *whee-sheeoo-titi-whee,* slightly dropping. Note, *vee-a* or *quee-a,* higher and more nasal than Veery's. **RANGE:** Ne. Siberia, Alaska, Canada, ne. U.S. Winters in W. Indies and n. S. America. **HABITAT:** Boreal forests, tundra scrub; in migration, woodlands.

BICKNELL'S THRUSH *Catharus bicknelli* (Not shown)   Scarce, restricted

M 329

6⅓" (16 cm) Slightly *smaller* than Gray-cheeked Thrush, warmer brown, *tail dull chestnut,* lower mandible *more than half yellow* (less than half in Gray-cheeked). *Legs more dusky* than toes (uniform pale in Gray-cheeked). **VOICE:** A melodic flutelike rolling from high to low to high, *whee-toolee-weee,* rising at the close. **RANGE:** Ne. U.S.; presumed to winter in hills of Hispaniola. **HABITAT:** Breeds in mountain fir forests of the Northeast, to shoreline in the Maritimes. In migration, forests.

SWAINSON'S THRUSH *Catharus ustulatus*   Fairly common

M 330

7" (18 cm) A spotted thrush that is uniformly gray-brown above without warm tones. *Buffy eye-ring* and buff cheeks and upper breast. (Gray-cheek lacks eye-ring, as does Bicknell's.) **VOICE:** Song, breezy flutelike phrases; each phrase sliding *upward.* Note, *whit.* In nocturnal migration, a short *heep* (recalls a Spring Peeper). **RANGE:** Alaska, Canada, w. and ne. U.S. Winters Mexico to Peru. **HABITAT:** Spruce forests. In woods in migration.

HERMIT THRUSH *Catharus guttatus*   Common

M 331

7" (18 cm) A spotted brown thrush with a *reddish* tail. When perched it has a habit of cocking its tail up and dropping it slowly. Also will flick wings. **SIMILAR SPECIES:** (1) Other brown thrushes, none of which has so contrasting a reddish tail to brown back (Bicknell's less contrasting). (2) Fox Sparrow (reddish tail) has a conical bill, is more streaked. **VOICE:** Note, a low *chuck;* also a scolding *tuk-tuk-tuk* and a harsh *pay.* Song, clear, ethereal, flutelike; 3 or 4 phrases at *different pitches,* each with a *long introductory note.* **RANGE:** Alaska, Canada, w. and ne. U.S. Winters U.S. to Guatemala. **HABITAT:** Conifer or mixed woods, forest floors; in winter, woods, thickets, parks.

VEERY *Catharus fuscescens*   Fairly common

M 327

6½–7½" (16–19 cm) Note *uniform warm brown or tawny* cast above. No strong eye-ring (may have a dull whitish ring). Of all our brown thrushes, the least spotted; spots are often indistinct, almost ghostlike. **VOICE:** Song, liquid, breezy, ethereal; wheeling downward: *vee-ur, vee-ur, veer, veer.* Note, a low *phew* or *view.* **RANGE:** S. Canada, n. and cen. U.S. Winters Cen. and n. S. America. **HABITAT:** Damp mixed woodlands, stream thickets.

WOOD THRUSH *Hylocichla mustelina*   Fairly common

M 332

8" (20 cm) *Rusty-headed.* Smaller than robin; plumper than other brown thrushes; distinguished by distinctly orange cast about the head and larger, more numerous, distinct, *round* spots. **VOICE:** Song with rounder phrases than other thrushes. Listen for flutelike *ee-o-lay.* Occasional guttural notes are distinctive. Call, a rapid *pip-pip-pip-pip.* **RANGE:** Se. Canada, e. U.S. Winters Mexico to Cen. America. **HABITAT:** Mainly deciduous woodlands, cool moist glades.

BROWN THRUSHES
Sexes similar

GRAY-CHEEKED THRUSH

SWAINSON'S THRUSH

HERMIT THRUSH

VEERY

WOOD THRUSH

juvenile

Excellent songsters; some mimic other birds. Strong-legged; longer tailed than true thrushes, bill usually decurved. **FOOD:** Insects, fruits. **RANGE:** New World; Canada to Argentina. **NO. OF SPECIES:** World, 35; East, 6.

BROWN THRASHER *Toxostoma rufum* — Fairly common

M 336

11½" (29 cm) *Bright rufous* above, *heavily streaked* below. Note wing bars, rather curved bill, long tail, yellow eye. **VOICE:** Song, a succession of deliberate notes and phrases resembling Gray Catbird's song, but more musical and each phrase usually repeated. Note, a harsh *chack!* **RANGE:** S. Canada to Gulf states; east of Rockies. **HABITAT:** Thickets, brush, shrubbery, thorn scrub. **SIMILAR SPECIES:** (1) **LONG-BILLED THRASHER** (*Toxostoma longirostre*, p. 322) 11½". Dark brown (not rufous) back, grayish head, long all-black bill. Undertail coverts streaked. Resident in extreme s. Tex. (2) **CURVE-BILLED THRASHER** (*Toxostoma curvirostre*, p. 322) 11". Grayish brown with mottled breast of spots, not streaks. Long, well-curved bill. Eye pale orange. Resident of sw. U.S. into Tex. (3) **SAGE THRASHER** (*Oreoscoptes montanus*) 8½" Grayish brown with streaking below (these can pale in older adults). Distinct face pattern and white iris. White corners to tail. Western species, east to Tex. in winter, with scattered records in the East. (4) Brown thrushes are spotted (not streaked) and have brown eyes.

GRAY CATBIRD *Dumetella carolinensis* — Common

M 334

9" (23 cm) Slate gray; slim. Note the black cap (*chestnut undertail coverts* may not be evident). Flips tail up. **VOICE:** Catlike mewing, distinctive. Also a grating *tcheck-tcheck*. Song, disjointed notes and phrases; not repeated as in songs of mockingbird and thrasher. **RANGE:** S. Canada, e. and cen. U.S. to Gulf states. Winters mainly s. U.S. to Panama, W. Indies. **HABITAT:** Undergrowth, brush, suburban gardens.

NORTHERN MOCKINGBIRD *Mimus polyglottos* — Common

M 335

9–11" (23–28 cm) Gray; slimmer, longer-tailed than robin. Note *large white patch* on wing and tail, conspicuous in flight. *Juvenile:* Spotted below, slight buff to underparts. **SIMILAR SPECIES:** (1) Shrikes have dark facial masks (see p. 254.) (2) In s. Fla. and Fla. Keys, vagrant Bahama Mockingbird (p. 324) is slightly larger, has streaked flanks, shows throat stripe, and lacks wing patch. (3) Sage Thrasher (above) looks similar to juvenile mockingbird but has distinct streaks, not spots, and lacks large white flashes in tail and wing. **VOICE:** Song, a varied, prolonged succession of notes and phrases, each repeated a half-dozen times or more before changing. (Thrasher usually repeats once, catbird does not repeat.) Often heard at night. Many mockingbirds are excellent mimics of other species. Note, a loud *tchack;* also *chair.* **HABITAT:** Towns, farms, roadsides, thickets.

TOWNSEND'S SOLITAIRE *Myadestes townsendi* (a thrush) — Vagrant

M 326

8" (20 cm) A thrush placed here based on similarity of appearance. A slim gray bird with a *white eye-ring, white tail sides,* and *buffy wing patches.* Pattern in wing and tail suggests a mockingbird, but note eyering, darker breast, and especially buff wing patches. **RANGE:** Alaska, nw. Canada to Calif., n. Mexico. Winters on cen. Great Plains. A very rare or casual fall and winter visitor farther east. **HABITAT:** Conifer forests; in winter, junipers and other berry-laden trees.

THRASHERS,
MOCKINGBIRDS

LONG-BILLED THRASHER

CURVE-BILLED
THRASHER

BROWN THRASHER

GRAY CATBIRD

NORTHERN
MOCKINGBIRD

juvenile

flight pattern

wing flashing

Shrike for comparison

TOWNSEND'S
SOLITAIRE

SAGE THRASHER

CROWS, JAYS, ETC. Family Corvidae.

Large perching birds with strong longish bills; nostrils covered by forward-pointing bristles. Crows and ravens are large and black. Jays are often colorful (usually blue). Magpies are black and white with long tails. Sexes alike. Most immatures resemble adults. **FOOD:** Omnivorous. **RANGE:** Cosmopolitan except for s. S. America, some islands, Antarctica. **NO. OF SPECIES:** World, 117; East, 11 (+ 1 accidental).

BLUE JAY *Cyanocitta cristata* — Common

M 290

11–12½" (28–31 cm) A showy, noisy, *blue* bird with a *crest*; larger than a robin. Bold white spots in wings and tail; whitish or dull gray underparts; black necklace. **SIMILAR SPECIES:** Florida Scrub-Jay lacks crest and white spotting on wings and tail. **VOICE:** A harsh slurring *jeeah* or *jay*; a musical *queedle, queedle*; also many other notes. Mimics calls of Red-shouldered and Red-tailed Hawks. **RANGE:** S. Canada, east of Rockies to Gulf states. Partially migratory. **HABITAT:** Oak and pine woods, suburban gardens, groves, towns.

FLORIDA SCRUB-JAY *Aphelocoma coerulescens* — Uncommon, restricted

M 291

11–12" (28–30 cm) Look for this crestless jay in Fla. in stretches of oak scrub. White forehead streaks and white eye-line. Back is pale gray and throat has a collar with streaking below. Wings and tail are solid blue (no white markings); back is brownish tan. **SIMILAR SPECIES:** (1) Western Scrub-Jay (*A. californica*). Interior form of this jay occurs on cen. Tex. plateau. Lacks white forehead of Florida Scrub-Jay, and back is dark gray. Breast-band is blue, not black. (2) Blue Jay, often present in same localities in Fla., has a *crest* and bold white spotting on wings and tail. **VOICE:** A rough rasping *kwesh . . . kwesh*. Also a low rasping *zhreek* or *zhrink*. **RANGE:** Fla., local. **HABITAT:** Mainly scrub, low oaks.

GRAY JAY *Perisoreus canadensis* — Uncommon

M 289

11–13" (28–33 cm) A large, fluffy, gray bird of cool northern woods; larger than a robin, with a *black* patch or partial cap across back of head and a *white forehead* (or crown); suggests a huge overgrown chickadee. Juveniles (first summer) are *dark sooty*, almost blackish; only distinguishing mark is a *whitish whisker*. Often very tame. **VOICE:** A soft *whee-ah*; also many other notes, some harsh. **RANGE:** Boreal forests of N. America. **HABITAT:** Spruce and fir forests.

BLACK-BILLED MAGPIE *Pica hudsonia* — Fairly common, restricted

17½–22" (44–55 cm); tail 9½–12" (24–30 cm) A large, slender, black-and-white bird with a long wedge-tipped tail. In flight, iridescent greenish black tail streams behind; large white patches flash in wings. **VOICE:** A harsh rapid *queg queg queg queg*. Also a querulous nasal *maag?* or *aag-aag?* **RANGE:** Eurasia, w. N. America. In winter, a few wander east, rarely to Great Lakes and accidentally to the Northeast. **HABITAT:** Rangeland, open woodland, conifers, streamsides, around human activity.

M 292

GREEN JAY *Cyanocorax yncas* see also p. 322 — Common, restricted

10½" (27 cm) The only green jay. Black throat, violet crown. Mainly Mexican. Resident of s. Tex. north to Nueces and Webb Cos.

BROWN JAY *Cyanocorax morio* see also p. 322 — Scarce

16½" (42 cm) A very large jay with brown upperparts and pale belly. Resident locally from lower Rio Grande Valley of Tex. to Panama.

JAYS, MAGPIES
sexes alike

BLUE JAY

FLORIDA SCRUB-JAY

GRAY JAY

adult

GRAY JAY

juvenile

GREEN JAY

BLACK-BILLED MAGPIE

BROWN JAY

FISH CROW *Corvus ossifragus* Fairly common

M 294

16–20" (40–50 cm) Slightly smaller and more delicately proportioned than American Crow but best identified by voice, as measurements of the 2 crows broadly overlap. **SIMILAR SPECIES:** American Crow has a different call. **VOICE:** A short nasal *car* or *ca*. Sometimes a two-syllabled *ca-ha*. (American Crow utters an honest-to-goodness *caw*.) Some calls of young American Crows may sound like those of Fish Crows. **HABITAT:** Often near tidewater, river valleys, lakes. Also farmfields, wood edges, and in towns and cities.

TAMAULIPAS CROW *Corvus imparatus* Rare, restricted

15" (38 cm) A small crow with a "stressed" voice (a harsh *awwwk*) found in garbage dumps near Brownsville, Tex., where no Fish Crows occur.

AMERICAN CROW *Corvus brachyrhyncos* Common

M 293

17–21" (43–53 cm) Completely black; glossed with purplish in strong sunlight. Bill and feet black. Often gregarious. **SIMILAR SPECIES:** (1) Fish Crow (see above) has a different voice. (2) Common Raven is larger; has a wedge-shaped tail, different voice. **VOICE:** A loud *caw* or *cah* or *kahr*; easily imitated. **HABITAT:** Woodlands, farmland, agricultural fields, river groves, shores. May form large night roosts. Partially migratory in the North.

CHIHUAHUAN RAVEN *Corvus cryptoleucus* Uncommon, restricted

M 295

19–21" (48–53 cm) A small raven of the arid plains, near size of American Crow. Flies with typical flat-winged glide of a raven; has a somewhat wedge-shaped tail. White feather bases on neck and breast show only when feathers are ruffled. **VOICE:** A hoarse *kraak*, flatter and higher than Common Raven's. **RANGE:** Sw. U.S. to cen. Mexico. **EAST:** Barely crosses 100th meridian eastward into w. Okla., w. Kans., and w. and s. Tex.

COMMON RAVEN *Corvus corax* Common

M 296

22–27" (55–68 cm) Note *wedge-shaped tail*. Larger than American Crow and inclined to be more solitary. Hawklike, it alternates flapping and sailing, gliding on flat swept-back wings; heavier bill. **SIMILAR SPECIES:** American Crow is smaller, has different voice. **VOICE:** A croaking *cr-r-ruck* or *prruk*; a metallic *tok*. **RANGE:** Widespread in N. America, Eurasia, Africa. Expanding, as forests mature, slowly southward in Northeast. **HABITAT:** Boreal and mountain forests, coastal cliffs, tundra.

EURASIAN JACKDAW *Corvus monedula* (see p. 328) Vagrant

13" (33 cm) Small crow, with a short bill, gray "shawl" and pale whitish eye. Recent vagrant from Europe to Maritimes and New England.

CROWS, RAVENS

Fish Crow

TAMAULIPAS CROW

FISH CROW

CHIHUAHUAN RAVEN

American
Crow

may show white on nape
when feathers are ruffled

AMERICAN CROW

Common
Raven

EURASIAN
JACKDAW

COMMON RAVEN

SHRIKES. Family Laniidae.

Songbirds with hook-tipped bills. Perch watchfully on treetops and wires. Prey may be impaled on thorns, barbed wire. **FOOD:** Insects, lizards, mice, small birds. **RANGE:** Widespread in Old World; 2 in N. America. **NO. OF SPECIES:** World, 30; East, 2.

NORTHERN SHRIKE *Lanius excubitor* — Scarce

M 279

9–10" (23–25 cm) Very similar to Loggerhead Shrike, but note *faintly barred* breast and *pale base* of lower mandible. Bill longer, heavier, more strongly hooked. Pale back; dark mask does not meet over bill. Young bird brown with *fine bars* on breast, duller mask. **SIMILAR SPECIES:** (1) Adult Loggerhead Shrike has a solid-black bill. Black mask meets over base of bill. Juvenile Loggerhead may have faint barring, but is grayer than young Northern. (2) Rapid wingbeat in undulating flight, shorter tail, and small white wing patches separate it from Northern Mockingbird (p. 248). **VOICE:** Song, a disjointed thrasherlike succession of harsh notes and musical notes. Note, *shek-shek*; a grating *jaaeg*. **HABITAT:** Semi-open country with lookout posts. Shrubby fields with hawthorns and fences for storing prey.

LOGGERHEAD SHRIKE *Lanius ludovicianus* — Uncommon to Rare

M 278

9" (23 cm) A big-headed, slim-tailed, gray, black, and white bird with a *black mask*; a bit smaller than a robin. Shrikes sit quietly on wires or bushtops; taking off, they fly low with flickering flight, showing white wing patches; swoop upward to perch. **SIMILAR SPECIES:** (1) Northern Shrike (above). (2) Northern Mockingbird (p. 248) has a longer tail, larger wing patches, and lacks mask. Flight less flickering (a rowing motion). **VOICE:** Song, harsh deliberate notes and phrases, repeated mockingbird-like 3–20 times; *queedle, queedle*, over and over, or *usurp-see-usurp-see*. Note, *shack, shack*. Declining in many areas. **HABITAT:** Open country, wires, scrub.

WAXWINGS. Family Bombycillidae.

Sleek; crested. Red waxy tips on secondaries. Gregarious. **FOOD:** Berries, insects. **RANGE:** N. Hemisphere. **NO. OF SPECIES:** World, 3; East, 2.

BOHEMIAN WAXWING *Bombycilla garrulus* — Scarce, irregular

M 340

8" (20 cm) Similar to Cedar Waxwing; larger, grayer (no yellow on belly); wings with strong white or *white and yellow* markings. Note *deep rusty* undertail coverts (white in Cedar Waxwing). Shape in flight very starlinglike. **VOICE:** *Zreee*, rougher than note of Cedar Waxwing. **RANGE:** N. Eurasia, nw. N. America. Winters to s. Eurasia, ne. and sw. U.S. **HABITAT:** Boreal forests, muskeg; in winter, irregular wanderings.

CEDAR WAXWING *Bombycilla cedrorum* — Common

M 341

7" (18 cm) Note *yellow band* at tail tip (can be *orange-red* in fall immature birds) A sleek, crested, brown bird, larger than a House Sparrow. Adults have *waxy red tips* on secondaries. Juvenile is grayer, softly streaked below. May have red tail tip depending on diet. Gregarious; flies in compact flocks. Often indulges in fly-catching, especially in late summer. **VOICE:** A high thin lisp or *zeee*; sometimes slightly trilled. **RANGE:** Se. Alaska, Canada, to s.-cen. U.S. Winters s. Canada to Panama. **HABITAT:** Open woodlands, fruiting trees, orchards; in winter, widespread, irregular movements.

SHRIKES
sexes similar

immature

NORTHERN SHRIKE

LOGGERHEAD SHRIKE

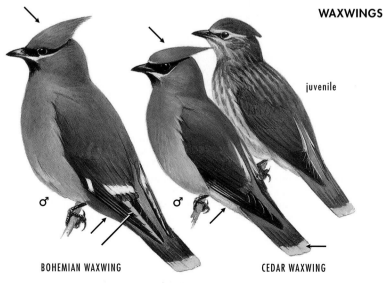

WAXWINGS

juvenile

♂

♂

BOHEMIAN WAXWING

CEDAR WAXWING

VIREOS. Family Vireonidae.

Small olive- or gray-backed birds, much like wood-warblers, but usually less active. Closely related to shrikes. Bills with a more curved ridge and a slight hook. May be divided into those with wing bars (and eye-rings) and those without (these have supercilia). Those with wing bars and eye-rings may be confused with *Empidonax* flycatchers (p. 226), but do not have the erect posture. **FOOD:** Mostly insects. **RANGE:** Canada to Argentina. **NO. OF SPECIES:** World, 52; East, 9 (+ 1 accidental).

RED-EYED VIREO *Vireo olivaceus*   Common

M 287

6" (15 cm) Note *gray cap* contrasting with olive back and strong *black-bordered white eyebrow stripe*. Red iris is not obvious at a distance. Iris is brown in immature birds. **SIMILAR SPECIES:** Warbling Vireo is paler, more uniform above; no black borders on eyebrow stripe. Song very different. **VOICE:** Song, short abrupt phrases of robinlike character, separated by deliberate pauses, repeated as often as 40 times per minute; monotonous. Note, a nasal whining *chway*. **RANGE:** Canada to Gulf states. Winters in Amazon Basin. **HABITAT:** Woodlands, shade trees, groves.

YELLOW-GREEN VIREO *Vireo flavoviridis*   Rare, restricted

6" (15 cm) Found in summer (rare) in extreme s. Tex. Vagrant elsewhere. Has yellow-green back and is much yellower beneath than Red-eye and has a more washed-out face pattern.

BLACK-WHISKERED VIREO *Vireo altiloquus*   Uncommon, restricted

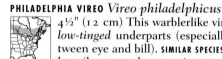

M 288

5" (13 cm) Narrow *dark whisker* on each side of throat. Otherwise similar to Red-eyed Vireo but duller overall and with slightly longer bill. **SONG:** Slightly slower than Red-eye. **RANGE:** Breeds W. Indies and s. Fla. Winters to n. S. America. **HABITAT:** Mangroves, low subtropical woods.

WARBLING VIREO *Vireo gilvus*   Fairly common

M 285

5" (13 cm) One of 3 common vireos that lack wing bars; in this one, note whitish breast and lack of black borders on eyebrow stripe, pale lores. **SIMILAR SPECIES:** (1) Philadelphia Vireo is yellowish on throat and breast, eye line crosses lores. (2) Red-eyed Vireo is larger, greener above, and has a bolder eyebrow stripe. **VOICE:** Song, a languid back-and-forth warble, unlike broken phrases of other vireos; suggests Purple Finch's song, but less spirited, with a burry undertone. Note, a wheezy querulous *twee*. **RANGE:** Canada to s. U.S., n. and w. Mexico. Winters Mexico and Guatemala. **HABITAT:** Deciduous and mixed woods, aspen groves, poplars, shade trees. *Particularly near water.*

PHILADELPHIA VIREO *Vireo philadelphicus*   Uncommon

4½" (12 cm) This warblerlike vireo combines unbarred wings and *yellow-tinged* underparts (especially across breast). *Dark loral spot* (between eye and bill). **SIMILAR SPECIES:** (1) Warbling Vireo usually lacks yellow (but may have a tinge on sides). (2) Fall Tennessee Warbler (p. 270) has clear white undertail coverts and a thin bill. **VOICE:** Song similar to Red-eyed Vireo's; higher, slower. **RANGE:** S. Canada, northeast edge of U.S. Winters in Cen. America. **HABITAT:** Second growth; poplars, willows, alders.

M 286

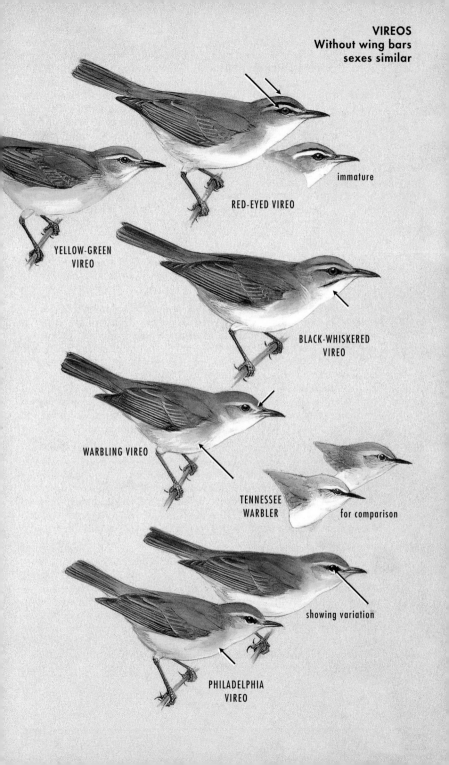

VIREOS
Without wing bars
sexes similar

immature

RED-EYED VIREO

YELLOW-GREEN
VIREO

BLACK-WHISKERED
VIREO

WARBLING VIREO

TENNESSEE
WARBLER

for comparison

showing variation

PHILADELPHIA
VIREO

YELLOW-THROATED VIREO *Vireo flavifrons*   Fairly common

M 283

5" (13 cm) *Bright yellow* throat, *yellow* "spectacles," and white wing bars. Our only vireo that is *bright* yellow. **SIMILAR SPECIES:** (1) Yellow-breasted Chat 2 in. longer and lacks wing bars. (2) Pine Warbler has some dusky streaks below, white tail spots. **VOICE:** Song, similar to Red-eyed Vireo's, but more musical, lower pitched; has a burry quality and longer pauses between phrases, swings back and forth with phrases that sound like *ee-yay, three-eight*. **RANGE:** E. U.S., se. Canada. Winters in tropical America. **HABITAT:** Deciduous woodlands, shade trees.

WHITE-EYED VIREO *Vireo griseus*   Fairly common

M 280

5" (13 cm) Note combination of *yellow* "spectacles," *whitish* throat. Other features are 2 wing bars, yellowish sides, *white eyes (dark in immatures)*. **SIMILAR SPECIES:** (1) Blue-headed Vireo has *white* "spectacles"; (2) Yellow-throated Vireo has a *yellow* throat; (3) See *Empidonax* flycatchers (p. 226). **VOICE:** Song, unvireolike, a sharply enunciated *chick'-a-per-weeoo-chick'*. Variable; usually starts or end with *chick*. **RANGE:** E. U.S. Winters s. U.S. to Nicaragua. **HABITAT:** Wood edges, brush, brambles, dense undergrowth.

BELL'S VIREO *Vireo bellii*   Uncommon

M 281

4½–5" (11–13 cm) Small, dull greenish with yellowish sides; nondescript. One or 2 light wing bars, pale yellowish-washed sides. **SIMILAR SPECIES:** (1) Distinguished from Warbling Vireo by overall size (especially tail), wing bar(s), and broken whitish eye-ring. (2) Immature White-eyed Vireo has more distinct wing bars and is whiter below. **VOICE:** Sings as if through clenched teeth; husky, unmusical phrases at short intervals: *cheedle cheedle chee? cheedle cheedle chew!* First phrase ends with a rising inflection; second phrase has a downward inflection. **RANGE:** Cen. and sw. U.S., n. Mexico. Winters Mexico to Nicaragua. **HABITAT:** Willows, streamsides, brush, dense undergrowth.

BLUE-HEADED VIREO *Vireo solitarius*   Fairly common

M 284

5–6" (13–15 cm) Note *white* "spectacles," *blue-gray* head, olive back, and *snow-white* throat. Two white wing bars. Usually earliest-arriving spring vireo. **VOICE:** Song, whistled phrases with short pauses. Similar to Red-eyed Vireo's song, but more deliberately spaced, higher, sweeter. **RANGE:** Canada, ne. U.S. and south in Appalachians. Winters s. U.S. to Costa Rica, Cuba. **HABITAT:** Mixed conifer-deciduous woods.

BLACK-CAPPED VIREO *Vireo atricapillus*   Scarce, local

M 282

4½" (11 cm) A small sprightly vireo with top and sides of head *glossy black* in male, slaty gray in female. Conspicuous "spectacles" formed by eye-ring and loral patch; 2 wing bars; eyes *red*. **SIMILAR SPECIES:** Female may be mistaken for Solitary Vireo, but eyes red. Endangered. **VOICE:** Song, hurried, harsh; phrases remarkable for variety and restless, almost angry quality. Alarm note, a harsh *chit-ah*. **RANGE:** Breeds cen. Okla., w. and cen. Tex. (Edwards Plateau) to Coahuila, Mexico. Winters in w. Mexico. **HABITAT:** Oak scrub, brushy hillsides, canyons. Local. Often hard to see.

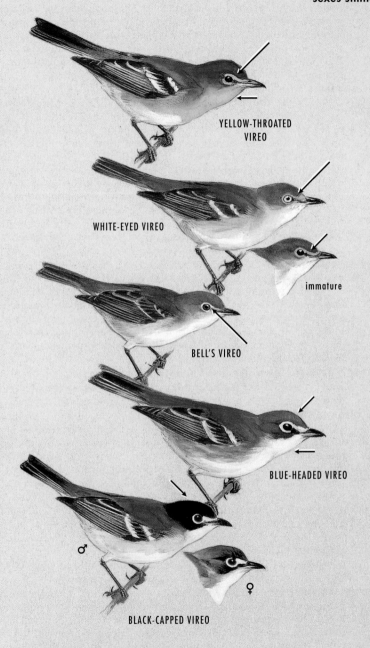

VIREOS
With wing bars
sexes similar

YELLOW-THROATED
VIREO

WHITE-EYED VIREO

immature

BELL'S VIREO

BLUE-HEADED VIREO

♂

♀

BLACK-CAPPED VIREO

WOOD-WARBLERS. Family Parulidae.

Active, brightly colored birds, usually smaller than sparrows, with thin pointed bills. The majority have some yellow. Identification in autumn may be a challenge (see pp. 278–281). For further identification tips, see *A Field Guide to Warblers of North America,* by Jon Dunn and Kimball Garrett. **FOOD:** Mainly insects. **RANGE:** Alaska and Canada to n. Argentina. **NO. OF SPECIES:** World, 116; East, 40 (+ 7 accidental).

NORTHERN PARULA *Parula americana*　　　　　　　　　　　　Common

M 347

4½" (11 cm) A bluish warbler with a yellow throat and breast and 2 conspicuous white wing bars. A suffused greenish patch on back (hard to see unless feeding low) is a clinching point. In male, most useful mark is a *dark band* across breast washed with orange (indistinct or lacking in female). **SIMILAR SPECIES:** Tropical Parula (*P. pitiayumi),* sometimes found in s. Tex., has a dark face mask and no eye-ring. **VOICE:** Song, a buzzy trill or rattle that climbs the scale and trips over at the top: *zeeeeeeeee-up.* Also a series of buzzy notes terminating in trill, *zh-zh-zh-zheeeeee.* **RANGE:** Se. Canada, e. U.S. Winters Fla., Mexico to W. Indies, Nicaragua. **HABITAT:** Breeds mainly in humid woods where either *Usnea* lichen or Spanish Moss hangs from trees (occasionally in some woods where neither is found).

YELLOW-THROATED WARBLER *Dendroica dominica*　　　　Fairly common

M 357

5–5½" (13–14 cm) A gray-backed warbler with a yellow throat. Black eye mask extending down side and white eyebrow stripe, 2 white wing bars, black stripes on sides. Sexes similar. Creeps about branches of trees. **VOICE:** Song, a series of clear slurred notes dropping slightly in pitch: *tee-ew, tew, tew, tew, tew, tew wi* (last note rising). **RANGE:** E. and cen. U.S. Winters s. U.S. to Costa Rica. **HABITAT:** Open woodlands, especially sycamores, live oaks, pines.

"SUTTON'S" WARBLER *Dendroica dominica × Parula americana*

Unusual hybrid between Northern Parula and Yellow-throated. Collected twice in W. Va. Several unconfirmed sightings. Not expected.

BLACK-THROATED GREEN WARBLER *Dendroica virens*　　　Common

M 355

4½–5" (11–13 cm) *Male:* Note bright *yellow face,* framed by black throat and olive-green crown. *Female:* Recognized by yellow face; much less black on throat. *Immature, fall:* See p. 278. **VOICE:** A lisping dreamy *zoo zee zoo zoo zee* or *zee zee zee zee zoo zee,* with *zee* notes on same pitch, *zoo* notes lower. **RANGE:** Canada, ne. U.S. and south in Appalachians. Winters s. Tex., Fla. to Colombia. **HABITAT:** Mainly conifers.

GOLDEN-CHEEKED WARBLER *Dendroica chrysoparia*　　　Scarce, local

M 354

5½" (14 cm) Restricted to cedar-clad hills and streamsides of the Edwards Plateau, Tex. *Male:* With yellow cheeks, black eye line, *black throat and back* and top of head. White below. *Female:* Same pattern but more drab. (Use caution with migrant Black-throated Green, which shows yellow on underparts.) **VOICE:** *Bzzz, layzee, dayzee.*

PROTHONOTARY WARBLER *Protonotaria citrea*　　　　Fairly common

M 367

5½" (14 cm) A golden bird of wooded swamps. Entire head and breast deep yellow to orangy. Wings blue-gray with no bars. Female duller. **VOICE:** Song, *zweet zweet zweet zweet zweet zweet,* on one pitch. **RANGE:** Great Lakes area to Gulf states. Winters se. Mexico to Colombia, Venezuela. **HABITAT:** Wooded swamps, backwaters, river edges.

NORTHERN PARULA

♀

♂

TROPICAL PARULA

♂

"SUTTON'S"
WARBLER
(hybrid)

YELLOW-THROATED
WARBLER
sexes similar

♂

immature

♀

BLACK-THROATED
GREEN WARBLER

GOLDEN-CHEEKED
WARBLER

♂

♂

♀

PROTHONOTARY WARBLER

BLACK-AND-WHITE WARBLER *Mniotilta varia*   Common

M 365

4½–5½" (11–14 cm) *Creeping* along trunks and branches of trees, this warbler is *striped lengthwise* with *black and white* and has a *striped crown*, white stripes on back. Female has whiter underparts. **VOICE:** Song, a thin *weesee weesee weesee weesee*; suggests one of American Redstart's songs, but higher pitched and longer. A second, more rambling song drops in pitch midway. **RANGE:** Canada to Gulf states. Winters s. U.S. to n. S. America. **HABITAT:** Woods.

BLACKPOLL WARBLER *Dendroica striata*   Common

M 363

5" (13 cm) *Male, spring:* A striped gray warbler with a *black cap* and *white* cheeks. *Female, spring:* Less heavily streaked, lacking black cap; greenish gray above, olive wash on breast. Distinctly pale legs and feet. *Autumn:* Olive above, greenish yellow below, faintly streaked; 2 wing bars, white undertail coverts, usually pale yellowish legs, or at least pale feet (see p. 278). **SIMILAR SPECIES:** (1) Black-and-white Warbler has white stripe through crown. (2) See fall Bay-breasted and Pine Warblers (p. 278). **VOICE:** Song, a thin high, mechanical *zi-zi-zi-zi-zi-zi-zi-zi-zi* on one pitch, becoming stronger, then diminishing. **RANGE:** Alaska, Canada, ne. U.S. Winters in tropical S. America. **HABITAT:** Conifers; in migration, other trees.

BLACK-THROATED GRAY WARBLER *Dendroica nigrescens*   Vagrant

4½–5" (11–13 cm) *Male:* Gray, with black throat, cheek, and crown patches separated by white. *Female:* Slaty crown and cheek, light throat. **RANGE:** W. N. America. Casual stray east to Atlantic states.

BLACK-THROATED BLUE WARBLER *Dendroica caerulescens*   Fairly common

M 352

5–5½" (13–14 cm) *Male:* Clean-cut; upper parts *blue*, throat and sides *black*, belly white. *Female:* Back olive-brown with a light line over eye and a small *white wing spot* (not always visible). Immature may lack white wing spot, but note *dark cheek*. See also p. 280. **VOICE:** Song, husky, lazy *zur, zur, zur, zreee* or *beer, beer, beer, bee* (ending higher). May be shortened to 2 or 3 notes. **RANGE:** E. N. America. Winters mainly W. Indies. **HABITAT:** Understory of deciduous and mixed woodlands.

CERULEAN WARBLER *Dendroica cerulea*   Uncommon

M 364

4½" (11 cm) *Male: Blue* above, white below. Overhead, note the *narrow black bar* across the chest. *Female:* Blue-gray and olive green above, whitish below; 2 white wing bars and white eyebrow stripe. **SIMILAR SPECIES:** Female suggests (1) Tennessee Warbler (p. 270), but latter has no wing bars; also (2) fall Blackpoll (p. 278), but greener above, whitish below, with a more conspicuous eyebrow. (3) Dull female Blackburnian has bolder back pattern. **VOICE:** Song suggests Parula's; rapid buzzy notes on same pitch, followed by a longer note on a higher pitch: *zray zray zray zreeeee*. Also has quality of Black-throated Blue's song. **RANGE:** E. N. America. Winters Colombia to n. Bolivia. **HABITAT:** High in deciduous forests, especially in river valleys and ridges.

WARBLERS
Black-striped,
gray, or bluish

BLACK-AND-
WHITE WARBLER

♀

♂

winter

BLACKPOLL
WARBLER

breeding ♂

♀

BLACK-THROATED
GRAY WARBLER

immature

♀

♂

BLACK-THROATED
BLUE WARBLER

♀

♂

CERULEAN WARBLER

♀

♂

MAGNOLIA WARBLER *Dendroica magnolia* Fairly common

M 350

4½" (11 cm) The "black and yellow" Warbler. Upperparts blackish, with large white patches on the wings and tail; underparts yellow, with heavy black stripes. In any plumage, note black tail bisected midway by a *broad white band*. From below, tail looks white with a broad black band at tip. *Immature:* See p. 278. **VOICE:** Song suggests Yellow Warbler's but shorter; *weeta weeta weetsee* (last note rising), or Hooded Warbler–like *weeta weeta wit-chew*. **RANGE:** Canada, ne. U.S. Winters Mexico, W. Indies to Panama. **HABITAT:** Low conifers; in migration, other trees.

YELLOW-RUMPED WARBLER *Dendroica coronata* Common

M 353

5–6" (13–15 cm) Recognized by bright *yellow rump* and call note (a loud *check*). *Male, spring:* Blue-gray above; heavy black breast patch (like an inverted U); yellow patch on crown and *below each wing*. *Female, spring:* Brownish; basic pattern similar. *Winter:* Brownish above, whitish below, streaked, with yellow patch at breast sides; *yellow rump*. Western form, "Audubon's" Warbler, casual in e. U.S., has a *yellow or yellowish* throat and lacks pale supercilium. **VOICE:** Song, a loose trill, but rising in pitch or dropping toward end. Call note, a loud *check*. **RANGE:** Alaska, Canada, ne. U.S. Winters to Panama. **HABITAT:** Conifer and mixed forests. In migration and winter, varied; woods, thickets, brush, bayberry scrub.

KIRTLAND'S WARBLER *Dendroica kirtlandii* Rare, restricted

M 359

6" (15 cm) Bluish gray above, streaked with black; yellow below, with black spots or streaks *confined to sides*. Male has a blackish mask. Female is grayer, lacks mask. In autumn, browner. Persistently *wags its tail* (as does Prairie Warbler). **VOICE:** Song, loud and low-pitched for a *Dendroica*, resembles Northern Waterthrush's song; at times suggests House Wren's. Typical song starts with 3 or 4 low staccato notes, continues with rapid ringing notes on a higher pitch, and ends abruptly. **RANGE:** N.-cen. Michigan, nesting in loose colonies in an area about 100 miles long, 60 miles wide. Winters Bahamas. **HABITAT:** Groves of young Jack Pines 5–18 ft. high with ground cover of blueberries, Bearberry, or Sweetfern. The Brown-headed Cowbird is having a distinct impact on Kirtland's population.

CANADA WARBLER *Wilsonia canadensis* Uncommon

5–5¾" (13–14 cm) The "necklaced" warbler. *Male:* Solid gray above, bright yellow below; with a *necklace of short black stripes. Female and immature:* Similar, but necklace fainter, upperparts duller. All have yellow and white "spectacles." Gray above, combined with lack of white in wings and tail, is conclusive. **VOICE:** Song, a staccato burst, irregularly arranged. *Chip, chupety swee-ditchety.* Note, *tchip*. **RANGE:** Canada, ne. U.S.; south in Appalachians. Winters n. S. America. **HABITAT:** Forest undergrowth, shady thickets.

M 379

WARBLERS
Grayish, striped

MAGNOLIA WARBLER

♀

♂

winter

♂ breeding

♀

YELLOW-RUMPED
("MYRTLE") WARBLER

KIRTLAND'S WARBLER

sexes
similar

♂
breeding

winter

YELLOW-RUMPED
("AUDUBON'S")
WARBLER

♀

CANADA WARBLER

♂

CAPE MAY WARBLER *Dendroica tigrina* Uncommon

M 351

5" (13 cm) *Male, spring:* Note *chestnut* cheeks. Yellow below, striped with black; rump dull yellow, crown black. *Female and autumn:* Lack chestnut cheeks; duller; breast often whitish, streaked. Dull *patch of yellow behind ear.* See also p. 278. **VOICE:** Song, a very high thin *seet seet seet seet,* easily confused with song of Bay-breast. **RANGE:** Canada, northeastern edge of U.S. Winters in Caribbean area. **HABITAT:** Spruce forests; in migration, other trees.

CHESTNUT-SIDED WARBLER *Dendroica pensylvanica* Fairly common

M 349

4½–5½" (11–14 cm) *Adult, spring:* Readily identified by combination of *yellow crown, chestnut sides.* *Autumn:* Lemon greenish above, mostly white below. Narrow white eye-ring, 2 pale yellow wing bars. Adults and some immatures retain some chestnut. *Immature:* See p. 278. **VOICE:** Song, similar to Yellow Warbler's; *see see see see Miss Beech'er* or *please please pleased to meet'cha,* penultimate note accented, last note dropping. Also a more rambling song. **RANGE:** S. Canada, ne. U.S.; south in Appalachians. Winters in Cen. America. **HABITAT:** Undergrowth, overgrown field edges, small trees.

BAY-BREASTED WARBLER *Dendroica castanea* Uncommon

M 362

5–6" (13–15 cm) *Male, spring:* Dark-looking with *chestnut throat, upper breast,* and sides. Note *large spot* of *pale buff* on neck. *Female, spring:* Paler, more washed out. *Autumn:* Olive green above; dull white below, 2 white wing bars. May have trace of bay on sides. Also, *buff* undertail coverts, dark legs and feet. See p. 278. **SIMILAR SPECIES:** See fall Blackpoll Warbler (p. 262). **VOICE:** A high sibilant *teesi teesi, teesi teesi* (notes doubled); resembles song of Black-and-white; thinner, shorter, more on one pitch. **RANGE:** Canada, northeastern edge of U.S. Winters Panama to Venezuela. **HABITAT:** Woodlands; conifers in summer.

BLACKBURNIAN WARBLER *Dendroica fusca* Fairly common

M 356

5" (13 cm) The "firethroat." *Male, spring:* Black and white, with *flaming orange* on head and throat. *Female:* Paler; some orange on throat. *Autumn:* Paler; note yellow head stripes, pale back stripes. **VOICE:** Song, *zip zip zip titi tseeeeee,* ending on a very high up-slurred note. Also a two-parted *teetsa teetsa teetsa teetsa zizizizizi,* more like Nashville's song. **RANGE:** Canada, ne. U.S.; south in Appalachians. Winters Costa Rica to Peru. **HABITAT:** Woodlands; conifers in summer.

AMERICAN REDSTART *Setophaga ruticilla* Common

M 366

5" (13 cm) Flutters like a falling leaf when feeding, runs on limbs, with drooping wings and spread tail. *Male:* Black; *bright orange patch* on wings and tail. *Female:* Olive to grayish; *yellow flash-patch* on wings and tail. *Immature male:* Like female, but patches tinged with orange. **VOICE:** Songs (often alternated), *zee zee zee zee zwee* (last note higher), *tsee tsee tsee tsee tsee-o* (last syllable dropping), and *teetsa teetsa teetsa teetsa teet* (notes paired), all rapid and hurried. **RANGE:** Canada, e. U.S. Winters Mexico, W. Indies to Brazil, n. Peru. **HABITAT:** Deciduous woods, saplings.

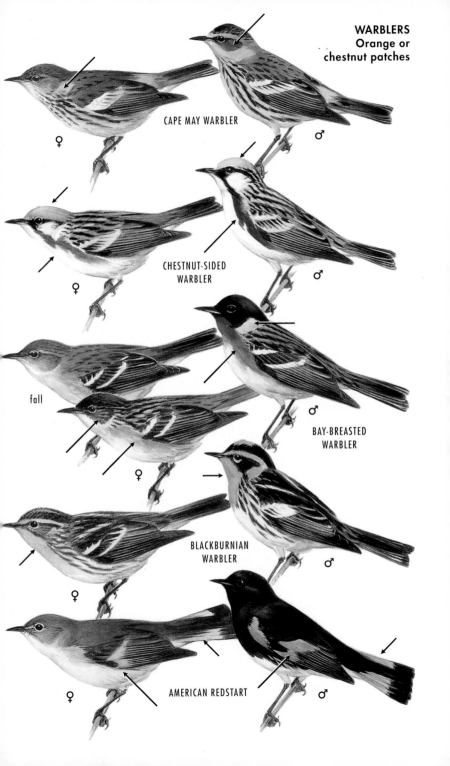

WARBLERS
Orange or chestnut patches

CAPE MAY WARBLER

♀

♂

CHESTNUT-SIDED
WARBLER

♀

♂

fall

BAY-BREASTED
WARBLER

♀

BLACKBURNIAN
WARBLER

♂

♀

AMERICAN REDSTART

♂

PINE WARBLER *Dendroica pinus* Common

M 358

5–5½" (13–14 cm) No other bright yellow–breasted warbler lacking other conspicuous field marks has two *white wing bars*. Breast dimly streaked, back *unstreaked*; white spots in tail corners, female duller than male. Immature and autumn females are duller; see fall warblers, p. 278. **VOICE:** Song, a trill on one pitch like Chipping Sparrow's song, but looser, more musical, slower. **RANGE:** E. N. America, W. Indies. Winters in southern part of range. **HABITAT:** Chiefly open pine woods, pine barrens.

PRAIRIE WARBLER *Dendroica discolor* Fairly common

M 360

5" (13 cm) This warbler *bobs its tail* (so does Palm Warbler); underparts yellow; black stripes *confined to sides*; 2 *black face marks*, 1 through eye, 1 below. At close range, chestnut marks may be seen on back of male (reduced in female). *Immature:* See p. 278. **VOICE:** Song, a thin *zee zee zee zee zee zee zee zee*; up scale. **RANGE:** E. N. America. Winters Fla. to Nicaragua. **HABITAT:** Brushy pastures, low pines, mangroves.

PALM WARBLER *Dendroica palmarum* Common

M 361

4½–5½" (11–14 cm) Note constant *bobbing* of tail. Brown above; yellowish or whitish below, narrowly streaked; *yellow* undertail coverts, white spots in tail corners. In spring, a *chestnut cap* (obscure in fall, winter; see p. 278). **VOICE:** Song, weak repetitious notes, *zhe-zhe-zhe-zhe-zhe-zhe*. **RANGE:** Canada, northeastern edge of U.S. Winters in s. U.S., Caribbean area. **HABITAT:** Ground loving. In summer, wooded and brushy borders of muskeg and bogs. In migration, low trees, bushes. Often on ground.

"BREWSTER'S" WARBLER Scarce
Vermivora chrysoptera × pinus or V. "leucobronchialis"

Golden-winged and Blue-winged Warblers hybridize where their ranges overlap, producing 2 basic types, "Lawrence's" (see p. 272) and "Brewster's" (the more frequent hybrid and more variable). Typical "Brewster's" is like Blue-wing with whitish underparts. Some have white wing bars, others yellow; some are tinged with yellow below. Black eye mark and white or largely white (not solid yellow) underparts are diagnostic. May sing like either parent.

BLUE-WINGED WARBLER *Vermivora pinus* Fairly common

M 342

4½–5" (11–13 cm) Note narrow *black line through eye*. Face and underparts yellow; wings with 2 *white bars*. **VOICE:** Song, a buzzy *beeee-bzzz* as if inhaled and exhaled. **RANGE:** E. U.S. Winters Mexico to Panama. **HABITAT:** Field edges, undergrowth, bushy edges, woodland openings.

YELLOW WARBLER *Dendroica petechia* Common

M 348

5" (13 cm) No other warbler is so extensively yellow. Even *tail spots are yellow* (white in many other species). Male has *rusty breast streaks* (in female, faint or lacking). *Fall:* See p. 278. *Note:* Mangrove subspecies, with distinct rusty hood, has occurred in Rio Grande Valley, Tex. **VOICE:** Song, a cheerful bright *tsee-tsee-tsee-tsee-titi-wee* or *weet weet weet weet tsee tsee*, given rapidly. Variable. **RANGE:** Alaska, Canada to cen. Peru. Winters Mexico to Peru. **HABITAT:** Bushes, swamp and stream edges, gardens.

WARBLERS
Olive or yellow with
streaks or wing bars

immature

PINE WARBLER

♂

♀

PRAIRIE WARBLER

♂

winter

"western" race

PALM WARBLER

♂

yellowish race

hybrid
(Blue-wing X
Golden-wing)

"BREWSTER'S" WARBLER

♂

♂

BLUE-WINGED WARBLER

♀

YELLOW WARBLER

♂

SWAINSON'S WARBLER *Limnothlypis swainsonii*   Uncommon

M 369

5" (13 cm) A skulker, difficult to see. Olive-brown above and plain buffy white below, with a *brown crown* and *light eyebrow stripe*. Sexes alike. **VOICE:** Song suggests Louisiana Waterthrush's, but shorter (5 notes: 2 slurred notes, 2 lower notes, and a higher note). **RANGE:** Se. U.S. Winters in W. Indies, Yucatán Peninsula. **HABITAT:** Cane thickets, swamps, bogs, stream bottoms, woodland brush; locally in rhododendron-hemlock tangles in cen. Appalachians.

WORM-EATING WARBLER *Helmitheros vermivorus*   Uncommon

M 368

5–5½" (13–14 cm) An unobtrusive forager of leaf-strewn wooded slopes and thick understory. Heard more often than seen. Dull olive, with *black stripes on a buffy head*. Breast rich buff. Sexes alike. **VOICE:** Song, a thin dry buzz; resembles trill or rattle of Chipping Sparrow, but thinner, more rapid, and insectlike. **RANGE:** E. U.S. Winters W. Indies, Cen. America. **HABITAT:** Dry wooded and rocky hillsides, undergrowth, ravines.

TENNESSEE WARBLER *Vermivora peregrina*   Uncommon

M 344

4½" (12 cm) Quite plain. *Male, spring:* Note white eyebrow stripe and gray head contrasting with greenish back. *Female, spring:* Similar; head less gray, underparts slightly yellowish. *Fall:* Greenish; note *unstreaked* yellowish breast, strong yellowish eyebrow stripe, and trace of a wing bar. See also p. 280. **SIMILAR SPECIES:** (1) See fall Orange-crowned Warbler (p. 280). (2) See also vireos without wing bars (p. 256). **VOICE:** Song, staccato, two- or three-parted: *ticka ticka ticka ticka, swit swit, chew-chew-chew-chew-chew*. Suggests Nashville Warbler's song, but louder, more tirelessly repeated. **RANGE:** Canada, northeastern edge of U.S. Winters Mexico to Venezuela. **HABITAT:** Deciduous and mixed forests; in migration, groves, wood edges.

ORANGE-CROWNED WARBLER *Vermivora celata*   Uncommon in East

M 345

4½–5½" (11–14 cm) A dingy warbler without wing bars or other distinctive marks; olive-green above, greenish yellow below. Note faint breast streaks, lack of wing bars, light eye line. "Orange" of crown seldom visible. Many birds in fall and winter are decidedly gray (see p. 280). **SIMILAR SPECIES:** See (1) fall Tennessee Warbler (p. 280); (2) Philadelphia Vireo (p. 256). **VOICE:** Song, a colorless trill, becoming weaker toward end. Often changes pitch, rising then dropping. **RANGE:** Alaska, Canada, w. U.S. Winters se. U.S. south to Guatemala. Uncommon in East, more regular in fall. **HABITAT:** Open woodland, brushy clearings, undergrowth.

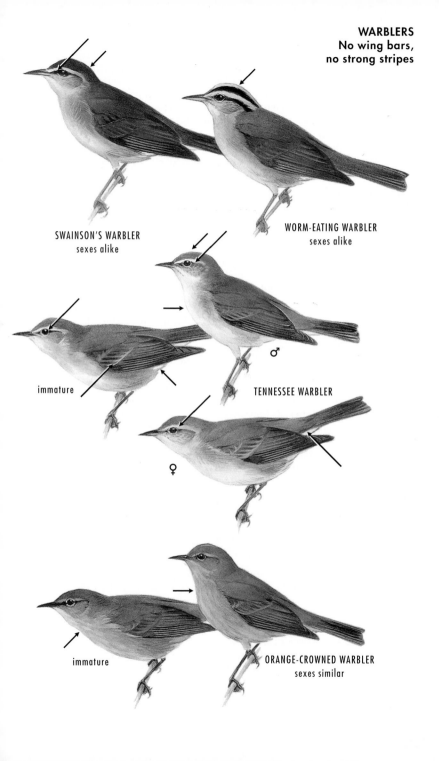

WARBLERS
No wing bars,
no strong stripes

SWAINSON'S WARBLER
sexes alike

WORM-EATING WARBLER
sexes alike

immature

♂

TENNESSEE WARBLER

♀

immature

ORANGE-CROWNED WARBLER
sexes similar

WILSON'S WARBLER *Wilsonia pusilla*   Uncommon

M 378

4½" (1 2 cm) *Male:* A yellow warbler with a *round black cap* and longish tail that is olive and unspotted. *Female* and *immature* male may show trace of a cap. Small, golden-looking, with a yellow stripe above a beady eye (see p. 2 8 0). Constantly moving and flitting about. **SIMILAR SPECIES:** (1) Female Hooded has white spots in tail; (2) Yellow Warbler, yellow spots in tail. **VOICE:** Song, a thin rapid little chatter dropping in pitch at the end: *chi chi chi chi chi chet chet.* Call note, a soft *chiup.* **RANGE:** Alaska, Canada, w. and ne. U.S. Winters Mexico to Panama. **HABITAT:** Thickets along wooded streams, moist tangles, low shrubs, willows, alders.

HOODED WARBLER *Wilsonia citrina*   Fairly common

M 377

5½" (1 4 cm) Black hood or cowl of *male* completely encircles yellow face and forehead. *Female* lacks this hood, although yellow face may be sharply outlined in some females. All have *white tail spots.* **SIMILAR SPECIES:** Female Wilson's Warbler lacks tail spots. **VOICE:** Note, a metallic *chink.* Song, a loud whistled *weeta wee-tee-o.* Also other arrangements; slurred *tee-o* is a clue. **RANGE:** E. and cen. U.S. Winters in Cen. America. **HABITAT:** Woodland undergrowth, laurels, wooded swamps.

BACHMAN'S WARBLER *Vermivora bachmanii*   Probably extinct

4½" (1 1 cm) Last known definite sighting 1 9 6 5. *Male:* Face and underparts yellow; *throat patch* and *crown patch black* (suggests a small Hooded with an incomplete hood). *Female:* Lacks black throat; forehead yellow; crown and cheek grayish; eye-ring yellow. **SIMILAR SPECIES:** (1) "Lawrence's" Warbler has wing bars, black ear patch. (2) Male Hooded has complete hood. (3) Female Hooded and (4) female Wilson's are similar to female Bachman's. Female Bachman's has gray crown and cheek, yellow eye-ring; lacks tail spots of Hooded. **VOICE:** Song, a rapid series of flat mechanical buzzes rendered on one pitch: *bzz-bzz-bzz-bzz-bzz-bzz-bzz-bzz.* Can be given in flight. **RANGE:** Se. U.S.; very local. Wintered in Cuba. Bred in se. Mo., ne. Ark., w. Ky., n. Ala., S.C., Va. (?), particularly in areas with cane. Migrated through Gulf states and Fla.

"LAWRENCE'S" WARBLER *Vermivora chrysoptera × pinus*   Rare

Recessive hybrid of Blue-wing–Golden-wing combination. Yellow below like Blue-wing, but with black head pattern of Golden-wing. Note black ear patch. **SIMILAR SPECIES:** See Bachman's Warbler. **VOICE:** Like either Golden-wing's or Blue-wing's.

GOLDEN-WINGED WARBLER *Vermivora chrysoptera*   Uncommon

M 343

5–5½" (1 3–1 4 cm) Gray above and white below. Male is the only warbler with combination of *yellow wing patch* and *black throat.* Note yellow forehead, black ear patch. In female, throat is gray. **VOICE:** Song, a buzzy note followed by 3 on a lower pitch: *bee-bz-bz-bz.* (Blue-wing sings a lazier *beee-bzzz.*) **RANGE:** E. U.S. Winters Guatemala to Colombia. **HABITAT:** Open woodlands, brushy clearings, undergrowth. Declining in many northeast and southern areas.

WARBLERS
Strong yellow and
black head patterns

WILSON'S WARBLER

♀ ♂

HOODED WARBLER

♀ ♂

BACHMAN'S WARBLER

♀ ♂

"LAWRENCE'S" WARBLER

"Lawrence's" Warbler
is a hybrid
(Blue-wing X
Golden-wing)

♂

GOLDEN-WINGED
WARBLER

♀ ♂

NASHVILLE WARBLER *Vermivora ruficapilla* Uncommon

M 346

4½" (12 cm) Note *white eye-ring* in combination with *yellow* throat. *Head gray*, contrasting with olive-green back. No wing bars. Males may show a dull chestnut crown patch. **SIMILAR SPECIES:** Connecticut Warbler also has a white eye-ring and lacks wing bars, but its throat is *grayish or brownish,* giving a hooded look, and is larger and walks rather than hops. **VOICE:** Song, two-parted: *seebit, seebit, seebit, seebit, titititititi* (ends like Chipping Sparrow's song). **RANGE:** S. Canada, w. and n. U.S. Winters s. Tex. to Guatemala. **HABITAT:** Open conifer and mixed woods with undergrowth, forest edges, bogs.

CONNECTICUT WARBLER *Oporornis agilis* Scarce

M 374

5½–6" (13–15 cm) A skulker. Similar to Mourning Warbler; adult has gray hood, yellow-and-olive body, and note complete, circular *white eye-ring* that gives a staring quality. Fall female and young are duller, lack gray hood, but have a suggestion of one (a brownish stain across upper breast). Eye-ring is always present. *Walks rather than hops.* **SIMILAR SPECIES:** (1) Breeding Mourning Warbler lacks eye-ring (but in fall, immature has a broken one). Male has a black throat. Also, Connecticut walks, Mourning hops. (2) Nashville Warbler also has an eye-ring, but it is much smaller and has a *yellow throat.* Nashville is a more active feeder. **VOICE:** A repetitious *chip-chup-ee, chip-chup-ee, chip-chup-ee, chip,* or *sugar-tweet, sugar-tweet, sugar-tweet* (W. Gunn). **RANGE:** Cen.-s. Canada, cen.-n. U.S. Winters n. S. America. **HABITAT:** Poplar bluffs, muskeg, Jack Pine, mixed woods near water; in migration, undergrowth (especially Touch-Me-Not, Ragweed, and Sweet Pepperbush).

MOURNING WARBLER *Oporornis philadelphia* Uncommon

M 375

5–5½" (13–14 cm) Olive above, yellow below, with a *gray hood* encircling head and neck; male with irregular *black bib. Immature:* See p. 280. **SIMILAR SPECIES:** See Connecticut Warbler; both are skulkers. **VOICE:** Song, *chirry, chirry, chorry, chorry* (*chorry* lower). Considerable variation. **RANGE:** Canada and ne. U.S. Winters Cen. and S. America. **HABITAT:** Bushy clearings, thickets (especially blackberry).

KENTUCKY WARBLER *Oporornis formosus* Uncommon

M 373

5½" (14 cm) Note broad black sideburns extending down from eye and yellow "spectacles." Sexes similar. Learn the song; 10 Kentuckies are heard for every 1 seen. **SIMILAR SPECIES:** (1) Common Yellowthroat (p. 276) lacks "spectacles"; (2) Canada Warbler (p. 264) has a dark necklace. **VOICE:** Song, a rapid rolling chant, *tory-tory-tory-tory* or *churry-churry-churry-churry,* suggestive of Carolina Wren's, but less musical (two-syllabled rather than three-syllabled). **RANGE:** E. U.S. Winters Mexico to n. S. America. **HABITAT:** Woodland undergrowth.

WARBLERS
No wing bars
or striping

NASHVILLE WARBLER

♀

♂

CONNECTICUT WARBLER

♀

immature

♂

MOURNING WARBLER

♀

immature

♂

Yellowthroat for comparison
(see p. 276)

KENTUCKY WARBLER
sexes similar

COMMON YELLOWTHROAT *Geothlypis trichas*   Common

M 376

4½–5½" (11–14 cm) A wrenlike warbler. *Male* with a black mask, or "domino"; throat yellow. *Female*, olive-brown with a rich yellow throat, buffy-yellow breast; no black mask. Immature male has faint black mask. Immature female may have no yellow below. Distinguished from similar warblers by *whitish belly*, brownish sides, and habitat. **VOICE:** A bright rapid chant, *witchity-witchity-witchity-witch;* sometimes *witchy-witchy-witchy-witch.* Note, a husky *tchep.* **RANGE:** Canada to s. Mexico. Winters s. U.S. to W. Indies, Panama. **HABITAT:** Swamps, marshes, wet thickets.

YELLOW-BREASTED CHAT *Icteria virens*   Uncommon

M 380

7½" (18 cm) Large for a warbler; large bill, longish tail, actions and habitat suggest a mimic thrush. Note *white* "spectacles," bright *yellow* throat and breast. No wing bars. **VOICE:** Song, clear repeated whistles, alternating with harsh notes and soft crowlike *caw's.* Suggests mockingbird, but repertoire more limited; much longer pauses between phrases. A single note, such as *whoit* or *kook,* is distinctive. **RANGE:** S. Canada to cen. Mexico, Gulf Coast. Winters Cen. America. **HABITAT:** Old fields with brushy tangles, briars, thickets.

NORTHERN WATERTHRUSH *Seiurus noveboracensis*   Common

M 371

6" (15 cm) Often *walks* along water's edge and teeters in manner of a Spotted Sandpiper. Brown-backed, with a *creamy, pale yellow, or buff* eyebrow stripe; *underparts striped,* often yellowish. *Throat striped.* **VOICE:** Note, a sharp *chink.* Song, a vigorous, rapid *twit twit twit sweet sweet sweet chew chew chew* (*chew's* drop in pitch). **RANGE:** Alaska, Canada, northern edge of U.S. Winters mainly in American Tropics. **HABITAT:** Swampy or wet woods, streamsides, lakeshores; in migration, also wet thickets.

LOUISIANA WATERTHRUSH *Seiurus motacilla*   Fairly common

M 372

6" (15 cm) Similar to Northern Waterthrush, but usually *whitish* below; bill slightly larger. Eyebrow stripe *pure white and flares noticeably behind eye.* Throat *lacks stripes in most cases.* Flanks buffy, legs pinkish. **SIMILAR SPECIES:** Some Northern Waterthrushes in fall (particularly western form, *S. m. notabilis*) have whitish eyebrow stripes. Northern has small spots or stripes on throat. **VOICE:** Song, musical and ringing; 3 clear slurred whistles, followed by a jumble of twittering notes dropping in pitch. **RANGE:** E. U.S. Winters Mexico, W. Indies to n. S. America. **HABITAT:** Brooks, ravines, wooded swamps.

OVENBIRD *Seiurus aurocapillus*   Common

M 370

6" (15 cm) A sparrow-sized warbler; usually seen walking on pale *pinkish* legs on woodland floor. Suggests a small thrush; olive above, but striped rather than spotted below. An *orangish patch on crown* visible at close range. Heard more often than seen. **VOICE:** Song, an emphatic *teach'er,* TEACH´ER, TEACH´ER, repeated rapidly in crescendo. In some areas, monosyllabic, with little change of emphasis, *TEACH, TEACH, TEACH,* etc., or *CHEAT, CHEAT, CHEAT.* **RANGE:** S. Canada, U.S. from Rockies eastward. Winters from se. U.S. to n. S. America. **HABITAT:** Near ground in leafy deciduous woods; in migration, woods and thickets.

WARBLERS
Aberrant species

COMMON
YELLOWTHROAT

♀

♂

YELLOW-BREASTED CHAT

sexes alike

yellowish race

sexes alike

NORTHERN
WATERTHRUSH

whitish
variation for
comparison

LOUISIANA
WATERTHRUSH

sexes alike

OVENBIRD

sexes alike

Most have streaks or wing bars.

RUBY-CROWNED KINGLET *Regulus calendula*   **P. 242**
(Not a warbler.) Broken eye-ring, pale wing bars.

CHESTNUT-SIDED WARBLER *Dendroica pensylvanica*   **P. 266**
Immature: Green above, whitish below; eye-ring.

BAY-BREASTED WARBLER *Dendroica castanea*   **P. 266**
Note dark legs and feet, buff undertail coverts. Fall adult may retain a
wash of bay on flanks. See Blackpoll Warbler.

BLACKPOLL WARBLER *Dendroica striata*   **P. 262**
Very similar to fall Bay-breast, but slimmer. It has (1) a greenish tinge
below and is streaked (Bay-breast is also yellowish, streaks indistinct
or lacking); (2) white (not buff) undertail coverts; (3) pale yellowish
legs and especially feet. (Bay-breast has dark legs, but so may some
Blackpolls. But Blackpoll's feet still pale.) Also, Bay-breast has fainter
back streaks.

PINE WARBLER *Dendroica pinus*   **P. 268**
Separate from 2 preceding species by unstreaked back. Note white undertail coverts (in Bay-breast, buff), fairly long tail, pale area behind
auricular, black legs (in Blackpoll, usually pale).

NORTHERN PARULA *Parula americana*   **P. 260**
Immature: Combination of bluish and yellow; wing bars.

MAGNOLIA WARBLER *Dendroica magnolia*   **P. 264**
Immature: Broad white band at midtail.

PRAIRIE WARBLER *Dendroica discolor*   **P. 268**
Immature: Jaw stripe, side stripes. Bobs tail.

YELLOW WARBLER *Dendroica petechia*   **P. 268**
Yellow tail spots. Some females and immature are so dusky that they
may resemble Orange-crowns (pp. 270, 280).

BLACKBURNIAN WARBLER *Dendroica fusca*   **P. 266**
Immature: Yellow throat, dark cheek; broad supercilium, pale back
stripes.

BLACK-THROATED GREEN WARBLER *Dendroica virens*   **P. 260**
Immature: Dusky outline frames yellow cheek. Plain greenish back.

PALM WARBLER *Dendroica palmarum*   **P. 268**
Brownish back, yellowish undertail coverts. Bobs tail.

YELLOW-RUMPED WARBLER *Dendroica coronata*   **P. 264**
Immature: Bright yellow rump, yellow spots on breast sides.

CAPE MAY WARBLER *Dendroica tigrina*   **P. 266**
Streaked breast, greenish yellow rump. Note pale neck spot (sometimes obscure in young birds).

CONFUSING FALL WARBLERS, etc.

♀

RUBY-CROWNED
KINGLET
not a warbler

immature
CHESTNUT-
SIDED

adult

PINE

immature

BAY-BREASTED

immature

PINE

BLACKPOLL

immature

immature

NORTHERN
PARULA

immature

MAGNOLIA

PRAIRIE

immature

YELLOW

immature

immature

BLACKBURNIAN

immature

BLACK-THROATED GREEN

immature

PALM

immature

YELLOW-RUMPED

CAPE MAY

Most of these lack streaks or wing bars.

ORANGE-CROWNED WARBLER *Vermivora celata*   P. 270
Dingy breast, yellow undertail coverts, faint eye line. Fall immature is greenish drab throughout, barely paler below; some birds often quite gray.

TENNESSEE WARBLER *Vermivora peregrina*   P. 270
Very similar to Orange-crowned (above) but differs in having (1) white undertail coverts; (2) a more conspicuous eyebrow stripe; (3) a greener look above; (4) paler underparts, with no hint of streaks; (5) a trace of a light wing bar.

PHILADELPHIA VIREO *Vireo philadelphicus*   P. 256
(Not a warbler.) "Vireo" song and actions (see p. 256). Note also thicker vireo bill.

HOODED WARBLER *Wilsonia citrina*   P. 272
Immature: Yellow eyebrow stripe, bold white tail spots.

WILSON'S WARBLER *Wilsonia pusilla*   P. 272
Immature: Like a small Hooded; no white in tail.

BLACK-THROATED BLUE WARBLER *Dendroica caerulescens*   P. 262
Dark-cheeked look, white wing spot. Some young birds and females lack this white spot and may suggest a Tennessee Warbler (above), but note *dark cheek.*

CONNECTICUT WARBLER *Oporornis agilis*   P. 274
Immature: Suggestion of a hood; complete eye-ring. *Walks.*

MOURNING WARBLER *Oporornis philadelphia*   P. 274
Immature and fall female: Suggestion of a hood; broken eye-ring. Brighter yellow below than Connecticut, including often on throat.

NASHVILLE WARBLER *Vermivora ruficapilla*   P. 274
Yellow throat, white eye-ring.

COMMON YELLOWTHROAT *Geothlypis trichas*   P. 276
Female: Yellow throat, brownish sides, white belly.

PROTHONOTARY WARBLER *Protonotaria citrea*   P. 260
Female: Dull golden head, gray wings.

CANADA WARBLER *Wilsonia canadensis*   P. 264
Immature: Lores yellow, eye-ring white, trace of necklace.

CONFUSING FALL WARBLERS, etc.

immature

ORANGE-CROWNED

TENNESSEE

PHILADELPHIA VIREO
not a warbler

WILSON'S ♀

immature

HOODED ♀

BLACK-THROATED BLUE ♀

immature

MOURNING

NASHVILLE

immature

CONNECTICUT

♀

COMMON
YELLOWTHROAT

♀

PROTHONOTARY

immature

CANADA

Male tanagers are brightly colored; females of U.S. species are greenish to grayish above, yellow below, suggesting large thick-billed warblers or vireos. Females may be confused with female orioles, but lack wing bars and have thicker bills. The rather stout bills are *notched* (hard to see). **FOOD:** Insects, fruits. **RANGE:** New World, most species in Tropics. **NO. OF SPECIES:** World, 256; East, 2 (+ 1 accidental).

SUMMER TANAGER *Piranga rubra* — Fairly common

M 381

7–7½" (18–19 cm) *Male: Rose red all over*, with a pale bill; no crest. *Female:* olive to grayish olive above, dingy mustard yellow below. Young males acquiring adult plumage (and a few females) may be patched with red and green. **SIMILAR SPECIES:** (1) Male cardinal has a crest, black face. (2) Male Scarlet Tanager has black wings and tail; female has darker wings and smaller, duskier bill. (3) Female orioles have wing bars and different bill shape. **VOICE:** Note, a staccato *pi-tuk* or *pik-i-tuk-i-tuk.* Song, robinlike phrases, less nasal and resonant than Scarlet Tanager's. **RANGE:** Cen. and s. U.S. to n. Mexico. Winters Mexico to Brazil. **HABITAT:** Woods (especially oaks), groves.

SCARLET TANAGER *Piranga olivacea* — Fairly common

M 382

7" (18 cm) *Male: Flaming scarlet*, with jet-black wings and tail. *Female, immature,* and *winter male:* Greenish above, yellowish below, with dark brownish or blackish wings. **SIMILAR SPECIES:** (1) Male Summer Tanager and (2) male cardinal (crested) are all red, lack black in wings and tail. (3) Female Summer Tanager has larger bill, wings are not as dark to dusky. **VOICE:** Note, *chip-burr.* Song, 4 or 5 short phrases (*hurry-worry-flurry-blurry*), robinlike but hoarse (suggesting a robin with a sore throat). **RANGE:** Se. Canada, e. U.S. Winters Colombia to w. Amazonia. **HABITAT:** Forests and shade trees (especially oaks), often stays high and overlooked.

WESTERN TANAGER *Piranga ludoviciana* — Casual in East (Vagrant)

7" (18 cm) The only U.S. tanager with strong *wing bars. Male:* Yellow, with black back, wings, and tail; 2 wing bars; and a *red face.* Red reduced in autumn and winter. *Female:* Yellowish below, dull gray with olive tint above, with white and yellow wing bars. **SIMILAR SPECIES:** Female resembles female orioles (p. 316), but tail and sides of face darker, bill less sharply pointed. *Caution:* A very few young Scarlet Tanagers in fall may have 2 thin yellowish wing bars, but these birds do not have "saddle-backed" look of immature or fall Western Tanager, whose grayish olive back contrasts with its paler head and rump. **VOICE:** Like Scarlet Tanager. Call a dry *pit-i-tic.* **RANGE:** W. N. America. Winters Cen. America. **EAST:** Casual, but there are numerous records from s. Canada to Gulf Coast, where it is very rare in late fall and winter, often at feeders.

TANAGERS

SUMMER TANAGER

♂ all seasons

♀

mature changing
to adult

SCARLET TANAGER

♂ changing

♂ winter

♀

♂ breeding

♂ orange
variant

WESTERN
TANAGER

♀

♂ breeding

♂ winter

GROSBEAKS, FINCHES, SPARROWS, BUNTINGS. Families Fringillidae, Emberizidae, Cardinalidae.

These birds have seed-cracking bills of 3 main types: (1) very large and thick (grosbeaks); (2) rather canarylike (finches, sparrows, bunting); (3) cross-tipped (crossbills). **FOOD:** Seeds, insects, small fruits. **RANGE:** Worldwide. **NO. OF SPECIES IN 3 FAMILIES:** World, 498; East, 50 (+ 10 accidental).

NORTHERN CARDINAL *Cardinalis cardinalis* — Common

M 417

7½–9" (19–23 cm) *Male:* An *all-red bird* with a *pointed crest,* and a black patch at base of its heavy triangular red bill. *Female:* Buff-brown, with some red on wings and tail. Crest, dark face, and heavy red bill are distinctive. *Juvenile:* Similar to female, but with a blackish bill. (See Pyrrhuloxia, p. 320). **SIMILAR SPECIES:** Male Summer Tanager, the other all-red bird of the southern and central states, has no crest. **VOICE:** Song, clear slurred whistles, lowering in pitch. Several variations: *what-cheer cheer cheer,* etc.; *whoit whoit whoit* or *birdy birdy birdy,* etc. Note, a short metallic *chip.* Female also sings. **RANGE:** S. Canada to Gulf states; sw. U.S., Mexico to Belize. **HABITAT:** Woodland edges, thickets, suburban gardens, feeders, towns.

RED CROSSBILL *Loxia curvirostra* — Uncommon, scarce

M 444

5½–6½" (13–16 cm) Size of a House Sparrow but looks bulkier. Large head and short tail. *Crossed mandibles,* often difficult to see. Sound made when it cracks open cones of evergreen trees often betrays its presence. It acts like a small parrot as it dangles while feeding. *Male:* Dull red, brighter on rump; wings and tail blackish. Young male is more orange. *Female:* Dull olive-gray; yellowish on rump and underparts. *Immature:* Striped above and below, suggesting a large Pine Siskin. **SIMILAR SPECIES:** White-winged Crossbill has white wing bars in all plumages. **VOICE:** Note, a hard *jip-jip* or *kip-kip.* Song, finchlike warbled passages, *jip-jip-jip-jeeaa-jeeaa,* or warbled passages, trills, and chips. **RANGE:** Conifer forests of N. Hemisphere. In N. America, south in mountains to Nicaragua; in East, locally to s. Appalachians. Erratic and irruptive wanderings, especially in winter. **HABITAT:** Conifers.

WHITE-WINGED CROSSBILL *Loxia leucoptera* — Uncommon, erratic

M 445

6–6½" (15–17 cm) Note wing bars, crossed mandibles. *Male:* Dull rose pink, with black wings crossed by 2 *broad white wing bars;* tail black. *Female:* Olive-gray, with a yellowish rump similar to female Red Crossbill's, but with 2 *broad white wing bars.* Wing bars are often quite evident in flight and help to pick out this species from mixed flocks of crossbills. **VOICE:** Notes, a liquid *peet* and a dry *chif-chif.* Song, a succession of loud trills on different pitches. **RANGE:** Boreal forests of N. Hemisphere. Erratic wanderings, especially in winter. **HABITAT:** Conifers.

RED FINCHES

♂

juvenile

♀

NORTHERN CARDINAL

♂

♀

immature

RED CROSSBILL

♂

♀

WHITE-WINGED
CROSSBILL

ROSE-BREASTED GROSBEAK *Pheucticus ludovicianus* Fairly common

M 418

7–8½" (18–21 cm) *Adult male:* Black and white, with a large triangle of rose red on breast and a *thick pale bill*. In flight, a pattern of black and white flashes across upperparts. Male in first-autumn plumage is similar to female but has a touch of red on a buffier breast. *Female:* Streaked, like a large sparrow or female Purple Finch (p. 292); recognized by large "grosbeak" bill, broad white wing bars, striped crown, and broad white eyebrow stripe. Wing linings yellow. **VOICE:** Song, rising and falling passages; resembles American Robin's song, but given with more feeling (as if a robin has taken voice lessons). Call note, a squeaky, metallic *kick* or *eek*. **RANGE:** S. Canada, e. and cen. U.S. Winters W. Indies, Mexico to nw. S. America. **HABITAT:** Deciduous woods, orchards, groves, thickets.

BLACK-HEADED GROSBEAK *Pheucticus melanocephalus* Vagrant in East

M 419

7–8½" (18–21 cm) *Adult male:* Size and shape of Rose-breasted Grosbeak, but breast, collar, and rump *dull orange-brown*. Black head, boldly marked black-and-white wings, and dark bill (darker than Rose-breasted). *Male, first fall:* similar to female with little or no streaking below. *Female:* Like female Rose-breast, but breast strongly washed with ocher; streaks much finer or nearly absent across chest; and darker billed. **SONG:** Very similar to Rose-breast. Call not as squeaky (*ik*). **RANGE:** Sw. Canada, w. U.S. to s. Mexico. Winters in Mexico. **EAST:** Breeds east to about 100th meridian in central parts of N.D., S.D., and Neb. Sometimes hybridizes with Rose-breast where ranges overlap. Strays rarely farther east, where it has wintered at feeders.

GREEN-TAILED TOWHEE *Pipilo chlorurus* Vagrant

6½" (16 cm) This slender western finch is identified by its *rufous cap* and *white throat*, bordered by a black mustache, gray chest, and plain *olive-green back*. It has strayed casually to at least 20 eastern states and provinces (strays usually recorded in winter at feeders).

EASTERN TOWHEE *Pipilo erythrophthalmus* Fairly common

M 384

7–8½" (18–21 cm) Readily recognized by *rufous sides*. Smaller and more slender than robin; rummages noisily among dead leaves. *Male:* Head and upper parts black; sides rufous rust, belly white. Flashes large white patches in the tail corners. Eye usually red (but white in birds of s. Atlantic Coast and Fla.). *Female:* Similar, but brown where male is black. *Juvenile, summer:* Streaked below like a large sparrow, but with diagnostic towhee wing and tail pattern. **SIMILAR SPECIES:** Spotted Towhee, below. **VOICE:** Song, *drink-your-tea*, last syllable higher, wavering. Call, a loud *chewink!* Southern white-eyed race gives a more slurred *shrink* or *zree*; song, *cheet cheet cheeeeee*. **RANGE:** S. Canada to Fla., Guatemala. Migrant in North. **HABITAT:** Open woods, undergrowth, brushy edges.

SPOTTED TOWHEE *Pipilo maculatus* Uncommon

M 383

7–8½" (18–21 cm) Replaces Eastern Towhee in West, is casual east of Mississippi R. It may be known by additional white wing bars and numerous white spots on back and different calls. **VOICE:** Song and call buzzier than Eastern Towhee. **HABITAT:** Undergrowth, brushy edges.

GROSBEAKS, TOWHEES

ROSE-BREASTED
GROSBEAK

♂

♀

BLACK-HEADED
GROSBEAK

♀

♂

GREEN-TAILED
TOWHEE

juvenile

♀

white-eyed
race ♂

♂

EASTERN
TOWHEE

SPOTTED
TOWHEE

BLUE GROSBEAK *Guiraca caerulea* Uncommon

M 420

6–7½" (15–19 cm) *Male:* Deep *dull blue,* with a thick silvery bill and 2 *broad rusty wing bars.* Often jerks or flips tail. Immature male a mixture of brown and blue. *Female:* About size of a Brown-headed Cowbird; warm brown, lighter below, with 2 rich *buff wing bars;* rump tinged with blue. **SIMILAR SPECIES:** Indigo Bunting is smaller and smaller billed, less distinct buffy wing bars when present. **VOICE:** Song, a rapid warble; short phrases rising and falling; suggests song of Purple Finch, House Finch, or Orchard Oriole, but slower and more guttural. Note, a sharp *chink.* **RANGE:** Cen. U.S. to Costa Rica. **HABITAT:** Roadsides, thickets, farmlands, brushy pastures.

INDIGO BUNTING *Passerina cyanea* Common

M 422

5½" (14 cm) *Male:* A small finch; rich deep blue *all over.* In autumn, male becomes more like brown female, but there is usually some blue in wings and tail. *Female:* Plain brown, breast paler, with indistinct streaks; a small brown finch devoid of obvious stripes. Wing bars, when present, are buffy. **SIMILAR SPECIES:** Blue Grosbeak (larger) has rusty wing bars. **VOICE:** Song, lively, high, and strident, with well-measured phrases at different pitches; notes usually paired: *sweet-sweet, chew-chew,* etc. Note, a sharp thin *spit.* **HABITAT:** Brushy pastures, edges.

LAZULI BUNTING *Passerina amoena* Rare in East

M 421

5–5½" (13–14 cm) *Male:* A small turquoise-blue finch, patterned somewhat like a bluebird (blue upperparts, pale cinnamon across breast and sides), but with 2 *white wing bars. Female:* Rather nondescript; a small finch with an unstreaked brown back, a trace of blue in wings and tail, 2 pale wing bars (more sharply defined than in female Indigo Bunting). Hybrids occur where ranges of Indigo and Lazuli Buntings overlap. **SIMILAR SPECIES:** Female Indigo Bunting has less pronounced wing bars and is richer brown above; usually shows faint blurry streaks on breast. **VOICE:** Song, similar to Indigo Bunting's; faster. **RANGE:** Breeds east to western edge of our area. **HABITAT:** Open brush, streamside shrubs.

PAINTED BUNTING *Passerina ciris* Uncommon

M 423

5½" (13 cm) The most gaudily colored N. American songbird. *Male:* A little finch the size of a Chipping Sparrow, with a patchwork of *blue-violet* on head, *green* on back, and red on rump and underparts. *Female and immature:* Vibrant green above, paling to lemon-green below; *no other small finch is so green* above. **VOICE:** Song, a bright pleasant warble; resembles song of Warbling Vireo, but more "wiry." Note, a sharp *chip.* **HABITAT:** Woodland edges, roadsides, brush, dune vegetation, towns, gardens.

BLUE BUNTING *Cyanocompsa parellina* Very rare visitor (Vagrant)

5½" (14 cm) *Male:* Deep dark blue finch. Much deeper blue than Indigo Bunting. Upper ridge on bill more curved. *Female: reddish brown* with no markings. Tail very dark. **RANGE:** Mexico. Rare visitor to the s. Tex. coast and Rio Grande Valley. **HABITAT:** Thickets and weedy areas.

VARIED BUNTING *Passerina versicolor* Rare, local

4½–5½" (11–14 cm) *Male: A small dark plum-colored* finch that looks black at a distance. Red patch at nape of neck. *Female:* Small, *uniform plain brown.* No wing bars or stripes. **RANGE:** Mexico, barely making it into Tex., N.M., and Ariz. Rare in Rio Grande Valley. **HABITAT:** Thickets and brush.

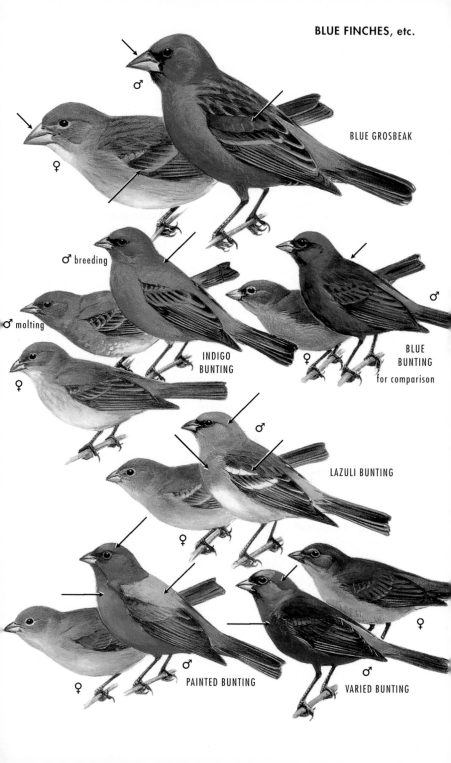

BLUE FINCHES, etc.

BLUE GROSBEAK

♂

♀

♂ breeding

♂ molting

♀

INDIGO BUNTING

♀

BLUE BUNTING
for comparison

♂

LAZULI BUNTING

♂

♀

♀

♂

PAINTED BUNTING

♀

♂

VARIED BUNTING

EVENING GROSBEAK *Coccothraustes vespertinus*   Uncommon, irregular

M 450

8" (20 cm) A chunky short-tailed finch, size of a starling, with a very large, conical, whitish or pale greenish bill. Undulating flight; its stocky shape and *large white wing patch* identify it as this species. *Male:* Dull yellow, with a dark head, yellow eyebrow stripe, and black-and-white wings; suggests an overgrown American Goldfinch. *Female:* Silvery gray, with just enough yellow, black, and white to be recognizable. Gregarious. **VOICE:** A ringing finchlike *chirp, cleer,* or *clee-ip* (suggesting a glorified House Sparrow's). Song, a short uneven warble. **RANGE:** Spruce belt of Canada, w. and ne. U.S., Mexico. Winters irregularly to se. U.S., Mexico. **HABITAT:** Conifer forests; in winter, Box Elders and other maples; fruiting shrubs, feeders.

AMERICAN GOLDFINCH *Carduelis tristis*   Common

M 449

5" (13 cm) A small finch with deeply undulating flight. *Male, summer:* Yellow, with *black wings,* tail, and forehead patch. *Female, summer:* Dull yellow-olive, darker above, with blackish wings and conspicuous wing bars; distinguished from other small olive-yellow birds by its short conical bill. *Winter, both sexes:* Much like summer female, but grayer. **SIMILAR SPECIES:** Yellow Warbler (p. 268) is yellowish all over, including the wings and tail. **VOICE:** Song, sustained, clear, light, canarylike. In flight, each dip often punctuated by *ti-dee´-di-di* or *per-chik-o-ree.* **RANGE:** S. Canada to s. U.S., n. Mexico. **HABITAT:** Patches of thistles and weeds, dandelions on lawns, roadsides, open woods, edges; also feeders stocked with thistle seeds.

PINE SISKIN *Carduelis pinus*   Uncommon, irruptive

M 448

4½–5" (11–13 cm) A small, dark, *heavily* streaked finch with a deeply notched tail, sharply pointed bill. A *touch of yellow* in wings and at base of tail is not always evident. In size and actions, resembles goldfinch. Most siskins are detected by voice, flying over. **SIMILAR SPECIES:** (1) Winter American Goldfinch lacks streaks. (2) Female House Finch has stubbier bill, less notch in tail. (3) Common Redpoll has red forehead. All lack yellow in wings and tail. **VOICE:** Call, a loud *clee-ip* or *chlee-ip;* also a light *tit-i-tit;* a buzzy *shreeee* (recalls a zipper sound). Song suggests Goldfinch's but coarser, wheezy. **RANGE:** S. Canada to s. U.S. Winters to n. Mexico. **HABITAT:** Conifers, mixed woods, alder, Sweet Gum, weedy areas, also feeders with thistle.

LESSER GOLDFINCH *Carduelis psaltria*   Scarce, restricted

3½–4½" (9–11 cm) *Male:* A very small finch with a *black cap,* black or greenish back, and bright yellow underparts; white on wing. Black cap retained in winter. Male of race *C. p. psaltria* (s. Rockies and w. Great Plains) has *black* back; male of western race *C. p. hesperophilus* has *greenish* back. *Female:* Similar to female American Goldfinch, but more greenish; *rump dark* (not pale), undertail yellowish, not white. **VOICE:** Sweet, plaintive notes *tee-yee* (rising) and *tee-yer* (dropping). Song, more phrased than American Goldfinch's. **RANGE:** Breeds from w. U.S. to Peru. Resident in west half of Tex. east to Coleman, Austin, Beeville. Winter s. Tex. to Peru. Scarce on central coast of Tex. **HABITAT:** Open brushy country, open woods, wooded streams, gardens.

YELLOW FINCHES, etc.

♂

♀

EVENING GROSBEAK

♂ winter

♂ breeding

♀

AMERICAN GOLDFINCH

♀

♂

LESSER GOLDFINCH

♂

♀

PINE SISKIN

COMMON REDPOLL *Carduelis flammea* Uncommon, irregular

M 446
5" (13 cm) A little, streaked, gray-brown "winter" finch with a *bright red cap* on forehead, a *black chin*, and a tiny yellow bill; dark streaks on flanks. Male is *pink-breasted.* In size, shape, and actions, resembles an American Goldfinch or a Pine Siskin. **SIMILAR SPECIES:** (1) Male House Finch and (2) male Purple Finch are larger and redder, and have red rumps; lack black chin. **VOICE:** In flight, a rattling *chet-chet-chet-chet.* Song, a trill, followed by rattling *chet-chet-chet-chet.* **RANGE:** Circumboreal. Winters irregularly to n. and cen. U.S. **HABITAT:** Birches, tundra scrub. In winter, weeds, brush, open areas; visits feeders.

HOARY REDPOLL *Carduelis hornemanni* Rare, irregular

M 447
5" (13 cm) Among Common Redpoll flocks look for a *"frostier"* bird with an *unstreaked whitish rump* and *less streaking below.* In males, rump may be pink tinged; bill more stubby than Common Redpoll's and hence appears shorter; undertail coverts unstreaked or barely streaked with a couple of marks. **RANGE:** Arctic; circumpolar. Winters irregularly to n. U.S. **HABITAT:** Dwarf willows and birches in tundra. Winter, open weed fields.

HOUSE FINCH *Carpodacus mexicanus* Common

M 443
5–5½" (13–14 cm) This Western transplant to our Eastern avifauna is often mistaken for Purple Finch, with which it may associate at feeders. It is smaller; male brighter red. Note dark *stripes* on sides and belly. The striped brown female is distinguished from female Purple Finch by its smaller bill and bland face pattern (no heavy mustache or dark cheek patch). **VOICE:** Song, bright, but loose and disjointed; frequently ends in a harsh nasal *wheer* or *che-urr.* Notes, finchlike; some suggest House Sparrow's, but more musical. **RANGE:** Historic w. U.S. to s. Mexico. Introduced in ne. U.S. about 1940. Spread to most of U.S. (see map). **HABITAT:** Cities, suburbs, farms. Is now a dominant species at many eastern feeders. Bacterial infection of eyes has reduced numbers in some areas.

PURPLE FINCH *Carpodacus purpureus* Uncommon

M 442
5½–6" (14–15 cm) Like a sparrow dipped in raspberry juice. *Male:* Dull rose red, brightest on head and rump, flanks unstreaked. *Female and immature:* Heavily striped, brown, sparrowlike. Distinguished from female House Finch by *broad dark malar stripe,* dark ear patch, broad light stripe behind eye, more deeply notched tail, and largish bill. **VOICE:** Song, a fast lively warble; note, a dull metallic *tick* or *pik.* **RANGE:** Canada, Pacific states, ne. U.S. Winters to s. U.S. **HABITAT:** Woods, groves; a few at feeders.

PINE GROSBEAK *Pinicola enucleator* Scarce, irregular

M 441
8–10" (20–25 cm) Near size of robin; a large tame winter finch with a longish tail. In flight, undulates. *Male, adult:* Dull rose red, dark wings with 2 white bars. *Male, immature:* Similar to female, but touch of reddish on head and rump. *Female:* Gray, with 2 white wing bars; head and rump tinged dull yellow. **VOICE:** Call, a whistled *tee-tew-tew,* suggesting that of Greater Yellowlegs, but finchlike; also a musical *chee-vli.* **RANGE:** Boreal forests of N. Hemisphere, wintering irruptively southward. **HABITAT:** Conifer forests; in winter, also mixed woods, fruiting trees, ash.

RED FINCHES, etc.

orange
variant

HOUSE
FINCH

COMMON
REDPOLL

HOARY
REDPOLL

PURPLE FINCH

immature ♂

PINE GROSBEAK

WHITE-THROATED SPARROW *Zonotrichia albicollis*   Common

M 408

6–7" (16–18 cm) A gray-breasted sparrow with a *white throat patch* and a *yellow lore spot* between eye and bill. Bill grayish. *Polymorphic;* some adults with *black-and-white head stripes,* others have *brown and tan head stripes. Winter:* Duller; darker head stripes varying shades of black, brown, tan. Immature birds may be somewhat streaked on the breast. *Note:* Has been known to hybridize with Dark-eyed Junco. **SIMILAR SPECIES:** White-crowned Sparrow (see below). **VOICE:** Song, several clear pensive whistles, easily imitated; 1 or 2 clear notes, followed by 3 quavering notes on a different pitch. Note, a slurred *tweet;* also a hard *chink.* **RANGE:** Canada, ne. U.S. Winters to s. U.S. **HABITAT:** Thickets, brush, undergrowth of conifer and mixed woodlands. Visits feeders, preferring to stay on ground.

WHITE-CROWNED SPARROW   Uncommon to fairly common
Zonotrichia leucophrys

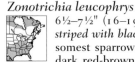

M 410

6½–7½" (16–19 cm) *Adult:* A clear pale grayish breast and a crown *striped with black and white,* often raised, make this one of the handsomest sparrows. Bill *pink. Immature:* Browner, with head stripes of dark red-brown and light buff; *bill pinkish.* The race *Z. l. gambelii* ("Gambel's" White-crown), which migrates through the Great Plains, can be separated from nominate race by white lores and by brighter orange-pink bill. **SIMILAR SPECIES:** White-throated Sparrow is browner, has a well-defined white throat, yellow spot before eye, *grayish* bill. **VOICE:** Song, 1 or more clear plaintive whistles (suggesting White-throat's), followed by husky trilled whistles. Variable. **RANGE:** Across Canada to Alaska; south through w. U.S. Winters w. and s. U.S., Mexico, Cuba. More common toward west, scarcer to east. **HABITAT:** Brush, edges, tangles, roadsides; in summer, boreal scrub.

HARRIS'S SPARROW *Zonotrichia querula*   Rare in East

M 409

7½" (19 cm) A large sparrow, size of a Fox Sparrow. In breeding plumage, has *black crown, face, and bib encircling a pink bill.* In winter adults, black crown is veiled with gray. Young in first winter have *white on throat,* less black on crown, buffy brown on rest of head; spots and streaks trace outline of bib on breast. In second winter, chin is black. **VOICE:** Song has quavering quality of White-throat's song; clear whistles on same pitch, or 1 or 2 at one pitch, the rest slightly higher or lower. Alarm note, *weenk* or *wink.* **RANGE:** N.-cen. Canada. Winters s.-cen. U.S. **HABITAT:** Stunted boreal forests; in winter, brush, hedgerows, field edges, open woods. Fairly common on central plains. Rare visitor farther east in winter.

GOLDEN-CROWNED SPARROW *Zonotrichia atricapilla*   Casual in East (Vagrant)

6–7" (15–18 cm) Similar to White-crowned Sparrow, but central crown dull yellow, bordered widely with black, duskier underparts and bill. Face of winter bird plain, suggesting large female House Sparrow, but longer-tailed, darker; usually with a dull yellow suffusion on forecrown; bill gray. **RANGE:** Nw. N. America, wintering through Pacific states. Casual or accidental in winter to East.

SPARROWS

tan-striped form

immature

WHITE-THROATED SPARROW

summer; similar in winter

white-striped form

summer; duller in winter

Gambel's form

immature

WHITE-CROWNED SPARROW

adult

immature

GOLDEN-CROWNED SPARROW

adult

adult breeding

HARRIS'S SPARROW

immature winter

CHIPPING SPARROW *Spizella passerina*   Common

5¼" (13 cm) *Breeding:* A small gray-breasted sparrow with a bright *rufous cap*, a *black line* through eye and a *white line* over it. *Winter:* Overall browner; cap and eyebrow line duller, and gray rump. *Immature:* Browner with a light central crown stripe, gray rump. **SIMILAR SPECIES:** Clay-colored Sparrow has a distinct face pattern (pale lores, whiter mustache mark) and brown, not gray, rump. **VOICE:** Song, a chipping rattle on one pitch. Note, a dry *chip*. **RANGE:** Canada to Nicaragua. Winters s. U.S. south to Mexico. **HABITAT:** Open woods, conifers, orchards, farms, towns.

M 388

FIELD SPARROW *Spizella pusilla*   Fairly common

5" (13 cm) Note *pink bill* of this rusty-capped sparrow. It has rather rusty upper parts and a clear breast; less noticeable facial striping than other rusty-capped sparrows. A narrow light *eye-ring* gives it a big-eyed expression. Juvenile has a finely streaked breast. **VOICE:** Song, opening on deliberate, sweet, slurring notes, speeding into a trill (which ascends, descends, or stays on same pitch). Note, *tsee*; has a querulous quality. **RANGE:** Se. Canada, U.S. (east of Rockies). Winters to ne. Mexico. **HABITAT:** Bushy pastures, brush, scrub.

M 390

SWAMP SPARROW *Melospiza georgiana*   Fairly common

5–5½" (13–14 cm) A rather stout, dark, rusty sparrow with a dull gray breast, outlined *white throat, reddish cap, gray face and nape.* In winter, duller crown and browner cheek. *Immature:* Dimly streaked and has little or no reddish on its crown. **SIMILAR SPECIES:** (1) Chipping Sparrow is slimmer and shows a white stripe over eye. (2) Field and (3) Tree Sparrows have prominent wing bars. (4) Also see Song Sparrow (p. 300). (5) Immature Swamp Sparrow is sometimes misidentified as Lincoln's Sparrow (p. 300) or Song Sparrow (p. 300). **VOICE:** Song, a loose trill, similar to Chipping Sparrow's, but slower, sweeter. Call note, a hard, nonmetallic almost phoebelike *chip*. **RANGE:** Canada (east of Rockies), ne. U.S. Winters to Gulf states. **HABITAT:** Fresh marshes with tussocks, bushes, or cattails; sedge swamps. Brushy areas, weedy fields, marshes, wet areas.

M 407

AMERICAN TREE SPARROW *Spizella arborea*   Fairly common

6–6½" (15–16 cm) To identify the "Winter Chippy," note single *dark spot* or "stickpin" on breast, and solid *red-brown cap.* Bill dark above, yellow below; 2 white wing bars. **VOICE:** Song, sweet, variable; opening on 1 or 2 high clear notes. Note, *tseet;* feeding note, a musical *teelwit.* **RANGE:** Alaska, n. Canada. Winters s. Canada to cen. U.S. **HABITAT:** Arctic scrub, willow thickets; in winter, brushy roadsides, weedy edges, marshes; patronizes feeders.

M 387

RUFOUS-CROWNED SPARROW *Aimophila ruficeps*   Uncommon, local

5–6" (13–15 cm) Note *black whiskers* bordering throat. A dark sparrow with a plain dusky breast, rufous cap, distinct eye-ring. **VOICE:** Song, stuttering, gurgling. Note, nasal *dear, dear, dear.* **RANGE:** Sw. U.S. **EAST:** Breeds east locally to e. Okla., w. Ark. **HABITAT:** Dry, open, brushy slopes.

M 386

RUSTY-CAPPED SPARROWS
sexes similar

winter

breeding

CHIPPING
SPARROW

juvenile

for comparison
with winter
Chipping Sparrow,
above

FIELD
SPARROW

juvenile

CLAY-COLORED
SPARROW
(see next page)

SWAMP
SPARROW

immature

RUFOUS-
CROWNED
SPARROW

AMERICAN
TREE SPARROW

LARK SPARROW *Chondestes grammacus*   Uncommon

5½–6½" (14–16 cm) Note *black tail with much white in corners* (as in Eastern Towhee, not as in a Vesper Sparrow); also *single central breast spot* and quail-like head pattern with chestnut ear patch, striped crown. **M 392** Juvenile like dull adult. Breast finely streaked, lacks central spot, ear patch duller. **SIMILAR SPECIES:** See Vesper Sparrow (p. 300). **VOICE:** A broken song; clear notes and trills with pauses between. **HABITAT:** Prairies, pastures, farms, roadsides. Strays to East Coast in fall and winter.

CLAY-COLORED SPARROW *Spizella pallida*   Fairly common

5½" (13 cm) A small pale sparrow of midcontinent; plain-breasted, Chipping Sparrow–like, but buffier. Note *light crown stripe and sharply outlined ear patch, pale lores, gray collar.* Chipping and Clay-colored Sparrows both have brown ear patches in fall and winter. **M 389** Clay-colored has crisper head markings and pale lores, contrasting with its gray collar, whiter mustache stripe. Rump brown in Clay-colored, gray in Chipping. **VOICE:** Song, insectlike; 3 or 4 low flat buzzes: *bzzz, bzzz, bzzz.* **HABITAT:** Scrub, brushy prairies.

GRASSHOPPER SPARROW *Ammodramus savannarum*   Uncommon, local

4½–5½" (11–13 cm) A small sparrow of open grasslands with a short sharp tail, flat head, *yellow loral spot, crown with a pale median stripe*; back striped with chestnut and black. Differs from other sparrows of meadows in having a relatively *unstriped buffy breast.* Flight feeble. **SIMILAR SPECIES:** See Le Conte's Sparrow. **VOICE:** Two songs: (1) 2 faint introductory notes and a thin dry buzz, *pi-tup zeeeeeeeeeeeee;* (2) a thin buzzy tumble of notes. **HABITAT:** Grassland, hayfields, prairies. Secretive. **M 396**

BACHMAN'S SPARROW *Aimophila aestivalis*   Scarce

5½" (14 cm) In dry open pine woods with grass and palmetto scrub of the South, this shy sparrow flushes reluctantly, then drops back into cover. Striped with reddish brown above, washed with dingy buff across its plain breast, with a gray bill. **SIMILAR SPECIES:** (1) Field Sparrow **M 385** is smaller, with *pink* bill. (2) Grasshopper Sparrow lives in meadows, has a light crown stripe and a short tail. (3) Young summer Bachman's suggests Lincoln's Sparrow, which would not be in the South in summer. It has an eye-ring and streaked buffy breast. **VOICE:** Song, variable; usually a clear liquid whistle, followed by a loose trill or warble on a different pitch; e.g., *seeeee, slip slip slip slip slip* (vaguely suggests Hermit Thrush's song). **HABITAT:** Open pine or oak woods, palmetto scrub. Declining in northern part of range.

BOTTERI'S SPARROW *Aimophila botterii*   Very local

5¼–6¼" (13–16 cm) Buffy breast and plain brown tail. Lateral throat stripe distinct. Unmarked throat and chest. **VOICE:** Song, a constant tinkling or *pitting* running into a dry trill. **SIMILAR SPECIES:** See Cassin's Sparrow, which is almost identical. **HABITAT:** Grass areas in s. Tex.

CASSIN'S SPARROW *Aimophila cassinii*   Fairly common

5½" (14 cm) A drab sparrow of open arid country. *Dingy unmarked underparts* except for faint streaks on flanks. *Throat lacks distinct lateral stripes.* Pale or *whitish tips on gray outer tail feather.* Best clue is the skylarking, which Botteri's does not do. **VOICE:** Song, 1 or 2 short notes, a high sweet trill, and 2 lower notes: *ti ti tseeeeeee tay tay.* **HABITAT:** Grasslands, brush east to cen. Tex. Casual vagrant farther east.

SPARROWS
(Mostly clear-breasted)
sexes similar

LARK SPARROW

adult

juvenile

Chipping Sparrow
(winter)
for comparison

breeding

CLAY-COLORED
SPARROW

winter

HENSLOW'S
SPARROW

adult

juvenile

BACHMAN'S
SPARROW

adult

GRASSHOPPER
SPARROW

(adult on
p. 302)

BOTTERI'S
SPARROW

CASSIN'S
SPARROW

adult

FOX SPARROW *Passerella iliaca* Fairly common

M 404

6½–7½" (17–19 cm) Larger than Song Sparrow, with a *rufous tail,* conspicuous in flight. Rust color combined with gray about neck gives bird its foxy look. Breast very heavily streaked with rust. Feeding is towheelike; rustles among dry leaves. **SIMILAR SPECIES:** Hermit Thrush (p. 246) has a reddish tail, but lacks streaks on back, is thin-billed, spotted, not striped. **VOICE:** Song, brilliant and musical; a varied arrangement of short clear notes and sliding whistles. **RANGE:** Alaska, Canada; w. mountains to cen.-w. U.S. Winters to s. U.S. **HABITAT:** Wooded undergrowth, brush; a few at feeders.

SONG SPARROW *Melospiza melodia* Common

M 405

5–6½" (13–16 cm) Note heavy breast streaks confluent into a *large central spot.* Long tail. **SIMILAR SPECIES:** (1) Savannah Sparrow (p. 302) is more of a field bird; it often shows yellowish over eye, has a shorter *notched* tail, pinker legs. (2) See Lincoln's Sparrow (below). (3) See Swamp Sparrow (p. 296) **VOICE:** Song, a variable series of notes, some musical, some buzzy; usually starts with 3 or 4 clear repetitious notes, *sweet sweet sweet,* etc. Call note, a low nasal *tchep.* **RANGE:** Alaska, Canada to cen. Mexico. **HABITAT:** Thickets, brush, marshes, roadsides, gardens.

VESPER SPARROW *Pooecetes gramineus* Uncommon

M 391

6" (15 cm) Note *white outer tail feathers,* conspicuous when bird flies. Less evident is *chestnut* at bend of wing. Otherwise suggests a Savannah Sparrow, but has a *whitish eye-ring.* **SIMILAR SPECIES:** Other field birds of comparable size with white tail sides: (1) pipits (p. 230), (2) longspurs (p. 308), (3) junco (p. 306). **VOICE:** Song, throatier than that of Song Sparrow; usually begins with 2 clear minor notes, followed by 2 higher ones. **RANGE:** Canada to cen. U.S. Winters to Mexico, Gulf Coast. **HABITAT:** Meadows, fields, prairies.

LINCOLN'S SPARROW *Melospiza lincolnii* Uncommon

M 406

5½" (14 cm) A skulker, "afraid of its shadow." Similar to Song Sparrow, but trimmer, side of face grayer, breast streaks *much finer* and sometimes not aggregated into a central spot. Note band of *creamy buff* across breast and narrow eye-ring. **SIMILAR SPECIES:** Immature Swamp Sparrow has a duller breast, with blurry streaks and a rustier wing. **VOICE:** Song, sweet and gurgling; suggests both House Wren's and Purple Finch's; starts with low passages, rises abruptly, drops. Note, a sharp *tik* or *chip.* **RANGE:** Alaska, Canada, w. and ne. U.S. Winters s. U.S. to Guatemala. **HABITAT:** Willow and alder thickets, muskeg, brushy bogs. In winter, thickets, weeds, bushes, wetlands.

STREAKED SPARROWS
sexes similar

FOX SPARROW

SONG SPARROW

VESPER SPARROW

LINCOLN'S
SPARROW

SWAMP SPARROW
(see p. 296)

immature

Purple Finch
♀

House Finch
♀

females for comparison with sparrows
(males shown on p. 292)

SAVANNAH SPARROW *Passerculus sandwichensis*   Common

M 394

4½–5½" (11–14 cm) This streaked open-country sparrow suggests a small Song Sparrow, but usually has a *yellowish* superciliary stripe, whitish crown stripe, short notched tail, and pinker legs. It may lack yellowish over eye. *Tail notch* is an aid when seen from rear. **SIMILAR SPECIES:** Song Sparrow's tail is longer, *rounded.* **VOICE:** Song, a dreamy lisping *tsit-tsit-tsit, tseeee-tsaaay* (last note lower). Note, a light *tsip.* **RANGE:** Alaska, Canada to Guatemala. Winters to Cen. America, W. Indies. **HABITAT:** Open fields, meadows, salt marshes, prairies, dunes.

"IPSWICH" SAVANNAH SPARROW   Uncommon, restricted
Passerculus sandwichensis princeps

M 395

6–6½" (15–16 cm) A large, pale, sandy-colored race of Savannah Sparrow. In spring, it has a pale yellow eyebrow stripe. **SIMILAR SPECIES:** It may suggest Vesper Sparrow, but has a white stripe through crown and lacks white outer tail feathers. **VOICE:** Similar to nominate Savannah Sparrow's. **RANGE:** Breeds on Sable Is., N.S. Winters along East Coast south to Ga. **HABITAT:** Dunes, beach grass, and edges of salt marshes adjacent to outer beaches.

BAIRD'S SPARROW *Ammodramus bairdii*   Uncommon, local

M 397

5½" (13 cm) An elusive prairie sparrow. Light breast is crossed by a *narrow band* of fine black streaks. Head yellow-brown, streaked with black. Key mark is a broad *ocher* median crown stripe; double whisker marks and 2 dark spots behind "ear." Secretive. **SIMILAR SPECIES:** (1) Savannah Sparrow has more extensive streaking below; has a narrow white median crown stripe and lacks dark marks at rear of auriculars and double whisker marks. (2) Henslow's Sparrow (below). **VOICE:** Song, begins with 2 or 3 high musical *zip's* and ends with a trill on a lower pitch; more musical than Savannah's. **RANGE:** N. Great Plains. Winters sw. U.S., n. Mexico. **HABITAT:** Native tall-grass prairies; local.

HENSLOW'S SPARROW *Ammodramus henslowii*   Uncommon, secretive

M 398

4¾–5¼" (12–13 cm) A secretive sparrow of fields, easily overlooked were it not for its odd song. Short-tailed and flat-headed, with a big pale bill; finely striped across breast. Striped olive-colored head in conjunction with reddish wings help identify it. Also note double whisker marks and spots behind "ear." Secretive. **SIMILAR SPECIES:** See Grasshopper Sparrow (p. 298). Young Henslow's Sparrow (summer) is practically without breast streaks, thus resembles adult Grasshopper. Conversely, young Grasshopper has breast streaks, but lacks adult Henslow's olive-and-russet tones. **VOICE:** Song, a poor vocal effort; a hiccuping *tsi-lick.* May sing on quiet, windless nights. **RANGE:** Cen. and ne. U.S. Somewhat "nomadic." **HABITAT:** *Very specific.* Partially overgrown fields with certain plant development of exacting components. Disappearing from many former haunts. Winters in dense cover in southern pine forests.

STREAK-BREASTED GRASS SPARROWS
sexes similar

SAVANNAH SPARROW

typical

SAVANNAH SPARROW

"IPSWICH" SAVANNAH SPARROW

BAIRD'S SPARROW

adult

HENSLOW'S SPARROW
(juvenile on p. 298)

GRASSHOPPER SPARROW
(adult on p. 298)

juvenile

SALTMARSH SHARP-TAILED SPARROW *Ammodramus caudacutus*   Fairly common

M 401

5–6" (13–15 cm) A short-tailed, often shy sparrow of coastal marshes. Note deep *ocher-yellow or orange of face,* which completely surrounds *gray ear patch.* Distinct streaks on breast, flat-headed appearance. **SIMILAR SPECIES:** (1) Nelson's Sharp-tailed Sparrow (see next species). (2) Juvenile Seaside Sparrow in late summer is much like Sharp-tail. (3) Le Conte's Sparrow (below). (4) Savannah Sparrow (p. 302) has a notched tail. **VOICE:** Song, a gasping buzz, *tuptup-sheeeeeeeee.* **RANGE:** Atlantic Coast. Winters coastally southward. **HABITAT:** Coastal salt marshes to cen. Fla.

NELSON'S SHARP-TAILED SPARROW *Ammodramus nelsoni*   Uncommon

M 400

5–6" (13–15 cm) Shy skulker of inland wetlands or coast in New England and Maritimes. *Distinctly yellowish ocher or bright orange* (interior population) with unstreaked gray nape, well-defined orange breast richer than Saltmarsh Sharp-tail. Chest stripes fine and not as distinct in Saltmarsh Sharp-tail. *Gray median crown stripe* and broad yellowish eye line. Birds of Me. and Maritime population grayer with less distinct stripes. Formerly considered a subspecies of Saltmarsh Sharp-tailed Sparrow. **VOICE:** A downward, slurred *pit-shhhhhh-uk.* **RANGE:** Canadian provinces, s. Hudson Bay, Maritime Provinces, coastal Me. **HABITAT:** Inland marshes, coastal marshes south to n. Mexico.

SEASIDE SPARROW *Ammodramus maritimus*   Fairly common

M 402

6" (15 cm) A dark, olive-gray sparrow of salt marshes, with a short *yellow area from bill to just above eye.* Whitish throat and white above dark malar. Shares marshes with both Sharp-tails. **SIMILAR SPECIES:** "Dusky" Seaside (now extinct) and "Cape Sable" Seaside Sparrows are distinct races of this species. **VOICE:** Song, *cutcut zhe´-eeeeeeee;* very similar to Saltmarsh Sharp-tailed Sparrow's song, but usually with a stronger accent (*zhe´*) in middle. Note, *chack* (like a little Red-winged Blackbird's). **RANGE:** Coastal marshes from s. New England to Fla. and along Gulf Coast to Tex. **HABITAT:** Salt marshes. (Occasional records inland during migration.)

"CAPE SABLE" SEASIDE SPARROW   Scarce, very restricted
Ammodramus maritimus mirabilis

6" (15 cm) Only race of Seaside Sparrow breeding in s. Fla. Green tint to brown above and more white below than northern race. Endangered. **HABITAT:** Coastal sedge/grass "prairies" in s. and sw. Fla.

M 403

LE CONTE'S SPARROW *Ammodramus leconteii*   Uncommon,

M 399

5" (13 cm) A secretive sparrow of weedy prairie marshes. Note *bright buff-ocher* eyebrow stripe and breast (with fine streaks *confined to sides*). Gray nape with reddish purple lines. White median crown stripe and boldly striped back. Secretive. **SIMILAR SPECIES:** (1) Nelson's Sharp-tailed Sparrow (above); (2) Grasshopper Sparrow (p. 298) has yellow in front of eye only and faint side streaks, if any. **VOICE:** Song, 2 extremely thin, grasshopper-like hisses. **RANGE:** S.-cen. Canada to n. prairie states. Migrant to Gulf. Very rare wanderer to East Coast. **HABITAT:** Marshes; tall-grass prairie, weedy fields.

MARSH SPARROWS
sexes similar

NELSON'S
maritime
("Acadian") race

SALTMARSH
SHARP-TAILED
SPARROW

NELSON'S
SHARP-TAILED
SPARROW

LE CONTE'S SPARROW

SEASIDE SPARROW

juvenile

"CAPE SABLE" SEASIDE
SPARROW

DARK-EYED ("SLATE-COLORED") JUNCO *Junco hyemalis* (in part)   Common

M 411

5½–6¼" (14–16 cm) This slate-gray, hooded, sparrow-shaped bird is characterized by white outer tail feathers that flash conspicuously as it flies away. Bill and belly are whitish. Male may have dark gray or blackish hood; female and immature are duller, some tinged brown (see "Oregon" Junco). Juvenile in summer is finely streaked on breast, hence, with its white outer tail feathers, might even suggest a Vesper Sparrow. **SUBSPECIES:** "Oregon" Junco *J. h. oreganus* (below). Very rare stray in the East. "White-winged" Junco (*J. h. aikeni*) of the Black Hills region (winters south to Colorado) known by its white wing bars, paler gray color, and more white in tail. **VOICE:** Song, a loose trill, suggestive of Chipping Sparrow's song, but more musical; note, a light *smack* or sharp *tik*; twittering notes. **RANGE:** Cool forests of Alaska, Canada; south in Appalachians to n. Georgia. Winters to Gulf states, n. Mexico. **HABITAT:** Conifer and mixed woods. In winter, open woods, undergrowth, roadsides, brush; also common at feeding stations, preferring to take its seeds on ground.

DARK-EYED ("OREGON") JUNCO *Junco hyemalis* (in part)   Vagrant in East

5½–6¼" (14–16 cm) *Male:* Resembles "Slate-colored" Junco, but back *red-brown*, contrasting sharply with black hood; sides *buffy* or *rusty*. *Female:* Head grayer; rusty back not so sharply defined, but "pink" or tawny sides are well separated from gray hood. Intergrades between subspecies are frequent, especially on Great Plains. **VOICE:** Very similar to that of "Slate-colored" Junco's. **RANGE:** Se. Alaska, sw. Canada, nw. U.S., Pacific states. Winters to n. Mexico and east to Great Plains. **EAST:** A very rare straggler, but occasional birds turn up nearly every winter as far east as Atlantic seaboard.

SNOW BUNTING *Plectrophenax nivalis*   Uncommon

M 416

6–7¼" (15–18 cm) No other songbird shows so much white. In winter, some individuals may look quite rusty brown, but when they fly, their flashing *white wing patches* identify them. Overhead, Snow Bunting looks almost entirely white, whereas American Pipits and Horned Lark have black tails. They often swirl over snowy fields in large flocks. In summer dress in the Arctic, male has a black back, contrasting with its white head and underparts. **SIMILAR SPECIES:** Beware of leucistic (partial albino) individuals of other species. **VOICE:** Note, a sharp whistled *teer* or *tew*; also a rough purring *brrt*. Song, a musical *ti-ti-chu-ree*, repeated. **RANGE:** Arctic; circumpolar. In winter to cen. Eurasia, cen. U.S. **HABITAT:** Tundra in summer. In migration and winter, prairies, fields, dunes, shores.

"SNOWBIRDS"

DARK-EYED
("SLATE-COLORED")
JUNCO

juvenile

♂

♀

DARK-EYED
("OREGON")
JUNCO

♂

♀

♀ winter

♂ winter

♂ breeding

SNOW BUNTING

LAPLAND LONGSPUR *Calcarius lapponicus*   Fairly common

M 413

6½" (16 cm) Lapland Longspurs, like Horned Larks and pipits, are birds of open country; in flight, they appear to have shorter tails than larks. *Male, summer: Black face outlined with white;* rusty collar. *Male, winter:* Sparse black streaks on sides, a rusty nape and wing coverts, and a dark smudge across breast help identify it. *Female, summer:* resembles winter male. *Female, winter:* More nondescript than male; note tail patterns (opposite). SIMILAR SPECIES: Other longspurs have more white in tail (opposite). Pipits and Horned Lark have thin bills and distinctly different plumages. VOICE: A musical *teew;* also a rattle and a whistle, *ticky-tick-tew.* Song (in display flight), vigorous, musical. RANGE: Arctic; circumpolar. Winters s. Canada to s. U.S. More numerous in Great Plains than farther east. HABITAT: Tundra; in winter, fields, prairies, shorelines. When found in East, often in with Horned Lark flocks.

CHESTNUT-COLLARED LONGSPUR *Calcarius ornatus*   Uncommon, restricted

M 415

5½–6½" (14–16 cm) *Male, summer:* Solid *black* below except on throat; nape *chestnut. Female and winter:* Sparrowlike; best field mark is tail pattern (a dark triangle on a white tail). VOICE: Song, short, feeble, but musical; suggestive of Western Meadowlark's. Note, a finchlike *kittle.* RANGE: S. Canadian prairies; n. prairie states. Winters sw. U.S., n. Mexico. HABITAT: Plains, prairies. Straggler to East Coast.

McCOWN'S LONGSPUR *Calcarius mccownii*   Uncommon, restricted/local

M 412

6" (15 cm) *Male, spring:* Crown and patch on breast black; tail largely white. Hindneck *gray* (brown or chestnut in other longspurs). *Female and winter male:* Sparrowlike and paler than other longspurs; note tail pattern (inverted black T on white). Large, fleshy bill. SIMILAR SPECIES: (1) Male Chestnut-collared Longspur in summer has a chestnut collar, black belly. (2) Horned Lark (similar breast splotch) has a thin bill, black face patch. VOICE: Song (in display flight), clear sweet warbles, suggesting Lark Bunting's song. Note, a dry rattle. RANGE: Prairies of s.-cen. Canada, n.-cen. U.S. Winters sw. U.S. to n. Mexico. HABITAT: Short-grass plains, prairies, plowed fields.

SMITH'S LONGSPUR *Calcarius pictus*   Uncommon, restricted/local

M 414

6" (15 cm) A *buffy* longspur; warm buff on entire underparts. Tail edged with white as in Lapland Longspur and Vesper Sparrow (no dark band at tip). *Male, summer: Deep buff;* ear patch with a *white spot,* strikingly outlined by a *black triangle. Female and winter:* overall buffy (warmest-toned longspur in a mixed flock); breast lightly streaked; some males may show white shoulder. Skulks and hard to see. SIMILAR SPECIES: See (1) Vesper Sparrow (p. 300), (2) Sprague's Pipit (p. 230), and (3) other longspurs (study tail diagrams opposite). VOICE: Rattling or clicking notes in flight. Song, sweet and warblerlike, terminating in a *we´ chew* like Chestnut-sided Warbler's. RANGE: N. Alaska to Hudson Bay. Winters s.-cen. U.S. HABITAT: Prairies, fields, airports; in summer, tundra.

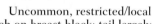

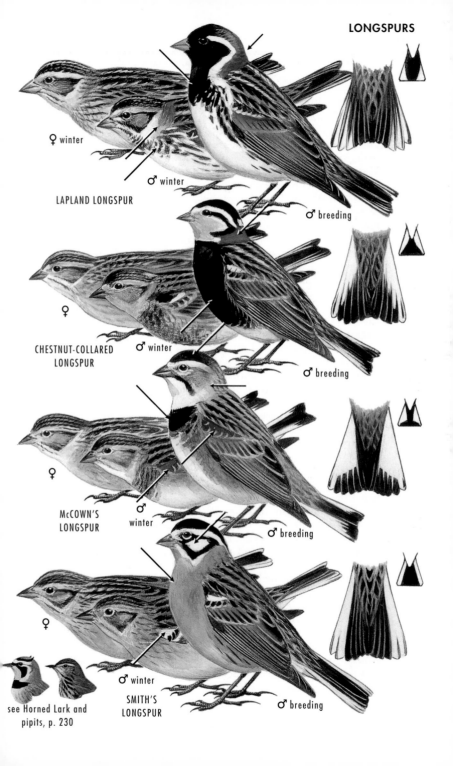

LONGSPURS

LAPLAND LONGSPUR

♀ winter

♂ winter

♂ breeding

CHESTNUT-COLLARED
LONGSPUR

♀

♂ winter

♂ breeding

McCOWN'S
LONGSPUR

♀

♂ winter

♂ breeding

SMITH'S
LONGSPUR

♀

♂ winter

♂ breeding

see Horned Lark and
pipits, p. 230

Varied color patterns; sharp bills. Some black and iridescent; orioles are highly colored. Sexes unlike. **FOOD:** Insects, small fruits, seeds, waste grain, small aquatic life. **RANGE:** New World; most in Tropics. **NO. OF SPECIES:** World, 97, East, 20 (+ 1 accidental).

RUSTY BLACKBIRD *Euphagus carolinus* Uncommon

M 430

9" (23 cm) Rusty only in fall and winter; suggests a short-tailed grackle. *Male, spring:* A robin-sized blackbird with pale yellow eyes. *Female, spring:* Slate-colored, with *light eyes. Winter adult and young:* Washed with rusty; males are *barred* below. **VOICE:** Note, a loud *chack.* "Song," a split creak like a rusty hinge: *kush-a-lee* alternating with *ksh-lay.* **RANGE:** Alaska, Canada, northeastern edge of U.S. Winters to se. U.S. **HABITAT:** River groves, wooded swamps; muskeg, bogs.

BREWER'S BLACKBIRD *Euphagus cyanocephalus* Scarce in East

M 431

9" (23 cm) *Male:* All black, with a whitish eye; in good light *purplish* reflections on head and greenish reflections on body. *Female:* Brownish gray, with a *dark* eye. **SIMILAR SPECIES:** Male Rusty Blackbird has longer, thinner-based bill. Female Rusty has a *light* eye. Brewer's does not acquire rusty look in winter. **VOICE:** Song, a harsh wheezy, creaking *quee-ee* or *ksh-eee.* **RANGE:** Sw. Canada, w. and n.-cen. U.S. Winters to s. Mexico. Wanders to East Coast. **HABITAT:** Fields, prairies, farms, parks.

COMMON GRACKLE *Quiscalus quiscula* Common

M 432

11–13½" (28–34 cm) A large iridescent blackbird larger than a robin. Breeding male has long wedge-shaped or keeled tail. Flight more level than that of other blackbirds. Male with iridescent purple on head, deep bronze or dull purple on back. "Bronzed" Grackle (New England and west of Appalachians) and "Purple" Grackle (seaboard south of New England) are separate, identifiable subspecies. **VOICE:** Note, *chuck* or *chack.* "Song," a split rasping note. **RANGE:** Canada, U.S., east of Rockies. **HABITAT:** Croplands, towns, groves (especially pines for nesting), streamsides.

BOAT-TAILED GRACKLE *Quiscalus major* Common, local

M 433

Male 16½" (41 cm); female 13" (33 cm) A very large blackbird; much larger than Common Grackle, with a longer, more ample tail. Female much smaller than male; much browner than female Common Grackle and with a pale brownish breast. Male Boat-tails of Atlantic Coast also have yellow eyes; those of Gulf region have brown eyes, but some males may have dull yellowish eyes. **SIMILAR SPECIES:** Louisiana westward, see Great-tailed Grackle. **VOICE:** A harsh *check check check;* harsh whistles and clucks. **RANGE:** Atlantic and Gulf Coasts from Conn. (rare) and Long Is. to cen. Tex. **HABITAT:** Resident near salt water along coasts; marshes. Some members of extreme northern population move south in winter. Also inland in Fla.

GREAT-TAILED GRACKLE *Quiscalus mexicanus* Common

M 434

Male 18" (45 cm); female 14" (35 cm) Very similar to Boat-tailed Grackle, but somewhat longer-tailed. Both sexes have *yellow* eyes. Flat-topped appearance to head. **VOICE:** More varied than Boat-tail's; loud *clock's;* a rising whistle. **RANGE:** Sw. U.S. to Peru. **HABITAT:** Whereas Boat-tail is restricted to coastal marshes and adjoining habitats (except in Fla.), Great-tail also frequents inland areas, parks, towns, farms, etc.

ICTERIDS (BLACKBIRDS, etc.)

♂ breeding

♀

RUSTY BLACKBIRD

♂ winter

BREWER'S BLACKBIRD

♀

♂ fall variant

♂

♂

♂

♀

purple race

bronze race

COMMON GRACKLE

♀

♂

GREAT-TAILED GRACKLE

♀

♂ Atlantic Coast

♂ Gulf states

BOAT-TAILED GRACKLE

RED-WINGED BLACKBIRD *Agelaius phoeniceus*   Common

M 426

7–9½" (18–24 cm) *Male:* Black, with *bright red epaulets*, most conspicuous in spring display. Often scarlet is concealed and only yellowish margin shows. *Immature male:* Sooty brown, streaked, but with reddish shoulders. *Female and young:* Commonly mistaken for a sparrow. Brownish; identified by sharp pointed bill, "blackbird" appearance, and *well-defined dark stripings* below. May have pink or buff tinge around throat. Very gregarious, traveling and roosting in large flocks. **VOICE:** Notes, a loud *check* and a high slurred *tee-err*. Song, a liquid gurgling *konk-la-ree* or *o-ka-lay*. **RANGE:** Canada to W. Indies, Costa Rica. **HABITAT:** Breeds in marshes, brushy swamps, hayfields; forages also in cultivated land, tidal areas, feeders, along edges of water, etc.

YELLOW-HEADED BLACKBIRD *Xanthocephalus xanthocephalus*   Common, local

M 429

8–11" (20–28 cm) *Male:* A robin-sized marsh blackbird with a *golden yellow* head and breast; shows a *white wing patch* in flight. *Female:* Smaller and browner; most of yellow is confined to throat and chest; lower breast streaked with white. Gregarious. **VOICE:** Song, low hoarse rasping notes produced with much effort; sounds like rusty hinges. Note, a low *kruck* or *kack*. **RANGE:** S. Canada, w. U.S., upper Mississippi Valley to nw. Mexico. Winters sw. U.S., Mexico. Rare wanderer to East Coast; rarely at feeders. **HABITAT:** Fresh marshes. Forages in fields, open country mixed in with other blackbirds in flocks.

BOBOLINK *Dolichonyx oryzivorus*   Fairly common

M 425

6–8" (15–20 cm) *Male, spring:* Our only songbird that is *solid black below and largely white above*, suggesting a dress suit on backward. Has a buff-yellow nape. *Female and autumn male:* A bit larger than a House Sparrow; *rich buff-yellow*, with dark stripes on crown and back. Bill is more like a sparrow's than a blackbird's. **SIMILAR SPECIES:** (1) Male Lark Bunting has white confined to wings, body all black; (2) female Red-winged Blackbird is heavily striped below; longer bill, less buff-yellow. **VOICE:** Song, in hovering flight and quivering descent, ecstatic and bubbling, starting with low, reedy notes and rollicking upward. Flight note, a clear *ink,* often heard as groups pass over in migration. **RANGE:** S. Canada, n. U.S. Winters in s. S. America. **HABITAT:** Hayfields, meadows. In migration, weedy fields, marshes.

STARLINGS. Family Sturnidae.

A varied family; some blackbirdlike. Sharp-billed, usually short-tailed. Gregarious. **FOOD:** Insects, seeds, berries. **NO. OF SPECIES:** World, 114; East, 1.

EUROPEAN STARLING *Sturnus vulgaris*   Common

M 337

7½–8½" (19–21 cm) A gregarious, garrulous, short-tailed "blackbird-like" bird; shape of a meadowlark. In flight, looks triangular; flies swiftly and directly, not undulating. In spring, iridescent; bill yellow. In winter, heavily speckled; bill dark. Immature is dusky brown, faint streaking and pale throat, short tail and long bill. Female cowbird is smaller and has more conical bill. **VOICE:** A harsh *tseeeer*; a whistled *whooee*. Also clear whistles, clicks, bill rattles and chuckles; sometimes mimics other birds. **RANGE:** Originally from Eurasia, where migratory to Africa. Introduced to N. America and widely elsewhere. **HABITAT:** Cities, parks, farms, fields, open country. Has had substantial impact on several native species.

ICTERIDS (BLACKBIRDS, etc.),
STARLING

Red-winged
immature ♂

♀

RED-WINGED
BLACKBIRD

♂

red epaulets
hidden

♂

YELLOW-HEADED
BLACKBIRD

♀

♂

BOBOLINK

♀

♂
breeding

fall

winter
adult

juvenile

EUROPEAN
STARLING

breeding

BLACKBIRDS, ORIOLES, ETC. Family Icteridae.

EASTERN MEADOWLARK *Sturnella magna* — Fairly common

M 427

9" (23 cm) In grassy country, a chunky, brown, starling-shaped bird. When flushed, shows a conspicuous patch of *white* on each side of its short tail. Several shallow, jerky wingbeats alternate with short glides. When bird perches on a post, chest shows bright yellow crossed by a *black V*. Walking, it flicks its tail open and shut. *Note:* Yellow of throat does not invade lower cheek behind bill. **VOICE:** Song, unlike flutelike gurgling of Western Meadowlark, is composed of 2 clear, slurred whistles, musical and pulled out, *tee-yah, tee-tair* (last note slurred and descending). Note, a rasping or buzzy *dzrrt;* also a guttural chatter. **RANGE:** Se. Canada to Brazil. **HABITAT:** Pastures, meadows, prairies, marsh edges.

WESTERN MEADOWLARK *Sturnella neglecta* — Fairly common

M 428

9" (23 cm) Nearly identical to Eastern Meadowlark but paler above and on flanks; yellow of throat invades lower cheek area behind bill. Perhaps best identified by song. **VOICE:** Song variable; 7–10 flutelike notes, gurgling and double-noted, unlike clear whistles of Eastern Meadowlark. Note, *chupp*, lower than rasping *dzrrt* of Eastern Meadowlark. **RANGE:** Sw. Canada to highlands of cen. Mexico. **HABITAT:** Grasslands, cultivated fields and pastures, meadows, prairies.

BROWN-HEADED COWBIRD *Molothrus ater* — Common

M 436

7½" (18 cm) A rather small blackbird with a short, sparrowlike bill. *Male:* Black, with a *brown head*. *Female:* Mouse gray with a lighter throat; note short finchlike bill. *Juvenile:* Paler than female — buffy gray, with soft breast streaks; often seen being fed by smaller birds whose nests have been parasitized. Young males in late summer molt; may be bizarrely patterned with tan and black. When flocking or with other blackbirds, cowbirds are smaller and feed on ground with their tails lifted high. **SIMILAR SPECIES:** Gray female Brown-headed Cowbird can be told from (1) female Brewer's Blackbird and (2) female Rusty Blackbird by its stubby bill and smaller size. (3) Young starling has a longer bill and a shorter tail. **VOICE:** Flight call, *weee-titi* (high whistle, 2 lower notes). Song, a bubbly and creaky *glug-glug-gleee*. Note, *chuck*. **RANGE:** S. Canada to Mexico. **HABITAT:** Farms, fields, barnyards, roadsides, wood edges, river groves. Parasitizes a wide variety of smaller bird nests. Never builds its own nest.

BRONZED COWBIRD *Molothrus aeneus* — Fairly common, restricted

7½–8½" (18–22 cm) Larger than Brown-headed Cowbird. Bill heavier, bulbous. Red eye visible at close range. *Male:* Does not have a brown head. In breeding season, a conspicuous *ruff* on nape. *Female:* Smaller, with a smaller ruff. Grayish black, not gray like female of other cowbirds. **VOICE:** High-pitched mechanical creaking. **RANGE:** Sw. U.S. to w. Panama. Resident in s. Tex. east to La.; a few winter east to Fla. **HABITAT:** Croplands, brush, semi-open country, feedlots.

SHINY COWBIRD *Molothrus bonariensis* — Scarce, restricted

M 435

7½" (18 cm) An invader to s. Fla. since 1985. Slowly spreading west and north with scattered records from as far north as N.B. and west to Okla. *Male:* Same size as Brown-headed Cowbird, but black with overall violet gloss, *thin pointed bill*. *Female:* Warm brown, slightly thinner bill compared to Brown-headed.

MEADOWLARKS,
COWBIRDS

EASTERN MEADOWLARK
sexes similar

WESTERN MEADOWLARK
sexes similar

BROWN-HEADED COWBIRD

♂

♀

immature ♂ molting

juvenile

♀

♂

BRONZED
COWBIRD

SHINY
COWBIRD

♂

Smaller, slimmer than American Robin; a brightly colored genus (*Icterus*) of the family Icteridae (blackbirds, etc.).

ORCHARD ORIOLE *Icterus spurius*   Fairly common

M 437

6–7" (15–18 cm) *Male:* An all-dark oriole. Rump and underparts deep chestnut; rest of bird black. *Immature male:* Dull greenish above, yellowish below, with a *black bib. Female and young:* Olive-green above, yellowish below; 2 white wing bars. **SIMILAR SPECIES:** (1) Female and young Baltimore Orioles are larger and not as greenish. Some female and immature Baltimores have black throats (as do immature male Orchards), but are more orange. (2) Female Scarlet and (3) female Summer Tanagers lack wing bars and have different bill shapes (p. 282). **VOICE:** A fast-moving outburst interspersed with piping whistles, guttural notes. Suggests Purple Finch's song. A strident slurred *wheeer!* at or near end is distinctive. Call, *chuck.* **RANGE:** Se. Canada, e. and cen. U.S. to cen. Mexico. Winters in Cen. and n. S. America. **HABITAT:** Wood edges, orchards, shade trees.

BALTIMORE ORIOLE *Icterus galbula*   Common

M 439

7–8" (18–20 cm) *Male:* Flame orange and black, with a solid-black head. *Female and young:* Olive-brown above, burnt orange-yellow below; 2 white wing bars. Some females may have traces of black on head, suggesting hood of male. Some immature females are paler yellowish with pale belly and grayer back. **SIMILAR SPECIES:** (1) See Bullock's Oriole. (2) Female Orchard Oriole is greener than female Baltimore. **VOICE:** Song, rich piping whistled notes. Note, a low whistled *hew-li.* Young (when begging), a plaintive *tee-deedee.* **RANGE:** Canada, e. and cen. U.S. Winters in American Tropics. **HABITAT:** Open woods, shade trees.

BULLOCK'S ORIOLE *Icterus bullockii*   Fairly common, restricted

M 440

7–8½" (18–21) *Male:* Distinguished from male Baltimore Oriole by its *orange cheeks, black line through eye, large white wing patch,* different tail pattern. *Female:* Differs from dull immature female Baltimore by dark line through eye and yellow brow over it. *Immature male:* Similar to female, but oranger and throat black. Hybridizes occasionally with Baltimore Oriole. **VOICE:** A series of accented double notes and 1 or 2 piping notes. Note, *skip;* also a harsh chatter. **RANGE:** Sw. Canada, w. U.S., n. Mexico, east to Great Plains. Winters Cen. America. Stragglers occur in winter along eastern seaboard, especially at feeders. Many past records have been reevaluated as dull Baltimores. **HABITAT:** Open woods, shade trees, river edges.

SPOT-BREASTED ORIOLE *Icterus pectoralis*   Uncommon, restricted

M 438

8" (20 cm) Note *orange crown,* black bib, and *black spots on sides of breast.* Much white in wing. No other oriole in our area has an orange crown. **RANGE:** Sw. Mexico to nw. Costa Rica. Established (by introduction or escape) in se. Fla. **HABITAT:** Flowering trees, residential areas.

ORIOLES FOUND IN S. TEX.: Audubon's, Hooded, etc. (see p. 320).

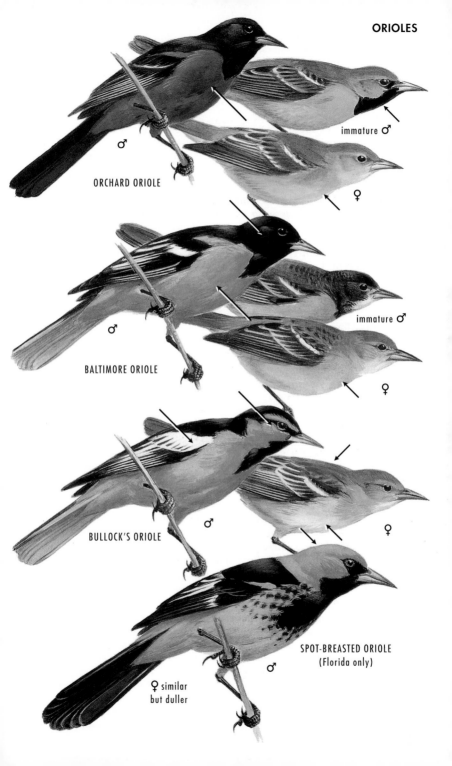

ORIOLES

ORCHARD ORIOLE

♂

immature ♂

♀

BALTIMORE ORIOLE

♂

immature ♂

♀

BULLOCK'S ORIOLE

♂

♀

SPOT-BREASTED ORIOLE
(Florida only)

♂

♀ similar
but duller

OLD WORLD SPARROWS. Family Passeridae.

Old World sparrows, unrelated to our native sparrows, which are in the Emberizidae family. Introduced House Sparrow is the best known. **FOOD:** Mainly insects, seeds. **RANGE:** Widespread in Old World. **NO. OF SPECIES:** World, 35; East, 2.

HOUSE SPARROW *Passer domesticus* — Common

M 451

6" (15 cm) Sooty city birds often bear a poor resemblance to clean country males with *black throat, white cheeks, chestnut nape.* Female and young lack black throat; have a plain *dingy breast* and a dull eye stripe. **RANGE:** Introduced to N. America. **HABITAT:** Cities, farms, human-disturbed areas.

EURASIAN TREE SPARROW *Passer montanus* — Restricted

M 452

5½" (14 cm) Both sexes resemble male House Sparrow, but black throat patch is smaller. Key mark a *black ear spot.* Crown *brown.* **VOICE:** Higher pitched than House Sparrow's. A metallic *chik* or *chup,* a repeated *chit-tchup.* In flight, a hard *tek, tek.* **RANGE:** Eurasia. Introduced around St. Louis area (see map). **HABITAT:** Farmland, weedy patches, locally in residential areas.

MISCELLANEOUS FINCHLIKE BIRDS

BROWN-HEADED COWBIRD *Molothrus ater* SEE P. 314

7" Gray-brown female and juvenile, with its soft streakings, may be taken for sparrows because of their short, finchlike bills.

DICKCISSEL *Spiza americana* — Fairly common

M 424

6–7" (15–18 cm) A grassland bird. During migration, may travel in large flocks. At feeders (especially wanderers to East), near size and appearance of House Sparrow. *Male:* Suggests a small meadowlark, with a black bib on a yellow chest. (In fall, bib is obscure or lacking.) *Female:* Very much like House Sparrow; paler, with a much lighter stripe over eye, a touch of yellow on breast, and a dull bluish bill. Chestnut shoulder is also an aid but hard to see. **VOICE:** Song, a staccato *dick-ciss-ciss-ciss* or *chup-chup-klip-klip-klip.* A short buzzing call often heard in migration. **RANGE:** Winters mainly from Mexico to n. S. America. **HABITAT:** Fields, meadows, prairies. May rarely winter in e. U.S. (at feeders). Wanders from place to place, establishing breeding sites but not returning the following year.

BOBOLINK *Dolichonyx oryzivorus* SEE P. 312

Because of short bill, female and autumn male Bobolinks may suggest sparrows or finches. A bit larger than House Sparrows; yellow buff, with dark stripes on crown and back. When flushed from grass or weedy areas, often gives a diagnostic *ink* call.

LARK BUNTING *Calamospiza melanocorys* — Fairly common, restricted

7" (18 cm) A gregarious prairie bird. *Male, spring: Black,* with a *large white wing patch (male Bobolink has white patches on back, not wings). Female, young, and winter male:* Brown, streaked; pattern suggests female Purple Finch. Usually some in flock show *whitish wing patch, white corner to tail.* **VOICE:** Song, cardinal-like slurs, unmusical chatlike *chug's;* piping whistles and trills; each note repeated 3–11 times. **HABITAT:** Plains, prairies, weedy fields. Wanders casually to East Coast.

M 393

FINCHLIKE BIRDS

EURASIAN TREE SPARROW

sexes similar

HOUSE SPARROW

♂

♀

juvenile BROWN-HEADED COWBIRD

♀

see p. 314

DICKCISSEL

♂

♀

fall

Bobolink for comparison (see p. 312)

♂ breeding

winter ♂ similar to ♀

LARK BUNTING

♀

ALTAMIRA ORIOLE *Icterus gularis*   Fairly common
8¼–9¼" (20.4–23 cm) Similar to Hooded Oriole but larger, with a thicker bill. *Upper wing bar yellow or orange,* not white. Sexes similar. **VOICE:** Song, disjointed whistled notes. A harsh "fuss" note. **RANGE:** Southern tip of Tex. to Nicaragua. **TEXAS:** Resident along lower Rio Grande Valley north to Zapata Co.

HOODED ORIOLE *Icterus cucullatus*   Fairly common
7–7¼" (18 cm) Orange and black with an *orange crown; 2 white wing bars.* More widespread in Tex. than Altamira Oriole. **RANGE:** Sw. U.S. to s. Mexico. **TEXAS:** Resident along Rio Grande Valley and along lower coast north to Kleberg Co.

AUDUBON'S ORIOLE *Icterus graduacauda*   Uncommon
9½" (24 cm) A *yellow* oriole with black wings, head and tail. *Yellowish back* is conclusive. Other male orioles have black backs. Sexes similar, but female duller. **VOICE:** Disjointed notes suggesting a child learning to whistle. **RANGE:** S. Tex. to cen. Mexico. **TEXAS:** Resident lower Rio Grande; occasionally north to Beeville and upriver to Eagle Pass. Casual, San Antonio, central coast.

GREAT KISKADEE *Pitangus sulphuratus*   Fairly common
9¾" (25 cm) A large big-headed flycatcher, like a Belted Kingfisher in actions, even catching small fish. Note striking head pattern; rufous wings and tail, yellow underparts and crown. **VOICE:** Loud *dee-kiss-ka-dee* or *ge dee-dek-ge-dee-deck* also a loud *wheep.* **RANGE:** S. Tex. to Mexico. Casual along Gulf of Mexico to La.

COUCH'S KINGBIRD *Tyrannus couchii*   Fairly common
9½" (24 cm) Very similar to Western Kingbird but *larger* bill, tail slightly *forked and dusky brown, not black,* without white edges. Dusky *gray ear patch.* Little or no gray across breast. **SIMILAR SPECIES:** Tropical Kingbird (which also occurs in Brownsville area) separated by voice, which is a staccato trill. **VOICE:** A nasal *queer* or *beeer* (suggests a Common Pauraque). **RANGE:** S. Tex. to Argentina. **TEXAS:** Resident in s. Tex. (south of a line from Falcon Dam at Raymondville). Occasional north to Laredo, Kingsville; strays farther east and north.

CLAY-COLORED ROBIN *Turdus grayi*   Scarce
9–9½" (22.5–24 cm) Scarce resident. Warm brown above, dull tan on chest, paling to light tawny buff on belly. Throat is streaked with light brown, not black. **RANGE:** Mexico to Colombia. Rare stray to s. Tex., where it has nested. Becoming more regular.

PYRRHULOXIA *Cardinalis sinuatus*   Fairly common
7½–8½" (19–21 cm) *Male:* Slender, gray and red with a crest and large parrotlike yellow-orange bill. *Female:* Lacks red on face and chest. **SIMILAR SPECIES:** Female cardinal, brown with red bill. **VOICE:** Song, clear *quink, quink, quink, quink* on one pitch. **HABITAT:** Mesquite and thorn scrub. **RANGE:** Rio Grande Valley west to Ariz.

PLAIN CHACHALACA *Ortalis vetula* (Family Cracidae)   Locally common
22" (53 cm) A large, *gray-brown turkeylike bird.* Small head, long rounded tail. Red gular skin. **VOICE:** Rollicking, loud, *chach-laca-chacha-laca.* **HABITAT:** Woods with dense underbrush. **RANGE:** Lower Rio Grande Valley.

SOUTH TEXAS SPECIALITIES

HOODED ORIOLE

ALTAMIRA ORIOLE

AUDUBON'S ORIOLE

PYRRHULOXIA

♂

♀

GREAT KISKADEE

COUCH'S KINGBIRD

CLAY-COLORED ROBIN

PLAIN CHACHALACA

LONG-BILLED THRASHER *Toxostoma longirostre*　　　　Fairly common
　10½–12" (22.5–30 cm) Darker than Brown Thrasher, breast stripes *blacker*, cheeks *grayer*, bill *longer*. **TEXAS:** Brush, mesquite north to Del Rio, San Antonio, Corpus Christi.

CURVE-BILLED THRASHER *Toxostoma curvirostre*　　　　Common
　10–11½" (25–28.5 cm) *Grayish;* deeply *curved bill,* light breast spots. **VOICE:** Note, a sharp *whit-wheet!* (like a whistle to get attention). **TEXAS:** Arid country of lower half of state, east rarely to Austin, San Antonio, Beeville.

GREEN JAY *Cyanocorax yncas*　　　　Common
　10½" (28–30 cm) The only *green* jay. Throat-patch black, crown violet, sides of tail yellow. **TEXAS:** Southern tip north to Norias; upriver to Laredo; colony at San Antonio. Casual to Alice, Kingsville, central coast.

BROWN JAY *Cyanocorax morio*　　　　Scarce
　16½" (35–45 cm) The largest jay. Sooty brown, darker on head; pale buff; bill black (adult) or yellow (young). **VOICE:** *Jhay, jhay, jhay!* Higher in pitch than Blue Jay's call. **TEXAS:** Lower Rio Grande Valley near Falcon Dam.

WHITE-COLLARED SEED-EATER *Sporophila torqueola*　　　　Scarce
　4" (10 cm) Tiny, with a stubby bill. *Male:* Dark cap, incomplete light collar, *white wing-spot.* Variable. *Female* buffy with eye-ring. **SONG:** High, then low *sweet, sweet, sweet, cheer, cheer, cheer.* **TEXAS:** A few along Rio Grande upriver from Falcon Dam.

BLUE BUNTING *Cyanocompsa parellina*　　　　Rare
　5½" (13.5 cm) *Male:* Deep blue-black, more blue on crown, shoulders, and rump. *Female* richer brown than female Indigo; no bars or streaks. Rare visitor s. Tex. Accidental La.

OLIVE SPARROW *Arremonops rufivirgatus*　　　　Common
　5½–6" (13.5–15 cm) Olive with 2 dull brown stripes on crown. **VOICE:** Song, dry notes on one pitch going into a Chipping Sparrow–like rattle. **TEXAS:** Bushy thickets of southern tip; a few north to Del Rio, Rockport.

GOLDEN-CROWNED WARBLER *Basileuterus culicivorus*　　　　Vagrant
　5" (13 cm) Yellow crown and eyebrow stripe bordered by black. Casual stray in s. Tex.

GRAY-CROWNED YELLOWTHROAT *Geothlypis poliocephala*　　　　Vagrant
　5½" (13.5 cm) Male has a *partial* Common Yellowthroat–type mask; has a *gray crown.* Both sexes have yellow on lower belly. **TEXAS:** Formerly resident along Rio Grande; now casual.

WHITE-COLLARED SWIFT *Streptoprocne zonaris*　　　　Vagrant
　8–8½" (20–20.5 cm) A large dark swift with a white collar and breast-band. **RANGE:** Mexico to S. America. Recorded Tex., La., Fla., Mich., Calif.

SOUTH TEXAS SPECIALITIES

LONG-BILLED THRASHER

CURVE-BILLED
THRASHER

juvenile

BROWN JAY

GREEN JAY

♀

♂

BLUE BUNTING

♀

WHITE-COLLARED
SEED-EATER

♂

OLIVE SPARROW

GOLDEN-CROWNED
WARBLER

♀

♂

GRAY-CROWNED
YELLOWTHROAT

WHITE-COLLARED
SWIFT

WHITE-TIPPED DOVE *Leptotila verreauxi* Uncommon
10–12" (25–30 cm) Large *stocky* dove with broad wings. Short tail has *white corners*. Spends a good deal of time *on the ground*. Often seen walking about in shadows of brushy tangles. Flies fast through woods. More regular than in the past. **VOICE:** Long, drawn-out, hollow *who— whoooooooooo*. **RANGE:** S. Texas to Argentina.

RED-BILLED PIGEON *Columba flavirostris* Scarce
13–14" (33–35 cm) A large *all-dark* pigeon (in good light a deep maroon color) including the underbelly. Bill all *red* or with small yellowish tip. *Shy*, mostly arboreal. Recent decline in numbers. **VOICE:** *Whoo, whoo, whoooooo*. **RANGE:** S. Texas to Costa Rica.

APLOMADO FALCON *Falco femoralis* Reintroduced/scarce
16" (40 cm) Striking long-tailed falcon. Bold face pattern. Pale throat, black chest, and rusty underbelly. **HABITAT:** Open country, grasslands. Often seen on wires, fences, and snags. Successful reintroduction program beginning at Laguna Atascosa Refuge.

FERRUGINOUS PYGMY-OWL *Glaucidium brasilianum* Rare
6½–7" (16–18 cm) Small with reddish brown breast streaks. Black *false eye spots* on nape of neck. Thin, barred, rusty tail. Crown striped. Ventriloquial quality of call makes it hard to spot in thicket. **VOICE:** Thin, fast, staccato *poip-poip-poip*. **RANGE:** S. Texas and se. Ariz. to s. tip of S. America.

NORTHERN BEARDLESS-TYRANNULET *Camptostoma imberbe* Scarce
4½" (12 cm) *Extremely small* flycatcher with *tiny blunt bill* and crest. Indistinct *gray-brown wingbars*, yellowish underbelly. Pale line over eye to bill. (Named for lack of rictal bristles other flycatchers have around base of bill.) Suggests a kinglet. **VOICE:** *Squee-up* or *peee-uk*. **RANGE:** S. Texas and se. Ariz. south to Costa Rica. **HABITAT:** Prefers dense brush, understory trees.

ROSE-THROATED BECARD *Pachyramphus aglaiae* Very rare
7¼" (19 cm) Sexually dimorphic. Male all gray with dark crown and *rosy pink throat* (at times hard to see). Female has cinnamon brown tail, brown back and cream underparts. Juvenile has all-cinnamon back. **NEST:** A large ball-like structure hanging from branch tip. **VOICE:** A thin, drawn-out *swee le*. **RANGE:** S. Texas and se. Ariz. south to Costa Rica. **HABITAT:** Favors river woodlands.

GREEN-BREASTED MANGO *Anthracothorax prevostii* Vagrant
4½–5" (11½–12½ cm) *Large*, with *long downcurved bill*. Sexually dimorphic. Male is dark emerald green above and has a velvety black throat edged in emerald. Center of belly a deep blue-green. Tail is *purple*. Female has a paler green back with median underparts white with *irregular dark stripe from throat to belly*. Dusky tail. Immature male (which accounts for most sightings north of the border) very similar to female plumage with lack of stripe on chin. **HABITAT:** Forest edges. All Texas records at feeders.

SOUTH TEXAS SPECIALTIES

RED-BILLED PIGEON

WHITE-TIPPED DOVE

APLOMADO FALCON

FERRUGINOUS PYGMY-OWL

NORTHERN BEARDLESS-TYRANNULET

♂ ♀

ROSE-THROATED BECARD

♀

GREEN-BREASTED MANGO

immature male similar to ♀

Some of these are of Mexican origin. For further information on identification, see *A Field Guide to Mexican Birds* by Roger Tory Peterson
and Edward L. Chalif. Others are of W. Indies origin. See *A Field
Guide to the Birds of the West Indies* by James Bond. Some are represented by a single record, others by many. The dynamics of appearance
of accidentals limit detailed lists. Below are some representative
records and comments. (Locations in parentheses indicate home
range.)

1. **CAVE SWALLOW** *Petrochelidon fulva* (Mex. to Tex.) See p. 232.

2. **BAHAMA SWALLOW** *Tachycineta cyaneoviridis* (W. Indies) S. Fla.

3. **ANTILLEAN PALM-SWIFT** *Tachornis phoenicobia* (W. Indies) Key West, Fla.

4. **BAHAMA MOCKINGBIRD** *Mimus gundlachii* (W. Indies) Fla. Keys, Dry Tortugas. Several records on se. Fla. mainland. Streaks on flanks; no white
wing patch.

5. **FORK-TAILED FLYCATCHER** *Tyrannus savana* (Mexico, S. America) Many
records from Fla. and Gulf Coast north to Maritime Provinces.

6. **ZENAIDA DOVE** *Zenaida aurita* (W. Indies or Mexico) Formerly bred Fla.
Keys; now accidental s. Fla.

7. **RUDDY QUAIL-DOVE** *Geotrygon montana* (W. Indies or Mexico) Dry Tortugas
and Fla. Keys, s. Tex.

8. **KEY WEST QUAIL-DOVE** *Geotrygon chrysia* (W. Indies) Key West (before
1900); recently recorded s. Fla.

9. **SCALY-NAPED PIGEON** *Columba squamosa* (W. Indies) Key West, Ga.

10. **RED-LEGGED THRUSH** *Turdus plumbeus* (W. Indies) Miami. Escape.

11. **BLACK-COWLED ORIOLE** *Icterus dominicensis* (W. Indies) Sight record Seal Island, N.S.

12. **TAWNY-SHOULDERED BLACKBIRD** *Agelaius humeralis* (W. Indies) Fla. Keys.

13. **YELLOW-GREEN VIREO** *Vireo flavoviridis* (Mexico) Tex., La., Fla., Que. (see p.
256).

14. **WESTERN SPINDALIS** *Spindalis zena* (W. Indies) S. Fla.

15. **CUBAN (MELODIOUS) GRASSQUIT** *Tiaris canora* (W. Indies) Miami, Fla. Keys.

16. **BANANAQUIT** *Coereba flaveola* (W. Indies) S. Fla.

17. **BLACK-FACED GRASSQUIT** *Tiaris bicolor* (W. Indies) S. Fla.

18. **CUBAN BULLFINCH** *Melopyrrha nigra* (W. Indies) Miami. Escape.

19. **GREATER ANTILLEAN BULLFINCH** *Loxigilla violacea* (W. Indies) S. Fla. Escape.

20. **GRAY-BREASTED MARTIN** *Progne chalybea* (not shown; see Mexican Field
Guide) Fla. Keys.

21. **THICK-BILLED VIREO** *Vireo crassirostris* (not shown; see W. Indies Field
Guide) Se. Fla.

ACCIDENTALS FROM
THE TROPICS

Field marks of the Eurasian strays listed below can be found in *A Field Guide to the Birds of Britain and Europe*. Some have been substantiated by specimens or photographs; others are convincing sight records but several are also certain escaped cagebirds. With continued coverage by birders, certainly others will appear.

1. **FIELDFARE** *Turdus pilaris* Breeds sw. Greenland. Recorded at numerous sites in Maritmes and Northeast.

2. **BRAMBLING** *Fringilla montifringila* Several sightings in the East.

3. **REDWING** *Turdus iliacus* Several sightings in the East.

4. **LINNET** *Carduelis cannabina* One eastern report.

5. **EUROPEAN GOLDFINCH** *Carduelis carduelis* Formerly established on Long Island. Occasional reports assumed to be escapes.

6. **COMMON GREENFINCH** *Carduelis chloris*

7. **TWITE** *Carduelis flavirostris* One eastern report.

8. **CHAFFINCH** *Fringilla coelebs* A few eastern records.

9. **HAWFINCH** *Coccothraustes coccothraustes* No substantiated eastern reports.

10. **EUROPEAN ROBIN** *Erithacus rubecula*

11. **EURASIAN BULLFINCH** *Pyrrhula pyrrhula*

12. **GREAT TIT** *Poecile major* Two eastern reports.

13. **BLUE TIT** *Poecile caeruleus* One eastern report.

14. **EURASIAN JACKDAW** *Corvus monedula* At least two small invasions to the Maritime Provinces and e. U.S. Has bred. No true colonization to date.

MAPS
INDEXES

RANGE MAPS

The maps on the following pages are approximate, giving the general out-lines of the range of each species. Within these broad outlines may be many gaps—areas that are ecologically unsuitable for the species. A Marsh Wren must have a marsh, a Ruffed Grouse a woodland or a forest. Certain species may be extremely local or sporadic for reasons that may or may not be clear. Some birds are extending their ranges, a few explosively. Others are declining or even disappearing from large areas where they were for-merly found. Winter ranges are often not as definite as breeding ranges. A species may exist at a very low density near the northern limits of its winter range, surviving through December in mild seasons but often succumbing to the bitter conditions of January and February. Varying weather condi-tions and food supplies from year to year may result in substantial variation in winter bird populations.

The maps are specific only for the area covered by this Field Guide. The Mallard, for example, is found over a large part of the globe. Its world range is briefly stated in the main text. The map shows only its range in eastern North America.

The maps are based on data culled from many publications (particularly from monographs detailing the status and distribution of a state or province's avifauna, as well as from breeding bird atlases), from such jour-nals as *North American Birds, Audubon Field Notes,* and *American Birds,* and from communication with many state and provincial experts from throughout eastern North America. The names of those authorities who provided information are found in the acknowledgments section.

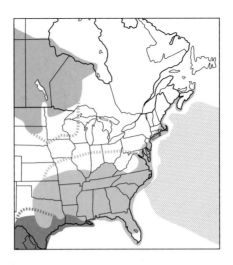

Key to Range Maps

RED: summer range
BLUE: winter range
PURPLE: year-round range
RED DASH LINE: approximate limits of irregular summer range and/or post-breeding dispersal
BLUE DASH LINE: approximate limits of irregular winter range
PURPLE DASH LINE: approximate limits of irregular year-round range
STRIPED AREA: pelagic range

Comments noting some population increases and declines, a species' regular winter or summer range if not found in eastern North America, and extralimital occurrences are included with many of the maps.

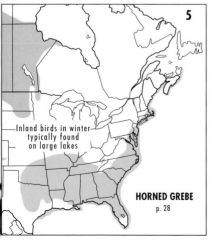

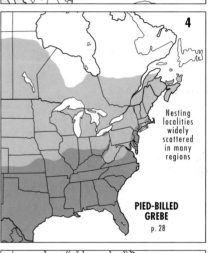

1

Rare migrant and winter visitor in interior and along Gulf Coast

RED-THROATED LOON
p. 26

2

Winters along Pacific Coast

Rare but regular migrant west of Mississippi River and winter visitor along Gulf Coast, casual to east

PACIFIC LOON
p. 26

3

Found inland in winter typically on large lakes

COMMON LOON
p. 26

4

Nesting localities widely scattered in many regions

PIED-BILLED GREBE
p. 28

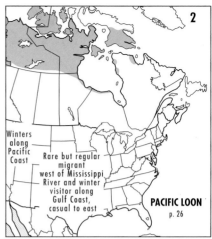

5

Inland birds in winter typically found on large lakes

HORNED GREBE
p. 28

6

Casual in southern states

RED-NECKED GREBE
p. 28

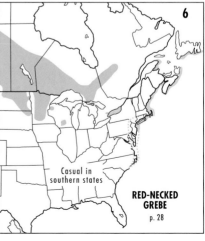

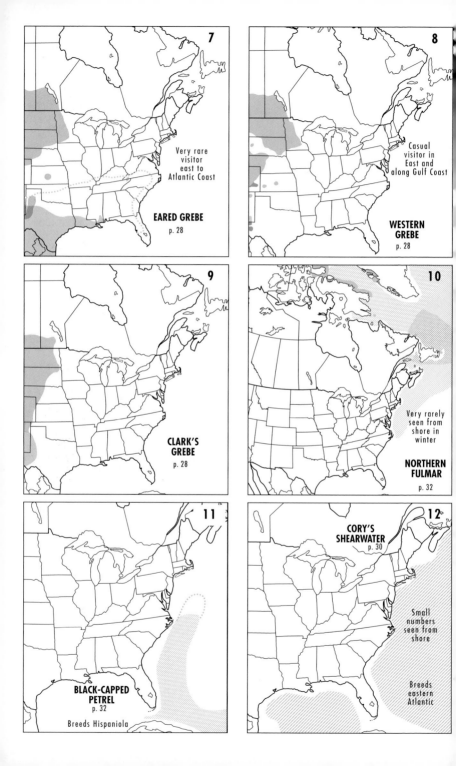

7

Very rare visitor east to Atlantic Coast

EARED GREBE
p. 28

8

Casual visitor in East and along Gulf Coast

WESTERN GREBE
p. 28

9

CLARK'S GREBE
p. 28

10

Very rarely seen from shore in winter

NORTHERN FULMAR
p. 32

11

BLACK-CAPPED PETREL
p. 32

Breeds Hispaniola

12

CORY'S SHEARWATER
p. 30

Small numbers seen from shore

Breeds eastern Atlantic

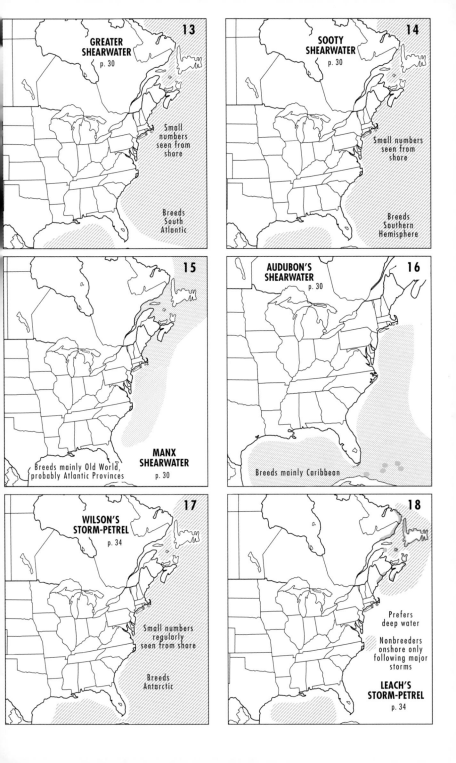

13

GREATER
SHEARWATER
p. 30

Small
numbers
seen from
shore

Breeds
South
Atlantic

14

SOOTY
SHEARWATER
p. 30

Small numbers
seen from
shore

Breeds
Southern
Hemisphere

15

Breeds mainly Old World,
probably Atlantic Provinces

MANX
SHEARWATER
p. 30

16

AUDUBON'S
SHEARWATER
p. 30

Breeds mainly Caribbean

17

WILSON'S
STORM-PETREL
p. 34

Small numbers
regularly
seen from shore

Breeds
Antarctic

18

Prefers
deep water

Nonbreeders
onshore only
following major
storms

LEACH'S
STORM-PETREL
p. 34

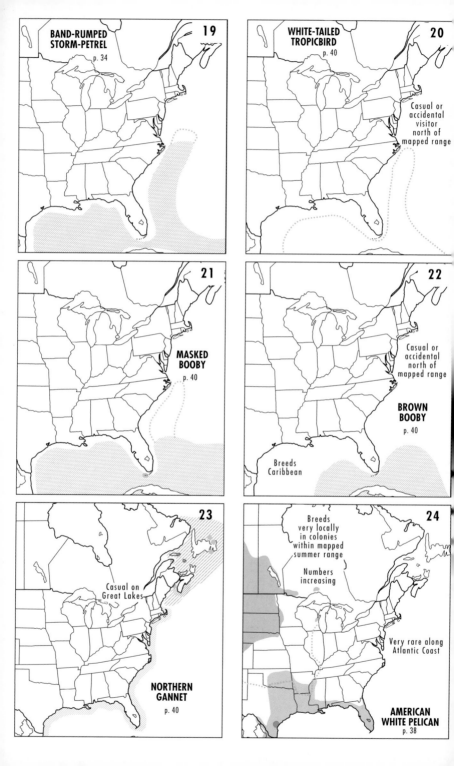

BAND-RUMPED STORM-PETREL p. 34 — **19**

WHITE-TAILED TROPICBIRD p. 40 — **20**
Casual or accidental visitor north of mapped range

MASKED BOOBY p. 40 — **21**

BROWN BOOBY p. 40 — **22**
Casual or accidental north of mapped range
Breeds Caribbean

NORTHERN GANNET p. 40 — **23**
Casual on Great Lakes

AMERICAN WHITE PELICAN p. 38 — **24**
Breeds very locally in colonies within mapped summer range
Numbers increasing
Very rare along Atlantic Coast

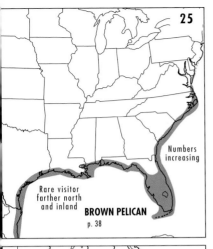

25

Numbers increasing

Rare visitor farther north and inland

BROWN PELICAN
p. 38

26

NEOTROPIC CORMORANT
p. 42

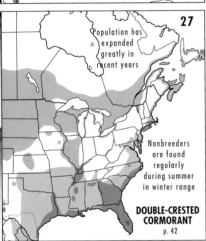

27

Population has expanded greatly in recent years

Nonbreeders are found regularly during summer in winter range

DOUBLE-CRESTED CORMORANT
p. 42

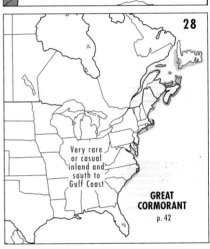

28

Very rare or casual inland and south to Gulf Coast

GREAT CORMORANT
p. 42

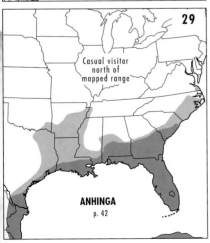

29

Casual visitor north of mapped range

ANHINGA
p. 42

30

Wanderers may be seen well north and inland, particularly after tropical storms

MAGNIFICENT FRIGATEBIRD
p. 38

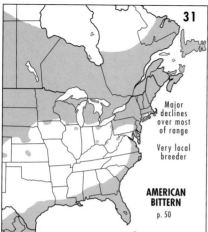

31

Major
declines
over most
of range

Very local
breeder

**AMERICAN
BITTERN**
p. 50

32

Found very
locally over
much of range

LEAST BITTERN
p. 50

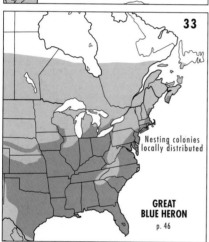

33

Nesting colonies
locally distributed

**GREAT
BLUE HERON**
p. 46

34

"GREAT WHITE" HERON
p. 48

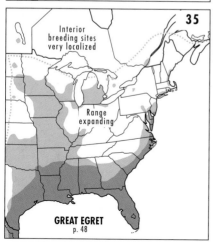

35

Interior
breeding sites
very localized

Range
expanding

GREAT EGRET
p. 48

36

SNOWY EGRET
p. 48

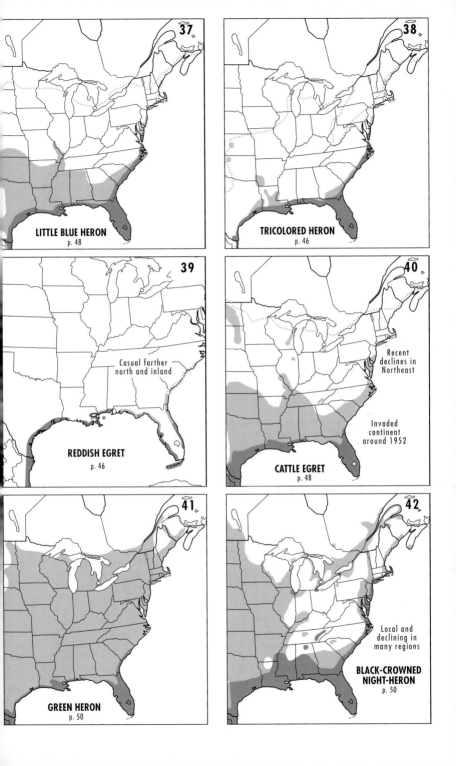

37 LITTLE BLUE HERON
p. 48

38 TRICOLORED HERON
p. 46

39 REDDISH EGRET
p. 46

Casual farther
north and inland

40 CATTLE EGRET
p. 48

Recent
declines in
Northeast

Invaded
continent
around 1952

41 GREEN HERON
p. 50

42 BLACK-CROWNED
NIGHT-HERON
p. 50

Local and
declining in
many regions

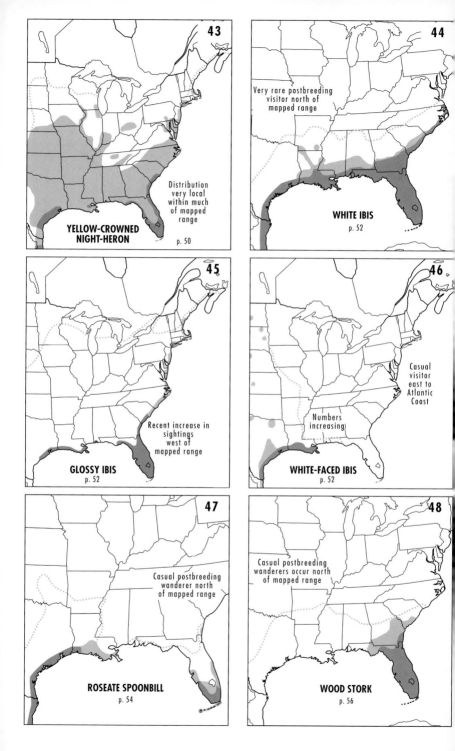

43

YELLOW-CROWNED NIGHT-HERON

p. 50

Distribution very local within much of mapped range

44

WHITE IBIS

p. 52

Very rare postbreeding visitor north of mapped range

45

GLOSSY IBIS

p. 52

Recent increase in sightings west of mapped range

46

WHITE-FACED IBIS

p. 52

Casual visitor east to Atlantic Coast

Numbers increasing

47

ROSEATE SPOONBILL

p. 54

Casual postbreeding wanderer north of mapped range

48

WOOD STORK

p. 56

Casual postbreeding wanderers occur north of mapped range

Very rare north of mapped range

Recent range expansion in Northeast

BLACK VULTURE
p. 92

49

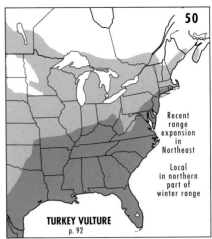

Recent range expansion in Northeast

Local in northern part of winter range

TURKEY VULTURE
p. 92

50

Wanderers occur very rarely well north of mapped range

Recent population increases and expansion

BLACK-BELLIED WHISTLING-DUCK
p. 66

51

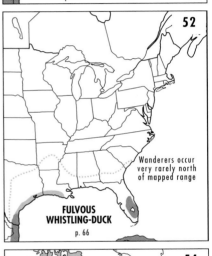

Wanderers occur very rarely north of mapped range

FULVOUS WHISTLING-DUCK
p. 66

52

Numbers have increased east of Great Plains

Rare visitor along East Coast

GREATER WHITE-FRONTED GOOSE
p. 62

53

Numbers have increased greatly in recent years

SNOW GOOSE
p. 60, 62

54

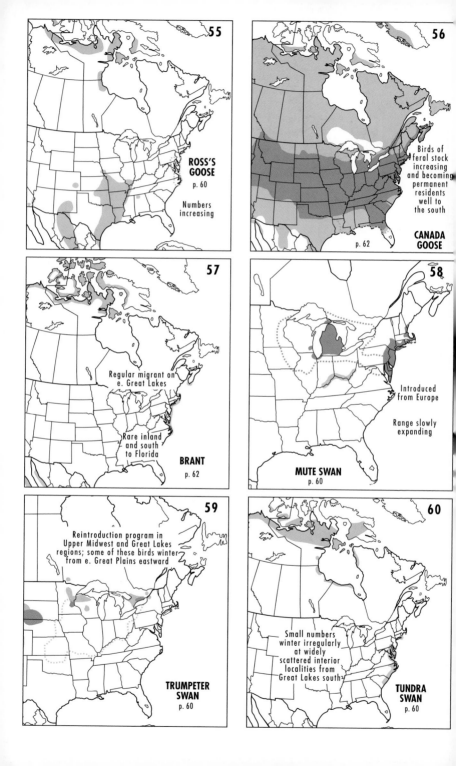

55

ROSS'S
GOOSE
p. 60

Numbers
increasing

56

Birds of
feral stock
increasing
and becoming
permanent
residents
well to
the south

CANADA
GOOSE

p. 62

57

Regular migrant on
e. Great Lakes

Rare inland
and south
to Florida

BRANT

p. 62

58

Introduced
from Europe

Range slowly
expanding

MUTE SWAN
p. 60

59

Reintroduction program in
Upper Midwest and Great Lakes
regions; some of these birds winter
from e. Great Plains eastward

TRUMPETER
SWAN
p. 60

60

Small numbers
winter irregularly
at widely
scattered interior
localities from
Great Lakes south

TUNDRA
SWAN
p. 60

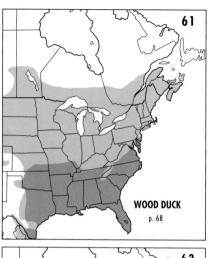

61

WOOD DUCK
p. 68

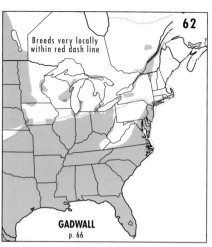

62

Breeds very locally within red dash line

GADWALL
p. 66

63

Regular visitor in Atlantic Provinces

Very rare but regular in interior

EURASIAN WIGEON
p. 68

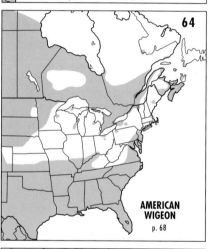

64

AMERICAN WIGEON
p. 68

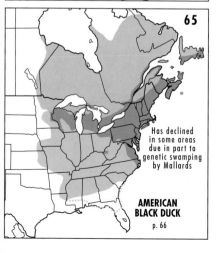

65

Has declined in some areas due in part to genetic swamping by Mallards

AMERICAN BLACK DUCK
p. 66

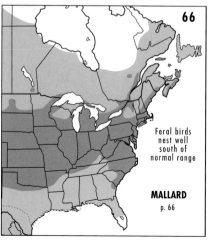

66

Feral birds nest well south of normal range

MALLARD
p. 66

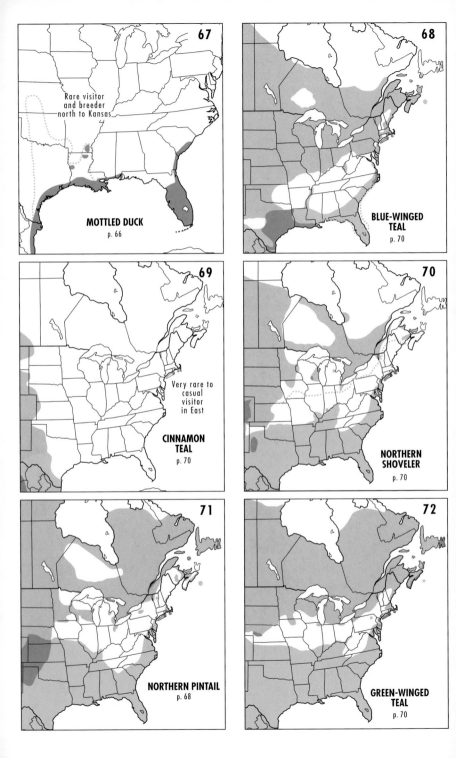

67 MOTTLED DUCK p. 66

Rare visitor and breeder north to Kansas

68 BLUE-WINGED TEAL p. 70

69 CINNAMON TEAL p. 70

Very rare to casual visitor in East

70 NORTHERN SHOVELER p. 70

71 NORTHERN PINTAIL p. 68

72 GREEN-WINGED TEAL p. 70

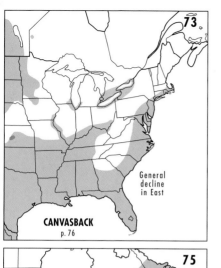

73

General
decline
in East

CANVASBACK
p. 76

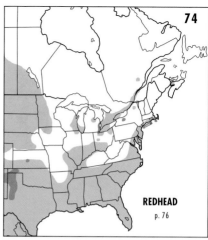

74

REDHEAD
p. 76

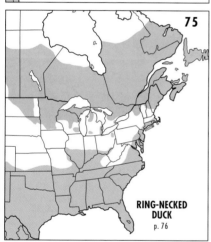

75

**RING-NECKED
DUCK**
p. 76

76

More common
winter scaup
in North

GREATER SCAUP
p. 76

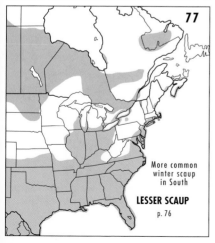

77

More common
winter scaup
in South

LESSER SCAUP
p. 76

78

Very rare to
casual inland

KING EIDER
p. 74

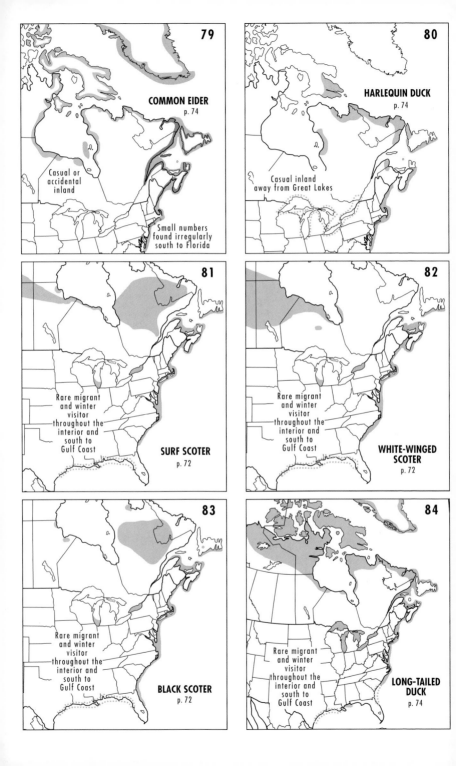

79
COMMON EIDER
p. 74

Casual or accidental inland

Small numbers found irregularly south to Florida

80
HARLEQUIN DUCK
p. 74

Casual inland away from Great Lakes

81
Rare migrant and winter visitor throughout the interior and south to Gulf Coast

SURF SCOTER
p. 72

82
Rare migrant and winter visitor throughout the interior and south to Gulf Coast

WHITE-WINGED SCOTER
p. 72

83
Rare migrant and winter visitor throughout the interior and south to Gulf Coast

BLACK SCOTER
p. 72

84
Rare migrant and winter visitor throughout the interior and south to Gulf Coast

LONG-TAILED DUCK
p. 74

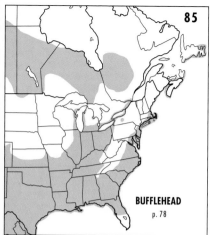

85

BUFFLEHEAD
p. 78

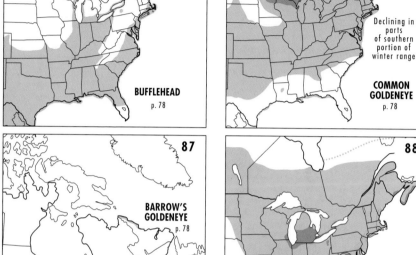

86

Declining in
parts
of southern
portion of
winter range

**COMMON
GOLDENEYE**
p. 78

87

**BARROW'S
GOLDENEYE**
p. 78

Very rare
south to
mid-Atlantic
and on
Great Lakes

88

Local and
irregular
breeder in
southern part
of range

**HOODED
MERGANSER**
p. 80

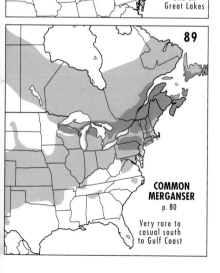

89

**COMMON
MERGANSER**
p. 80

Very rare to
casual south
to Gulf Coast

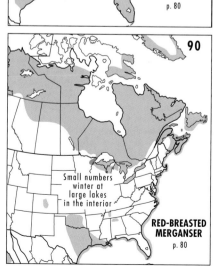

90

Small numbers
winter at
large lakes
in the interior

**RED-BREASTED
MERGANSER**
p. 80

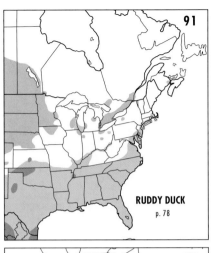

91

RUDDY DUCK
p. 78

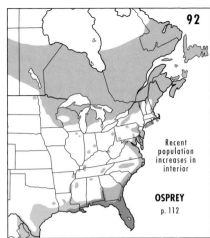

92

Recent
population
increases in
interior

OSPREY
p. 112

93

Very rare
visitor north
of mapped range

**SWALLOW-TAILED
KITE**
p. 96

94

Accidental north
of mapped range

**WHITE-TAILED
KITE**
p. 96

95

Numbers and range
fluctuate depending
on water levels and
food supply

Endangered in U.S.

SNAIL KITE
p. 96

96

Range
expanding
northward

Very rare
spring and
summer
visitor north
and east
of mapped
range

**MISSISSIPPI
KITE**
p. 96

Winters S. America

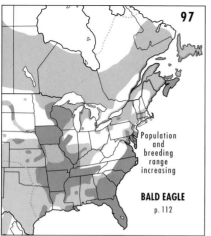

97

Population and breeding range increasing

BALD EAGLE
p. 112

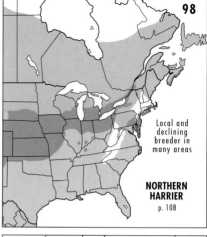

98

Local and declining breeder in many areas

NORTHERN HARRIER
p. 108

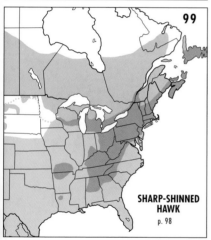

99

SHARP-SHINNED HAWK
p. 98

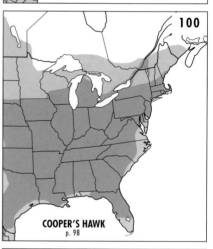

100

COOPER'S HAWK
p. 98

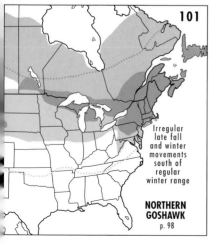

101

Irregular late fall and winter movements south of regular winter range

NORTHERN GOSHAWK
p. 98

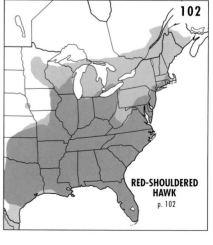

102

RED-SHOULDERED HAWK
p. 102

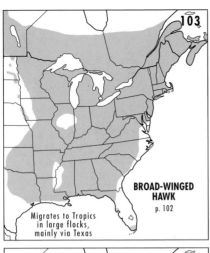

BROAD-WINGED HAWK
p. 102

Migrates to Tropics
in large flocks,
mainly via Texas

Casual in Texas

SHORT-TAILED HAWK
p. 102

Very rare
fall and
casual
spring
visitor
to East

SWAINSON'S HAWK
p. 100

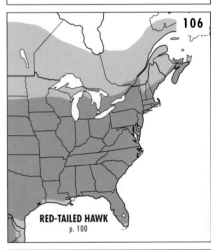

RED-TAILED HAWK
p. 100

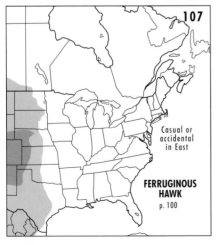

Casual or
accidental
in East

FERRUGINOUS HAWK
p. 100

Numbers
of birds
and southern
limits in
winter
vary from
year to year

ROUGH-LEGGED HAWK
p. 102

109

?

?

?

?Breeding range poorly known

?

Sparse and local in winter east of Great Plains

GOLDEN EAGLE
p. 112

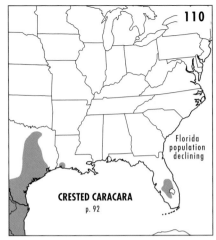

110

Florida population declining

CRESTED CARACARA
p. 92

111

Declining over much of its eastern range

AMERICAN KESTREL
p. 116

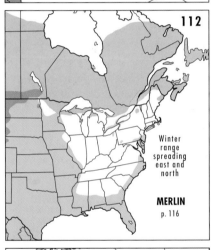

112

Winter range spreading east and north

MERLIN
p. 116

113

GYRFALCON
p. 116

114

PEREGRINE FALCON
p. 116

Reintroduced birds nest at many locations, including urban sites, south of mapped summer range; many of these birds are permanent residents

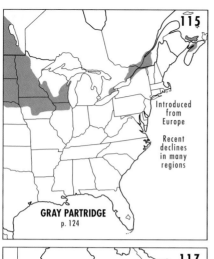

115

Introduced
from
Europe

Recent
declines
in many
regions

GRAY PARTRIDGE
p. 124

116

Introduced
from
Eurasia

Some
populations
result of
annual releases

Declining
in much of
Northeast

**RING-NECKED
PHEASANT** p. 120

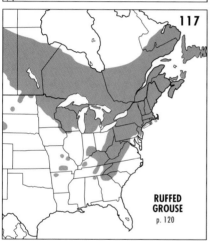

117

**RUFFED
GROUSE**
p. 120

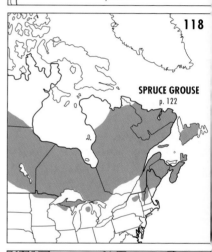

118

SPRUCE GROUSE
p. 122

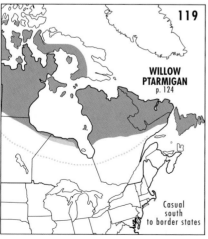

119

**WILLOW
PTARMIGAN**
p. 124

Casual
south to
border states

120

**ROCK
PTARMIGAN**
p. 124

Casual
south to
U.S. border

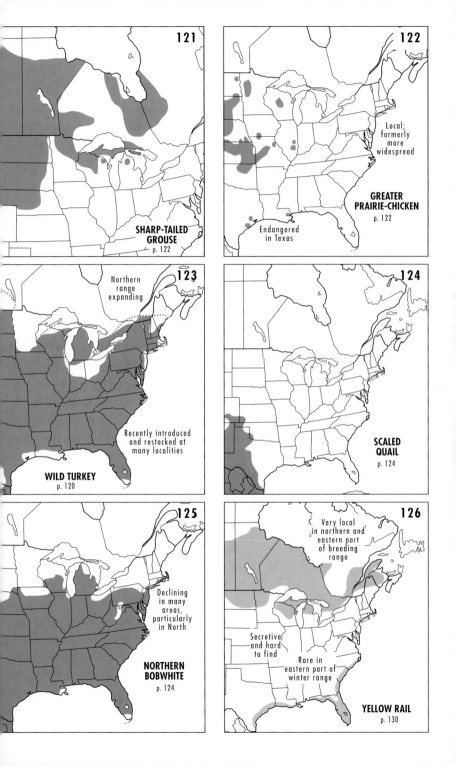

121 SHARP-TAILED GROUSE p. 122

122 GREATER PRAIRIE-CHICKEN p. 122

Local; formerly more widespread

Endangered in Texas

123 WILD TURKEY p. 120

Northern range expanding

Recently introduced and restocked at many localities

124 SCALED QUAIL p. 124

125 NORTHERN BOBWHITE p. 124

Declining in many areas, particularly in North

126 YELLOW RAIL p. 130

Very local in northern and eastern part of breeding range

Secretive and hard to find

Rare in eastern part of winter range

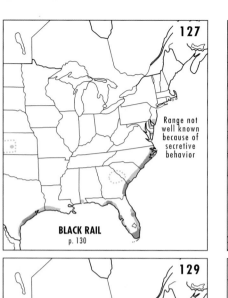

127

Range not
well known
because of
secretive
behavior

BLACK RAIL
p. 130

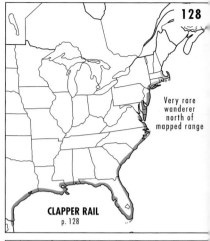

128

Very rare
wanderer
north of
mapped range

CLAPPER RAIL
p. 128

129

Declining in
many areas

Very local
within
most of
mapped
range

KING RAIL
p. 128

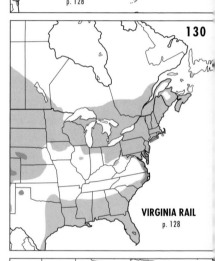

130

VIRGINIA RAIL
p. 128

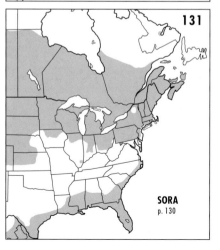

131

SORA
p. 130

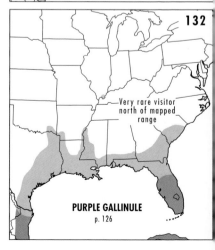

132

Very rare visitor
north of mapped
range

PURPLE GALLINULE
p. 126

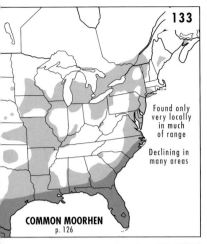

133

Found only
very locally
in much
of range

Declining in
many areas

COMMON MOORHEN
p. 126

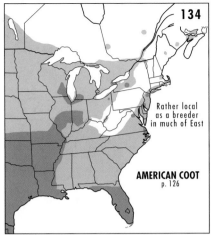

134

Rather local
as a breeder
in much of East

AMERICAN COOT
p. 126

135

Accidental
north
of mapped range

LIMPKIN
p. 52

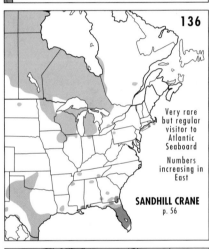

136

Very rare
but regular
visitor to
Atlantic
Seaboard

Numbers
increasing in
East

SANDHILL CRANE
p. 56

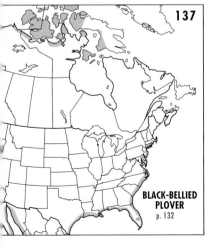

137

**BLACK-BELLIED
PLOVER**
p. 132

138

Fall migration
both inland
and down/off
Atlantic Coast

Spring
migration
mainly
via Great
Plains and Midwest

Winters
S. America

**AMERICAN
GOLDEN-
PLOVER**
p. 132

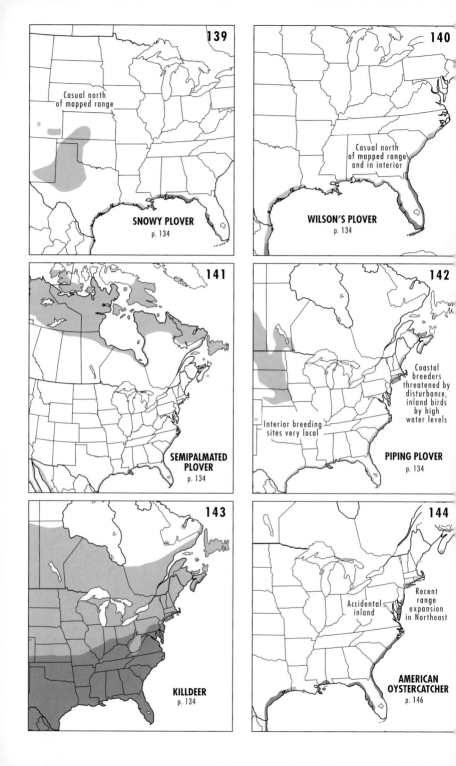

139

Casual north of mapped range

SNOWY PLOVER
p. 134

140

Casual north of mapped range and in interior

WILSON'S PLOVER
p. 134

141

SEMIPALMATED PLOVER
p. 134

142

Coastal breeders threatened by disturbance, inland birds by high water levels

Interior breeding sites very local

PIPING PLOVER
p. 134

143

KILLDEER
p. 134

144

Accidental inland

Recent range expansion in Northeast

AMERICAN OYSTERCATCHER
p. 146

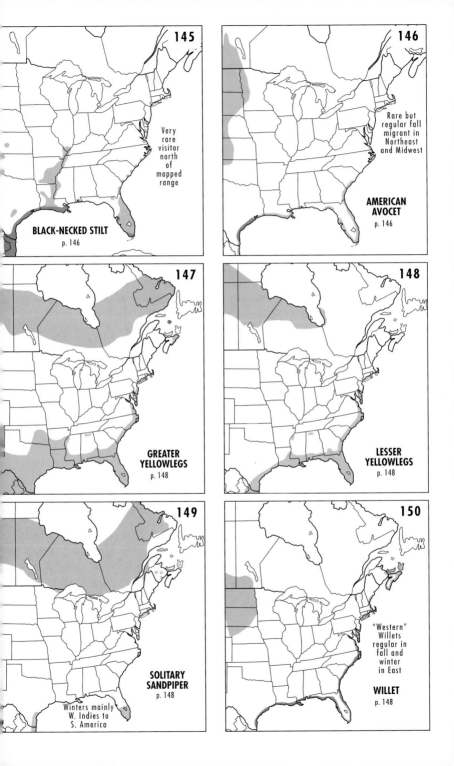

145

Very
rare
visitor
north
of
mapped
range

BLACK-NECKED STILT
p. 146

146

Rare but
regular fall
migrant in
Northeast
and Midwest

**AMERICAN
AVOCET**
p. 146

147

**GREATER
YELLOWLEGS**
p. 148

148

**LESSER
YELLOWLEGS**
p. 148

149

**SOLITARY
SANDPIPER**
p. 148

Winters mainly
W. Indies to
S. America

150

"Western"
Willets
regular in
fall and
winter
in East

WILLET
p. 148

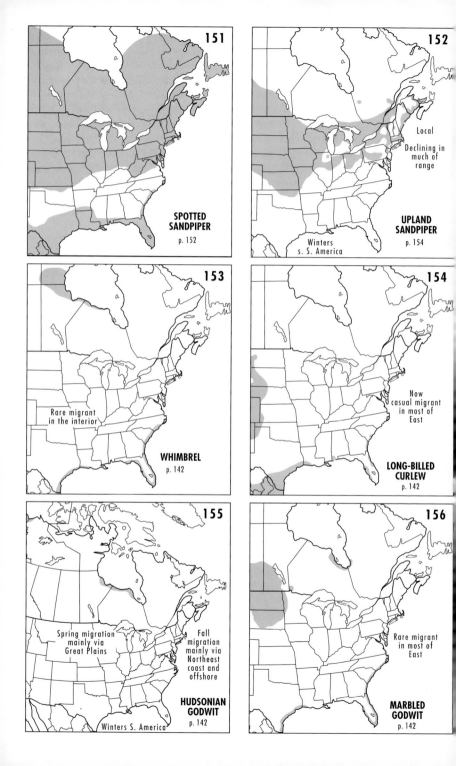

151
SPOTTED
SANDPIPER
p. 152

152
Local
Declining in
much of
range
UPLAND
SANDPIPER
p. 154
Winters
s. S. America

153
Rare migrant
in the interior
WHIMBREL
p. 142

154
Now
casual migrant
in most of
East
LONG-BILLED
CURLEW
p. 142

155
Spring migration
mainly via
Great Plains
Fall
migration
mainly via
Northeast
coast and
offshore
HUDSONIAN
GODWIT
p. 142
Winters S. America

156
Rare migrant
in most of
East
MARBLED
GODWIT
p. 142

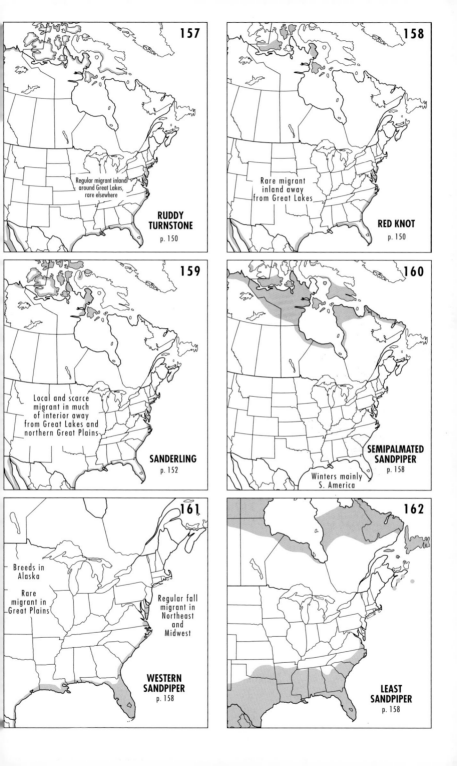

157

Regular migrant inland
around Great Lakes,
rare elsewhere

**RUDDY
TURNSTONE**
p. 150

158

Rare migrant
inland away
from Great Lakes

RED KNOT
p. 150

159

Local and scarce
migrant in much
of interior away
from Great Lakes and
northern Great Plains

SANDERLING
p. 152

160

Winters mainly
S. America

**SEMIPALMATED
SANDPIPER**
p. 158

161

Breeds in
Alaska

Rare
migrant in
Great Plains

Regular fall
migrant in
Northeast
and
Midwest

**WESTERN
SANDPIPER**
p. 158

162

**LEAST
SANDPIPER**
p. 158

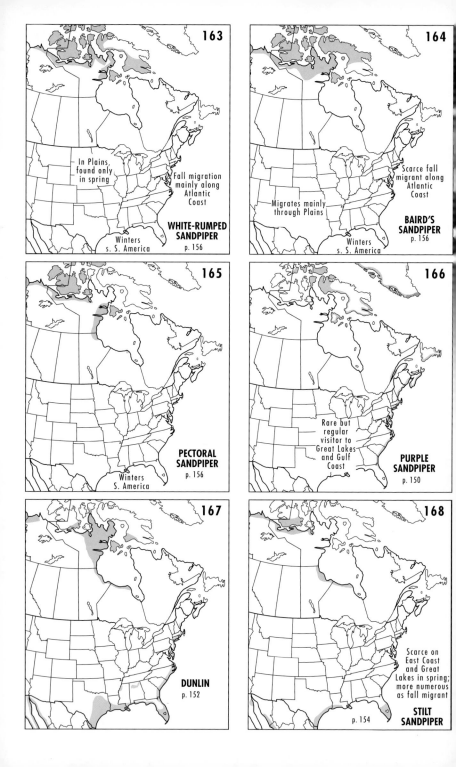

163

In Plains, found only in spring

Fall migration mainly along Atlantic Coast

WHITE-RUMPED SANDPIPER
p. 156

Winters s. S. America

164

Scarce fall migrant along Atlantic Coast

Migrates mainly through Plains

BAIRD'S SANDPIPER
p. 156

Winters s. S. America

165

PECTORAL SANDPIPER
p. 156

Winters S. America

166

Rare but regular visitor to Great Lakes and Gulf Coast

PURPLE SANDPIPER
p. 150

167

DUNLIN
p. 152

168

Scarce on East Coast and Great Lakes in spring; more numerous as fall migrant

STILT SANDPIPER
p. 154

169

BUFF-BREASTED SANDPIPER
p. 154

Spring migration largely via Great Plains

Small numbers of fall migrants in East

Winters S. America

170

Scarce migrant through Great Plains

SHORT-BILLED DOWITCHER
p. 140

171

Breeds nw. Arctic

LONG-BILLED DOWITCHER
p. 140

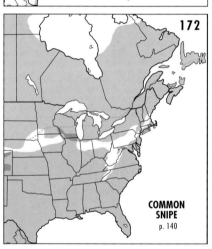

172

COMMON SNIPE
p. 140

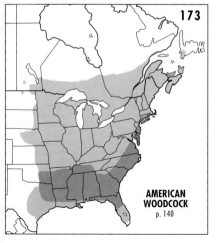

173

AMERICAN WOODCOCK
p. 140

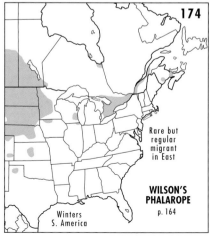

174

Rare but regular migrant in East

WILSON'S PHALAROPE
p. 164

Winters S. America

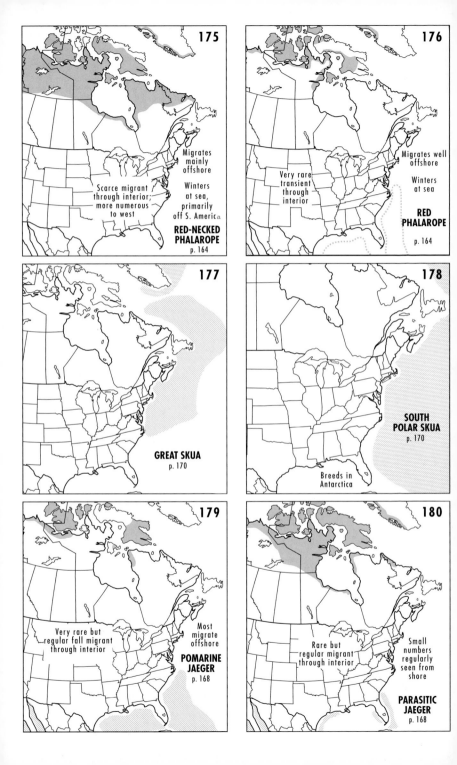

175

Migrates mainly offshore

Winters at sea, primarily off S. America

Scarce migrant through interior; more numerous to west

RED-NECKED PHALAROPE
p. 164

176

Migrates well offshore

Winters at sea

Very rare transient through interior

RED PHALAROPE
p. 164

177

GREAT SKUA
p. 170

178

SOUTH POLAR SKUA
p. 170

Breeds in Antarctica

179

Very rare but regular fall migrant through interior

Most migrate offshore

POMARINE JAEGER
p. 168

180

Rare but regular migrant through interior

Small numbers regularly seen from shore

PARASITIC JAEGER
p. 168

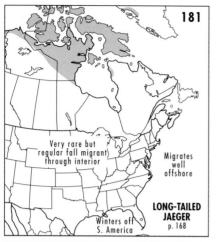

181

Very rare but regular fall migrant through interior

Migrates well offshore

Winters off S. America

LONG-TAILED JAEGER
p. 168

182

Wanders north to Atlantic Provinces

Regularly wanders inland in summer and early fall

LAUGHING GULL
p. 180

183

Very rare but regular visitor east to Atlantic Coast

Winters mainly off S. America

FRANKLIN'S GULL
p. 180

184

Breeds very locally and irregularly from Hudson Bay to Great Lakes region

Occurs very rarely west of mapped range

LITTLE GULL
p. 180

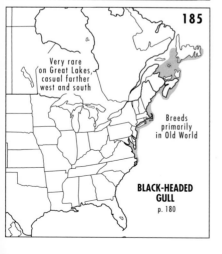

185

Very rare on Great Lakes, casual farther west and south

Breeds primarily in Old World

BLACK-HEADED GULL
p. 180

186

May winter on Great Lakes in mild years

BONAPARTE'S GULL
p. 180

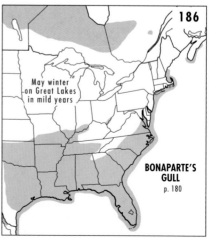

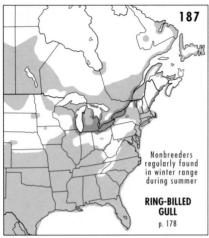

187

Nonbreeders regularly found in winter range during summer

RING-BILLED GULL
p. 178

188

Very rare to casual east to Atlantic Seaboard

Winters mainly along Pacific Coast

CALIFORNIA GULL
p. 178

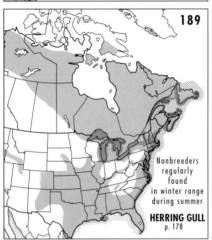

189

Nonbreeders regularly found in winter range during summer

HERRING GULL
p. 178

190

Winters mainly along Pacific Coast

THAYER'S GULL
p. 178

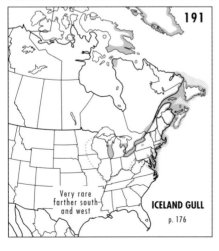

191

Very rare farther south and west

ICELAND GULL
p. 176

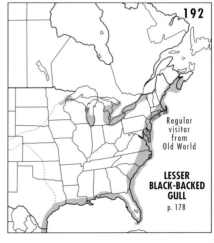

192

Regular visitor from Old World

LESSER BLACK-BACKED GULL
p. 178

193

GLAUCOUS GULL
p. 176

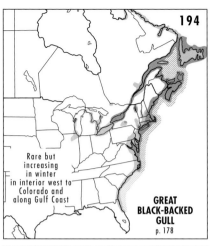

194

Rare but
increasing
in winter
in interior west to
Colorado and
along Gulf Coast

**GREAT
BLACK-BACKED
GULL**
p. 178

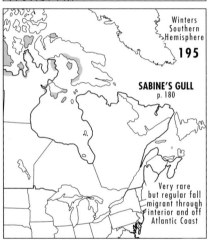

Winters
Southern
Hemisphere

195

SABINE'S GULL
p. 180

Very rare
but regular fall
migrant through
interior and off
Atlantic Coast

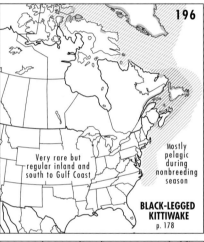

196

Mostly
pelagic
during
nonbreeding
season

Very rare but
regular inland and
south to Gulf Coast

**BLACK-LEGGED
KITTIWAKE**
p. 178

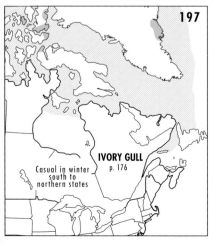

197

IVORY GULL
p. 176

Casual in winter
south to
northern states

198

A few
wander inland
in late summer

GULL-BILLED TERN
p. 186

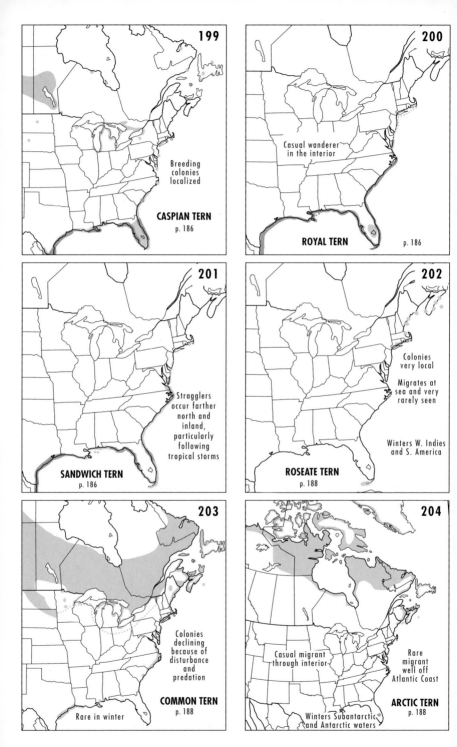

199
Breeding
colonies
localized

CASPIAN TERN
p. 186

200
Casual wanderer
in the interior

ROYAL TERN
p. 186

201
Stragglers
occur farther
north and
inland,
particularly
following
tropical storms

SANDWICH TERN
p. 186

202
Colonies
very local

Migrates at
sea and very
rarely seen

Winters W. Indies
and S. America

ROSEATE TERN
p. 188

203
Colonies
declining
because of
disturbance
and
predation

Rare in winter

COMMON TERN
p. 188

204
Casual migrant
through interior

Rare
migrant
well off
Atlantic
Coast

Winters Subantarctic
and Antarctic waters

ARCTIC TERN
p. 188

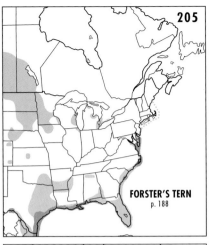

205

FORSTER'S TERN
p. 188

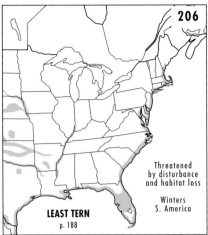

206

Threatened
by disturbance
and habitat loss

Winters
S. America

LEAST TERN
p. 188

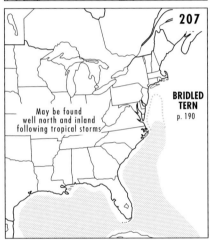

207

**BRIDLED
TERN**
p. 190

May be found
well north and inland
following tropical storms

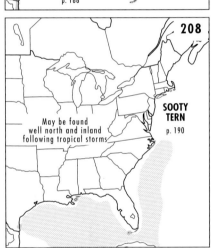

208

**SOOTY
TERN**
p. 190

May be found
well north and inland
following tropical storms

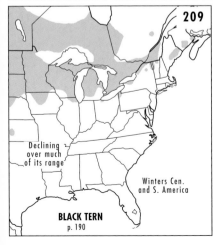

209

Declining
over much
of its range

Winters Cen.
and S. America

BLACK TERN
p. 190

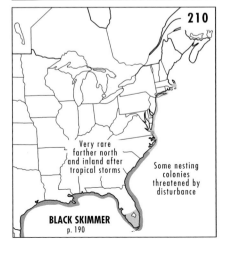

210

Very rare
farther north
and inland after
tropical storms

Some nesting
colonies
threatened by
disturbance

BLACK SKIMMER
p. 190

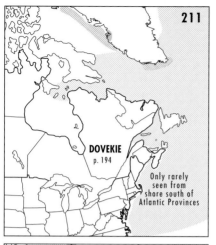

DOVEKIE
p. 194

Only rarely
seen from shore
south of
Atlantic Provinces

211

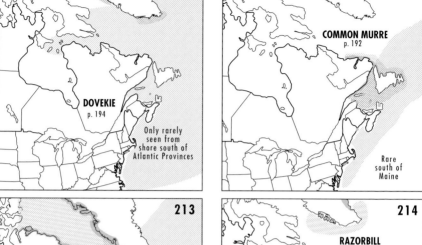

COMMON MURRE
p. 192

Rare
south of
Maine

212

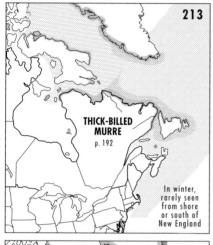

**THICK-BILLED
MURRE**
p. 192

In winter,
rarely seen
from shore
or south of
New England

213

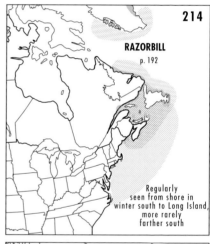

RAZORBILL
p. 192

Regularly
seen from shore in
winter south to Long Island,
more rarely
farther south

214

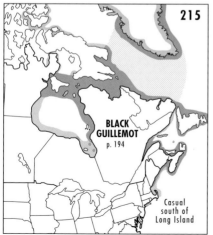

**BLACK
GUILLEMOT**
p. 194

Casual
south of
Long Island

215

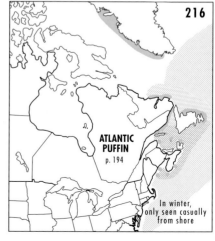

**ATLANTIC
PUFFIN**
p. 194

In winter,
only seen casually
from shore

216

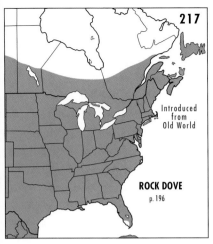

217

Introduced
from
Old World

ROCK DOVE
p. 196

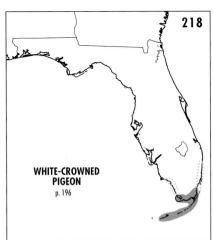

218

**WHITE-CROWNED
PIGEON**
p. 196

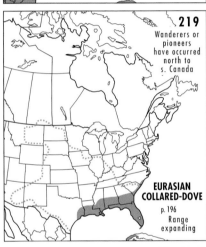

219

Wanderers or
pioneers
have occurred
north to
s. Canada

**EURASIAN
COLLARED-DOVE**
p. 196
Range
expanding

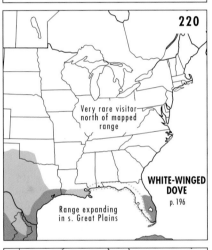

220

Very rare visitor
north of mapped
range

**WHITE-WINGED
DOVE**
p. 196

Range expanding
in s. Great Plains

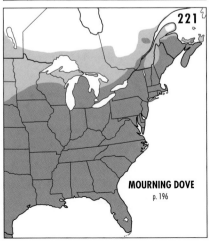

221

MOURNING DOVE
p. 196

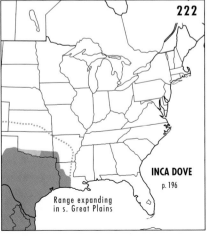

222

INCA DOVE
p. 196

Range expanding
in s. Great Plains

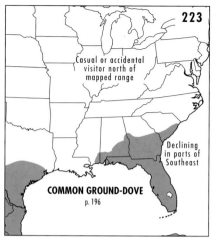

223

Casual or accidental visitor north of mapped range

Declining in parts of Southeast

COMMON GROUND-DOVE
p. 196

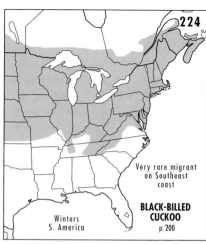

224

Very rare migrant on Southeast coast

Winters S. America

BLACK-BILLED CUCKOO
p. 200

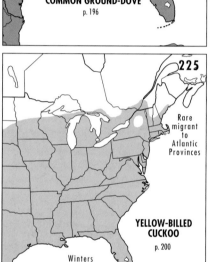

225

Rare migrant to Atlantic Provinces

Winters S. America

YELLOW-BILLED CUCKOO
p. 200

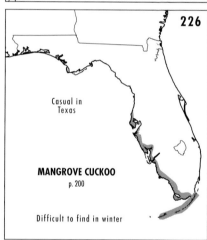

226

Casual in Texas

MANGROVE CUCKOO
p. 200

Difficult to find in winter

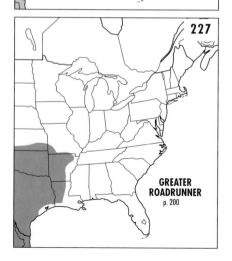

227

GREATER ROADRUNNER
p. 200

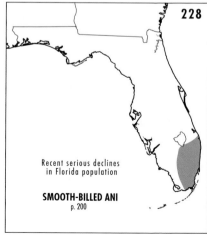

228

Recent serious declines in Florida population

SMOOTH-BILLED ANI
p. 200

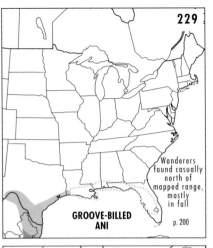

229

Wanderers found casually north of mapped range, mostly in fall

GROOVE-BILLED ANI
p. 200

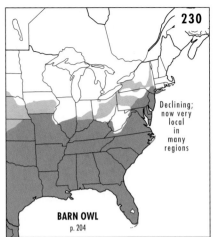

230

Declining; now very local in many regions

BARN OWL
p. 204

231

EASTERN SCREECH-OWL
p. 202

232

GREAT HORNED OWL
p. 202

233

Cyclic winter irruptions south to dash line and casually beyond

SNOWY OWL
p. 204

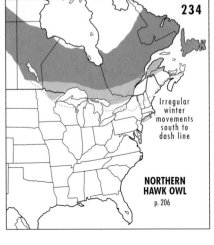

234

Irregular winter movements south to dash line

NORTHERN HAWK OWL
p. 206

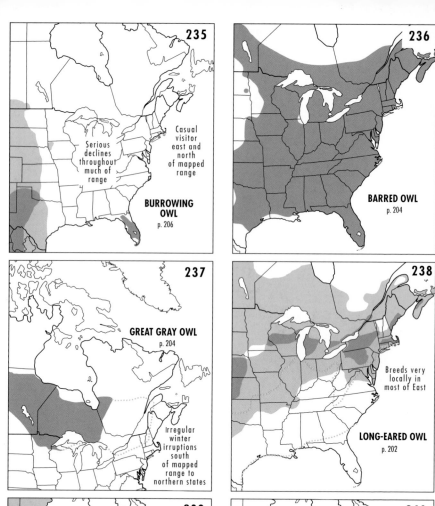

235

Serious declines throughout much of range

Casual visitor east and north of mapped range

BURROWING OWL
p. 206

236

BARRED OWL
p. 204

237

GREAT GRAY OWL
p. 204

Irregular winter irruptions south of mapped range to northern states

238

Breeds very locally in most of East

LONG-EARED OWL
p. 202

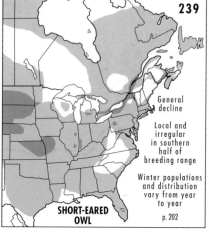

239

General decline

Local and irregular in southern half of breeding range

Winter populations and distribution vary from year to year

SHORT-EARED OWL
p. 202

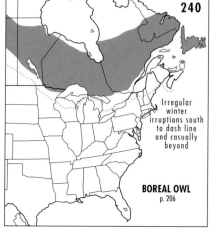

240

Irregular winter irruptions south to dash line and casually beyond

BOREAL OWL
p. 206

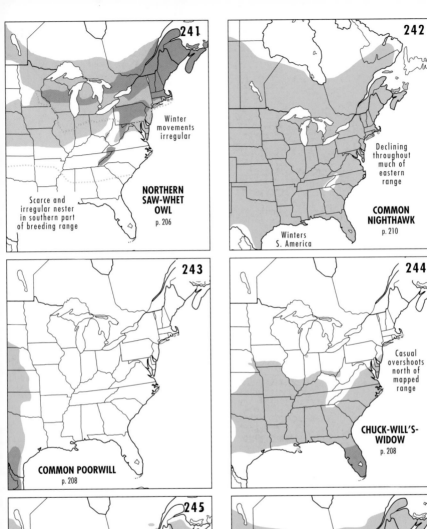

241

Winter movements irregular

Scarce and irregular nester in southern part of breeding range

NORTHERN SAW-WHET OWL
p. 206

242

Declining throughout much of eastern range

Winters S. America

COMMON NIGHTHAWK
p. 210

243

COMMON POORWILL
p. 208

244

Casual overshoots north of mapped range

CHUCK-WILL'S-WIDOW
p. 208

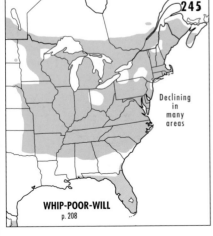

245

Declining in many areas

WHIP-POOR-WILL
p. 208

246

CHIMNEY SWIFT
p. 234

Winters S. America

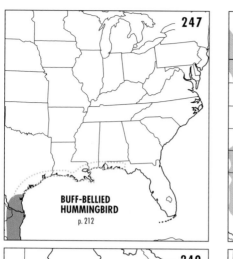

247

BUFF-BELLIED HUMMINGBIRD
p. 212

248

Small numbers winter at southeastern feeders

RUBY-THROATED HUMMINGBIRD
p. 212

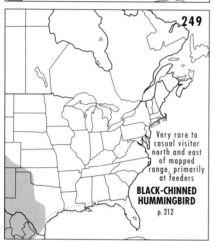

249

Very rare to casual visitor north and east of mapped range, primarily at feeders

BLACK-CHINNED HUMMINGBIRD
p. 212

250

Breeds in Northwest

Occurs rarely but regularly north and east of mapped range, mostly in fall

Recent increases in small wintering population at southeastern feeders

RUFOUS HUMMINGBIRD
p. 212

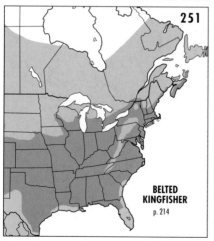

251

BELTED KINGFISHER
p. 214

252

Recent declines in Northeast

RED-HEADED WOODPECKER
p. 216

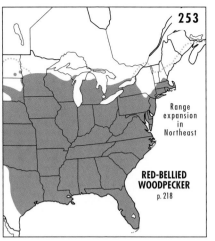

253

Range
expansion
in
Northeast

**RED-BELLIED
WOODPECKER**
p. 218

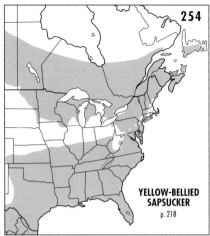

254

**YELLOW-BELLIED
SAPSUCKER**
p. 218

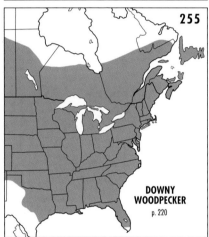

255

**DOWNY
WOODPECKER**
p. 220

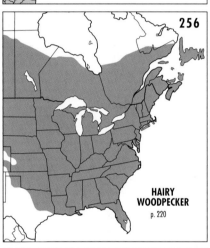

256

**HAIRY
WOODPECKER**
p. 220

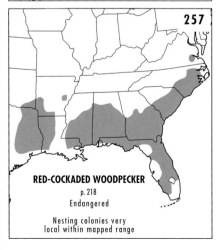

257

RED-COCKADED WOODPECKER
p. 218
Endangered

Nesting colonies very
local within mapped range

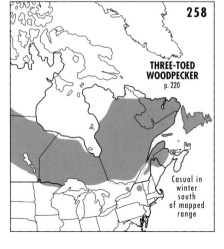

258

**THREE-TOED
WOODPECKER**
p. 220

Casual in
winter
south
of mapped
range

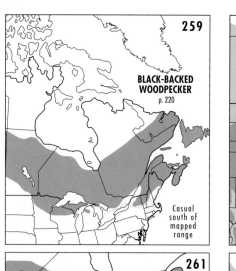

259

BLACK-BACKED WOODPECKER
p. 220

Casual south of mapped range

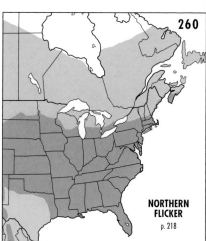

260

NORTHERN FLICKER
p. 218

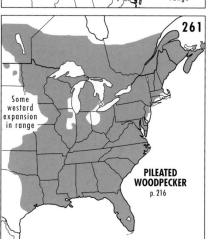

261

Some westard expansion in range

PILEATED WOODPECKER
p. 216

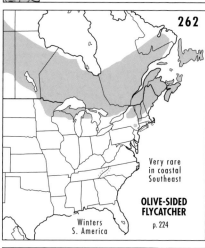

262

Very rare in coastal Southeast

OLIVE-SIDED FLYCATCHER
p. 224

Winters S. America

263

EASTERN WOOD-PEWEE
p. 224

Winters Cen. and S. America

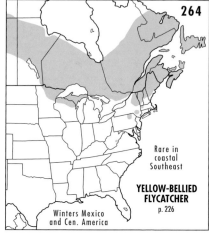

264

Rare in coastal Southeast

YELLOW-BELLIED FLYCATCHER
p. 226

Winters Mexico and Cen. America

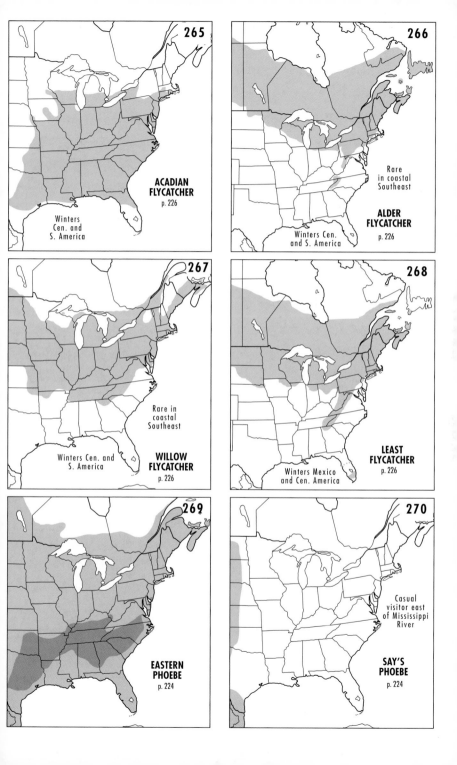

265

ACADIAN FLYCATCHER p. 226

Winters Cen. and S. America

266

Rare in coastal Southeast

ALDER FLYCATCHER p. 226

Winters Cen. and S. America

267

Rare in coastal Southeast

Winters Cen. and S. America

WILLOW FLYCATCHER p. 226

268

LEAST FLYCATCHER p. 226

Winters Mexico and Cen. America

269

EASTERN PHOEBE p. 224

270

Casual visitor east of Mississippi River

SAY'S PHOEBE p. 224

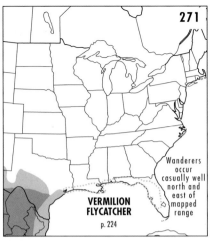

271

Wanderers occur casually well north and east of mapped range

VERMILION FLYCATCHER

p. 224

272

Wanderers occur casually well north and east of mapped range, particularly in late fall

ASH-THROATED FLYCATCHER

p. 222

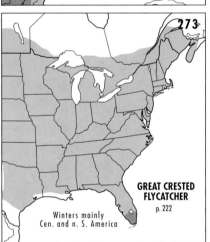

273

GREAT CRESTED FLYCATCHER

p. 222

Winters mainly Cen. and n. S. America

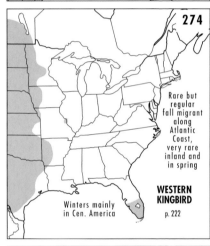

274

Rare but regular fall migrant along Atlantic Coast, very rare inland and in spring

WESTERN KINGBIRD

p. 222

Winters mainly in Cen. America

275

Spring overshoots north to Newfoundland

EASTERN KINGBIRD

p. 222

Winters S. America

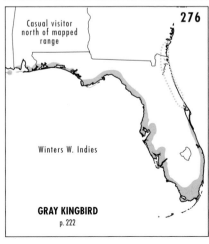

276

Casual visitor north of mapped range

Winters W. Indies

GRAY KINGBIRD

p. 222

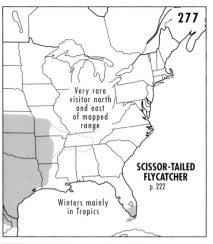

277

Very rare
visitor north
and east
of mapped
range

SCISSOR-TAILED
FLYCATCHER
p. 222

Winters mainly
in Tropics

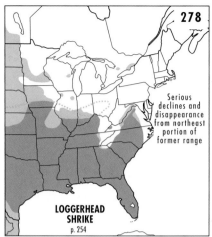

278

Serious
declines and
disappearance
from northeast
portion of
former range

LOGGERHEAD
SHRIKE
p. 254

279

Irruptive
fall and
winter
visitor to
dash line,
very rarely
beyond

NORTHERN
SHRIKE
p. 254

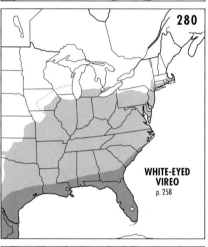

280

WHITE-EYED
VIREO
p. 258

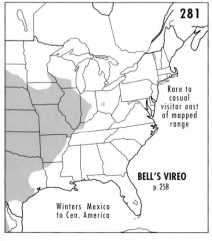

281

Rare to
casual
visitor east
of mapped
range

BELL'S VIREO
p. 258

Winters Mexico
to Cen. America

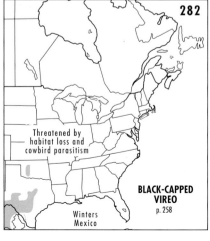

282

Threatened by
habitat loss and
cowbird parasitism

BLACK-CAPPED
VIREO
p. 258

Winters
Mexico

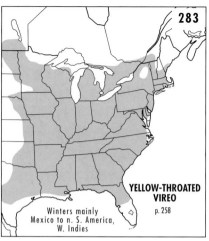

283

YELLOW-THROATED VIREO

Winters mainly Mexico to n. S. America, W. Indies

p. 258

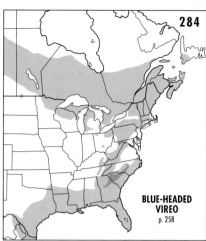

284

BLUE-HEADED VIREO

p. 258

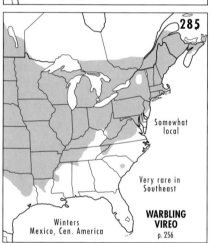

285

Somewhat local

Very rare in Southeast

Winters Mexico, Cen. America

WARBLING VIREO

p. 256

286

Rare in Southeast

Winters Mexico to S. America

PHILADELPHIA VIREO

p. 256

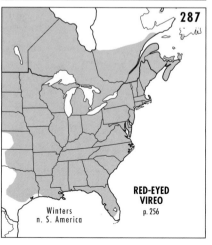

287

RED-EYED VIREO

Winters n. S. America

p. 256

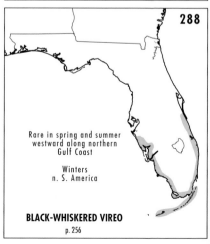

288

Rare in spring and summer westward along northern Gulf Coast

Winters n. S. America

BLACK-WHISKERED VIREO

p. 256

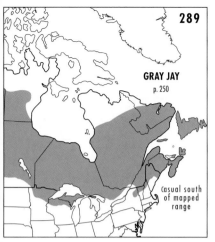

289

GRAY JAY
p. 250

Casual south of mapped range

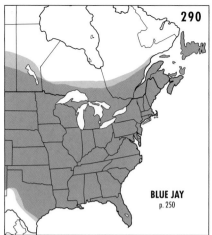

290

BLUE JAY
p. 250

291

Very local within mapped range

Population declining

FLORIDA SCRUB-JAY
p. 250

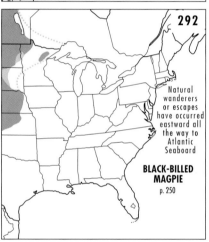

292

Natural wanderers or escapes have occurred eastward all the way to Atlantic Seaboard

BLACK-BILLED MAGPIE
p. 250

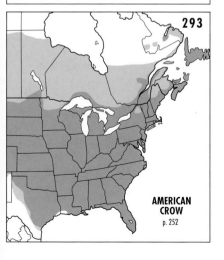

293

AMERICAN CROW
p. 252

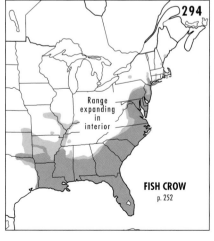

294

Range expanding in interior

FISH CROW
p. 252

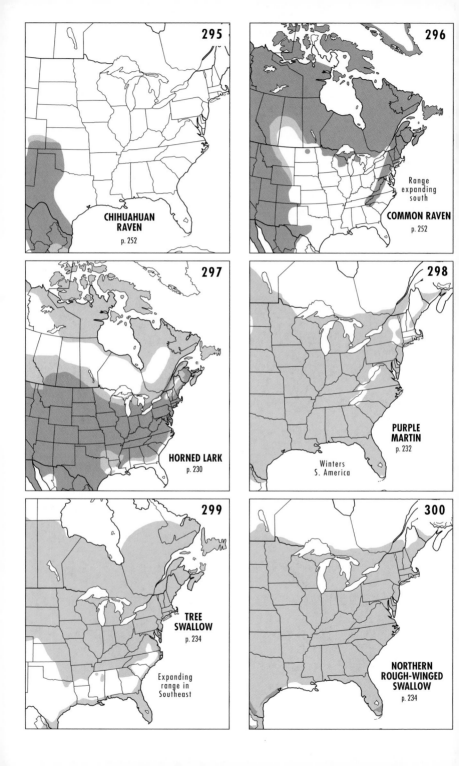

295 CHIHUAHUAN RAVEN p. 252

296 COMMON RAVEN p. 252
Range expanding south

297 HORNED LARK p. 230

298 PURPLE MARTIN p. 232
Winters S. America

299 TREE SWALLOW p. 234
Expanding range in Southeast

300 NORTHERN ROUGH-WINGED SWALLOW p. 234

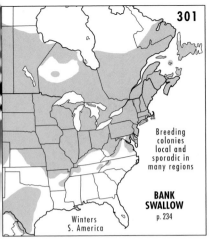

301

Breeding
colonies
local and
sporadic in
many regions

**BANK
SWALLOW**
p. 234

Winters
S. America

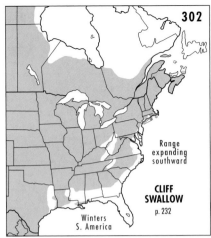

302

Range
expanding
southward

**CLIFF
SWALLOW**
p. 232

Winters
S. America

303

Wanderers
found well
north and east
of mapped range

Texas population
spreading

CAVE SWALLOW
p. 232

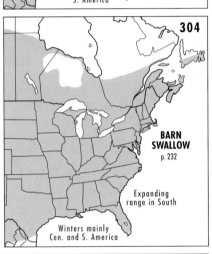

304

**BARN
SWALLOW**
p. 232

Expanding
range in South

Winters mainly
Cen. and S. America

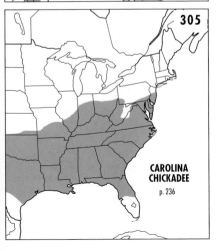

305

**CAROLINA
CHICKADEE**

p. 236

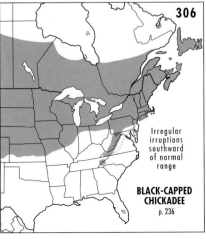

306

Irregular
irruptions
southward
of normal
range

**BLACK-CAPPED
CHICKADEE**
p. 236

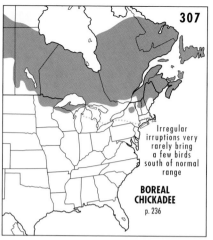

307

Irregular
irruptions very
rarely bring
a few birds
south of normal
range

**BOREAL
CHICKADEE**
p. 236

308

**TUFTED
TITMOUSE**
p. 236

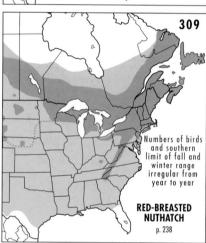

309

Numbers of birds
and southern
limit of fall and
winter range
irregular from
year to year

**RED-BREASTED
NUTHATCH**
p. 238

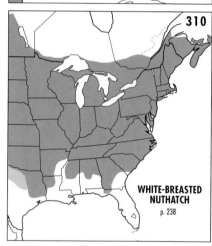

310

**WHITE-BREASTED
NUTHATCH**
p. 238

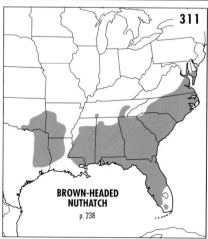

311

**BROWN-HEADED
NUTHATCH**
p. 238

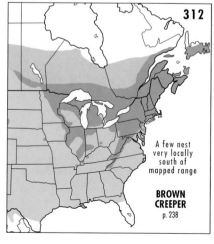

312

A few nest
very locally
south of
mapped range

**BROWN
CREEPER**
p. 238

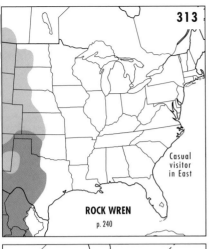

313

Casual
visitor
in East

ROCK WREN
p. 240

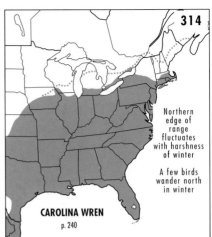

314

Northern
edge of
range
fluctuates
with harshness
of winter

A few birds
wander north
in winter

CAROLINA WREN
p. 240

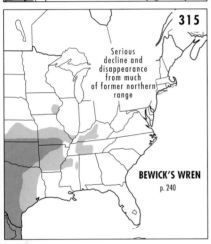

315

Serious
decline and
disappearance
from much
of former northern
range

BEWICK'S WREN
p. 240

316

HOUSE WREN
p. 240

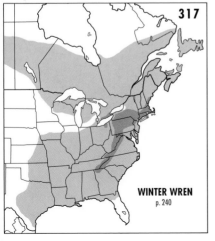

317

WINTER WREN
p. 240

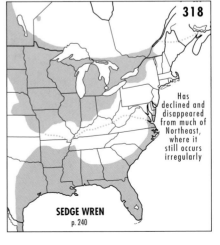

318

Has
declined and
disappeared
from much
of Northeast,
where it
still occurs
irregularly

SEDGE WREN
p. 240

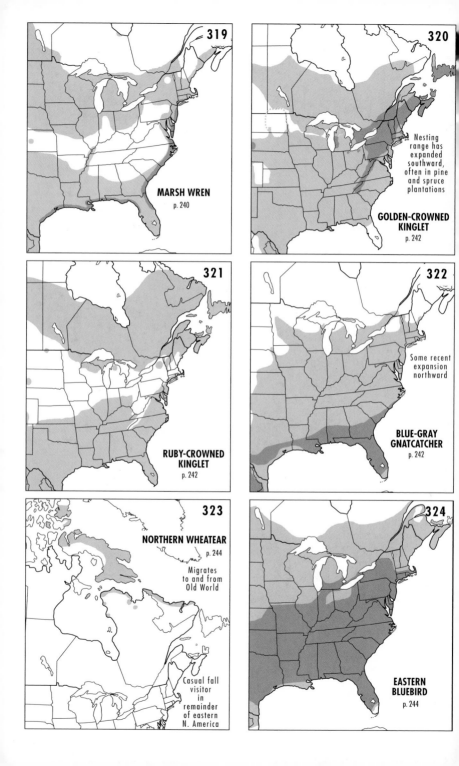

319

MARSH WREN
p. 240

320

Nesting range has expanded southward, often in pine and spruce plantations

GOLDEN-CROWNED KINGLET
p. 242

321

RUBY-CROWNED KINGLET
p. 242

322

Some recent expansion northward

BLUE-GRAY GNATCATCHER
p. 242

323

NORTHERN WHEATEAR
p. 244

Migrates to and from Old World

Casual fall visitor in remainder of eastern N. America

324

EASTERN BLUEBIRD
p. 244

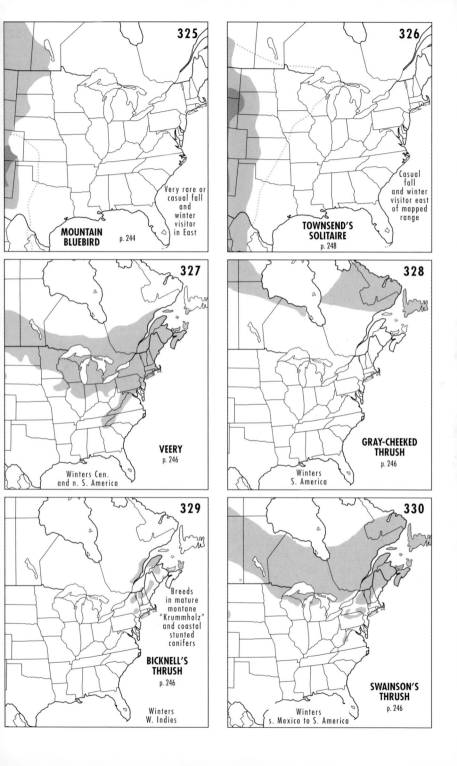

325

MOUNTAIN
BLUEBIRD   p. 244

Very rare or
casual fall
and
winter
visitor
in East

326

Casual
fall
and winter
visitor east
of mapped
range

TOWNSEND'S
SOLITAIRE
p. 248

327

VEERY
p. 246

Winters Cen.
and n. S. America

328

GRAY-CHEEKED
THRUSH
p. 246

Winters
S. America

329

Breeds
in mature
montane
"Krummholz"
and coastal
stunted
conifers

BICKNELL'S
THRUSH

p. 246

Winters
W. Indies

330

SWAINSON'S
THRUSH
p. 246

Winters
s. Mexico to S. America

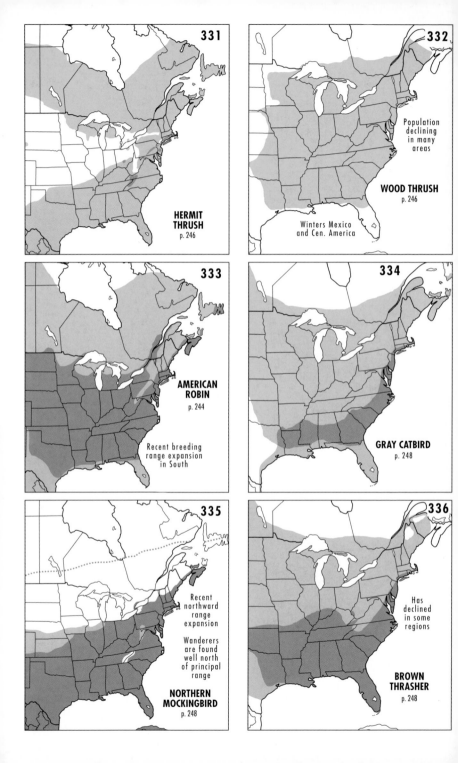

331
HERMIT THRUSH
p. 246

332
Population declining in many areas
WOOD THRUSH
p. 246
Winters Mexico and Cen. America

333
AMERICAN ROBIN
p. 244
Recent breeding range expansion in South

334
GRAY CATBIRD
p. 248

335
Recent northward range expansion
Wanderers are found well north of principal range
NORTHERN MOCKINGBIRD
p. 248

336
Has declined in some regions
BROWN THRASHER
p. 248

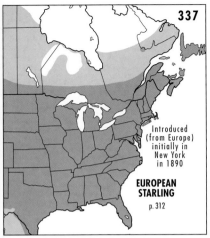

337

Introduced (from Europe) initially in New York in 1890

EUROPEAN STARLING

p. 312

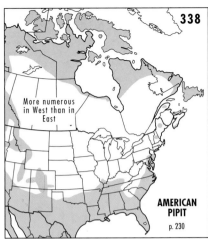

338

More numerous in West than in East

AMERICAN PIPIT

p. 230

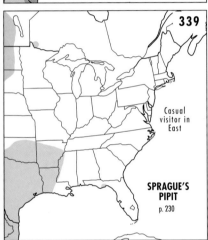

339

Casual visitor in East

SPRAGUE'S PIPIT

p. 230

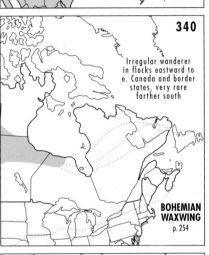

340

Irregular wanderer in flocks eastward to e. Canada and border states, very rare farther south

BOHEMIAN WAXWING

p. 254

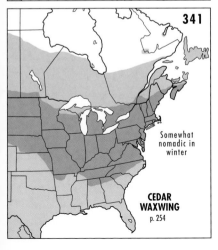

341

Somewhat nomadic in winter

CEDAR WAXWING

p. 254

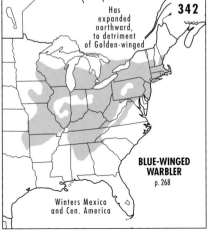

342

Has expanded northward, to detriment of Golden-winged

BLUE-WINGED WARBLER

p. 268

Winters Mexico and Cen. America

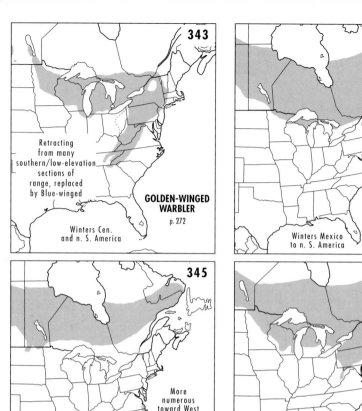

343

Retracting from many southern/low-elevation sections of range, replaced by Blue-winged

Winters Cen. and n. S. America

GOLDEN-WINGED WARBLER
p. 272

344

Recent overall population declines, possibly cyclic

Winters Mexico to n. S. America

TENNESSEE WARBLER
p. 270

345

More numerous toward West than in East

ORANGE-CROWNED WARBLER
p. 270

346

Very rare in Southeast

Winters mainly in Mexico and Cen. America

NASHVILLE WARBLER
p. 274

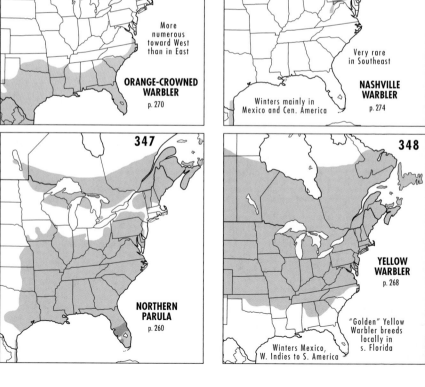

347

NORTHERN PARULA
p. 260

348

YELLOW WARBLER
p. 268

"Golden" Yellow Warbler breeds locally in s. Florida

Winters Mexico, W. Indies to S. America

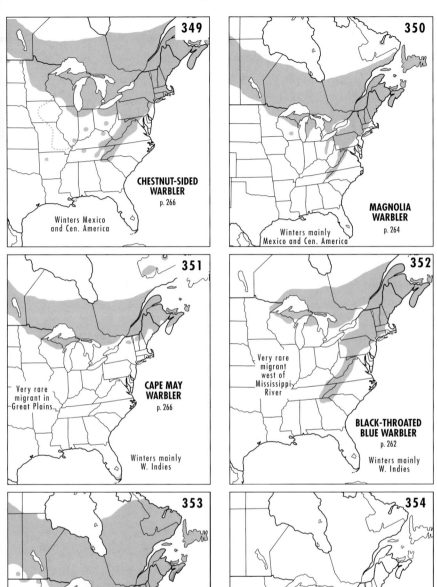

349
CHESTNUT-SIDED WARBLER
p. 266
Winters Mexico and Cen. America

350
MAGNOLIA WARBLER
p. 264
Winters mainly Mexico and Cen. America

351
CAPE MAY WARBLER
p. 266
Very rare migrant in Great Plains
Winters mainly W. Indies

352
BLACK-THROATED BLUE WARBLER
p. 262
Very rare migrant west of Mississippi River
Winters mainly W. Indies

353
YELLOW-RUMPED WARBLER
p. 264
"Audubon's" subspecies nesting in w. N. and S. Dakota and Nebraska

354
GOLDEN-CHEEKED WARBLER
p. 260
Winters s. Mexico and Cen. America

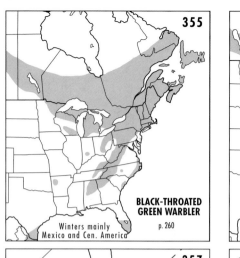

355

BLACK-THROATED GREEN WARBLER

p. 260

Winters mainly Mexico and Cen. America

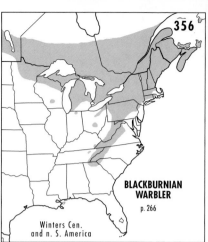

356

BLACKBURNIAN WARBLER

p. 266

Winters Cen. and n. S. America

357

Very rare north of mapped range

YELLOW-THROATED WARBLER

p. 260

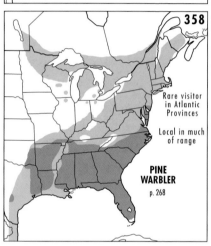

358

Rare visitor in Atlantic Provinces

Local in much of range

PINE WARBLER

p. 268

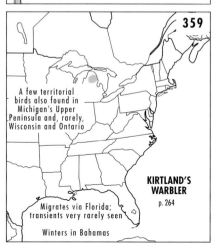

359

A few territorial birds also found in Michigan's Upper Peninsula and, rarely, Wisconsin and Ontario

KIRTLAND'S WARBLER

p. 264

Migrates via Florida; transients very rarely seen

Winters in Bahamas

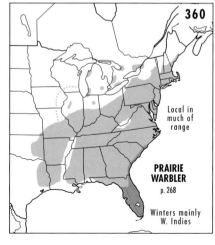

360

Local in much of range

PRAIRIE WARBLER

p. 268

Winters mainly W. Indies

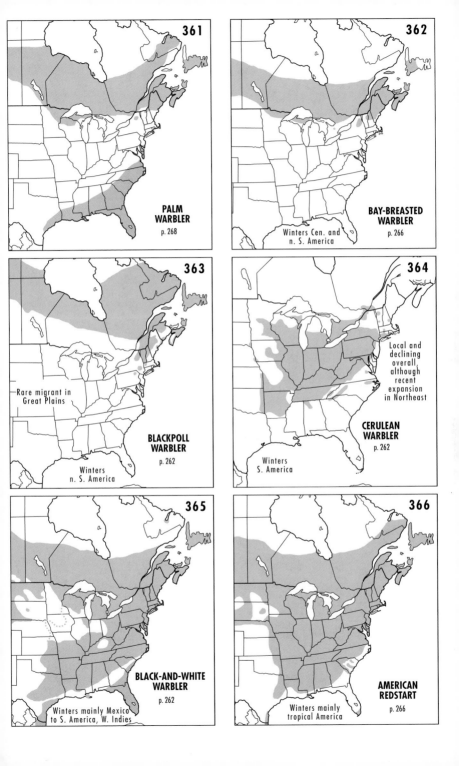

361
PALM WARBLER
p. 268

362
BAY-BREASTED WARBLER
p. 266
Winters Cen. and n. S. America

363
BLACKPOLL WARBLER
p. 262
Rare migrant in Great Plains
Winters n. S. America

364
CERULEAN WARBLER
p. 262
Local and declining overall, although recent expansion in Northeast
Winters S. America

365
BLACK-AND-WHITE WARBLER
p. 262
Winters mainly Mexico to S. America, W. Indies

366
AMERICAN REDSTART
p. 266
Winters mainly tropical America

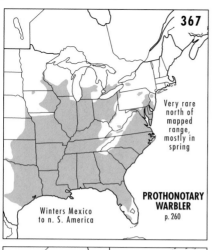

367

Very rare
north of
mapped
range,
mostly in
spring

**PROTHONOTARY
WARBLER**
p. 260

Winters Mexico
to n. S. America

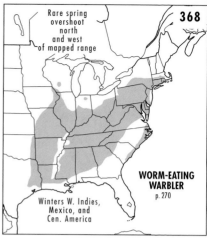

368

Rare spring
overshoot
north
and west
of mapped range

**WORM-EATING
WARBLER**
p. 270

Winters W. Indies,
Mexico, and
Cen. America

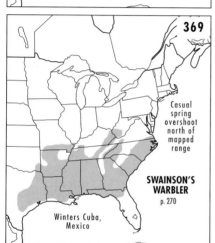

369

Casual
spring
overshoot
north of
mapped
range

**SWAINSON'S
WARBLER**
p. 270

Winters Cuba,
Mexico

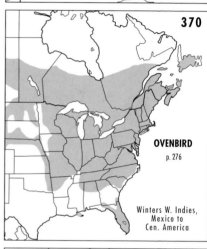

370

OVENBIRD
p. 276

Winters W. Indies,
Mexico to
Cen. America

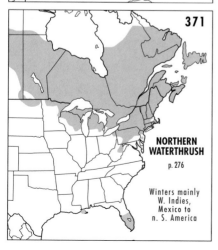

371

**NORTHERN
WATERTHRUSH**
p. 276

Winters mainly
W. Indies,
Mexico to
n. S. America

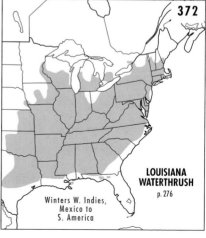

372

**LOUISIANA
WATERTHRUSH**
p. 276

Winters W. Indies,
Mexico to
S. America

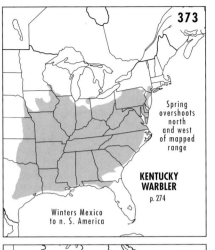

373

Spring
overshoots
north
and west
of mapped
range

**KENTUCKY
WARBLER**
p. 274

Winters Mexico
to n. S. America

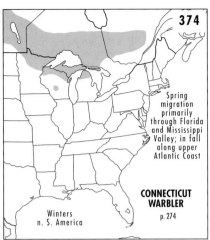

374

Spring
migration
primarily
through Florida
and Mississippi
Valley; in fall
along upper
Atlantic Coast

**CONNECTICUT
WARBLER**
p. 274

Winters
n. S. America

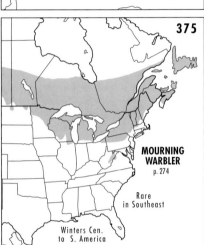

375

**MOURNING
WARBLER**
p. 274

Rare
in Southeast

Winters Cen.
to S. America

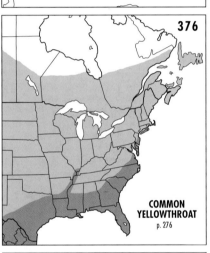

376

**COMMON
YELLOWTHROAT**
p. 276

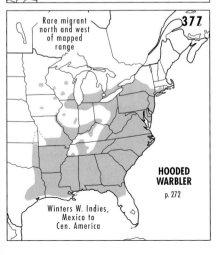

377

Rare migrant
north and west
of mapped
range

**HOODED
WARBLER**
p. 272

Winters W. Indies,
Mexico to
Cen. America

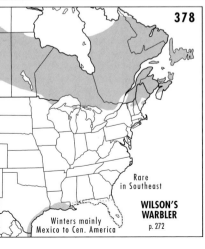

378

Rare
in Southeast

**WILSON'S
WARBLER**
p. 272

Winters mainly
Mexico to Cen. America

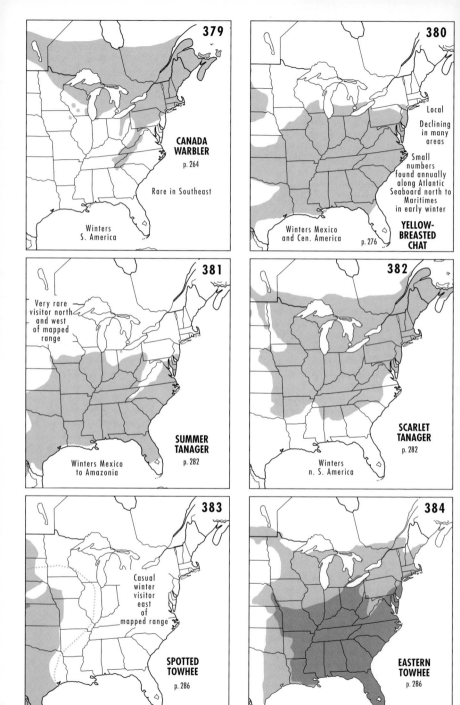

379

CANADA WARBLER

p. 264

Rare in Southeast

Winters S. America

380

Local

Declining in many areas

Small numbers found annually along Atlantic Seaboard north to Maritimes in early winter

Winters Mexico and Cen. America

YELLOW-BREASTED CHAT

p. 276

381

Very rare visitor north and west of mapped range

SUMMER TANAGER

p. 282

Winters Mexico to Amazonia

382

SCARLET TANAGER

p. 282

Winters n. S. America

383

Casual winter visitor east of mapped range

SPOTTED TOWHEE

p. 286

384

EASTERN TOWHEE

p. 286

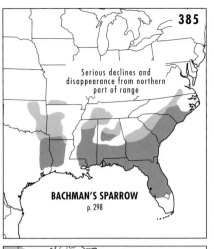

385

Serious declines and disappearance from northern part of range

BACHMAN'S SPARROW
p. 298

386

RUFOUS-CROWNED SPARROW
p. 296

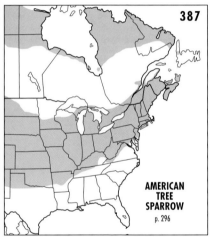

387

AMERICAN TREE SPARROW
p. 296

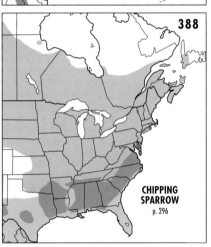

388

CHIPPING SPARROW
p. 296

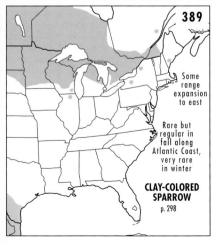

389

Some range expansion to east

Rare but regular in fall along Atlantic Coast, very rare in winter

CLAY-COLORED SPARROW
p. 298

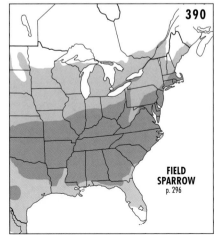

390

FIELD SPARROW
p. 296

391

Declining
and
very local
in much of
Northeast

**VESPER
SPARROW**
p. 300

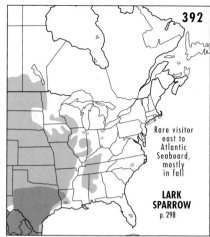

392

Rare visitor
east to
Atlantic
Seaboard,
mostly
in fall

**LARK
SPARROW**
p. 298

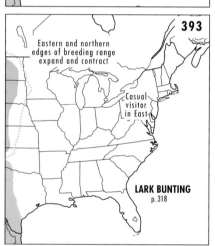

393

Eastern and northern
edges of breeding range
expand and contract

Casual
visitor
in East

LARK BUNTING
p. 318

394

**SAVANNAH
SPARROW**
p. 302

395

Breeds
Sable
Island

Found
primarily
along marsh
edge and in
dune habitat

**"IPSWICH"
SAVANNAH
SPARROW**
p. 302

396

Local and
declining in
parts of
eastern
range

**GRASSHOPPER
SPARROW**
p. 298

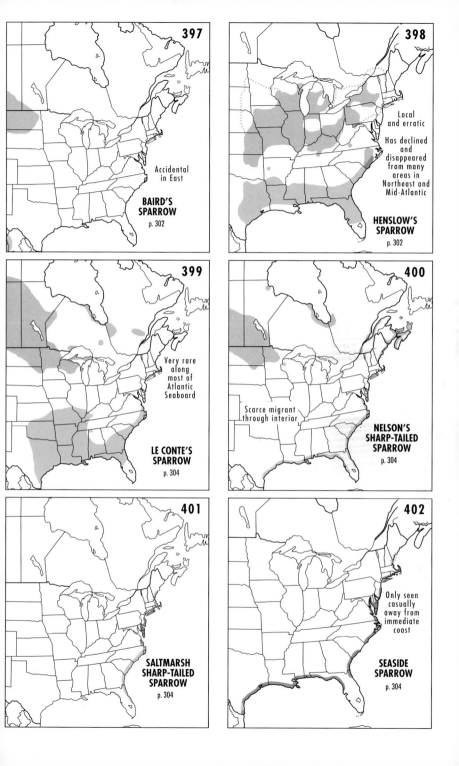

397

Accidental in East

BAIRD'S SPARROW
p. 302

398

Local and erratic

Has declined and disappeared from many areas in Northeast and Mid-Atlantic

HENSLOW'S SPARROW
p. 302

399

Very rare along most of Atlantic Seaboard

LE CONTE'S SPARROW
p. 304

400

Scarce migrant through interior

NELSON'S SHARP-TAILED SPARROW
p. 304

401

SALTMARSH SHARP-TAILED SPARROW
p. 304

402

Only seen casually away from immediate coast

SEASIDE SPARROW
p. 304

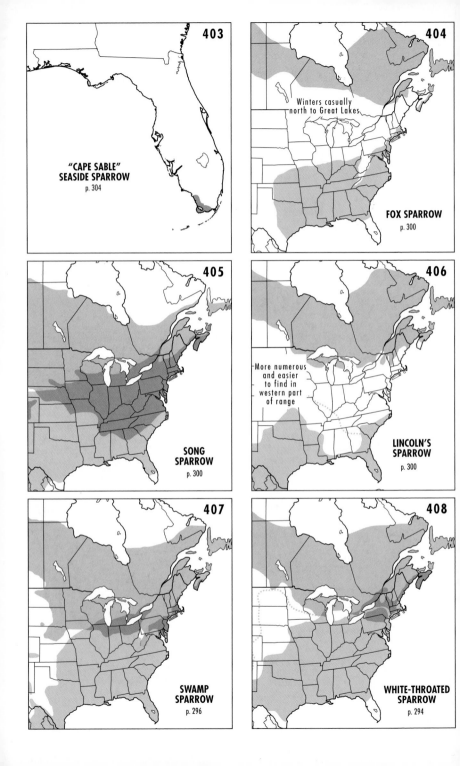

403 "CAPE SABLE" SEASIDE SPARROW p. 304

404 FOX SPARROW p. 300
Winters casually north to Great Lakes

405 SONG SPARROW p. 300

406 LINCOLN'S SPARROW p. 300
More numerous and easier to find in western part of range

407 SWAMP SPARROW p. 296

408 WHITE-THROATED SPARROW p. 294

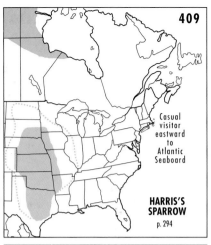

409

Casual visitor eastward to Atlantic Seaboard

HARRIS'S SPARROW
p. 294

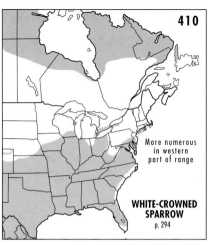

410

More numerous in western part of range

WHITE-CROWNED SPARROW
p. 294

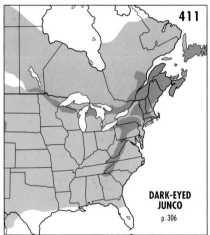

411

DARK-EYED JUNCO
p. 306

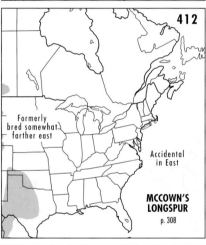

412

Formerly bred somewhat farther east

Accidental in East

MCCOWN'S LONGSPUR
p. 308

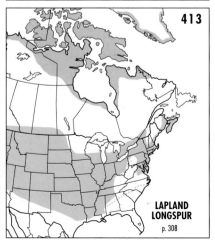

413

LAPLAND LONGSPUR
p. 308

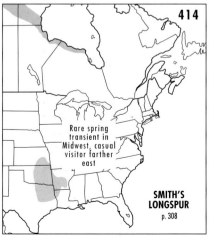

414

Rare spring transient in Midwest, casual visitor farther east

SMITH'S LONGSPUR
p. 308

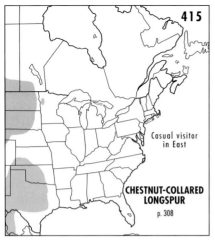

415

Casual visitor
in East

**CHESTNUT-COLLARED
LONGSPUR**

p. 308

416

SNOW BUNTING

p. 306

417

**NORTHERN
CARDINAL**

p. 284

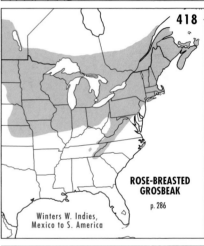

418

**ROSE-BREASTED
GROSBEAK**

p. 286

Winters W. Indies,
Mexico to S. America

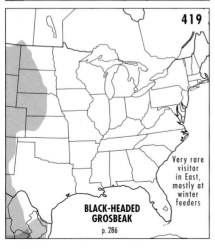

419

Very rare
visitor
in East,
mostly at
winter
feeders

**BLACK-HEADED
GROSBEAK**

p. 286

420

Some
northward
expansion in
breeding range

Rare visitor
farther north

BLUE GROSBEAK

p. 288

Winters Mexico,
Cuba, and Cen. America

421

Casual or accidental visitor in East

LAZULI BUNTING
p. 288

422

Rare migrant in Atlantic Provinces

INDIGO BUNTING
p. 288

Winters mainly W. Indies, Mexico, and Cen. America

423

Very rare visitor north of mapped range, sometimes at feeders

PAINTED BUNTING
p. 288

Winters mainly W. Indies, Mexico, and Cen. America

424

Eastern and northern borders of breeding range expand and contract

Regular fall migrant and rare winter visitor along Atlantic Coast

DICKCISSEL
p. 318

Winters mainly Mexico to n. S. America

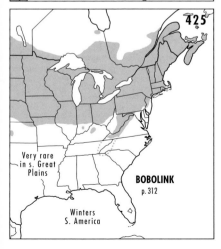

425

Very rare in s. Great Plains

BOBOLINK
p. 312

Winters S. America

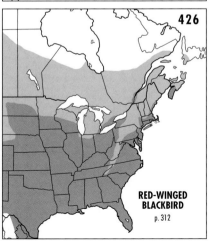

426

RED-WINGED BLACKBIRD
p. 312

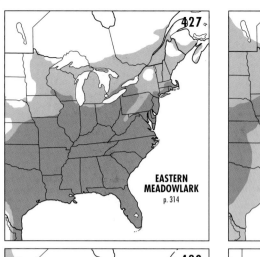

427

EASTERN
MEADOWLARK
p. 314

428

Sparse
breeder
in East

Casual
east to
Atlantic
Seaboard

WESTERN
MEADOWLARK
p. 314

429

Rare but
regular
visitor
east to
Atlantic
Seaboard

YELLOW-HEADED
BLACKBIRD
p. 312

430

Has recently
declined
over much
of winter
range

RUSTY
BLACKBIRD
p. 310

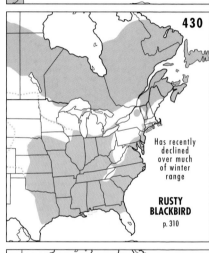

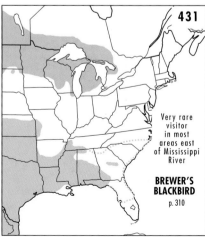

431

Very rare
visitor
in most
areas east
of Mississippi
River

BREWER'S
BLACKBIRD
p. 310

432

COMMON
GRACKLE
p. 310

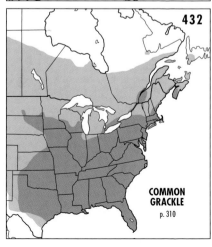

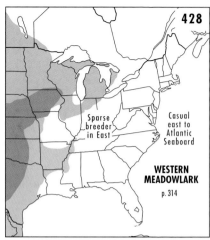

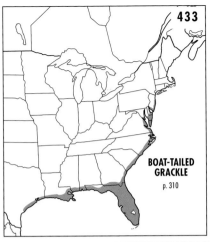

433

BOAT-TAILED GRACKLE

p. 310

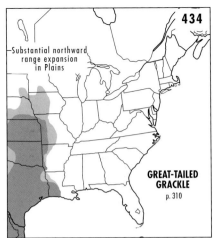

434

Substantial northward range expansion in Plains

GREAT-TAILED GRACKLE

p. 310

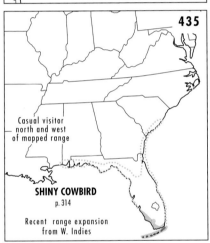

435

Casual visitor north and west of mapped range

SHINY COWBIRD

p. 314

Recent range expansion from W. Indies

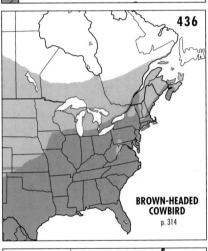

436

BROWN-HEADED COWBIRD

p. 314

437

ORCHARD ORIOLE

p. 316

Winters Mexico to n. S. America

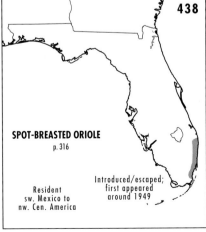

438

SPOT-BREASTED ORIOLE

p. 316

Resident sw. Mexico to nw. Cen. America

Introduced/escaped; first appeared around 1949

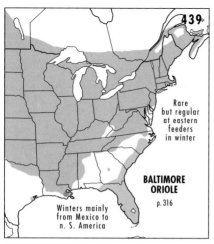

439

Rare but regular at eastern feeders in winter

BALTIMORE ORIOLE

p. 316

Winters mainly from Mexico to n. S. America

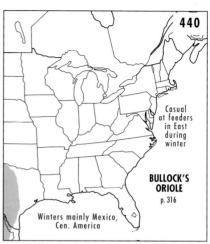

440

Casual at feeders in East during winter

BULLOCK'S ORIOLE

p. 316

Winters mainly Mexico, Cen. America

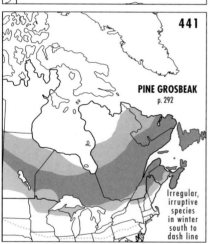

441

PINE GROSBEAK

p. 292

Irregular, irruptive species in winter south to dash line

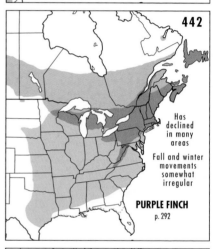

442

Has declined in many areas

Fall and winter movements somewhat irregular

PURPLE FINCH

p. 292

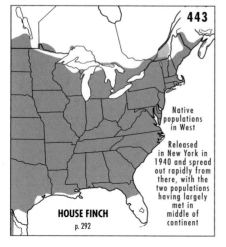

443

Native populations in West

Released in New York in 1940 and spread out rapidly from there, with the two populations having largely met in middle of continent

HOUSE FINCH

p. 292

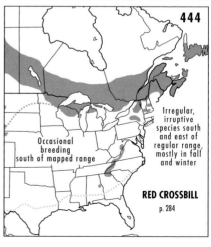

444

Irregular, irruptive species south and east of regular range, mostly in fall and winter

Occasional breeding south of mapped range

RED CROSSBILL

p. 284

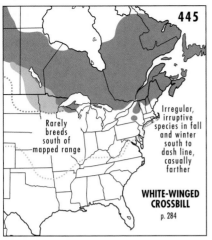

445

Rarely breeds south of mapped range

Irregular, irruptive species in fall and winter south to dash line, casually farther

WHITE-WINGED CROSSBILL
p. 284

446

Irregular, irruptive species in fall and winter south to dash line, very rarely farther

COMMON REDPOLL
p. 292

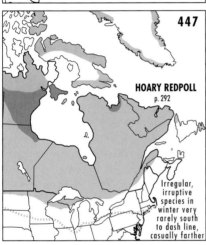

447

HOARY REDPOLL
p. 292

Irregular, irruptive species in winter very rarely south to dash line, casually farther

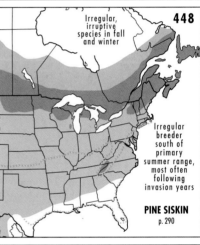

448

Irregular, irruptive species in fall and winter

Irregular breeder south of primary summer range, most often following invasion years

PINE SISKIN
p. 290

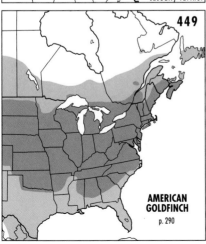

449

AMERICAN GOLDFINCH
p. 290

450

Irregular, irruptive species in fall and winter south to dash line, casually beyond

Recent reductions in numbers south of principal range

EVENING GROSBEAK
p. 290

451

Introduced
(from Europe)
initially in
New York
in 1850

**HOUSE
SPARROW**

p. 318

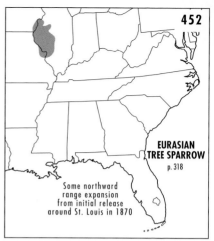

452

**EURASIAN
TREE SPARROW**

p. 318

Some northward
range expansion
from initial release
around St. Louis in 1870

INDEX OF SCIENTIFIC NAMES

A

Accipiter cooperii, 98, 118, M100
 gentilis, 98, 118, M101
 striatus, 98, 118, M99
Actitis macularia, 152, 162, M151
Aechmophorus clarkii, 28, M9
 occidentalis, 28, M8
Aegolius acadicus, 206, M241
 funereus, 206, M240
Agapornis personatus, 198
Agelaius humeralis, 324
 phoeniceus, 312, M426
Aimophila aestivalis, 298, M385
 botterii, 298
 cassinii, 298
 ruficeps, 296, M386
Aix sponsa, 68, 84, M61
Ajaia ajaja, 54, M47
Alca torda, 192, M214
Alle alle, 194, M211
Amazilia yucatanensis, 212, M247
Amazona oratrix, 198
 viridigenalis, 198
Ammodramus bairdii, 302, M397
 caudacutus, 304, M401
 henslowii, 302, M398
 leconteii, 304, M399
 maritimus, 304, M402
 maritimus mirabilis, 304, M403
 nelsoni, 304, M400
 savannarum, 298, M396
Anas acuta, 68, 84, M71
 americana, 68, 84, M64
 bahamensis, 90
 clypeata, 70, 84, M70
 crecca, 84

crecca carolinensis, 70, M72
crecca crecca, 70
cyanoptera, 70, M69
discors, 70, 84, M68
formosa, 90
fulvigula, 66, M67
penelope, 68, M63
platyrhynchos, 66, 82, M66
querquedula, 90
rubripes, 66, 82, M65
strepera, 66, 84, M62
Anhinga anhinga, 42, M29
Anous stolidus, 190
Anser albifrons, 62, 64, M53
 anser, 90
 brachyrhynchus, 90
 erythropus, 90
 fabalis, 90
Anthus rubescens, 230, M338
 spragueii, 230, M339
Aphelocoma coerulescens, 250,
 M291
Aquila chrysaetos, 112, 114, M109
Aramus guarauna, 52, M135
Aratinga canicularis, 198
 chloroptera, 198
 holochlora, 198
Archilochus alexandri, 212, M249
 colubris, 212, M248
Ardea alba, 48, M35
 herodius, 46, 48, M33, M34
Arenaria interpres, 136, 150, M157
Arremonops rufivirgatus, 322
Asio flammeus, 202, M239
 otus, 202, M238
Asturina nitida, 104, 108

U

Uria aalge, 192, M212
  lomvia, 192, M213

V

Vanellus vanellus, 166
Vermivora bachmanii, 272
  celata, 270, 280, M345
  chrysoptera, 272, M343
  chrysoptera x pinus, 268, 272
  peregrina, 270, 280, M344
  pinus, 268, M342
  ruficapilla, 274, 280, M346
Vireo altiloquus, 256, M288
  atricapillus, 258, M282
  bellii, 258, M281
  crassirostris, 326
  flavifrons, 258, M283
  flavoviridis, 256, 326
  gilvus, 256, M285
  griseus, 258, M280
  olivaceus, 256, M287
  philadelphicus, 256, 280, M286
  solitarius, 258, M284

W

Wilsonia canadensis, 264, 280,
  M379
  citrina, 272, 280, M377
  pusilla, 272, 280, M378

X

Xanthocephalus xanthocephalus,
  312, M429
Xema sabini, 180, 184, M195

Z

Zenaida asiatica, 196, M220
  aurita, 326
  macroura, 196, M221
Zonotrichia albicollis, 294, M408
  atrocapilla, 294
  leucophrys, 294, M410
  querula, 294, M409

Index of Common Names

THE PETERSON SERIES®

PETERSON FIELD GUIDES®

BIRDS

ADVANCED BIRDING North America 97500-x
BIRDS OF BRITAIN AND EUROPE 0-618-16675-0
BIRDS OF TEXAS Texas and adjacent states 92138-4
BIRDS OF THE WEST INDIES 0-618-00210-3
EASTERN BIRDS Eastern and central North America 74046-0
EASTERN BIRDS' NESTS U.S. east of Mississippi River 93609-8
HAWKS North America 67067-5
HUMMINGBIRDS North America 0-618-02496-4
WESTERN BIRDS North America west of 100th meridian and north of Mexico 91173-7
WESTERN BIRDS' NESTS U.S. west of Mississippi River 0-618-16437-5
MEXICAN BIRDS Mexico, Guatemala, Belize, El Salvador 97514-x
WARBLERS North America 78321-6

FISH

PACIFIC COAST FISHES Gulf of Alaska to Baja California 0-618-00212-x
ATLANTIC COAST FISHES North American Atlantic coast 97515-8
FRESHWATER FISHES North America north of Mexico 91091-9

INSECTS

INSECTS North America north of Mexico 91170-2
BEETLES North America 91089-7
EASTERN BUTTERFLIES Eastern and central North America 90453-6
WESTERN BUTTERFLIES U.S. and Canada west of 100th meridian, part of northern Mexico 79151-0

MAMMALS

MAMMALS North America north of Mexico 91098-6
ANIMAL TRACKS North America 91094-3

ECOLOGY

EASTERN FORESTS Eastern North America 92895-8
CALIFORNIA AND PACIFIC NORTHWEST FORESTS 92896-6
ROCKY MOUNTAIN AND SOUTHWEST FORESTS 92897-4
VENOMOUS ANIMALS AND POISONOUS PLANTS) North America north of Mexico 93608-x

PLANTS

EDIBLE WILD PLANTS Eastern and central North America 92622-x
EASTERN TREES North America east of 100th meridian 90455-2
FERNS Northeastern and central North America, British Isles and Western Europe 97512-3
MEDICINAL PLANTS AND HERBS Eastern and central North America 98814-4
MUSHROOMS North America 91090-0
PACIFIC STATES WILDFLOWERS Washington, Oregon, California, and adjacent areas 91095-1
ROCKY MOUNTAIN WILDFLOWERS Northern Arizona and New Mexico to British Columbia 93613-6
TREES AND SHRUBS Northeastern and north-central U.S. and southeastern and south-central Canada 35370-x
WESTERN TREES Western U.S. and Canada 90454-4
WILDFLOWERS OF NORTHEASTERN AND NORTH-CENTRAL NORTH AMERICA 91172-9
SOUTHWEST AND TEXAS WILDFLOWERS 93612-8

EARTH AND SKY

GEOLOGY Eastern North America 0-618-16438-3
ROCKS AND MINERALS North America 91096-x
STARS AND PLANETS 93431-1
ATMOSPHERE 97631-6

REPTILES AND AMPHIBIANS

EASTERN REPTILES AND AMPHIBIANS Eastern and central North America 90452-8
WESTERN REPTILES AND AMPHIBIANS Western North America, including Baja California 93611-x

SEASHORE

SHELLS OF THE ATLANTIC Atlantic and Gulf coasts and the West Indies 0-618-16439-1
PACIFIC COAST SHELLS North American Pacific coast, including Hawaii and the Gulf of California 18322-7
ATLANTIC SEASHORE Bay of Fundy to Cape Hatteras 0-618-00209-x
CORAL REEFS Caribbean and Florida 0-618-00211-1
SOUTHEAST AND CARIBBEAN SEASHORES Cape Hatteras to the Gulf Coast, Florida, and the Caribbean 97516-6

PETERSON FIELD GUIDE COLORING BOOKS

AUDIO AND VIDEO

EASTERN BIRDING BY EAR
cassettes 97523-9
CD 97524-7

WESTERN BIRDING BY EAR
cassettes 97526-3
CD 97525-5

EASTERN BIRD SONGS, Revised
cassettes 53150-0
CD 97522-0

WESTERN BIRD SONGS, Revised
cassettes 51746-X
CD 97519-0

BACKYARD BIRDSONG
cassettes 97527-1
CD 97528-X

EASTERN MORE BIRDING BY EAR
cassettes 97529-8
CD 97530-1

WATCHING BIRDS
Beta 34418-2
VHS 34417-4

PETERSON'S MULTIMEDIA GUIDES: NORTH AMERICAN BIRDS
(CD-ROM for Windows) 73056-2

PETERSON FLASHGUIDES™

ATLANTIC COASTAL BIRDS 79286-X
PACIFIC COASTAL BIRDS 79287-8
EASTERN TRAILSIDE BIRDS 79288-6
WESTERN TRAILSIDE BIRDS 79289-4
HAWKS 79291-6
BACKYARD BIRDS 79290-8
TREES 82998-4
MUSHROOMS 82999-2
ANIMAL TRACKS 82997-6
BUTTERFLIES 82996-8
ROADSIDE WILDFLOWERS 82995-X
BIRDS OF THE MIDWEST 86733-9
WATERFOWL 86734-7
FRESHWATER FISHES 86713-4

PETERSON FIELD GUIDES can be purchased at your local book-
store or by calling our toll-free number, (800) 225-3362.

When referring to title by corresponding ISBN number,
preface with 0-395, unless title is listed with 0-618.